The Myth of Japanese Homogeneity:

Social-Ecological Diversity in Education and Socialization

The Myth of Japanese Homogeneity:

Social-Ecological Diversity in Education and Socialization

Herman W Smith

University of Missouri-St. Louis

NOVA SCIENCE PUBLISHERS, INC.

H-Y LIB
(W)

HN
723.5
.S 55
1994

HARVARD-YENCHING LIBRARY
HARVARD UNIVERSITY
2 DIVINITY AVENUE
CAMBRIDGE, MA 02138

AUG 2 8 1996

YANKEE

Art Director: Christopher Concannon
Graphics: Elenor Kallberg and Maria Ester Hawrys
Manuscript Coordinator: Roseann Pena
Book Production: Tammy Sauter, and Michelle Lalo
Circulation: Irene Kwartiroff and Annette Hellinger

Library of Congress Cataloging-in-Publication Data

Smith, H. W (Herman W), 1943-
    The myth of Japanese homogeneity : social ecological
diversity in education and socialization / by Herman
W Smith.
        p. cm.
    Includes bibliographical references and index.
    ISBN 1-56072-169-3
    1. Japan--Social conditions--1945- 2. Social status--
Japan. 3. Socialization--Japan. 4. Education--Japan.
I. Title.
HN723.5.S55   1994   94-2156
306'.0952--dc20   CIP

© *1995 Nova Science Publishers, Inc.*
6080 Jericho Turnpike, Suite 207
Commack, New York 11725
Tele. 516-499-3103 Fax 516-499-3146
E Mail Novasci1@aol.com

All rights reserved. No part of this book may be reproduced, stored in a retrieval system or transmitted in any form or by any means: electronic, electrostatic, magnetic, tape, mechanical, photocopying, recording or otherwise without permission from the publishers.

Printed in the United States of America

Dedicated to my Japanese teachers, particularly Ms. Kazuko Saito of Kyōto who first stimulated and nurtured my incessant curiosity about things Japanese.

TABLE OF CONTENTS

List of Tables and Figures xi

Acknowledgements xv

Introduction 1

Chapter 1- **Honne** and **Tatemae** in Education 5

The origins of contemporary education in Japan 6
Debunking stereotypes of japanese education 8
Educational homogeneity or heterogeneity? 10
Education as "cultural capital" 15
Education as an impersonal sorting machine 19
The objectives of education versus schooling 20
An overview of the structure of japanese education 31
Summary 38

Chapter 2 - **The Educational Race Starts in the Cradle** 39

The preschool system 39
    early childhood socialization 40
    day-care centers 43
    kindergartens 45
    do hoikuen and yochien serve the same function? 46
    class size and the myth of <u>shudan seikatsu</u> 52
    teacher recruits 56
Elementary schools 57
    public and private expenses 58
Junior high: The apex of pressures to succeed 60
    results of indoctrination in its rawest form 61
        bullying 62
        absenteeism 64
        truancy 65
        cram schools 68
Summary 69

Chapter 3 - High School and Beyond: The Final Laps 71

Yobikō and rōnin status 79
Undergraduate university structure 80
   public versus private universities 81
   social stratification and cultural capital 84
   institutionalized sex discrimination 87
   the structure of the select 45 universities 88
      the national universities 88
      public versus private universities 90
      features peculiar to japanese universities 95
      regional patterns of recruitment of college graduates 99
Post-baccalaureate education 101
   the role of women 106
   adult education 107
Summary 109

Chapter 4 - Socialization, Marital Ideals, and the Marriage Squeeze 111

Sex ratios and marriage markets 113
The strength of the Japanese (female) yen 123
Summary 139

Chapter 5 - Family Change and Stability 141

Alien worlds of work and family 142
Status and power inherent in family versus work identities 155
Family formation and process 159
   ideal family size 160
   desired family size 160
   actual family size 160
   contraception and abortions 162
Child rearing and juvenile delinquency 167
Divorce japanese style 171
Summary 177

Chapter 6 - Prehistoric and Historic Roots of Ethnic Pluralism 181

De-constructing "internationalism" 182
   prehistoric traces 182
   historic traces 185
   opening of japan during the meiji era 190
      learning 190
      immigration 191
      invasion 193
Burakumin: "The invisible race" 196
Okinawans 205
Ainu 206
Summary 207

**Chapter 7 - Insiders and Outsiders: Boundaries
         to "Internationalization"** **209**

Indicators of internationalism 210
Korean-Japanese 213
Chinese-Japanese 218
Resident aliens 219
The unevenness of internationalization 222
     sister ties 222
     Japanese overseas volunteers corps 227
     passport holders and foreign trips 228
     returnees from long-term overseas assignments 233
     internationalization and foreigners living in Japan 238
Summary 239

Japanese Glossary **241**

Bibliography **247**

Subject Index **261**

LIST OF TABLES AND FIGURES

Figure 1—1   Ratings of Goodness, Powerfulness, and Liveliness across the Educational Life Course Roles

Figure 1—2   Ratings of Goodness across the Educational Life Course Roles by Sex of Raters and Ratings

Figure 3—1   The Percent of Graduates from the Top 400 High Schools in 1988, as Defined by the Sunday Asahi Magazine

Figure 3—2   Tree Diagram Linkages for the Top 45 Universities in Japan, including Status as a Member of the Top 7 (Imperial), Public, Private, Women's and Tōkyō (T)—Osaka (O) Area

Figure 4—1   The Percent of the Male Population Who Can Be Expected Never to Marry, Based on 1985 Data.

Figure 4—2   Males per 100 Female High School Students Matriculating to Colleges in 1984

Figure 4—3   The Number of Males per 100 Female High School Graduates in 1988

Figure 4—4   The Percentage of Employed Persons Age 15 and Older Who Were Engineers in 1988

Figure 4—5   The Percentage of Employed Persons Age 15 and Older Who Were Employed in Managerial and Technical Occupations in 1988

Figure 4—6   Path Diagram of the Major Determinants of Marriage for Women Age 20-24

Figure 4—7   The Differences in Mean Age at First Marriage in 1985

Figure 4—8   Crude Marriage Rates for the United States and Japan from 1920-1985

Figure 5—1   The Percent of Home Owners in 1986

xi

Figure 5—2   The Crude Birth Rate per 1000 Population in 1983

Figure 5—3   Abortions per 1000 Live Births in 1987

Figure 6—1   Percent Burakumin in 1987

Figure 7—1   Korean-Japanese per 10,000 Population in 1988

Figure 7—2   Chinese-Japanese per 10,000 Population in 1988

Figure 7—3   Sister Ties per Million Population in 1989

Figure 7—4   The Percent of the Population Holding a Valid Passport in 1988

Figure 7—5   The Increase in "Long-Term" Overseas Expatriates 1969 through 1986

Table 1—1   Semantic Differential Ratings for a Subset of Deviant Educational Roles

Table 1—2   Semantic Differential Ratings for a Subset of Educator Roles

Table 2—1   Correlations between Percent of Children in Day Nurseries and Kindergarten in 1987 and Some Possible Causes (N=47 Prefectures)

Table 2—2   Results of a Regression of Population Density, Percent Nuclear Families, Percent Females in Labor Force, and Percent Managers on Percent Nursery School Attendance

Table 2—3   Results of a Regression of Percentage Females in Labor Force, Percentage Farmers, Percentage Laborers, and Percentage Self-employed on the Percent of Nursery School Attendance

Table 2—4   Results of a Regression of Percent of High School Graduates from Top High Schools, Percent Professional and Technical Workers, Percent Females in the Labor Force, and Percent of Self-employed on Kindergarten Attendance.

Table 2—5   Correlations and Beta Weights for a Regression on Ratios of Children in Day Nurseries during 1987

Table 2—6   Correlations and Beta Weights for a Regression on the Ratios of Children in Kindergartens during 1987

Table 3—1   Probabilities of Entry into the 44 Most Elite Universities from Prefectures Containing the Top 400 High Schools

Table 3—2   Basic Univariate Measures of Average and Distribution for the National Universities, Standardized per 10,000 High School Graduates in 1988

Table 3—3   Factor Analysis Results using Varimax Rotation of the Top-Ranked 45 Universities, Sorted by Factor 1 Loadings

Table 4—1   Results of a Regression of the Male-to-Female Ratio for College Matriculation and Suzuki's Marriage Squeeze index on the Age-Specific Marriage Rate for Men Ages 25—29

Table 4—2   Correlations for Types of Occupations with the Age-Specific Marriage Rate for Women Ages 20—24 and the Mean Average Age at Marriage for Women

Table 5—1   Comparison of Average Family and Kinship Identities from American and Japanese SD Lexicons

Table 5—2   Comparison of Japanese Women's Fundamental Sentiments Concerning Selected Marital and Work-Related Roles

Table 5—3   Zero-Order Correlates of the Abortion Rate per 1000 Live Births

Table 5—4   Correlations between Delinquency Rates for Persons Age 14 to 18 and Glue Sniffing and Some Possible Causes (N=47 Prefectures)

Table 6—1   Correlations between the Percent Burakumin and Various Measures Indicative of their Social Status

Table 7—1   Results of a Regression of Population Size, Japanese Overseas Tourists per 1000 population, and the Number of Library Books Lent per 100 Population on Sister Ties per Million Population

Table 7—2   Results of Zero-Order Correlations between the Percentage of Japanese with Passports and Selected Indicators of Status

ACKNOWLEDGEMENTS

There are a number of colleagues and students to whom I am grateful for various types of help at different stages of the research that led to this book. I am first and foremost grateful to Carolyn Yang, retired director of the Japanese-United States Education Commission for giving me the opportunity for a Fulbright experience at Tōhoku University during the 1989-1990 academic year. At Tōhoku University, my host, Prof. Michio Umino, loaned me the use of his Behavioral Studies Laboratory where I conceptualized the data collection requirments of this book. My undergraduate and graduate students in his lab helped locate, code, and verify much of the data. I am also grateful to Prof. Makio Morikawa of Dōshisha University for presenting me with the opportunity to extend my Japanese stay during the 1990-1991 academic year, and to my department chairman, Prof. K. Peter Etzkorn, and Dean Terry Jones, for allowing me an extended leave of absence in Kyōto. My sociology undergraduate and graduate students at Dōshisha presented numerous opportunities for discussion of the ideas presented in these chapters. I also owe Joel Glassman, Director of the UM-St. Louis Center for International Studies and co-director of the UM-St. Louis Washington University Joint Center for East Asian Studies my gratitude for Center release time to complete the manuscript, and to Joseph Allen, Director of the Washington University East Asian Studies Program for the opportunity to refine this manuscript through a graduate course at Washington University during the Winter Semester of 1993. Most importantly, I owe much to my wife, Mary Burrows, who read and critiqued each draft of this manuscript.

INTRODUCTION

Calder (1988) makes a distinction between two competing stereotypesto answer the question "Where does power lie within the Japanese polity?": the Everest-ites and Miracle Men. Everest-ites want to know many things, but the Miracle Men want to know only one big thing: How has Japan succeeded? The miracle men regard Japan as an omni-efficient economic and social superpower. Ezra Vogel's Japan as Number One (1979) and Chalmers Johnsons' MITI and the Japanese Miracle (1982) provide the classic miracle-man stereotypes. These scholars have encouraged us to revise the study of the Japanese.

The Japanese "Revisionists" label assumes that Japan is a country with different values and should be treated differently from other democracies and market economies, A competing indigenous argument of Japanese uniqueness, nihonjinron, is extremely popular in Japan. Nihonjinron is a school of cultural particularism or relativism run rampant. Unlike the revisionists, nihonjinron and its offshoots (e.g., bunmeiron, nihon bunkaron), lack theoretical frameworks for understanding Japan in their obsession with identifying what is unique about Japan.

For example, many Japanese believe that ninjō are uniquely Japanese human feelings that cannot be understood by foreigners. They believe that Japanese are ultra- sensitive to each other's needs and have a special gift for wordless communication, or that they are a "race apart" from other peoples. Some authors have gone so far as to suggest a special quality of the Japanese brain that makes them want to suppress their individual selves, labeled the yamatogokoro (soul of the earliest Japanese). For such people "homogeneity" is a code word for uniqueness. Their dominant image is one of a classless and conflictless society without individual distinctions.

The result is what Gluck (1990) terms the "mythistory" of Japan. A typical example of how Westerners often fall into the nihonjinron trap is an editorial in the New York Times (April 12, 1990) by Nicholas Wade. Wade demonstrates the typical inability of the West to penetrate myths about Japan when he lauds the Japanese government for decisions based on "excellent information and well-formed consensus," calls Japanese goods "the high-level products of a highly functional society," and states that "the order and efficiency of Japanese life flow from strong pressures to conform." Popular books do little better. Witness Boye DeMente's 1990 book, Japan's Secret Weapon: The Kata Factor—The Cultural Programming that

Made the Japanese a Superior People. He claims Japanese uniqueness resides in the concept of kata as in shikata, (ways of doing things); kata ni hamaru (to apply form); or kata ni hamaranai (out of form). Kata refers to the way things are suppose to be done. According to DeMente, Japan has no genuine philosophy; and form replaces substance. Doing things the right (read: Japanese) way replaces logic and reason. There is no room for deviation, change, or creativity in DeMente's world. One wonders how the stuttifying nature of kata explains major changes such as the radical post-war simplification of the Chinese characters. Or more universally, whether the form of Japanese norms and values are more unbending than those of other cultures. What lies underneath appearances? Do we believe what people say or what they do?

On the other hand, the Everest-ites, with whom Calder identifies, view Japan as pluralistic and centerless--having many conflicting and competing sources of power that create a vacuum for action. Thus, Calder (1988) underscores classic Everest-ite themes: that Japan is economically weak and politically unstable. This view sees nothing particularly Herculean about the cohesiveness of Japan's industrial and trade policies. Rather, this view suggests that endemic power crises require constant compensatory actions.

The Japanese have an expression keizai ikkyū seiji sankyū (A first-rate economy with third-rate politics) that underscores the competing Dr. Jeckyl and Mr. Hyde stereotypes. How can a country have undergone an economic miracle to become an omni-efficient economic superpower while its government is a political basket case? Neither stereotype is credible, but how does one reconcile them?

Part of the problem lies in sloppy methodology. Bernard Finifter notes that there is

> . . . a curious inconsistency in the way researchers interpret results from attempted replications when discrepancies crop up. Failure to reproduce a finding in the same culture usually leads the investigator to question the reliability, validity, and comparability of the research procedures used in the two studies for possible methodological artifacts. But failure to corroborate the same finding in a different culture often leads to claims of having discovered "cultural" differences, and substantive interpretations are promptly devised to account for the apparent differences. (1977, p. 155)

Thus, a legitimate comparative discourse requires the application of consistent methods and the testing of universal theory. It also entails the testing of ideas and arguments rather than assuming their a prioi legitimacy.

The idea is to rescue Japan studies from the oblivion of particularism. The goal of this work is to root social science research in methodological and theoretical frameworks that promote comparative discourse; to deconstruct prevailing myths; to look beyond appearances; and to test for universal causes of all human experiences and practices. Chapters One through Three explore the educational life cycle. The dominant theory tested is social-capital theory. Chapter Four turns to the post-educational life cycle rites of passage of finding and marrying a mate through an exploration of the influence of sex-ratio theory. Chapter Five follows up on later stages of the marital life-cycle through comparisons of Western and Japanese attitudes and behaviors toward work, marriage, and divorce. Chapters Six and Seven address the issue of insiders and outsiders. Historical and contemporary data aid understanding of pressures toward conformity and reactions to non-conformity through a consideration of out-groups: Ainu, Burakumin, Korean-Japanese, Chinese-Japanese, other foreigners living in Japan, and signs of internationalization.

Most current work on Japan focuses upon power. Power relations are important to understanding any culture, and provide a major part of the framework in these chapters. However, status relationships have been seriously neglected in Japanese studies. Power and status are fundamental relational dimensions across societies. Power involves relational issues of control, compliance, coercion, force, threat, manipulation, and dominance; status concerns acceptance and positive association. Power always involves some form of involuntarism while status implies voluntarism. Thus, this book attempts to focus upon membership, willingness, deference, acceptance, liking, loving, and other markers of the conferral of status. For ultimately, the voluntarism underlying status is more powerful than the outside coercion implied by power.

The statuses conferred by acceptance into Tōkyō University, registration of one's marriage in the town registry, hiring as an engineer at Mitsui, or recognition as a Japanese national are powerful symbols of who a person is. There is no rational self-interest in failing to get into a major university, unemployment, divorce, or countrylessness, regardless of the society. Duty, obligation, and tradition are important components of status in all cultures, but rational self-interest is a stronger motivator to conform.

For most people, the natural unit of observation is the individual. However, sociologists emphasize the system level. The status of wife exists only in conjunction with the status of husband; One cannot be a mother without a child, a subordinate without a superior, or a Japanese without alternative cultures. Thus, this book also emphasizes the relationships between statuses in contemporary Japan. Most humans feel uncomfortable with power because of its ugly asocial connotations. If one person has power, another must have less. But high status can be conferred by one person or group on another with no loss of status for others. The beauty of status is its non-zero-sum nature.

Status relationships provide an important means of understanding the context of sociology. Joan Huber (1990) in her 1989 Presidential Address to the American Sociological Association pointed out that ". . . few scholars debated macro and micro relations until the 1960s when Homans tried to reduce sociology to social behaviorism." Such scholars usually did not take social structure into account. Social organization and structure can be studied quite nicely without reference to social psychology. Macro theory must account for patterns of social relations not on the basis of motives but on the basis of external constraints and opportunities for social relations created by population composition and the structure of positions in the social environment. This becomes another task of this book.

The population composition of Japan has been too long ignored as a source of social dynamics. The massive de-population of the rural areas and increasingly concentrated urban populations; the increasingly skewed numbers of marriageable men to women; and the fast-aging characteristics of the Japanese are only a few of the major composition structures that this book addresses to help understand who the Japanese are becoming.

Finding differences is one of a scientist's mandates. The myth of a harmonious, homogeneous society serves as a very powerful rational means for the establishment to exert control over the masses. One of the first status-defining concepts taught to Japanese children is the necessity of wa: a readiness to sacrifice one's personal welfare for the sake of communal harmony. At least, this is the "front-stage" behavioral expectation.

One of the common mistakes resulting from contact with only English-speaking Japanese and Japanese in public settings is the error of assuming their public face reflects their private actions. The public Japanese face overemphasizes the polite fictions of unity, homogeneity, harmony, and cooperation. But like the American expression "Don't hang your dirty laundry out in public" suggests, there is tension between public and private selves. Clear conflicts of status (urban-rural, married-single, Tōkyō University graduate or not, citizen-foreigner) are always just below the surface ready to erupt in predictable ways. More importantly, these status differences give insights into the diversity of the Japanese that exist under the public face. What most foreigners take for Japanese culture is only the tip of the iceberg.

Books on Japanese and Japan have become popular, but many of them are written by persons who have not made any attempt to reach basic vernacular materials. They quote from the same sources over and over again, leading to a proliferation of technical errors committed at the source. The end result is exaggeration of truth with famous concepts like "culture of shame," "developmental state mentality," Japan's "xenophobia", etc. These sources rarely go back to the basics of looking at original data, or making standard comparisons between Japanese or of Japan with other cultures. This book sets an example for future research by illustrating some of the ways in which better comparisons can be made through standardization of raw population data. It illustrates similarities and differences within Japan with social-ecological maps. The book calls attention to the results of cross-cultural methods using better reliability and validity checks than those with which many readers may be familiar. Finally, it places findings, as much as possible, within the comparative structure of universal sociological theory. The result, I hope, is a furthered appreciation of both the diversity of the Japanese and an understanding of how they are both similar and different.

Chapter 1

HONNE AND TATEMAE IN EDUCATION[0]

A merican lay persons, educators, and scholars alike have become obsessed with the Japanese educational system over the past decade. Numerous individuals note such evidence of declining educational standards in the United States as poorer SAT scores, although the past several years have shown modest gains. Others charge that the American educational system is no longer competitive with Japan's and those in other Western nations. Most people believe that quality education is crucial to overall industrial competitiveness. As education is an important form of human capital (Coleman 1993) the next three chapters will focus upon Japanese education.

However, the quality of formal education is only one of numerous factors that affect industrial competitiveness. Hart (1992) demonstrates that the way in which a country organizes its state and its society is more important than economic or cultural variables as a means of attaining international competitiveness. He suggests that strong business and government combined with weak labor movements aid state industrial policies in Japan. In essence, the Japanese business-government-labor connection allows for the high speed diffusion of new technologies. This connection traces back to the industrial and social unrest of 1919 when government and business formed the Kyōchōkai (Cooperation and Harmony Society) (Kinzley 1990). Also, Nakatani (1990) suggests that keiretsu (horizontally organized groups) are better able than conglomerates to distribute risk and to gain preferential access to capital markets.

By contrast, Germany has a relatively weak government, but strong business and labor with a major commitment to upgrading the skill levels of its work force. Both Germany and Japan have distinct advantages over the United States and Britain in periods of technological transition. The latter two nations lack centralized policies and mechanisms for coordination of capital, labor, education, industries, and so on. Thus, educational quality is

---

[0]Japanese use Honne to refer to "real intentions" versus Tatemae for "official party line."

important, but the reader should not think that it is the only, or even the most important factor, underlying international competitiveness. Furthermore, Taira and Levine (1992) point out that direct on-the-job training of adult workers is probably more important to the development of labor skills in Japan than the formal educational system.

This chapter focuses upon the arrangement of formal education in Japan. It begins with a cursory look at the historic origins of contemporary Japanese education. Then it debunks the numerous claims concerning how education works in Japan, including the myth of homogeneity. The underlying concept arises from the vast sociological literature on education as a form of cultural capital, and education systems for impersonally sorting students rather than teaching them. This leads into a consideration of the functions of education and ends with a survey of the structure of Japanese education.

THE ORIGINS OF CONTEMPORARY EDUCATION IN JAPAN

In the first years of the Meiji Reformation (1866—1912) the Japanese government made sweeping legal changes by establishing de jure educational opportunities for all citizens. On September 2, 1871, it created a powerful ministry of education with the authority to establish a centralized, nationwide school system (Rubinger, 1989). The next year the Meiji government passed the 1872 Decree for Encouragement of Learning. This degree mandated that "from this time onward, everyone irrespective of class origins such as nobility, military, farmer, artisan or merchant, and irrespective of one's sex, ought to learn, so that there should be no family without learning through the village and no person without learning in the family. . . ." (Fujita, 1989, pp. 128—129).

This decree radically broadened educational opportunity. Before the Meiji Reformation education was intended for the privileged few: priests, bureaucrats, royalty, and others of upper stations. Within 15 years of the decree, Japan could boast of a fully literate samurai (leadership) class and close to 17,000 schools including terakoya (parish schools), gōgaku (local schools), and shijuku (private academies) extending beyond urban areas so that even rural commoners were afforded some opportunities that were previously beyond their means. Even more impressively, the Meiji government abolished elementary school tuition in 1900, effectively underwriting mass education as evidenced in a sharp rise in school enrollments (Rubinger, 1989, p. 230). By 1880, Japan had as many primary schools as exist today with approximately one-third of today's population (White, 1987, p. 59). By 1900, 98% of all children attended elementary school, as is still true today.

Numerous scholars have concluded that such policy changes successfully democratized a previously feudalist set of educational opportunities because the creation of an efficient education system that reaches all echelons of society is a key element of modernization. Lebra

(1984, p. 321) states that education has become democratized in educational opportunities to enter "top institutions." Likewise, Iwama (1989, p. 76) and Cogan (1984, p. 464) assert that Japan has a standardized educational system that preserves Japanese homogeneity and monoculturality, affords equality of educational opportunity, and socializes Japanese youth into the kind of consensus-seeking that characterizes adult life in Japan.

Somewhat closer to the truth is the observation that tension and conflict became institutionalized when Japan replaced temple schools with a more modern national educational standard. Conflict continues unabated between advocates of tight government control and their more liberal minded opponents who promote the schools' independence and the curbing of government influence. Nikkyōso (the Japanese Federation of Teachers) has persisted for decades in opposing centralized control from Monbushō (The Ministry of Education, Science and Culture) and in fighting for independent education (Duke, 1986; Ota, 1989; Rohlen, 1983). Japanese education is not, and never has been, as democratized or conflict-free as many scholars or lay persons assume (Duke, 1989).

The decentralization caused by contemporary student use of the private juku (cram school) system has also worked against democratization, as Rohlen (1983; 1985) has argued. Although White (1987, p. 143) gives the figure of some "90% of ninth-grade children in urban areas" to demonstrate the "fairness" of the juku system, those "urban areas" refer to official Prime Minister's Office survey figures for the Kantō (Greater Tōkyō Metropolitan Area), masking wide variations across Japan. Urban families in the Kantō area, as I shall demonstrate later, have a much greater chance of placing their children in the top university (Tōkyō University) as well as the other leading 44 universities than do other areas of Japan which have a smaller proportion of highly ranked high schools and a lower percentage of students attending cram schools. Furthermore, the juku system would not even be needed if the public school system were as high quality as supporters of the system try to portray it.

Of course, it would be a mistake to assume that the Japanese or any other country's educational system has ever been fully democratized and open. As this chapter will demonstrate, Japanese education is not the meritocracy Shields (1989, p. 101) calls it; nor are White (1987, p. 73) and Goldberg (1989, p. 176) correct in stating that Japanese schools provide the same education regardless of variation in pupil ability or interest. Rohlen (1983) found great differences in the quality of five high schools in the Osaka-Kōbe area in his pioneering participant observation study of Japanese high schools. Yet he argues, without an empirical basis, that Japanese education offers greater basic equality than American reformers have dreamed possible until high school, and then somehow becomes competitive and elaborately hierarchical.

Instead, Japanese sociologists have found persistent differences in educational stratification since World War II. Fujita (1989) summarizes this relatively unchanging pattern of differences in academic achievement by father's occupation, which have persisted over the decennial (1955, 1965, and 1975) Japanese Social Stratification and Mobility (SSM) studies.[1] Fujita's (1989) empirical data demonstrates two clear, unchanging effects of social stratification on educational opportunity in Japan: First, the higher the father's educational level, the higher the son's academic achievement. Second, parents' background, father's occupation, and family income show effects on status attainment in Japan similar to that in the United States. Even Rohlen's (1983) less encompassing study indicates that few students from poor families entered elite universities in the mid-1970s, and suggests that delinquency rates closely correlate with academic rank of high schools, reflecting differences in family background.

Rohlen states that these stratification differences have only recently become pronounced, yet a stratified system of education — that mirrors the society at large — has deep roots in Japanese culture. Hierarchy historically defines the ways in which Japanese deal with each other much more so than in the West. A primary historical basis of Japanese stratification is age. Japanese schools, colleges, and universities — like individuals — rank according to their age. The seven oldest, national universities (the former imperial universities) stand at the apex and more recently established ones sit at the bottom.

Age ranking creates a vicious circle of self-ratification of institutional status. The general Japanese population rates older institutions at the top so that they naturally want their children to attend these "time-tested" schools, colleges, and universities; academics aspire to teach at these top-ranked institutions; and the government is most likely to continue educational support based on this self-fulfilling prophesy. The result is an age-stratified educational system that is highly resistant to change.

DEBUNKING STEREOTYPES OF JAPANESE EDUCATION

A persistent claim is that a uniform curriculum linked to national tests in Japan, a lifetime job system, and similar country-wide pay scales for teachers lead to virtually no variability in teacher quality, and uniform and predictable high, nation-wide levels of achievement in mathematics and other tests (Duke, 1986; White, 1987, p. 73). The standard hypothesis is that the Japanese educational system has a human "capital" advantage. Schaub and Baker (1991) have demonstrated that this hypothesis is fundamentally incorrect. Pay for teaching is equivalent across Japan and United States.

---

[1]The SSM is a cooperative venture of Japanese sociologists using a national probability sample drawn independently of official government samples in years ending with a "5" to test a variety of sociological questions contributed by cooperative members. The SSM exists because the Japanese government neither allows the public sharing of census-type data, nor non-governmental contributions to official censuses and surveys. Therefore, the SSM provides a unique source of exceptionally high-quality sociological data for the post-World War II period that is virtually unknown and unexplored by non-Japanese scholars. The SSM generally shows a much less rosy picture of Japanese life than the Japanese government normally portrays with its English-language releases of official statistics, white papers, and press reports.

Japanese teachers do not receive more training and are no more experienced. Japanese students receive less yearly instruction in mathematics. Student bodies are no more homogeneous educationally in Japan. Japan spends no more resources on education. Japanese children are no more intelligent. Japanese parents are no more involved in their children's schooling. And Japanese mathematics teachers assign less homework.[2]

What Schaub and Baker did find is that the classroom milieu and pedagogical practices play important roles in giving Japanese students an advantage over time. American teachers spend less time on new materials and more on review because of the huge differences in level of knowledge of incoming American students. American mathematics teachers might well borrow the Japanese methods of organizing instructional time to impart new, relevant material. Their analysis indicates that the American practices of streaming by ability groups and use of class time for ill-advised activities (e.g., school meal preparation, building maintenance, large numbers of tests, individual-level instruction at expense of group instruction) leads to a poorer atmosphere for student learning.

One of the functions of this chapter is to debunk stereotypes of the Japanese educational system. It is a diverse system, not unlike the U.S.A., although would-be experts often present Japanese education as a monolithic utopia to the outside world. Only a few studies by non-Japanese scholars (Beauchamp & Rubinger 1989; Passin 1970; Rohlen 1983) go beyond lauding the apparent successes of the Japanese system. For example, Beauchamp and Richards point out that Japanese scholars focus on a wide variety of festering problems calling for drastic reform of Japanese education including

> . . . the inegalitarian effects of entrance exam pressures and juku (cram school) attendance; the sacrifice by young children of their emotional and physical well-being; the increase in school violence, bullying, and dropouts; the need to internationalize the curriculum, and to better integrate students from abroad; and the need for greater flexibility in the system as a whole. (1989, p. 258)

Probably because the Japanese economy has continued to expand in an unprecedented fashion for over 30 years, the primary and secondary educational systems in Japan have attracted wide admiration abroad. The untested assumption is that the educational system has contributed greatly to this unabated economic expansion. There are probably numerous extra-

---

[2]These misunderstandings emanate largely from a study by Stevenson (1989) which used only Japanese students from Sendai, Japan in comparison with Taiwanese and the Chicago metropolitan area in Illinois. Of course, a comparison of students from only two non-randomly chosen geographical areas could easily turn up better, more homogeneous mathematics scores in samples. A more recent study based on stratified random samples of classrooms for both nations (Schaub & Baker 1991) indicates that what are significantly different are the ranges, or standard deviations. American students have a range of mathematics-aptitude scores much lower and much higher than Japanese students in their study. It is time to use only truly representative cross-national studies, rather than those based on unrepresentative samples to guard against problems of sample comparability.

educational reasons for the exceptionally strong growth of the Japanese economy after World War II.

After the war, Fukutake (1976) argues that Japan experienced abnormally high rates of urbanization and industrialization, leaving a shell of farming communities and traditional rural life. According to Fukutake's thesis, the rapid disintegration in the social fabric of rural Japan, which included a hollowing out of the quality of the rural school system, widens differences in rural-urban educational opportunities. In a later chapter I shall present data suggesting some strong deleterious effects of these rural-urban inequities on Japanese education.

EDUCATIONAL HOMOGENEITY OR HETEROGENEITY?

To the outsider, the Japanese educational system appears to be incredibly homogeneous. Casual observations easily verify an inordinately homogeneous picture. For example, most schools require a standard uniform. It can be a little unnerving for first-time foreign visitors to see all 40 children from the same nursery school dressed in the same yellow cap; porting the same regulation school back pack with exactly the same number of pens, crayons, pencils, or whatever inside; wearing the same exact shoes, socks, pants, and shirt; and sporting the same haircut. The image, from nursery school through high school, is one straight out of an old-style American or British military school.

Numerous casual observations reinforce the impression of uniform military-like schooling. A high degree of synchronization of group activity characterizes education in Japan. Schools and universities observe the same holidays, use the same textbooks, enforce the same standards for pace of learning of basic Chinese characters, and so on, because Monbushō is a highly centralized ministry with the authority to set and enforce national educational standards.[3]

Again, if one inspects rates of advancement to high school and high school graduation, the statistics indicate highly uniform and high quality results of this system. For example, high-school-graduation rates in the United States range from a low of roughly two-thirds of students in Louisiana to a high of close to 95% in the North Central states of North Dakota, South Dakota, and Minnesota. By contrast, the high school graduation rates in Japan in 1984 had a mean of 95% with only a few percentages of variation (based upon tenth grade entrance rates). Similarly, the 1984 rate of male junior high school students entering high schools ranged from 89.3% in Ryūkyū (Okinawa) Prefecture to 96.9% in Toyama Prefecture. The statistics are similar for girls — a low of 90.1% in Aichi and a high of 98.3% in

---

[3]The School Education Law of 1947 returned preparation and publication of textbooks to private hands, after 40 years of state-run system. In 1955 the ruling Liberal Democratic Party promoted "textbook revisions" of social studies textbooks setting up a long term battle with the Japan Teacher's Union over control of education. By 1963 through laws passed favoring large publishers, government efforts to control textbooks had resulted in standardized texts for the entire country.

Toyama Prefectures.[4] Both Western and Japanese observers point to such widely known statistics as signs of (a) high standards of Japanese schooling and (b) exceptionally high equality of educational opportunities in Japan. Most of the statistics officially issued by <u>Monbushō</u> uphold these images of high quality education and educational opportunities. By contrast, the American system with its decentralized community-based system of close to 15,000 independent school boards appears to be much more highly variable in quality and quantity than the Japanese system. Widely available statistics indicate that only a few private and public high schools in the U.S.A. consistently produce high numbers of college entrants, and engineering, science, and mathematics majors, while other high schools produce large numbers of dropouts.[5] However, a basic thesis of this chapter is that the Japanese system, in spite of its apparent homogeneity, is extremely variable in quality and quantity. Monbushō holds tight control over the entire system from appropriate textbooks and content[6] for each grade level to teacher qualifications. Still, tremendous differences exist in equality of education in terms of who gets into the top universities, which translates eventually into the most-sought-after jobs, prestige, and wealth.

High-school-entrance and graduation rates (and many other official statistics) are poor measures of quality and quantity of Japanese education. The reason is simple. The pervasive myth of homogeneity leads educators to ignore individual differences which adds pressure to pass students who would otherwise fail in the American system. Virtually no student fails in Japan — not necessarily because of high quality of education — but because Japanese beliefs in homogeneity impel educators to ignore real individual differences.

If school quality were as homogeneous as official statistics report, we should expect homogeneous rates of going to colleges and universities across all prefectures. However, high schools are well known for extreme variation in the production of top-university material. Every April the <u>Sunday Mainichi</u> magazine publishes a widely-read series of issues on the "top 400 high schools" (those that produce the vast majority of successful entrants into the top-44 ranked universities) out of a total of 5512 high schools in Japan by name of student, sex, high school, prefecture, university acceptance. They also include the 10-year-running average for top high school success rates. That less than 7% of the high schools produced all successful test takers for the 44 universities at the apex of the status-ladder suggests extreme inequality of educational opportunity.

---

[4]Unless I indicate otherwise, my statistics all come from the <u>1989 Nihon Tōkei Nenkan. (1989 Japan Statistical Yearbook)</u>. Ed. by Sōrichō Tōkeikyoku (Statistical Bureau, Prime Minister's Office). Tōkyō: Nihon Tōkei Kyōkai. However, much of their data is in raw form only so I have standardized it with percentages, ratios, and other appropriate measures to highlight differences normally obscured by raw statistics.

[5]Extreme differences in quality of schools are also true of Japan, but people outside Japan rarely learn of these statistics.

[6]Ministry policy has gone so far as to censor history texts that do not expose the official line toward the Japanese invasion of China and the conquest and colonization of Korea (Cho 1987).

Data for 1988[7] indicate wide variation in quality of schools at the prefectural level. Only 4.3% of Saitama's top-rated high school graduates entered the elite 44 universities compared to 33.14% in Tokushima Prefecture at the other extreme. A Tokushima student had 8 times the chance of a Saitama student of entering one of the top-44 universities. Similarly, success-rates for the applicants to the elite seven (the original so-called Imperial) universities demonstrate high differentiation. These seven universities only admitted 43 out of every 10,000 graduating high school seniors from Ryūkyū Prefecture compared to 2060 from Toyama Prefecture. So a Toyama senior had 48 times the chance of admittance to one of these universities as a Ryūkyū senior. Even if we ignore these prestigious universities, widespread geographic differences remain in college attendance across the entire archipelago: 17.6% of Gunma high school seniors advanced on to a university in 1984 compared to 37.1% at the other extreme in Hiroshima.[8]

A related myth that crops up in academic (Shields, 1989) as well as non-academic discussions of Japanese educational quality is the belief that the Japanese system caters to students of average ability while the American system serves better those of high and low ability. This belief ignores well-known differences in treatment of females, Burakumin[9], Koreans, students who go abroad for a year or more, and the physically and emotionally handicapped compared to males of more "traditional" Japanese background (Hawkins, 1989; Upham, 1987). It is worthwhile considering each of these groups in turn.

Japanese perceive higher education as "the male track" (otoko no michi). Fujimura-Fanselow (1989, p. 166) cited the results of an NHK (Japan Broadcasting Corporation) poll suggesting how parental aspirations influence sex discrimination in education. Thirty-four percent of a national sample of Japanese adults thought an upper-secondary school education was sufficient for their daughters; 24% chose junior college and 24% a university education. For sons, the corresponding figures were 15%, 9%, and 68%, with an additional 6% desiring graduate-level education for their sons. There is still a widespread belief that women's educational experiences should make them better wives and mothers, and a husband ought to be better educated than his wife. This is as true of mothers as fathers in Japan. Lebra's (1984, pp. 161, 185) ethnographic account describes Japanese respondents who are

---

[7]Special issue of Sande- Mainichi (Sunday Mainichi) April 16, 1988. Through the month of April of each year this magazine publishes scores of pages of statistics on university admittance patterns. One of the issues also carries data on the total 1360 high schools that contribute to the top 45 universities. However, the top 400 account for over 80% of these students and all of the new freshman at the top seven universities.

[8]Of course, one could make the argument that some of these differences are due to "individual motivation, personal skills and interests," or other such factors. However, supporters are not inclined to make such arguments. The myth represents all students as having equal educational opportunities. I shall address this issue again more directly later in this chapter.

[9]Literally, this means "village people," but it is actually the official euphemism for the original Tokugawa Period outcaste group known as the eta.

intensely filiocentric with mothers of boys being strong supporters of male dominance. These discriminatory beliefs are inconsistent with actual educational outcomes. Although one would expect these sexist beliefs to lead to sex discrimination against women, government statistics show a more complex picture. From the standpoint of general education, women outperform men in advancing from junior high school to high school and from high school to higher education. First, in all 47 prefectural units fewer boys than girls pass from junior into senior high schools. The sex ratio ranged from 95.9 to 99.3 boys per 100 girls in 1984. Second, there are only seven prefectures in which more male students pass from high school into higher education. The ratio ranged from a low of 60.9 males per 100 females in Kōchi Prefecture to 113.9 in Tottori Prefecture. The mean ratio for this 1984 data is 85.6 males per 100 females.[10]

Still, these government statistics are deceptive because they mix junior and senior college data, resulting in inflated numbers of women in higher education. Japanese perceive junior colleges as "finishing schools" for women. They place junior colleges at the bottom of the status pyramid in part because most are relatively new (over 200 of the 500-odd junior colleges were established in the 1960s and 1970s) and they stereotype them as the "women's track" (onna no michi). In 1989, over 95% of all junior college students were women while less than 40% of university students were women.

In spite of the fact that more female than male students enter high school and college, colleges accept fewer women students the higher the status of the university. For example, the 1989 rates of coeds entering top-ranked Tōkyō, Kyōto, and Ōsaka University were 12, 6, and 11%.[11] A good portion of the lower percentages of women students is due to a small number of well-known private, male-only high schools that specialize in entering Tōkyō University and other top-ranked universities. Forty percent of the students who entered Tōkyō University in 1989 attended private all-male high schools, according to tabulations based on the Sunday Mainichi statistics.

Sex discrimination also is institutionalized at the career level, acting as a further damper on women's college entrance aspirations. Lebra (1984, p. 241) points out that the Ministry of Finance and the Ministry of Health and Welfare have turned down women with Tōkyō University specialization in economics. Furthermore, the one woman graduate from Tōdai's law school to

---

[10]In another chapter I plan to show the serious implications these previously unrecognized data have for marriage prospects in Japan where the average unmarried male expects to marry a woman with less education than himself while the average woman expects to marry a man with more education than herself.

[11]I am indebted to Kaoru Bergland and Naoto Inoue for helping me differentiate between Japanese male and female given names. This data comes from the 1989 special annual issue of the Sande-Mainichi [1988] magazine on top high schools and colleges in Japan. The results are conservative in the sense that we coded names that could be either male or female as female names. In all three cases, the difference is only one-half percentage point between the lowest and highest estimates my informants counted.

pass the civil service exam one year was rejected. Courts assign women to family courts only and consider women inept for criminal cases. The judiciary also rules out women as presiding judges or court directors. Such structural barriers make university attendance a relatively pointless exercise for women interested in careers rather than short-term jobs. The few women who do manage to attend four-year institutions are pressured to major in literature, home economics, and education. The annual report of the Sunday Mainichi on elite high schools suggests therefore that virtually all of the few women who do make it to the top universities end up in the bungakubu (liberal arts) or kyōikubu (educational) tracks.[12]

There is also widespread educational discrimination against the sizeable populations of Chinese and Korean heritage. As of September, 1989 the Tōkyō Metropolitan Government reported only 7 high schools that would accept the 105 children of World-War-II-displaced persons of Chinese or Korean descent who have come to Japan in recent years. It set quotas for transfers from other prefectures for students accepted on the strength of recommendations by junior high school authorities to 367 of Chinese descent and 165 of Korean descent, according to The Japan Times (May 17, 1990).

The remarks of Mombushō's Minister Hori (The Japan Times, April, 24 1990) indicate the pervasive exclusion of non-Japanese from mainstream education. Hori stated that the Ministry might finally allow adult foreign residents to participate in annual national sports meets. The Japan Amateur Sports Association limits participation in national athletic contests to those with Japanese nationality. In 1981 high school students with foreign-resident status were allowed to join in national sports meets, and junior high students in 1988, but no college student or adult has yet been allowed (as of 1993). These include third and fourth-generation residents who have never traveled outside of Japan.

The barriers to non-Japanese participation in mainstream education are remarkably consistent across the various minorities. Close to 95% of Japanese nationals enter and graduate from high school, but Korean, Ainu, Okinawan, and Burakumin populations all range well below the national average. The Hokkaidō Prefectural government estimated that slightly more than 78% of Ainu attained a high school diploma in 1988; the Ōsaka Municipal government has reached even lower estimates of around two-thirds of Koreans in Ōsaka.

For Burakumin, the story is similar: In 1963, less than 10% of the parents had attended senior high school and 30% of children, compared with 60 to 70% of the Japanese public. By 1973 Burakumin senior high attendance had improved to 64% attending compulsory-level schools but they still lagged behind the Japanese general cohort figure of 95% (Hawkins, 1989, p. 199). Hawkins also notes that a mere 4.2% of Burakumin graduate from

---

[12]Unlike American universities, students in Japan are admitted to schools within universities based on test scores. College admissions test scores place students into law, engineering, science, liberal arts, education, etc, in relative order of prestige. Within schools, admissions tests further rank students. Thus, sociology is ranked lower than political science, so some students with low test scores who want to enter political science might be admitted to sociology and major in the sociology of politics.

college. Part of the reason is due to blatant discriminatory policies on the part of universities, some of which have bought lists of known Burakumin ghettos, the only plausible use of which is to weed out prospective "undesirable" college applicants (Sueo & Miwa 1986). Local school authorities, under pressure from local Burakumin groups, have instituted affirmative-action programs with improvements in increased staffing and equipment, remedial classes, and additional counseling in recognition of the continued de facto discrimination. During the late 1960s local school districts in the Osaka area attempted to prevent cross-district registration by students at schools outside their own district — a phenomenon analogous to "white flight" from increasingly black inner cities in American schools (Upham 1987:93).

EDUCATION AS "CULTURAL CAPITAL"

Katsillis and Rubinson (1990) speak of the role of cultural capital — a metaphor based on the economic concept — in relating social background, inequalities, and educational attainment. As numerous sociologists of education have noted, parent's education is an important type of cultural capital in the reproduction of a social hierarchy. Those individuals with higher education are more able to pass on their status advantages.

Although the pressures for meritocratic selection and equality of educational opportunity are great in modern nation-states, there are still clear counterpressures to reproduce and legitimate the traditional ascriptive power of class, sex, and ethnic statuses. For Greek high school seniors Katsillis and Rubinson found that both father's class position and family socioeconomic status determine a student's cultural capital, but they found no evidence that cultural capital has either direct or indirect effects on educational achievement. Similarly, Horan and Hargis (1991) used 1890 survey data to demonstrate the timelessness of how higher levels of family resources and lower levels of demand on those resources induce higher rates of children's participation in school after controlling for alternative explanations.

No social scientist to my knowledge has rigorously tested the cultural-capital thesis to date in Japan, but (1) the blatant discriminatory policies and practices against minority groups and (2) sex stratification in the willingness of parents to pay for college educations give good reason to entertain this idea in later sections of this chapter. For example, Steelman and Powell (1991, p. 1525) note that while there is no guarantee that an American son or daughter will repay college debts incurred by a parent while Japanese sons (but not daughters) are under obligation to repay parents, to work in family-owned businesses, and to support their parents in old age.

Student ability and effort are, ironically, the major mechanisms maintaining and legitimating the educational process (Katsillis & Rubinson 1990). In other words, because the general public perceives that individual student ability and effort are the major reasons for individual educational attainment, it is easy for the general public to rationalize that differences between ascriptive groups (i.e., Koreans and Japanese, men and women) are due to effort, ability, and skill rather than luck or social background. Baker and Stevenson (1988) found that Japanese perceived family socioeconomic status and quality of tutorial schooling as just another form of student effort, rather than as a characteristic ascribed to the family into which a student is born. The social positions of families in Japan, however, are much more ascribed than in the U.S.A.

Also, Japanese children have powerful incentives to learn well in school because the consequences of not bearing down are greater than in the U.S.A. where a student always has the belief in a "second chance" if he or she fails the first time. Such perceptions aid the status quo in Japan. Individuals believe that student effort and ability are the main factors allowing them to enter juku (cram schools) with a reputation for placement into Tōkyō University, legitimating the system as a fair and just one. Such perceptions of fairness and justness override perceptions that ascriptive social background characteristics have anything to do with the process.[13]

One peculiarly Japanese social institution of particular interest to the cultural capital argument is tanshin-fu'nin. This phrase means "taking up a new post in another city or country, unaccompanied by one's family." Tanshin-fu'nin is particularly common among middle-aged Japanese businessmen with children of high school age. Although every school in Japan is under very narrow restrictions as to what it may teach, making for a high degree of apparent homogeneity across all schools, in actuality Japanese parents are well aware of the extreme disadvantages that may accrue from change of schools.

Ranking of high schools is a national mania manifest in the enormous amount of newspaper and magazine coverage given to the results of university entrance tests each winter. Consequently, once a child enters a high-status high school, great pressures practically insure that the father posted to a place outside commuting distance from home will leave his family behind and live the life of a bachelor in a separate household. The greatest likelihood of this happening appears among men with greater cultural capital such as white-collar workers and university professors. Rather than give up the investments in their children's (particular their sons') educations, parents who have greater cultural capital to invest are

---

[13] As one demonstration of this, consider the typical reaction I have received when presenting data to Japanese university students and colleagues showing that no Okinawan has ever been accepted to Tôdai and that the chances of a student from Toyama Prefecture going to one of the top seven universities is 48 times that of one from Okinawa Prefecture. The immediate response is invariably that "smart" Okinawan parents send their children to famous boarding schools on Honshū island like Nada in Kōbe which is known for its high-pass rate on the Tōdai entrance examination, totally disregarding alternative hypotheses based on ascriptive factors such as the income, occupation, and education of parents. Parents may not have the funds necessary to make such an expensive sacrifice, no matter how intelligent their child might be. Again, when the best universities ban or limit Koreans, Chinese, Burakumin, Okinawans, Ainu, or women, such factors as skill and ability make absolutely no difference.

likely to keep their sons in those schools that are most able to insure replication of the fathers' statuses. Many fathers then find it necessary to move elsewhere for the purpose of earning enough to support their sons following in their footsteps.

As a rule, Japanese feel very strongly that only a standardized, national curriculum is fair to all children, who — with similarly good teachers — all have an equal chance at the rewards education brings. Teachers share in the status of their school, because the general public avidly follows the results of test scores and school rankings published in newspapers and magazines. Such strong standardization of curriculum helps maintain the illusion of a nearly total meritocracy in which only individual effort and skill cause differences in educational outcomes. Such effects of families and external resources as private schools, juku and, yobikō (cram schools) are easily explained away as resources used only by students of high caliber who also are the most dedicated students. Of course, if the systems were truly meritocratic we would not expect to find the huge differences in educational outcomes that occur between prefectures replicated year after year, nor the persistent class differences noted earlier in the SSM survey results. Explanations of truly individual differences are at odds with explanations of cultural-capital explanations because purely individual differences should be random across time and large geographic units.

Mothers are another component of the cultural-capital explanation. Social pressures compel mothers to participate in PTAs which meet during the day and to take their turns at various offices in their local PTAs. These norms act as dampers on the desires of mothers to work. Mothers also work very hard preparing elaborate lunches, making things for their children to use in schools, and attending school functions. Therefore, mothers view their childrens' successes at school as their own personal achievement (Iwamura 1987, p. 20). Mothers, therefore, come to perceive personal responsibility for their children's educational outcomes rather than attribute the results to the effects of other forces.

Language provides another powerful means for "explaining" educational outcomes. Japanese most often attribute lack of achievement to failure to work hard rather than lack of ability or personal and environmental obstacles. Singleton (1989, p. 8) states that Japanese emphasize "Gambaru" (persistence) in explaining and organizing education versus Americans who emphasize ability (IQ, intelligence, talent.). The point is not whether Japanese or Americans are correct. Both may be wrong. Of greatest concern is the lack of interest in testing such explanations. Researchers continue to assume these individual differences are more important than social structural ones without conducting fair tests.

The problem, then, is neglect of the subtle, multifaceted intervening influences of family, peers, and culture on young people. Lynn (1988) suggests that Japanese children appear to work voluntarily. They stay in school after the years of compulsory schooling. They go to non-compulsory juku; and they do much more homework than their Western counterparts. Yet these facts ignore the social and cultural environment surrounding children including peer as well as adult pressures. They also overlook the realities of the talent-selection system.

Another part of cultural capital is the willingness to pay for education and the foresight to understand its long-term value. The hidden costs of primary and secondary education grew between 4% and 80%, respectively, from 1977 to 1987, depending on student's ages, according to Monbushō's annual "white paper" (1989).[14] In 1987, parents paid nearly ¥184,000 ($898) per primary student annually, ¥225,000 ($1098) in junior high school, and ¥294,000 ($1434) in high school.[15] During the same period, consumer's prices rose 34.4%. Especially outside school costs — special tutorings and cram schools for entrance examinations — increased every year and more than doubled during the decade indicating the growing importance of juku and yobikō to educational success.

The disproportionately rising costs have increased the likelihood that unfairness of educational opportunities will occur in Japan because they insure greater opportunities only for those with the ability to afford these costs.[16] These costs start as early as pre-school and differ by private and public education. In 1988, public-kindergarten students averaged ¥180,000 ($878) in total costs. Private-kindergarten costs reached ¥340,000 ($1659). Private high school students paid ¥605,000 ($2951), or nearly twice the public school rate.[17]

Marked differences across prefectures suggest inequitable valuation of education that is a necessary, if not sufficient, condition for the cultural capital argument. For example the 1987 prefectural low for total pupil expenditures was close to half of the high: ¥226,800 in Saitama versus ¥429,200 in Akita. These differences persist across breakdowns into elementary, junior high, and senior-high expenditures. The prefecture with the lowest expenditures per pupil in each breakdown is close to half that of the prefecture with the highest amount. Per-pupil expenditures depend in part upon political decisions concerning what proportion of budgets are allotted for educational versus non-educational items. This suggests the possibility that some prefectures are much more interested in supporting

---

[14]Although schooling is free at these levels, such things as uniforms and school supplies are not.

[15]These figures, and all others in this book, are based on economic purchasing power parities (p.p.p.) of ¥205=$1.00. The current exchange rate fluctuates too widely and does not accurately reflect the purchasing power in each country. In 1990 average figures showed about 130 to 150 yen to the dollar. However, the National Science Foundation uses conversion tables developed by economists that show the dollar is much stronger than normal conversion tables indicate. Economists equalize price levels among countries through P.P.P.'s. The aim is to make the clout of differing currencies roughly equal in terms of goods that are traded internationally. In 1989, this method showed the dollar was worth about 205 yen rather than the actual market value of 138 yen.

[16]One of the great ironies is that examinations originally aided fairness. There is no room for competitive examinations in a feudal society, because social rank and privilege is inherited rather than distributed on the basis of merit or academic excellence.

[17]Unlike students in the U. S. A., Japanese students attending public high schools must pay tuition fees.

their youth than others. In essence, cultural capital appears to operate as much at the prefectural, as the familial, level.

EDUCATION AS AN IMPERSONAL SORTING MACHINE

The view of education as a form of cultural capital that one's offspring can inherit is not a very popular idea among people with little educational capital to pass on, because this idea does not allow for much possibility that effort and persistence will produce high educational outcomes for the children of parents with poorer economic resources. It also is not a popular idea among elites who prefer that the masses not know the differences educational capital makes to academic success, out of fear that such knowledge works against the status quo. However, there is another metaphor much used in the sociology of education with an even more sinister possibility. This is the conception of education as an impersonal, monolithic sorting machine.

Few people realize the recency of mass education throughout the entire world. Instead, they take it for granted. University education originally was intended for the elites. The great universities of Europe (Oxford, Bologna, Heidelberg, etc.) were not established for the masses. Likewise, such early colleges in the U. S. A. as Harvard, William and Mary, and Pennsylvania were conceived of as finishing schools for sons of the wealthy. Higher education for the masses is a phenomenon of the twentieth century. The American version obtained its main impetus from returning veterans of World War II who received veteran's benefits allowing a whole class of persons to attend college who had never before had the financial resources to do so.

The need for efficient ways for choosing who should go to college paralleled the fast-rising numbers of students. Given the limited number of students any given school system could afford to admit, educators turned to objective testing systems for making university-entrance decisions. Such tests as the A.C.T. and S.A.T. have become institutionalized in the U. S. A. as a way of sorting large masses of college-hopefuls. Japan, likewise, developed a parallel system after World War II for sorting students through adaptation of the Western mass-testing function. One important result of mass testing, charged by Japanese critics (Amano 1989) is that schools are no longer a place where children learn and gain important knowledge but have become a place where educators evaluate what they have done at home and in classes after school.

From this view, tests act as a sorting mechanism for placement in the hierarchy of schools and universities in Japan. These tests do not evaluate ability to draw conclusions, to abstract from facts, to connect abstractions, to organize thoughts through essays, to express one's self in another language, or ask questions. These tests show no patience with originality. Their emphasis is on rote memorization of trifling details (Amano 1989; Rohlen

1983). Tests do not necessarily evaluate the contributions of schools to student achievement either. Reports abound of nursery and kindergarten schools that have devised tests to sort three to five-year-old children into "desirable" and "undesirable" students, increasing the pressures on both children and parents to conform to school expectations at unreasonably early ages.

The result is of elite educational institutions trying to pick students who have already shown they have memorize huge amounts of materials rather than that they have tried to educate students. As von Wolferen (1989, p. 379) charges, the emphasis in Japanese education is on "automatic, endless, non-reflective repetition." Although students may appear to start out with equal opportunities to conform to educational expectations to learn to regurgitate the mass of facts needed to pass college entrance examinations, by high school there are huge nonrandom differences in their chance of going to top-rated universities. Educational opportunity for everyone is very much a myth in modern Japan, which translates into important consequences in later life.

THE OBJECTIVES OF EDUCATION VERSUS SCHOOLING

Is Japanese education a success or failure? The answer to this question depends on the stated objectives. At the lowest level of objectives are basic, functional literacy and numeracy. On this point the Japanese government has asserted for years that their educational system is a complete success. Over 95% of Japanese youth graduate from high school placing Japan first in the world, so it would be easy to assume that illiteracy and innumeracy have been largely eradicated in Japan. However, a good part of the Japan's high secondary school-graduation rate is due to the Japanese loathing to admit student failure and the desire of its leadership to perpetuate the myth of a homogeneous race. Singleton (1989, p. 12—13) notes that both failing and jumping grades are "unthinkable in Japan." Iwamura (1987, p. 20), likewise, charges that both the gifted and those in need of remedial work suffer from lack of instructions because of this ultimate failure to grade students. This makes the high Japanese passing rates and assertion that Japan has no illiteracy particularly suspect. The substantial differences in successful entry into top-ranked universities are a clear sign of the chimera of consistently high-quality education across the span of Japan.

Nevertheless, the Japanese mass media spends considerable effort in attacking the "poor" educational system in the U. S. A. For example, former Prime Minister Nakasone's infamous charge that racial and ethnic heterogeneity is the root cause of American educational problems, giving Japan's "unique" and "homogeneous" race the advantage. The Japanese press continues to play up this "blame the victim" type of explanation while pretending that no problems of a similar nature exist in Japan.

As a point of reference, consider the story in The Japan Times (April 7, 1990) that Motorola Corporation will reportedly spend $35 million in 1990, four times its investment in a new state-of-the-art plant, to teach basic reading skills to employees. In 1989, Motorola Corporation rejected approximately half of 3000 applicants for its Arlington Heights, Illinois plant. The rejected applicants could not do fifth-grade mathematics or read at the seventh-grade level on employment tests. According to the story, Motorola can no longer afford employees without the skills necessary to run efficiently and correctly an increasingly sophisticated and complex operation.

This story implies that Motorola's horror story could not take place in Japan because of its elimination of basic illiteracy and innumeracy. That may be the case, but because Monbushō maintains that illiteracy has been completely solved, there are no official statistics in Japan to test the idea. However, the extreme differences in educational opportunities that exist in Japan continue to be treated as due to lack of individual effort rather than systemic dysfunction, so the educational inequity problem in Japan appears to be very much an open question.

Rohlen's (1983) ethnographic study of Japanese high schools was perhaps the first non-Japanese study to comment on illiteracy in modern Japan. Rohlen expressed great shock at the number of adults he observed taking night-school courses who could not read basic Chinese characters that he himself had mastered as a non-native after only a few years of study. Ken Motoki (1989), a professor of education at Ōsaka University, is one of the rare Japanese academics who has studied this problem. He charged that it is difficult to get accurate figures because many people in Japan as in the U.S.A conceal their problem. Motoki believes that as many as three million Japanese may be illiterate at sixth-grade levels of reading and writing. His argument suggests a profile of illiteracy consisting predominately of females, Burakumin, the elderly, and Koreans. This profile is consistent with national figures on high school graduation rates that are markedly lower for minority group members and with the idea of strong male biases in educational tracking.

Three million Japanese illiterates seems relatively small in a population of 130 million. After all, that is only slightly more than 2% of the total population. However, a sixth-grade level of reading and writing in Japanese amounts to only 881 of the 2000-odd characters deemed essential to read an average daily newspaper in Japan.[18] While an English-native can look up any English word in a dictionary, looking up unknown Chinese characters is infinitely more demanding, requiring knowledge of close to 200 primitive building blocks of the characters known as radicals. Monbushō claims that most children can read and write the minimal set of standard

---

[18]The Japanese government recognizes three levels of literacy: the lowest level consists of 881 "education" kanji; the middle one of "general purpose" ones encountered in daily newspapers; and the most difficult level of thousands of other kanji including scholarly words that few readers ever even partially master. In reality, illiteracy is part of a broader continuum.

(tōyō)1850 kanji by the end of high school. However, Yamada (1992) has shown that this is not true. For example, he found that even children in Grade 6 can read only 61%, and can write only 68%, of Grade-3 kanji. This problem worsens with time because there is no analytic correspondence between grapheme and sound in kanji, and because of interactions between the large numbers of multiple readings, homophony, and graphic complexity.

Many Japanese, including academics who should know better, reify Chinese characters by making the claim that they are inherently easier to read than alphabetic-based printed matter: They claim a built-in advantage for Japanese over English literacy. Several false notions underlie this claim. One is that kanji (Chinese characters) are pictographs (shōkeimoji). In actuality, they are ideographs (kaiimoji). A true pictograph should be an obvious representation of some thing as many early Chinese characters were — mountain, moon, sun, eye, and hand being good examples for which confirmed archaeological pictographs readily exist. However, the kanji evolved into more abstract graphic representations that continue to be modified and simplified. Such simple characters as ue (up) and shita (down) had alternative forms of a dot above a line and a dot below a line in their early evolution. This suggests the relative nature of their representation compared to present rules that portray "up" with two straight strokes above a bottom line, and "down" with an inversion of the same character.

Another good indicator of the relative, ideographic nature of the kanji is the fact that Chinese and Japanese compounds have evolved in increasingly divergent ways. Completely different ideographs can express the same idea. A good example is the expression for an incorporated business. The Chinese use two characters read as kōshi in Japanese, while the Japanese employ four other Chinese characters which they read as kabushigaisha. True pictographs should at least employ the same characters.

Another false notion is that the Chinese characters have consistent usage. Paradis, Hagiwara, and Hildebrandt (1985, pp. 6—7, 172—173) point to at least two nonstandard aspects of kanji usage by Japanese that create problems for attaining full literacy by native readers. First, over one-third of the first 2000 characters have nonstandard readings. For example, daidokoro (kitchen) is a combination of a Chinese (dai) and a Japanese (dokoro) reading. Second, there is at least one example of 23 different morphemes that may be represented by the same kanji. Thus, the same kanji may use the sound hagemu to represent "be diligent," the reading hagemasu to mean "to encourage," or as rei in combination with a kanji "kō" signifying "to come" to mean "enforce strictly." As Paradis and his colleagues state, "Poorly educated adults tend to use more kana when they write and are always able to read words spelled in kana but not all words written in kanji." They give numerous citations and examples (p. 172—173) of native Japanese confusion of the expected Japanese reading of kanji with the incorrect Chinese reading.

The Japanese language is so unlike the Chinese language that the borrowing of the kanji was somewhat akin to fitting square pegs into round holes. Many Japanese words borrowed kanji not for their meaning but for their sounds — omoshiroi (interesting) and daijobu (okay) are classic examples of Japanese use of kanji compounds that the Japanese borrowed for their sounds in complete defiance of their original Chinese meanings. Particularly kanji which are used for verbs are susceptible to meanings based on context rather than ideographic expression.

In spite of these obvious complexities, myths abound that ideographic systems are superior to alphabetic ones. This is an important assertion, because if it were true, ideographic systems would have an important advantage over alphabetic systems for promoting literacy. Psychologists who have tested these claims (see Paradis et al., 1985 for a critical review) have not found any substantiating evidence. The roots of Western languages (e.g., Greek, Latin) appear to carry just as much information as the radicals in Chinese characters. Any English-native with a modest grasp of Latin or Greek etymology should be able to make as good a guess at a previously unknown English word as a Japanese can with a previously unseen kanji compound. New dictionaries of contemporary newspaper Japanese compounds appear each year because the average Japanese reader has as little idea of the meaning of complex scientific, economic, and business terminology as the average American does with their English equivalents.

Furthermore, the 881 characters taught through the sixth-grade are not completely synonymous with the most frequently used character compounds needed by adults to understand newspapers and other mass media.[19] Consequently, even Motoki's (1989) figures are probably highly conservative because knowing the 881 characters taught through the first six grades make up less than half of the characters necessary to read adult-level materials without necessarily having learned how to look up any of the remaining unknown characters for meaning and pronunciation help. By contrast, it is possible for a 12-year-old English native sixth-grader to use a dictionary to look up both pronunciation and meaning of any unknown English word they encounter in reading. This difference probably puts Japanese illiterates at a distinct disadvantage compared to English illiterates.

We can obtain a more accurate idea of the actual extent of illiteracy in Japan by focusing on that percentage of the adult population who have only completed an elementary school education in Japan. Using government figures on the percentage of the population over age 14 who have finished only an elementary school education shows a huge number of adults who must be functionally illiterate. The average rate of the adult population with only an elementary-school education in 1980 was 41.8%. This figure ranged from a low in Tōkyō of 25.9% to 53.5% in Aomori. Correlations between the government figures broken down by sex are r = 0.96, suggesting that Motoki is wrong in hypothesizing that illiteracy is more a female than male problem.

Illiteracy probably relates to depopulation and the brain drain with older, illiterate groups remaining in the hinterlands. Prefectures with higher

---

[19]The 881 "essential" Chinese characters taught through the first six grades in Japan are listed in order in Sakade, Emori, Friedrich, and Ohashi (1959). Kikuoka (1970) has compiled the 1000 most used Japanese newspaper compounds.

rates of elementary-school education are all in the most populace urban areas: Tōkyō, Kanagawa, Hiroshima, Nara, Kyōto, Ōsaka, and Fukuoka. Rural prefectures such as Aomori, Iwate, Niigata, Ryūkyū, Akita, Fukushima, Miyazaki, and Mie have the lowest percentages of elementary-school graduation rates. Although an adult Japanese with a sixth-grade education may have learned to read higher-level kanji — making this definition an inflated estimate of illiteracy — there are many reasons for suspecting these educational attainment figures are a good proxy for measuring illiteracy.

A highly literate nation should be a nation that reads literate materials. Japan ranks dead last among the industrial nations in libraries and books read per capita. For example, it has one-fourth the number of public libraries with one-half the number of library volumes per capita of the United States. The Japanese government totes the 39 million copies sold for the five major national dailies as the highest newspaper readership per capita in the world, but this assumes that Japanese read them. The typical commuter-reading fare on trains and subways is not newspapers or literary works but such low-level reading as manga[20] or sports dailies that focus on baseball trivia and Playboy-type centerfolds by salaried workers, and harlequin-type romances for women. The reading level of this material is certainly no higher than the Reader's Digest level in the United States, and the intellectual content is equal to the National Inquirer. This is not the level one would expect of a highly literate nation.

Theoretically, a student entering one of the prestigious national universities ought to have the reading level of the Nihon Keizai Shinbun (the Japan Economic Journal), which is the Japanese equivalent of the Wall Street Journal and New York Times combined. However, students at Tōhoku and Dōshisha Universities consistently report to me they find it too difficult to read, and are awed that any foreigner would work daily at building ability to read it.[21]

According to the Japan Newspaper Publishers and Editors Association, television has won the competition with newspapers in Japan as it has in the U.S.A. The typical Japanese spends three- and-one-half hours per day in front of the television set but only about 30 minutes with the newspaper. This trend toward more television watching and less newspaper reading has occurred in Japan, as in other highly industrialized countries, since the post-World War II era started.

---

[20]Adult comic books quite often have the syllabic readings next to common Chinese characters, suggesting that many readers do not know how to read them without help. See Powers, Kato, and Stronach (1989) for an introduction to these and other components of popular culture in contemporary Japan.

[21]As a point of reference, from my own experience I would estimate that if a person can read 90% of the characters in the Asahi, Nikkei comprehension is about 60%, making the Nikkei level of reading difficulty close to 50% more difficult than the typical Japanese daily. The Nikkei also is more demanding in it frequent use of statistical graphs and tables and infrequent use of photographs relative to the big five dailies.

Readership data supports the impression that this newspaper is at the high end of literacy. The Nikkei, as abbreviated in daily conversations, had a total circulation of 2.9 million copies in May 1989, which is only 7% of total newspaper circulation, affirming the elite-literate status of this newspaper. Eight-five percent of its circulation is in the Greater Tōkyō and the Ōsaka-Kōbe-Kyōto areas, suggesting that its readership is mostly among business leaders who are exceptionally literate and interested in the highly specialized spheres of international economics and politics.

Books checked out of libraries per capita, public libraries per capita, and newspaper circulation per capita also provide indicators of literacy. Data from 1987 underscores the more impressionist accounts in previous paragraphs: Tōkyō stands out at the pinnacle on all three measures. Tōkyō residents checked out almost 13 times as many books as residents of Miyazaki Prefecture in 1987: Four books per capita compared to less than one-third of a book per person. Similarly, Tōkyō residents are blessed with over six times as many public libraries per 100,000 residents as the lowest-ranked prefecture. Finally, daily newspaper circulation in Tōkyō is over twice that of Nagasaki Prefecture, which has the lowest rate. The strong negative correlation between newspaper readership per 100,000 population and eighth grade or fewer years of education also suggests the argument is sound: $r = -0.76$. Fewer persons subscribe to newspapers in Japan where those rates of less than a junior high school education are highest. Tōkyō is what statisticians call an outlier or deviant case for newspaper readership. It is more than three standard deviations above the mean for all three indicators. This suggests that Tōkyōites are quite unrepresentative of Japanese: A fact I shall replicate over and over again. Tōkyō acts like a huge magnet, attracting the best and brightest of Japanese. The result is a continuous brain drain hemorrhaging outlying areas, with the less skilled, older population left to fend for themselves far from the political and financial capital. Government surveys, which focus on samples drawn from the Greater Tōkyō Metropolitan Area, paint a rosy picture of a highly skilled, literate, well-educated population with little or no variation, masking serious problems in more rural areas.

The unrepresentativeness of Tōkyō also masks another point. Although the Japanese government focuses on the high-newspaper readership in Japan as a sign of the success of their educational system, it uses the mean average of 562 newspapers sold daily per 1,000 inhabitants (1983 data). However, the median rate, which is unaffected by the two extreme scores of Tōkyō and Ōsaka, drops below all of the remaining so-called "Group of Seven" largest industrial powers (the former U.S.S.R., France, Germany, and Great Britain) except the United States and Canada.

Also running against the interpretation of newspapers in Japan as a sign of high literacy is the dramatic drop in newspaper circulation to less than half of its 1949 post-war high. As measured by newspaper readership, literacy is on the decline, contrary to government claims that it has improved over the post-war years. Traditional newspapers have stiff competition from a variety of much less demanding sources: television, radio, and manga, to name only three. These sources give easier visual or auditory clues to the reader or listener than newspapers. The general public has increasingly opted for less literary sources of information that require less demanding skills.

If variations in libraries, book readership, and newspaper circulation are signs of educational quality, we should expect to find positive correlations between these indicators and education. The most prestigious schools and universities are most likely to attract students with the capabilities to read more difficult Chinese characters. However, five of the six correlations between percentage of top high school graduates or the percentages of top 45 universities with libraries per capita, book loan rate per capita, and newspaper circulation rate per capita are close to zero, indicating essentially no relationship between these measures of literacy and educational quality.

On the other hand, there is a 0.54 correlation between prefectures producing students who enter the top-ranked 44 universities and newspaper circulation rates. The fact that two-thirds of the top-ranked universities are located in the two financial and business centers of Japan — metropolitan Tōkyō and the Ōsaka-Kōbe-Kyōto area — largely explains this correlation. Graduates from these universities expect to work and live in these two areas with abnormally high rates of newspaper circulation after university graduation. The implication is that students entering the more prestigious universities are the ones most likely to be able to read and comprehend newspapers, which is not surprising. However, the converse, but less pleasant principle, is also true in that case; prefectures that have schools with lower rates of students entering the top universities produce few newspaper-literate Japanese.

In essence, it should be clear that literacy is not the simple dichotomy assumed by official statistics. There are certainly as many gradations of literacy (and illiteracy) in Japan as the United States. The international comparisons of student achievement in science and mathematics have been providing highly misleading indicators of the actual quality of education systems and student expertise. For example, according to the International Association for the Evaluation of Educational Achievement (Rotberg 1990), Hungary ranks near the top in 8th-grade math achievement. However, by the 12th grade, Hungary falls to the bottom of the list because it enrolls more students (50%) than any other country in advanced math. By contrast, Hong Kong comes in first, but only 3% of its 12th graders take math. Rotberg points out that the higher the proportion of students who take any standardized test the lower the mean test scores. The above sampling design compares 80% of American upper-secondary students with only 12% of Japanese, insuring that Americans will come out lower in the final comparisons.

Most studies have focused on children without considering long-term effects on adult populations. The first large-scale survey comparing public understanding of science in Japan and the United States (Langreth 1991) suggests that, except for questions on the Big Bang and evolutionary theories (which demonstrate the negative impact of Christian fundamentalism) Americans outperformed the Japanese. For example, only 8% of Japanese compared to 30% of Americans knew that "antibiotics kill viruses as well as bacteria" while only 14% of Japanese disagreed with the statement that "lasers work by focusing sound waves" compared to 37% of Americans. Interestingly, Americans in their forties out-performed all the other age groups in both countries, suggesting a decline in American science education since the Sputnik era when the 40-49 age group went to high school.

A second educational objective is to impart practical knowledge related to occupations or professions. Certainly the ability to read a newspaper of the quality of the Nikkei would be such a useful skill for persons aspiring to positions in the business world. However, the Nikkei makes special demands on readers: high degrees of (a) numeracy to read its sophisticated statistics and tables, and (b) literacy to understand its wide usage of unusual Chinese characters, character compounds, and technical vocabulary. The data I presented earlier show that few Japanese attain this high degree of literacy, even though literacy is of high practical value to the business world. Furthermore, special dictionaries published each year explain particularly difficult, specialized vocabularies, suggesting recognition of a huge market demand for aids to overcoming illiteracy in business, scientific, international, and other specialized areas.

Part of the reason that individuals read such technically useful newspapers so little is because the educational system does not impart knowledge directly related to specific occupations or professions. The ultimate goal maximizes opportunities to sort students into those who can and cannot pass specific college entrance tests. Leaders in Japanese businesses assume that entrance into college is evidence prima facie of a "good employee." Businesses in the primary sector with the most status do not really care whether or not most new white-collar employees directly out of college (engineers may be a notable exception) have specific skills (Rohlen 1974). Upon entry of new college recruits every April, upper management in the world of the large corporations use a cynical phrase to describe freshman employees: "ekijō terebikai mitai, benri sō da ga, usui dake" This translates roughly as "like a liquid crystal television screen which is transparent (superficial) but useful."

The educational structure in Japan does not exist for the purpose of educating a highly skilled work force; it exists to mold workers who will be suppliant, meek servants of the industrial captains of Japan. It might be more apt to call it a national indoctrination system rather than educational system because its major successes are the imbuing of partisan, sectarian opinions about yamato damashi (uniquely Japanese spirit), not dissimilar from the turn-of-the-century "white-man's burden" in the West. The educational system is extremely good at fulfilling this purpose. Japan has no effective union or consumers' movements to oppose industry. Teaching the virtue of obeyance to authority effectively creates precisely the type of white-collar worker industry desires.

The Japanese educational system has not produced a consumer's, citizen's, or rights-of-worker's literacy movement as has occurred in all other members of the Group of Seven most economically powerful nations. Popular opinion attributes this to wa[22]: Upham (1987) has documented the institutionalization of legal informality in Japanese society as the most plausible reason explaining how the Japanese government controls attempts to create social or political movements that might upset industrial policy or historic discriminatory patterns.

Monbushō has created a populace fragmented by their own personalistic concerns for educational credentialism without concern for education that liberates individuals or stimulates creativity. The government-controlled curriculum emphasizes non-academic activities such as neatness, cooperativeness, efficiency, and perseverance as a way of socializing students into the values of major corporations (Tsuneyoshi, 1992).

White (1987) suggests that "Monbushō is distinctively Japanese in its consistent concern for children (p. 50)." She implies that Japanese students like schools because schools care for children. An alternative reason is that schools do not fail students. Also, teachers rarely intervene in student affairs. Daily in-class education, in other words, makes few demands upon students. These demands emerge from the university-entrance-examination system rather than the formal educational system. Therefore, students view schools as benevolent means to pass an examination beyond their control, even though the examination system exists only as a sorting machine for college entrance.

Another indicator of practical education is the mastery of English. In recognition of English as the language of communication in the international business world, Monbushō requires study of the English language starting in the seventh grade. This requirement effects six years of secondary study followed up by at least two more years during freshman and sophomore years of university. However, few students master basic English (Chambers & Cummings 1990). Few university students know how to spell, look words up in dictionaries, speak so that a native can understand their accents, ask more than the most basic questions, or write an entire paragraph in comprehensible English. Except for the few students who had the chance to study abroad, my students at two of the top universities could not understand a basic college-level lecture or read from an introductory textbook without translation.[23]

In spite of the failure of the educational system to teach basic, functional English, Mouer and Sugimoto (1985) claim that Japanese are infinitely better at learning foreign languages than Americans. They base

---

[22]Usually dictionaries translate wa as a uniquely Japanese trait of unity or group spirit, but it has a strong sense of a plea of "please don't rock the boat" in daily usage.

[23]To be fair, I should point out that the Western teaching of Japanese as a foreign language provides a mirror image in its attempt to teach Japanese through romanization and listening skills rather than the kana and kanji.

their statement on the observation that some 10,000 Japanese businessmen work in the Greater New York area who have mastered English while less than 100 American businessmen in the Tōkyō area have mastered Japanese. This is certainly an unreasonable conclusion. Japan has close to 11 million students attending junior and senior high schools each year and roughly 900,000 freshman and sophomores in college, all of whom have studied English for six to eight years, respectively, while the United States has only a few hundred schools and 66 universities that offer even the most rudimentary instruction in the Japanese language. A recent publication of national comparisons on TOEFL test results confirms the poor mastery of English by Japanese (Educational Testing Services, 1992). The combined TOEFL test results for 1989 through 1991 placed Japanese in the second to last place with an average score below the 450 points necessary for passing.

Furthermore, numerous Japanese businesses send their employees to the United States under terms of paid leave to learn English and to take college and graduate-level courses for up to four years. There is no comparable system in the United States, although such a system would clearly aid the learning of Japanese. The reasons for differences of such magnitude in numbers of bilingual individuals are due primarily to differential educational opportunities rather than national character. Given the huge advantage Japanese students and employees have over Americans for foreign language instruction it is more interesting that they have produced so few graduates with any proficiency in English rather than so many.

Foreign language instruction in Japan has no practical orientation. The college-entrance-testing system does not require listening or speaking skills, or practical business or diplomatic English — the equivalents of Japanese teineigo (formal, polite language). Chauvinistic insistence that only Japanese have formal, polite language is a basic hindrance toward mastering practical, business English. Because Japanese students learn that English is a rude, direct language without the "emotive" content of Japanese they are not taught basic everyday English expressions that would aid smoother business or international relationships. They have great difficulty in accepting that English also has equivalent evasive or polite language.

The public secondary school and college-entrance-English-test systems work at a huge disadvantage in part because they do not generally employ native English speakers. The result is a large number of Japanese teachers of English and English-test makers who neither pronounce English intelligibly nor write coherent test questions; strange, unintelligible "loan words" from English such as "suto" (strike), "temu" (theme), and "ofureko" (off-the-record); dictionaries that use only the Japanese syllabary which lacks such fundamental distinctions as that between "l" and "r" and "b" and "v", or diphthongs like "th" and "dr;" and a fundamental lack of understanding of basic English grammar and rules of politeness. As an example, school texts teach that it is entirely appropriate to say "You had better. . ." which is a particularly offensive, rude expression to native English speakers except in those few rare situations such as when a parent is talking down to a child. In such cases, a native speaker would most likely use the softer "It might be a good idea if . . ." or "It would be better if . . ." [24]

Private schools are at a distinct advantage over public institutions because they are more likely to employ native speakers as English teachers. However, even these schools and the private juku that employ native English teachers rarely use teachers with proper TOEFL qualifications. The typical English teacher is a native speaker just out of college who has no training in English grammar and rules of politeness, and with no formal preparation in how to teach English as a foreign language. The result is a perpetuation of poor English instruction and myths about the English language and American culture.

Creativity is a third honored aim of education. There are some international yardsticks for measuring creativity. One is the Nobel Prize which many people consider the epitome of creative science and scientific excellence. By this measure, Japan's schools are homogeneous in their lack of qualifying alumni. Susumu Tonegawa, the 1987 winner in physiology and medicine stated flatly that he could not have done his work in Japan. He charged that the entire Japanese educational system stifles the necessary creativity. (He did his work in the United States.) No other Japanese has ever won that particular Nobel Prize compared to 38 native-born Americans over the past 90 years. Twenty-seven Americans and one Japanese have won the Nobel Prize in Chemistry. Fifty Americans and four Japanese have been honored with the Nobel Prize in Physics. Twelve Americans and no Japanese have ever won the Economics Nobel Prize first established in 1969.

These figures count only native-born Americans. The data are even more lopsided when one counts immigrants to the United States. The Japanese government has even created their own version of the Nobel Prize, calling it the Japan Prize. They have yet to award one to a Japanese national. The West continues to set the standards of creativity and eminence in science.[25]

---

[24]One of my former Japanese language teachers gave me a copy of the 1990 college entrance examination question for admittance to Tōkyō University in which the "correct" answer to one question was the use of a dangling participle. According to her account, Japanese high schools teach that such "no nos" are acceptable practice. I personally was amazed to find that none of my students at either Tōhoku or Doshisha Universities had ever been taught simple rules like breaking words between syllables (they invariably break them in random places as if they were Chinese characters). According to an informant who has been a high school teacher in Japan for more than 20 years, part of the reason such basic mistakes occur is that a Japanese professor making up such tests would "lose face" if a native speaker changes too many of his test questions so the few native speakers who aid test construction end up changing only a few of the most basic errors with an explanation of "your English is good but there is a slightly more natural way to say the same thing" or some such face-saving device.

[25]Bartholomew (1989) gives a much less sanguine view of the contribution of Japanese to science. He points out that several well-known Japanese ought to have been given the Nobel Prize. Nevertheless, the same is true of many non-Japanese scientists. A careful reading of his argument shows that the historical institutional impediments to science still exist in Japan. Citation-count analyses (Garfield & Welljams-Dorof 1992) confirm that American scientists are over twice as likely as their Japanese counterparts to publish Nobel-quality research that never receives that prize.

Another measure of scientific prominence is the number of publications per scientist. The Institute for Scientific Information (ISI) published figures from a study of the papers of scientists listed in their article databases for the 1980s (Garfield & Welljams-Dorof 1992). From 1981 until 1990 they found that 9 of the 20 most prolific scientists were Americans, 4 were (formerly) Soviet, four were British, one was German, one was Belgian, and one was Japanese (Science Watch 1992). ISI data also show that the U.S.A. accounted for 35.6% of the world's technical publications in 1986 whereas Japan, the United Kingdom, and the former Soviet Union accounted for about 8% each (Rotberg 1990, p. 300). These figures hold up across every area of science and engineering. These new data mesh well with the Nobel statistics in illustrating the continued prominence of American compared to Japanese basic science.

AN OVERVIEW OF THE STRUCTURE OF JAPANESE EDUCATION

The remaining portions of this chapter analyze Japanese education from the standpoint of a life-course perspective. It follows the natural course from pre-school through post-college education. Before focusing on individual stages of the system, it is worthwhile broadly surveying each stage. This section uses a simple, but powerful technique known as the semantic differential (SD) to describe the life course of Japanese education. Cross-cultural psychologists and sociologists [for early and recent summaries see Osgood, Suci, Tannenbaum (1957) and Inoue and Kobayashi (1985)] have long respected its robustness.

The SD technique supplies the fundamental connotations of words, as opposed to normal dictionaries that provide only denotations. It is a simple, yet robust, method for collecting data on fundamental attitudes. The SD summarizes three dimensions of status (good-bad), power (powerful-powerless), and liveliness (active-inactive). This Japanese lexicon is particularly rich in terms representing educational statuses.

Figure 1—1 compares nine typical statuses in the Japanese educational life cycle. The value of SD comparisons of educational statuses stands out across all three dimensions in Figure 1—1.[26] Goodness (represented by the

---

[26]Although the samples used to compute SD ratings may seem very small and unrepresentative, over 40 years of use by cross-cultural psychologists demonstrates their robustness compared to survey research which needs much larger samples. One needs only about 30 males and 30 females to compute various stimuli accurately for an entire culture. Only a few stimuli are adversely affected by particular sub-cultures in these types of studies. For example, strong behaviors such as rape are rated quite differently by females than males, necessitating the need for separate ratings by each sex for certain intimate behaviors. Likewise, members of deviant subcultures will rate specific behaviors central to their subculture differently than general populations but not behaviors which are non-central. For example, cocaine users will rate cocaine use as a good thing while the general population rates it as an evil thing; but on issues like "motherhood" or "apple pie," both deviant and non-

"star" icon) hovers on the slightly negative side of zero until graduate school and graduation to alumni status. Until entrance into high school, it shows a slight trend toward unfavorable ratings, confirming well-known problems with school violence that peak in junior high school and probably due to the competitive pressures of getting into the "right" high school. These ratings then start to rise slightly (although they still remain slightly unfavorable) once children are firmly sorted into senior high-level tracks. After university graduation, former students jump in status — a rise of over 1.24 (13%) on a 9-point scale.

It is also instructive to compare these differences with childhood roles in the United States. Children in the U.S.A. are much more highly valued at all levels. Similarly constructed SD ratings (Heise & Lewis 1988) in the U.S.A. show comparable powerfulness and liveliness scores for children's roles.

Figure 1—1 indicates an inverse relationship between the other two dimensions: the more powerful the role the less lively. Japanese children are highly active, impotent creatures who do not really have power until they enter the work force after completing their education. Furthermore, school-study and work-world pressures create increasing demands to become sedentary. The same statements are true of the United States.

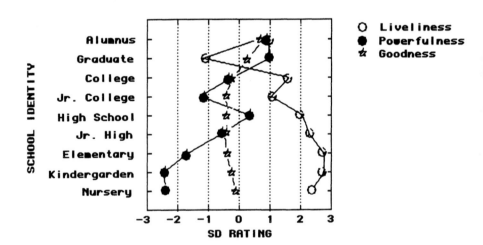

Figure 1—1. Ratings of Goodness, Powerfulness, and Liveliness across the Educational Life Course Roles
(Ns of 25 male and 25 female undergraduates at Tōhoku University)
Source: Umino, Matsuno, and Smith (1991)

---

deviant subcultures rate stimuli similarly. Our technique uses a nine-point scale from +4.0 (infinitely good) to -4.0 (infinitely bad). The standard deviations for our stimuli averaged around 1.0 on a 9-point scale, demonstrating low variation in SD ratings among our Japanese sample of Tōhoku University students.

The greatest value of SD comparisons lies in cross-cultural comparisons of the goodness dimension. First, normal childhood roles in the United States show much higher statuses than in Japan. Whereas all normal childhood roles are slightly negative in the Japanese data (including those not shown such as "infant"), all normal childhood roles in the United States connote fairly positive (~1.0) statuses (Heise & Lewis 1988). Children would appear to be slight status burdens in Japan, also evidenced by declining birth rates, which in 1990 were down to around 1.5 children per family.

Second, the Japanese data is useful as a critique of studies indicating that Japanese students "like" school. These studies (White 1987, for example) usually employ government-run survey results, and paint a Pollyannish impression of student roles in Japan in which students are happy with the system. One of the most cited "objective proofs" of satisfaction offered by Monbushō officials is the extremely low percentage of Japanese students who drop out of school — currently less than 3% of all students. However, drop-out rates are not necessarily a good indicator of happiness with the educational system. Japan is a country with extremely strong social pressures to conform. These social pressures make deviant school roles very unlikely, regardless of individual feelings of happiness with the school system.

Studies run independently of the government also have not used probability-sampling methods. For example, Stevenson, Chen, and Lee (1993, p. 57) use non-probabilistic samples from Sendai area data to generalize student satisfaction and well-being to all Japanese students. The Sendai (Miyagi Prefecture) area, as Chapters 2 and 3 will demonstrate, does not represent the "typical" Japanese educational profile. Miyagi Prefecture is exceptional in sending disproportionately high percentages of students to the top universities without relying greatly on the stress-inducing juku or yobiko systems so prevalent in the Kantō and Kansai areas.

As a demonstration of this, consider the data in Table 1—1, which presents SD ratings for a subset of deviant educational roles. All deviant status ratings on the goodness dimension are much below those for normal childhood roles. Social psychologists have long used the concept of the comparison-level alternative (CLalt) to demonstrate why individuals will choose a relationship with a poor reward-cost ratio (Thibaut & Kelly 1959). Given alternative roles, individuals most likely will also choose the one that has the best reward-cost ratio. There is no profit in a normal child aspiring to any deviant role (other than honor student) from among the list in Table 1—1 because a choice of such a role implies a huge drop in goodness status of close to one point on a nine-point scale.

Similarly, several of these deviant roles (bully, bully's victim, school laggard, and school delinquent) have powerlessness or inactivity ratings close to pre-school levels, yet are roles associated with junior-high-school level or older roles in Japan. To take on such a role in Japanese society should be regarded as particularly costly. Semantically, such roles cluster with other deviant roles such as hothead, traitor, drinker, sissy, coward, and retardate in Japan.

The most plausible explanation for the high rate of conformity in Japan appears to reflect more the draconian consequences of taking on deviant roles than any inherent liking for the school system, which is well known for its competitive pressures and junior high school-bullying problems. As Shields (1989, p. 7), states, ". . .the emphasis Japanese parents and teachers place on an exact behavior in public . . . provides a good basis for understanding . . . the cognitive roots of school failure and other antisocial behavior."

Table 1—1
Semantic Differential Ratings for a Subset of Deviant Educational Roles

Role	Goodness	Powerfulness	Liveliness
bully	-1.69	1.46	2.22
bully's victim	-1.22	-2.84	-1.14
school dropout	-1.32	-1.44	0.60
school laggard	-1.46	-2.08	-0.30
suspended student	-1.60	-1.32	0.94
teacher's pet	-1.54	0.64	0.98
delinquent from school	-1.72	0.08	2.04
flunk out	-1.50	-1.76	0.18
university reject (rōnin)	-0.62	-1.18	-0.34
student (honors)	0.99	1.60	-1.47
classmate	0.62	0.48	1.00
student (overall ratings)	0.06	-0.16	1.22

(Ns of 25 male and 25 female undergraduates at Tōhoku University)
Source: Umino, Matsuno, and Smith (1991)

Fundamental attitudes also cause honor students problems in Japan. Although they have very high status (0.99 compared to the average 0.06), the honor-student role is more powerful and much more inactive than average student roles. This may explain why particularly good students in Japan will go to great lengths to hide their studious habits from classmates in spite of the cultural imperative to gambaru [persist, not give up, keep trying] (Singleton 1989). The power differential between honor students and more average classmates is over one point greater than that for normal student roles. Likewise, their inactivity levels are roughly two points lower than one would expect.

Another widespread phenomenon in Japan is the huge number of students who spend several years after graduation trying to pass entrance examinations into the top universities. Parents of former rōnin currently spend as much as a million yen ($4878) a year to help their children pass these examinations. The SD scores for rōnin in Table 1—1 are 0.68 below the average high school student's goodness scores, 1.34 lower in powerlessness, and 1.56 lower in liveliness than the average student rating. This means that rōnin are a particularly deviant group of youth. Although they hold the most-prized aspiration (admittance to an elite university) society basically scorn them — unless they attain their goals, which few do.

Table 1—1 also demonstrates that there are much worse student identities than rōnin. School flunk outs and delinquents, have even worse evaluations and consequent lower status. The point is that the relative differences between normal and deviant identities are so disparate in Japan that it becomes easy to understand why the "social glue" that holds students to acceptable student roles is a "super glue" at that. Few youths are willing to take on roles outside the cultural accepted one, regardless of liking for school, quality of education, or fundamental inequities of the school system.

Table 1—2
Semantic Differential Ratings for a Subset of Educator Roles

Role	Goodness	Powerfulness	Liveliness
teacher (nursery school)	1.16	0.26	0.68
teacher (kindergarten)	0.96	0.26	1.04
teacher (elem school)	0.96	0.60	0.72
teacher (jr. high)	0.74	0.58	0.14
high school teacher	0.58	1.04	-0.62
teacher (head)	0.74	0.92	-0.94
graduate assistant	0.82	-0.06	0.20
instructor	1.08	1.28	-0.76
lecturer	1.14	0.68	-0.62
assistant professor	1.18	0.76	-0.86
professor	1.52	1.86	-1.86
scholar	1.52	1.56	-1.88
university president	1.32	2.20	-2.10
educator	1.26	1.38	-1.24
educational staffer	0.86	0.78	-0.44
researcher	1.36	0.58	-1.68
principal	1.16	2.18	-2.08
teacher (sensei)	1.16	1.50	-1.10
teacher (of blind)	1.82	0.74	-1.46
teacher (of handicapped)	1.68	0.88	-1.30
teacher (of deaf)	2.12	0.94	-1.54

(Ns of 25 male and 25 female undergraduates at Tōhoku University)
Source: Umino, Matsuno, and Smith (1991)

The high status of educator roles is another important reason why more children stay in school in Japan compared to the United States. Table 1—2 gives SD ratings for various educator roles in Japan. Professional roles in the United States are all much less highly evaluated than in Japan (although similar in power and activity). For example, a university professor in the United States ranks about 1.05 in goodness, while a full professor in Japan has an average rank of 1.52.

Japanese professors are more powerful than their American counterparts — 1.86 versus 1.13. It doesn't take long for newly arrived foreigners to Japan to pick up on the reverence and awe attached to the general word for teacher: sensei. Both teachers and professors in Japan are highly powerful roles, giving them the authority to make exceptional demands on students, who are very impotent compared to American students. The general difference in power between students and teachers averages 1.5 on a 9-point SD scale in Japan by comparison to 1.0 in the U.S.A.

Another interesting comparison between Japan and the United States are the roles of scholar and researcher. These are roles that Americans do not evaluate highly.   The role of "scholar" has fallen into such disrepute among students, that editors and reviewers ask writers to replace the word with that of "researcher," "sociologist," etc. However, in Japan "scholar" connotes a quite esteemed, powerful role, bestowing authority that should be the envy of scholars in the United States. The irony is that Japan has really few scholars by American publication standards.

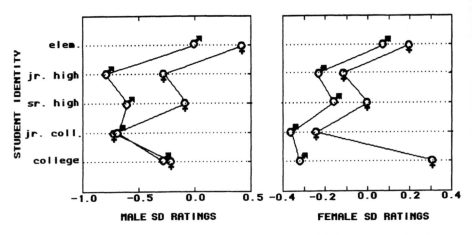

Figure 1—2. Ratings of Goodness across the Educational Life Course Roles by Sex of Raters and Ratings
(Ns of 25 male and 25 female undergraduates at Tōhoku University)
Source: (Umino, et al. 1991)

Earlier in this chapter I mentioned that gender differences play an important role in Japanese education. More women than men enrolled in school until high school graduation, but general societal attitudes consign the majority of women to lower educational status than men. SD data again confirms these sex role identities. Figure 1—2 indicates that Japanese differentially evaluate male and female elementary school children, and this difference continues through the secondary school years. It becomes particularly marked by a large gender gap in attitudes during the junior high years for males and during college for females. In both junior and senior high school, boys rate girls' statuses close to 0.5 higher than boys' statuses. Girls also rate boys higher in goodness, although not to the same extent. This is understandable if one recalls that boys have higher pressures placed upon their need for success (creating a large degree of failure) and higher delinquency rates.

The chances of boys attaining entrance into universities is not good. Forty percent of applicants are accepted in universities in general, but only 49% of students attending one of the elite 400 high schools went to one of the top 45 universities. Only 10% of all graduating students were able to enter one of these top-ranked universities in 1988. Thus, the probabilities of male student success in attaining top-university admittance are small. It is likely that this 90% failure rate must play a significant role in the gap between male and female student roles throughout secondary schooling.

Figure 1—2 also indicates the strong interaction effects of sex of student identity and sex of raters for junior college and university student identities. For male raters, the goodness ratings for each college group are insignificant. Female raters assess the status of female junior college students higher than male junior college students, and they rate women's university student identities over 0.6 points higher in status than comparable male identities.

Because the results of random surveys demonstrate negative feelings toward women who go to college but encouragement for male college aspirations, this is a particularly interesting datum. Similarly, the general public perceives junior colleges as "finishing schools" for women, and this low status is evident for both men and women. For both males and females, there is over a 0.5 gain in status by entering a four-year college rather than a two-year one. As these ratings are only for acceptance into the average junior college or university, we can guess that the gain in status must be even higher for students attending the most prestigious universities.

Comparisons with high school student statuses are also enlightening. In the case of male raters, a woman always loses status by going further in school, although the loss is particularly serious if she ends up at a junior college. However, women students assess such changes in life cycle quite differently. Women raters view attendance at junior colleges as a loss in status but attendance at a university as a gain. This is an important difference. It means that a girl in high school would be better off to set her sights on a university rather than a junior college. It also suggests that official attempts to restrict women to junior colleges will ultimately fail if women act in their own self interests.

SUMMARY

This excursion into the educational role system of Japan, and its differences with the United States, should aid understanding of variations in Japan and cross-national differences. I will return to some of these SD ratings in the next chapter as they provide information on the Japanese educational system beyond these more general implications. The next chapter focuses upon the earliest portion of the Japanese educational life cycle.

The picture of Japanese education presented in official Monbushō statistics and much of the academic and popular press assumes homogeneity and paints a Pollyannish picture. This chapter challenges these views in several ways. First, it debunks the stereotypes of Japanese education by tracing its historic roots in the so-called Meiji Reformation, which suggests an inaccurate picture of a homogeneous transformation toward equality. Second, it pursues this line of analysis by emphasizing education as "cultural capital" and showing how various aspects of Japanese life discriminate against those persons with less cultural capital.

Third, this chapter compares American and Japanese semantic differential data using educational identities from elementary school through university graduation broken down by sex of identities and raters. The SD, which is an extremely robust method of displaying two fundamental dimensions of social life — status and power — indicates significant patterned life course variation and interaction of sex of identities and raters in Japan.

In general, Japanese educator identities have higher status and power than their American counterparts. By contrast, socially accepted Japanese student roles are lower in status and power than their American equivalents. The power of conformity of the Japanese educational system is most apparent when one contrasts SD ratings for deviant and socially accepted roles. Finally, the interaction of sex of raters and identities becomes most apparent in ratings of college roles where Japanese women gain status in their own eyes by attending four-year institutions but lose status in the eyes of Japanese men illustrating basic gender-based conflicts in modern Japan.

Chapter 2

THE EDUCATIONAL RACE STARTS
IN THE CRADLE

During the 1950s and 1960s respected researchers like Ruth Benedict, William Caudill, and Takeo Doi contributed much work on Japanese childhood and education. It is curious, thus, that in the first fourteen years of the Journal of Japanese Studies, not one article appeared concerning children, child-rearing, or early education (Rohlen 1989). Cultural transmission and generational differences are important to understanding any nation or culture. This chapter examines the Japanese educational system according to its important rites de passage. This tactic aids in understanding some of the main points of Chapter 1. In particular, this highlights the effects of cultural capital, economic capital, and sorting mechanisms for the spoils of elite education, that commence as early as preschool education, although most individuals do not perceive their effects until high school.

THE PRESCHOOL SYSTEM

Preschools have become a necessity because mothers in modern countries are increasing part of the labor force — presently 60% in the U.S.A. and 40% in Japan. Preschool has become an important agent of socialization both reflecting and bringing about social changes of which few individuals show awareness. Women with only one or two children have become less willing to accept lives as full-time mothers. Also, women who have to work to make a living or who value their careers highly are more likely to decide to have only one or two children. For these mothers, preschools offer acceptable solutions to the dilemmas of the double burden of child rearing and professional life. Thus ever more children are growing up in a world where the family is being replaced as the center of their lives at an early age, and where preschools are expected to take over many of the functions that used to be carried out by the family. This raises important questions: How do preschools work? What roles do they play? How do they fit into the overall educational system? What are their advantages and disadvantages?

EARLY CHILDHOOD SOCIALIZATION

Japanese conceptions of childhood differ radically from American ones. Japanese use the expressions "masshiro" (pure white) and "hakushi" (white sheet) to describe the nature of a newborn infant. These words appear to conceptualize the Western philosophical concept of tabula rasa (blank sheet), but the Japanese take their expressions more seriously than Americans take tabula rasa. Recall from Chapter 1 that the main difference between American and Japanese SD ratings was the goodness dimension: Americans rate infants as quite good while Japanese rate them close to neutral in goodness.

These ratings summarize parental and teacher reaction to bad behavior on the part of young children. A naughty or difficult child in the United States is likely to result in disciplining of the child because such a child has not confirmed preconceived notions of childhood identities as fundamentally good. American parents use discipline to internalize "correct" child behaviors, so that the child will act as he or she is "suppose" to act. By contrast, Japanese parents and teachers externalize blame on forces they presume to be beyond the child's control.

One of the most-heard Japanese expressions of externalized blame among children's authority figures is kan no mushi (provoked by a bug). This expression would be a little like "the devil made me do it" excuse if was not for the fact that the American expression occurs most often as a joke, while kan no mushi is a seriously offered excuse. The perception is that because a child is neither good nor bad, he or she couldn't possibly have done something bad. In broader terms, Japanese rely on excuses that acknowledge young children's bad behavior as undesirable or wrong, but deny personal responsibility for conduct; Americans apply justifications that admit personal responsibility but deny the act's wrongness.

As a consequence, Japanese are not likely to discipline children when they are bad. Rather, they lean on amae, which usually translates as "dependence" but which generally has a more positive sense than the

English translation. Amae and its verb form <u>amaeru</u> are closer to "indulgence" or "tolerance" of another's behavior. Amae functions by creating dependence through shame.[0]

The earliest years of child rearing for a newborn Japanese stand in stark contrast to an American's. Hendry (1986) has documented important differences in early childhood socialization. A Japanese first-born sleeps with its mother or between the mother and father unlike an American baby who is most likely to sleep in a separate bedroom from its parents. The addition of a second-born child is likely to result not in transference to separate quarters but instead to the father's bed. Japanese parents do not like cribs. They perceive cribs as restricting a child's development. Similarly, Japanese parents reject baby-sitting. The result is that Japanese infants spend much more time in the company of their mothers, which restricts the couple's social and sexual life to a much greater extent than do American infants.

Japanese mothers stay home with their infants while fathers go out to restaurants or bars at nighttime. Similarly, because Japanese give their infants much freer reign to crawl and walk than crib-bound American infants, Japanese mothers must be much more vigilant for dangers such as electric outlets and hot stoves. Due to the belief that a mother should always be with her infants it is not unusual to see a mother going shopping on a bicycle or motor scooter with two infants in hand — one in a baby carrier attached to the back of the bike, and another straddled precariously in front of her. The result is that Japanese infants spend much more time with their mothers than American infants do, even when comparing women who are full-time housewives.

There are also strong societal pressures for Japanese mothers to stay home with their children until they are old enough to enter elementary school. These pressures show in relatively low rates of nursery school and kindergarten attendance in Japan. The median 1987 attendance figure for day-nursery attendance in Japan was 14% for children up to age five. Similarly, 44% of children age four and five attended a kindergarten in 1987.[1]

The study of day nurseries and kindergartens is of great interest because they give public display to many facets of socialization that are less visible within the privacy of Japanese households. Kindergartens and day nurseries are places where "children are nationali[z]ed, begin to be Japanese citizens, [and] learn the art of group interaction and daily habits" (Hendry, 1986, p.

---

[0]Doi (1963) presents the classic disscussion of the concept of amae as a key to Japanese culture.

[1]It is necessary to use different population bases to standardize each figure because day nurseries have a much larger client population. The kindergarten figure is higher, not because fewer parents use preschool facilities for three- through five-year-olds than for children younger than age four, but because the day nurseries service parents with children from roughly one- to six-years of age and children at older ages are more likely to go to preschool. Mombushō (1989) continued to claim throughout the 1980s that close to two-thirds of Japanese five-year-olds attended kindergarten, but this is an impossibly high figure for the whole country, although it is true for particular regions. The reason is the high variation in prefectural enrollment figures which ranges from 2 to 49% for kindergartens and from 4.5 to 48% for day nurseries. Government figures ignore the huge variation between prefectures. Some prefectures have very small percentages of children in preschool education while others have a clear majority.

143). One of the first habits that Japanese preschools inculcate is that fun and friendship are only for cooperators. Non-cooperators quickly learn that the other children ostracize them, resulting in quite effective social control over the majority of children.

Japanese conceptions of socialization help explain much of the activity that goes on in preschools. Parents and teachers often employ shitsuke as the primary objective of socialization. The original meaning of shitsuke employs one Chinese character that has two parts: "body" and "beautiful." Consequently, the genesis implies beautifying the body. The primary definition given in dictionaries suggests the instilling of habits necessary for daily living. However, there is a homonym for shitsuke made up of two kanji that can be a pun meaning "attend" and "attach." Hendry's (1986: 11) informants often used the following two expressions to describe this meaning: kata ni hameru [to fit into a mold] and kitaeru [to discipline]. Thus, body beautification is a very broad concept in Japan, including the mastery of manners, correct behavior, arts, and other forms of gracefulness that must become automatic, habituated, and routine.

Shitsuke is one of the moral pillars of Japanese education: Throughout the inculcation of both physical sports like baseball (White, 1987) and mental habits throughout the school years, Japanese education emphasizes learning without asking questions or giving reasons. This is both a strength and a weakness of the educational system. Schooling emphasizes the blind following of almost any order to memorize, mimic, or routinize a teacher's instructions or example. Thus, shitsuke allows only scant margin for creativity or imagination.

A comparison of American, Chinese, and Japanese preschools by Tobin, Wu, and Davidson (1989) is informative in further distinguishing characteristics of Japanese preschool education. Tobin and his colleagues found that parents in all three cultures put their children in preschool with the expectation that they will acquire basic academic skills, but parents stressed academic instruction much more in China and the United States than in Japan: 67% of Chinese parents and 51% of American parents mentioned "a good start academically" as one of the top three reasons for a society to have preschools, yet only 2% of Japanese were so inclined. Chinese parents stressed the academic function the most, Japanese stressed play, while American parents divided between these two purposes of preschool.

A stress on play with minimal teacher intervention is certainly a unique characteristic of the Japanese system that draws the attention of foreigners on their first visit to Japan. The noise and liveliness levels in Japanese preschool activities are incredible as confirmed by the Figure 1—1 rate for preschool activity rating of 2.68 on a scale from -3 to +3, comparable to a colicky baby's activity rating in the United States. Typical Japanese adult reactions to preschool trips on Japanese trains are instructive. As soon as a troop of 30 preschoolers board, panic sets in among the helpless adult passengers who sit frozen in their seats trying to ignore the excruciating decibel levels. Of most interest to a foreign observer is that no adult will ask the accompanying teachers to tame the bedlam. The only resistance to child behavior that I have ever observed in these situations is teachers who will passively block their little charges from debarking at the wrong train stations or putting their arms out the windows because of possibilities of injuries.

In confirmation of these observations, Tobin and his colleagues found that the typical Japanese preschool was the noisiest and liveliest of the three cultures. Chinese preschools they observed were reminiscent of a boot camp where teachers controlled and guided more or less every movement through their authority. From their vantage, the typical American preschool looks like a "psychological counseling center" where a great deal of emphasis is placed on verbalizing the reasons for behaving, or misbehaving, in one way or another.

Japanese teachers pay bare attention to Japanese preschoolers compared to their American or Chinese peers. This noninterventionist disposition among Japanese preschool teachers allows Japanese preschoolers to interact more with age mates. Japanese allow preschoolers to form groups and create their own sources of group cohesion with a minimum of adult interference. It seems to matter little to Japanese preschool teachers whether the resulting groups resemble a flock of screaming banshees or if individual members misbehave.

Japanese teachers assume a more laissez-faire philosophy because they expect the children's group will eventually bring deviant members into line in the long run. In many cases, the short-run rights of adults or other children are not sufficient reasons for adult intervention in children's group activities. By contrast, American teachers inform researchers that they intervene in children's activities when they perceive those activities impinge on the rights of other individuals. In this regard, Chinese and American teachers are very much alike: Both groups believe, contrary to Japanese teachers' beliefs, that young children need adult supervision and guidance to discover goodness and morality.

Throughout this discussion, one common theme is clear in research on pre-schooling: Regardless of the society, adults communicate the attitudes and beliefs that form the ideological basis of their society to their offspring at very early ages. Preschool teachers are part of an institution that plays an important role in teaching the dominant ideology of any state.

DAY-CARE CENTERS

To this juncture, I have lumped all preschools — day nurseries (hoikuen) and kindergartens (yōchien) — together. Many Japanese pre-school authorities (Hendry, 1986, pp. 126, 128) claim there are few major differences between them once children are of kindergarten age. However, each type of preschool arose to meet unique circumstances mandated by different government ministries. I shall demonstrate that these different needs do in fact lead to major macroscopic differences between hoikuen and yōchien which are not observable in studies of individual preschools, no matter how carefully researched.

The concept of hoikuen was first established in 1918 as a way to care for children from infancy until first grade. In 1926 there were only 65 public and 228 private hoikuen. At the end of World War II there were still only 2000 such institutions in spite of the widespread need for child care while mothers contributed to the war effort. However, over the course of the four decades following the war, the Kōseishō rapidly increased the total to a high of 22,899 in 1985. Because of the declining birth rate in Japan both hoikuen and yōchien have started to drop slowly in numbers since 1985.

Entry into hoikuen is more exclusive than into yōchien. Parents must demonstrate lack of family care because both parents normally work.[2] Hoikuen are open longer than yōchien: nine-hour days everyday except Sundays and holidays for about 300 days a year. By contrast, yōchien may operate four to five hours a day Monday through Saturday, 220 days per year, following the normal school calendar. Hoikuen must also provide meals and snacks that are optional at yōchien. Most Japanese regard hoikuen as having a lesser education role than yōchien (DeCoker, 1989). Hoikuen administrators recruit primarily young females with junior college certificates as teachers.[3]

The size of day nursery groups depends on the ages of the children. The Health and Welfare Ministry mandates national standards carried out by prefectural authorities of one adult per three babies up to one-year-old, six infants per caretaker from age one to three, up to twenty children age three per caretaker, and up to 30 four- and five-year-olds per adult. These regulations appear to be followed fairly closely: In 1988 the national average was 10 children per adult and about 33 four- and five-year-olds per supervisor.

Lewis (1989: 33) suggests that the most striking feature of nursery schools is small, fixed-membership groups within each class. Whereas American teachers assign children wth personal desks and responsibilities, Japanese teachers assign children to group tables that frequently are the basis of group chores. Another interesting strategy employed in Japanese nursery schools Lewis (1989: 35) mentions is distribution by teachers of "able" children among groups. In only 22% of Lewis' observations did teachers interact with the class as a whole. Teachers delegated hand waving and other forms of competition for adult attention to groups rather than to individuals. Japanese nursery school teachers appear to opt for allocation of their time as equally as possible to individual students through groups.

Noise and chaos level were the most astonishing aspect of Lewis's observations of preschool classes, as with other studies cited earlier by

---

[2]Most will not accept infants until about 10 months of age when they can eat solid foods.

[3]The Japanese call them "hobo" which literally means "protective mother" but more figuratively translates into the function of "mother-figure." The typical recruit is a junior college graduate who will stay on the job only a few years before marrying and starting her own family.

foreign observers. Lewis (1989: 36) writes that children were within the teachers' sight "in only 54%" of her observations and that ". . .in 13% of the cases, none of the children were within the teacher's sight in classroom" confirming the strong beliefs expressed by Japanese teachers that children are capable of self-control and self-regulation.

Lewis suggests that the use of discipline to teach children correct behavior does not internalize good behavior. It only internalizes the knowledge that various adults can apply sanctions if the child does not behavior appropriately. By attributing an undesirable act to some outside influence, adults may re-inforce the "good child" image.

KINDERGARTENS

Yōchien are under the direction of Mombushō and admit children from age three until admission to first grade. Monbushō allows up to 40 children per class, which seems excessive by Western standards. Kindergartens have a longer history than day nurseries in Japan. The first one started in 1876 at Tōkyō Women's Normal School (present-day Ochanomizu Women's University) for upper-class families. They mushroomed after the Second World War, but have leveled off to cater to just over 2 million children in slightly more than 15,000 establishments through the 1980s. Most were Christian organizations before World War II. During the war, Buddhist temples, Shinto shrines, libraries, and schools opened new ones to meet the demands of working women.

One of the most important questions concerns the purpose of kindergartens and nursery schools. Although Tobin, Wu, and Davidson (1989) suggest that academic preparation plays a minor role in Japanese preschools, other researchers are more ambivalent on the issue. Only a few of Hendry's (1986: 63) respondents told her of their concerns with academically oriented preschool education, yet her data also suggest academic undercurrents. For example, children of doctors seemed particularly under pressure to go to kindergarten in her (p. 67) study. Similarly, she notes that private kindergartens are more prevalent in urban areas.[4] Both of these observations are consistent with academic pressures, regardless of what her respondents told her (p. 131).

Mothers of young children appear to be under social pressures to prepare their children with basic academic skills before entering kindergartens. Increasingly kindergartens use entrance examinations that test for maternal preparation of their children. They prefer children who can print their names in the kana syllabary, know the kana, draw or fold paper in origami style, and so on. Furthermore, if kindergartens were just a place for play there would be little need for mother participation, yet

---

[4]Actually this is not true. I will discuss private kindergartens in more detail shortly.

kindergartens often expect mothers to be available to help their children. Kimura (1981, p. 119) quoted from a 1972 survey showing that 87.9% of five-year-olds could read at least 60 of the 90-odd syllabic (kana) characters. Impressionistic observations since confirm unusually large numbers of children whose mothers have already taught them most of the kana.[5]

Several other trends appear to support the increasing social pressures toward preschool attendance. First, there has been a consistent trend toward earlier entry into kindergartens. In 1965, only 4.1% of kindergartners were three-year olds. This percentage has surged to 12.1 in 1988, a three-fold increase in only 23 years. Second, four-year-olds also have increased in percent of enrollment over the same period; an increase from 34.8% to 40.5% over the same period. Third, an increasing percentage of kindergartners have entered private kindergartens. In 1950, 50.8% of preschoolers attended private kindergartens, and has mounted every year; it now stands at 76.8% of enrollees.[6] Because earlier attendance and private preschool attendance increases parental educational costs significantly, these figures suggest that parents feel under increasing pressure to start their children up the educational ladder.

Do Hoikuen and Yōchien Serve the Same Functions?

Hendry (1986:146) argues that there are no real differences between hoikuen and yōchien in spite of the fact that ministries with different regulations and goals administer them. A test for a correlation between the percentage of children enrolled in each type of institution across all of the 47 prefectural units provides useful information. If they serve the same functions we would expect a high positive correlation between each variable as a minimum necessary requirement. However, there is a correlation of -0.39 between the two variables which indicates they do serve different populations.

Hoikuen (day nurseries) disproportionately serve mostly the rural populations of Kyūshū, Shikoku, and the Japan Sea with the lowest numbers in the Kansai (Ōsaka-Kōbe-Kyōto) and Kantō (Greater Tōkyō) regions. By contrast, yōchien are generally stronger in the urban areas of the Kantō and Kansai and weaker in other areas of the country. There is also wide variation in populations served by each type of preschool within prefectures.

Hoikuen data are highly skewed. Attendance ranges from 4.5% to 48% of infants, but 29 of the 47 prefectures are at the low end of the median, yet within one negative standard deviation (s.d.=10.3%) of the mean of 14%. By contrast, eleven of the prefectures have percentages greater than one

---

[5]Hendry (1986:56) points out that fathers play virtually no role in the education
[6]These figures are from Mombushō's (Ministry of Education) 1990 Kyōiku Tōkei Nenkan (1990 Educational Statistics Annual), pp. 43, 89.

standard deviation higher than the mean average. Three prefectures (Kōchi, Ishikawa, and Nagano) are over two standard deviations greater than normal. The univariate statistics for yōchien attendance produces a virtual mirror-image of the above results: The prefectures with greatest and lowest percentages reverse in many cases. For example, the three prefectures with the highest percentages of day nurseries are among the seven lowest with kindergarten population.

Table 2—1 summarizes correlations between each type of preschool and various variables that the preceding arguments have suggested as possible explanations for the wide differences that exist in preschool enrollments across prefectures. In particular I have chosen variables suggested by the cultural-capital thesis, grouped by general type. Nursery schools have 12 possible candidates out of the total 15 relationships that are significant

Table 2—1

Correlations between Percent of Children in Day Nurseries and Kindergarten in 1987 and Some Possible Causes (N=47 Prefectures)

Variable Name	Hoikuen%	Yōchien%
Population density (km²)	**-0.342	-0.048
Child Dependency ratio	-0.216	-0.003
Elderly Dependency ratio	**0.581	0.143
%Nuclear Families	**-0.467	0.081
% Females in the Labor Force	**0.625	-0.188
%Professional/Technical	*0.245	*0.248
%Managers	**0.402	0.041
%Farmers	**0.406	0.036
%laborers	**0.430	-0.130
%Self-employed	**0.451	0.133
Per capita educational spending	**-0.438	-0.131
Gross Prefectural Profits	**-0.362	-0.090
%Owners (of businesses)	**0.386	-0.008
%Graduates from top high schools	0.123	**0.509
%Private kindergartens	0.097	**-0.702

Source: Sōricho, Nihon Tōkei Nenkan, 1989.

* significance level ≥ 0.05
**significance level ≥ 0.01

statistically while kindergartens have three different statistically significant correlations, further suggesting different sources of student populations.

Although there are 12 possible statistically significant relationships with nursery schools shown in Table 2—1, most of them are spurious, reducing to zero or near zero when tested with regression analysis.[7] Thus, asking why there is an inverse relationship between population density and nursery school enrollments is not profitable. It is more informative to look at the results of a few selective regression analyses, so as to demonstrate some of the more easily detected spurious causes of preschool attendance as well as to indicate (1) more likely causes and (2) differences between nursery and kindergarten attendance.

Table 2—2 displays the results of regressing population density, percentages of families that are nuclear, percentages of females in the labor force, and percentages of managers on nursery school attendance percentages. Only the percentage of women in the labor force withstands the regression analysis. All other correlations are spurious as their beta weights reduce to near zero. In this test, one variable — the percentage of females in the labor force — explains 40% of the differences in hoikuen attendance across the 47 prefectures. This regression demonstrates that the Ministry of Health and Welfare's policies are effective. After all, the primary purpose of hoikuen is suppose to be service to families where both parents work and should have nothing at all to do with population characteristics, families in general, or type of father's occupation. Hoikuen enrollments appear to be little influenced by these proxies for cultural capital.

Table 2—2

Results of a Regression of Population Density, Percent Nuclear Families, Percent Females in Labor Force, and Percent Managers on Percent Nursery School Attendance

Variable	Betas
Population Density	0.08
%Nuclear Families	0.05
%Females in Labor Force	*0.61
%Managers	-0.05

$r^2 = 0.40$

*at least twice the standard error of the beta

---

[7]There are numerous hidden relationships that sinple correlations do not reflect. Regression analysis is a type of what-if query that asks: If none of the independent variables were associated, what would be the true net effects of each independent variable?

All other occupational categories, except the percentage of self-employed, are spurious relationships, further establishing the Koseishō's bureaucratic powers to discriminate between families that are truly in need of day care and those that do not. Table 2—3 further supports this position. Self-employment status may sometimes indicate a family-run business that needs the wife and children to help run the business. Nevertheless, the percentage of females in the labor force is almost twice as powerful an explanation as the percentage of self-employment because the beta is close to twice as large.

Although farm occupations may appear to be a weak causal factor, its sign changed from plus to negative, indicating that it is probably spurious. Farming is a type of self-employment status (confirmed by a correlation of 0.76 between these two variables) so this regression indicates that it is self-employment status rather than farm status that contributes to nursery school attendance. Self-employment status adds very little to the total prediction of nursery school attendance. The total explained variation increases from 0.40 to 0.45 with its addition.

All other variables listed earlier in Table 2—1 are spurious. This gives credence to beliefs that hoikuen education is relatively fair. That is, such socio-economic factors as per capita educational spending, gross prefectural product (a form of GNP at the prefectural level), and type of occupation make no difference in attendance in nursery schools. These results also add credence to Hendry's contention that day nurseries exist because their "long hours are convenient for working mothers" and are "more readily available in areas where most mothers do in fact work" (1986: 61).

Table 2—3

Results of a Regression of % Females in Labor Force, %Farmers, %Laborers, and %Self-employed on %Nursery School Attendance

Variable	Betas
%Females in Labor Force	*0.55
%Self-employed	0.28
%Farmers	-0.16
%Laborers	-0.09

$r^2 = 0.45$

*at least twice the standard error of the beta

On the other hand, a regression analysis of principle causes of attendance in Monbushō's kindergartens suggests the considerable influence of educational stratification. Table 2—4 imparts the strong force of quality of educational institutions on kindergarten attendance. Parents who live in prefectures with high school programs most likely to send children on to the elite 45 universities are the most likely to enroll their children in kindergartens. These elite high schools are remarkably stable over time, and are well known to parents, many of whom put huge effort into enrolling their children into their programs. It is not completely clear whether quality of high school causes kindergarten enrollments to go up, or high kindergarten enrollments lead to better chances of high graduation rates from high schools at the apex of the educational ladder.

The transportation infrastructure of the Kansai and Kantō areas allow parents in those areas particularly wide choices of quality schools within commuting distance, significantly increasing their cultural-capital advantage over other areas of Japan. Research by Peak (1992) also demonstrates the definitive advantage given to Tōkyō over provincial residency. First graders in her work from Tōkyō started pre-school up to a year and a half earlier and were much more likely to have attended enrichment lessons including exam preparation classes for entrance into the first grade.

Table 2—4

Results of a Regression of Percent of High School Graduates from Top High Schools, Percent Professional and Technical Workers, Percent Females in the Labor Force, and Percent of Self-Employed on Kindergarten Attendance

Variable	Betas
%Top high school	*0.28
%Professional/technical	0.37
%Females in the labor force	0.25
%self-employed	0.33
%Private kindergarten	*-0.43
%Nursery school	*-0.60

$r^2 = 0.77$

*at least twice the standard error of the beta

There is also a cultural-capital effect of professional and technical workers. High-status workers appear more concerned than those of lower status in making sure their children get a head start through kindergartens. Also, self-employed workers are likely to enroll their children in preschools of either kind. Husband's occupational status, as the cultural-capital argument predicts, also appears to be important. Although official policy forbids the use of yochien as preparatory for elementary school skills, one Monbushō informant estimates that 98% of kindergartens teach letters and numbers. The same official points out that academic pressures lead prestigious kindergartens to accept fewer than one in five applicants .

The effect of female labor force participation, as with the effect for nursery schools, appears to encourage attendance in kindergartens. Families with mothers who work are most likely able to afford to send their children to kindergartens, which is the opposite of what we would expect of true kyōiku mama's. The kyōiku mama role encourages mothers to stay at home and guide their children's education themselves. However, the increasing financial burdens of education may be making this an impossibility.

Two opposing predictors are private kindergartens and day nurseries. Day nurseries, as we have seen, compete with kindergartens. They have numerous advantages that female workers may appreciate, including long hours. Private kindergartens are significantly more expensive and have the largest effect of all six independent variables. Although three-fourths of kindergartners presently attend private kindergartens, this beta weight suggests the strong capping pressure of private education as social capital: If cheaper public alternatives were available, significantly more children would probably attend preschools.

In total, the variables in Table 2—4 account for 77% of the differences in preschool attendance across prefectures. All of them are fair proxies for the cultural-capital thesis. Two of them — private kindergartens and nursery schools — may also be indicators of early sorting mechanisms. These two factors have the strongest effects on kindergarten attendance in Japan.

Table 2—4, thus, demonstrates a quite different educational path for kindergartners as opposed to the path for nursery school attendees suggested by Table 2—3. Mombushō-controlled preschools have a strongly stratified flavor not apparent in the Kōseishō-controlled preschools. Mombushō preschools appear designed to appease the conservative status quo dominated by the strong effects of privilege and status, while Kōseishō preschools target households where both adults are likely to have to work. Furthermore, the strong relationship of top high school graduation rates to Monbushō's kindergartens suggests that these types of preschools have a latent academic function, while the lack of association with Koseisho's nursery schools do not.

The overall pattern confirms that preschools in Japan are indeed varied and have conflicting goals centering at least around differences between Mombushō and Kōseishō policies. These results encourage attention to this source of heterogeneity because public kindergartens presently cost only 61% of private ones, raising further issues of fairness of educational opportunity at very early ages. Even if preschools serve primarily social rather than academic functions, the privilege of receiving social experiences is greater for certain classes of people.

The great heterogeneity among preschools should also give warning to researchers who continue to assume falsely that small case studies give accurate representation for all of Japan. For example, Miyagi Prefecture, the site of Stevenson's (1989) pioneering study of comparative mathematical ability, is the fourth lowest in ratio of hoikuen students and in the top-third in yōchien attendance. Comparing a preschool system so obviously skewed toward high-performance academic orientation with one (Chicago metropolitan area) with no obvious representation of the total United States should be particularly suspect in light of the wide variation in preschools in Japan.[8]

CLASS SIZE AND THE MYTH OF SHUDAN SEIKATSU

One of the most consistent characteristic descriptions of Japanese preschools is the large size of classes by comparison to Western preschools. Tobin, Wu, and Davidson (1989:59) point out that class-size allowances far exceed American prescribed limits on students per teacher. Tobin and his colleagues comment (p. 67) that this "class size system only dates from the Meiji era one hundred years ago and was borrowed from the West."

Researchers like White (1987, pp. 68, 176) accept the naturalness of large class size as part of Japanese culture in spite of the historical evidence that they are new to Japanese culture. Japanese teachers themselves think that it is good for children to learn to relate to large numbers of age-mates although (1) there has never been any research conducted to test this hypothesis in Japan and (2) both social psychological research on group size as well as common sense would suggest that there must be limits to the benefits of increasing group size. The purpose of this section is to explore reasons Japanese teachers give for large class size and to assess the benefits for Japanese preschool children.

Tobin and his coworkers (Tobin and others 1989: 70) suggest that

> . . . large student/teacher ratios seem to function effectively (in Japan) when preschools employ methods of instruction and teacher-student interaction specifically suited to a large-group format. . . including (1) delegating authority to children; (2) intervening less quickly in children's fights and arguments; (3) having lower expectations for children's noise level and comportment; (4) using more musical cues and less verbal ones; (5) organizing more highly structured, large-group daily activities such as taiso (morning group exercise); (6) using a method of choral recitation for answering teacher's questions rather than calling on individuals; and (7) making more use of peer-group approval and opprobrium and less of teacher's positive and negative reactions to influence children's behavior.

---

[8]Stevenson (personal communication) states that he drew a stratified random sample of schools from the Chicago metropolitan area, and has since found essentially the same data with stratified random samples from several other metropolitan areas in the United States, so that this is not a problem. However, the fact remains that his method loses tremendous variation in Japan by ignoring differences between a relatively high-performance prefecture (e.g., Miyagi) versus low-performance ones (e.g., Niigata). It also does not reflect the wide variation in the United States.

In essence, this quote assumes that shudan seikatsu (group life) is a unique and essential part of Japanese culture in spite of evidence already given that it is relatively new to Japanese education. Moreover, the seven points listed above do not necessarily have any relation to extraordinarily large group size. Why, for example, should it be better to have a child in a class of 40 students than one of 30 or 20 students? Surely all of the above points could be just as successfully carried out with a class of 20 students as double that size.

In fact, some of these points can be otherwise interpreted. For example, point 7 fits well with the Japanese educational abhorrence of teachers judging students. Students rarely fail in Japan. I suspect that this point may have less to do with class size (it could be used with any size group) so much as with confirmation of the teacher's role as someone who never really individually is called upon to judge students.

Students of group size have long known that while the number of possible dyads grows exponentially at the rate of $(n*(n-1)/2)$ time, space, activities, and a host of other variables severely limit the number of actual dyads. A class of 20 students has 190 possible dyads while a class of 40 students has 800. No child is likely to make friends with a fraction of those possibilities.

Moreover, the most basic weakness of this position is that it assumes that all Japanese preschools have the same basic large group size. This is patently false. The 1987 infants-to-day-nursery worker ratio ranged from 6.86 in Tōkyō to 14.6 in Nagano with a mean of 10.9. Likewise the 1987 kindergartner-to-teacher ratio varied from 21.7 in Miyagi Prefecture to 29.5 in Nagano Prefecture with a mean average of 25.1 and an essentially student's t-distribution (almost flat).

Mapping of this variation indicates that the lowest ratios of infants-to-nurses are in the immediate Tōkyō, Osaka-Kōbe-Kyōto and Fukuoka areas. The further from these areas into rural areas, the higher the ratios. Because day nurseries are publicly supported institutions, it would appear that richer urban areas benefit by considerably smaller infant ratios. Recall, also, that these areas are precisely the areas with the least amount of illiteracy (as measured by amount of education below junior high school).

Correlations in Table 2—5 support this interpretation. Lower population densities, more women in the labor force, more farmers, lower prefectural per capita student spending, and lower gross prefectural product are all statistically significant at the .01 level or higher. Higher numbers of females in the labor force are the strongest possible reason for high day-nursery class size. This raises the interesting possibility that geographic areas with fewer working-women clients may allow more opportunities for alternative care with more favorable children-to-teacher ratios.

Of course, there is another plausible explanation. Women who work may have smaller families for which they prefer to compensate by having their offspring experience larger numbers of other peers. This possibility is certainly in line with beliefs expressed by Japanese kindergarten teachers that larger numbers of children make for a more well-rounded education. If so, it may be true that large classes promote traditional values of "group-centeredness." However, if this is so, the effects of population density which is an indicator of wealthier populations and school districts counteracts this tendency.

Table 2—5

Correlations and Beta Weights for a Regression on Ratios of Children in Day Nurseries during 1987

Variable Name	Correlations	Beta Weights
Population density (km^2)	**-0.550	***-0.36
% Females in the Labor Force	**0.617	***0.47
%Farmers	**0.471	0.01
Per capita educational spending	**-0.470	*
Gross Prefectural Profits (GPP)	**-0.461	*

$R^2 = 0.49$

Source: Sōricho, Nihon Tōkei Nenkan, 1989. The entire codebook is listed in Appendix X at the end of this book.

* Left out because of high auto-correlations of 0.853, 0.943, and 0.915 between these variables. The results of the first three independent variables are essentially the same without these two additional variables which means that population density is an adequate proxy for the two discarded variables.
**significance level ≥ 0.01
***at least twice the standard error of the beta

Population density remains robust: The larger the population density the lower the class size. The correlations for pupil spending and GPP (Gross Prefectural Profit) with population density are extremely high and positive, indicating the power of urbanized areas in Japan to support education, including relatively large reductions in class size (the largest class size is 34% larger than the smallest). Farming is a spurious factor in Table 2—5 so that the first two factors alone explain nearly half of the differences between prefectures. Therefore, even if class size is much larger than in Western countries, large differences do exist in Japan and these differences appear to be related to socio-economic differences rather than any inherently Japanese cultural uniqueness.

The public-private issue is important because it permits variation in individual choice. Private institutions are 64% more expensive than public ones. Hence, parents who can afford private institutions probably trade off financial costs for perceived benefits. There are 3.2 times as many students attending private as public kindergartens, confirming the strong tendency to send young children to private institutions. There are also small differences in student-to-teacher ratios. Public institutions average 21.3 students per teacher, and private ones average 18.3.

Because of the distinct sources of kindergarten and day nursery enrollments, it is unlikely that the same variables explain student-to-teacher ratios as was true of infant-to-nurse ratios. For example, none of the indicators of prefectural wealth used previously — population density, per capita income, or GPP — have statistically significant correlations with kindergarten child-to-teacher ratios.

Table 2—6

Correlations and Beta Weights for a Regression on the Ratios
of Children in Kindergartens during 1987

Variable Name	Correlations	Beta Weights
%Private kindergartens	*-0.28	***-0.25
% Nuclear families	**-0.48	***-0.23
%Females in labor force	* 0.44	***0.24
Per capita educational spending	-0.37	-0.06

$R^2 = 0.31$
Source: Sōricho, Nihon Tōkei Nenkan, 1989. The entire codebook is listed in Appendix X at the end of this book.

*significance level ≥ 0.05
**significance level ≥ 0.01
***at least twice the standard error of the beta

The private-public distinction is indeed a factor in explaining differences in kindergarten-class size. The higher the percentage of private ownership, the lower the class size. If this effect is accurate, it implies that part of the extra costs of private kindergartens is going for smaller classes contrary to the "big is better" argument. Likewise, the relationship of nuclear families to class size is the opposite of the shudan-keisatsu thesis. The usual argument is that smaller families necessitate giving children large group experiences, yet the regression analysis in Table 2—6 suggests the opposite.

Finally, working women appear to have no control over class size. The positive relationship can be interpreted as showing that they have no bargaining power. Working women may simply need to find a place — any place — where they can leave their children while they work. While the analysis explains only 31% of the variation, it does indicate that the shudan seikatsu argument is oversimplified at best. The analysis raises counter-arguments about the value of group size for keeping down institutional costs. Larger student-teacher ratios mean higher profits to institutions. Also, because large ratios most often occur in less well-educated regions, more educated areas appear less likely to have bought arguments of the value of larger classes.

Careful studies of family size and school achievement in the United States by Blake (1989) support the argument in favor of small group size. American children from small families fare well compared to children from large families. They go further in school, have less likelihood of dropping out, and benefit from enhanced verbal skills. These children and their parents hold higher expectations for their ultimate educational attainment because they test better and get higher grades in school. They are more likely to engage in a rich variety of intellectually and culturally broadening activities at home (to have music and dance lessons, to travel abroad, to be read to by their parents early in life) and at school (to be active in student government, on the school newspaper, in drama groups, etc.). They also seem more confident of their academic ability.

Blake's studies suggest an interesting and quite plausible possibility that students of Japanese education appear not to have seriously considered: the cultural capital effect of small family size in Japan that now averages only 1.6 children and has extremely low variation. Therefore, while conservatives in the Diet lament small family size and working mothers in Japan, these very features of the Japanese education system may be one of its hidden cultural-capital strengths.

Another cultural-capital strength of the Japanese system is inherent in the placing of children in school groups that will stay together for several years. Having the same set of teachers and peers to work with over a relatively long period of time probably builds a child's sense of attachment and belonging, thereby increasing the child's sense of security and contribution to the group. It seems reasonable that this would create a better learning environment, help shape desirable behaviors, and reduce problems of intolerance, violence, and vandalism that seem to be such a part of the American school system. On the negative side, students who do not feel a sense of belonging to such groups because their parent move to a new area or because they become victims of bullies suffer much greater distress than students with equivalent statuses in the United States.

TEACHER RECRUITS

In 1974 Mombushō (Pp. 4—5) started to keep statistics on teacher ratios of women to men when barely over half (54%) were women and they like to point out yearly that the number of women teachers is increasing. However, the reason women teachers outnumber men is due primarily to preschool and elementary school figures. At the junior high school level less than one-third of teachers are women and less than 20% at the high school level. At the university level, virtually no full-time faculty are women. Employment of women at the nursery school level in Japan has the character of part-time work. The typical "career-pattern" is for 20- or 21-year-old single women, fresh out of junior college, to work for a couple of years before settling down to raise their own families. The short-term, female-dominated nature of this work helps to keep costs of preschool education down. It also helps indoctrinate young women into the "advantages" of the Japanese-style of preschool with its large class sizes. Field workers consistently report that these young "teachers" are strong supporters of the system. Teachers are likely, therefore, to support the same types of experiences for their own future children leading to a perpetuation of the untested benefits of large group experiences.

ELEMENTARY SCHOOLS

On the surface, Japanese elementary schools also appear to be extremely egalitarian. There is virtually no variation across prefectures in rates of elementary-school-aged children in school — it is about 98% from Hokkaidō to Okinawa. Similarly, there is no private elite elementary school system in Japan; 99.3% of elementary students attend public schools, and this figure has been unchanged since the end of World War II. Rates of student absenteeism and failure rates are only a fraction of 1% in all prefectures. These figures are always the ones that Mombushō publishes in its English-language press releases and white papers.

Such statistics have naturally much impressed Western observers. The urge is to want to learn from the Japanese system by asking the invariable question: How do Japanese teachers manage to instruct much larger classes than in the U.S.A. while devoting comparatively less time to matters of social control. Stevenson's (1989) work on teaching mathematics and science in primary schools in Sendai indicate that teachers devote a significantly higher percentage of total class time to the subject than their Minneapolis counterparts.

Counter-intuitively, his most recent observations (Lee, Graham, Stevenson in press) suggest that the methods the Sendai teachers engage students more in the learning process because teachers break lessons up into smaller segments than their Minneapolis counterparts. The Sendai teachers also used much more concrete objects to illustrate difficult concepts, elicited more explanations from students, provided more examples that applied directly to the students' own experiences, and used more word problems. The impression left with the Sendai observers was that Sendai teachers used classroom time more productively than in Minneapolis.

Also, the Sendai teachers were fresher because they were not overburdened by lengthy periods of teaching. While Minneapolis teachers had classes throughout the school day, Sendai teachers taught no more than four hours in a school day, leaving adequate time for preparation for lessons. Ironically, the group-orientation of the Sendai teachers allowed them more time to handle individual problems than the individual-orientation of the Minneapolis teachers. The result was that the Japanese students normally left class understanding the solutions to problems that the American students did not know.

Singleton (1989: 11) observed that teachers refused to assess slow learners as "underachievers" and fast learners as "overachievers." Although schools retain IQ scores on file for students, he also found that teachers rejected availing themselves of that information in their student evaluation. Teachers do not like to consider individual variations; they feel that slow learners simply have to try harder to pull their grades up while fast learners are proof of the Japanese gambaru (effort and persistence) system. The system leaves no allowance for alternative explanations of differences between individuals. The irony is that the same causal variables explain individual differences as in the United States. For example, Jacobson and Takamura (1986) demonstrate that the best cultural-capital predictor of mean scores on an international test of core science in both countries are the number of books in a student's home. Interestingly, the correlation in both cases is 0.29. Also, in the fifth grade test, they found that the number of books in the home — a measure of cultural capital — was the single best predictor of mean scores on the International Core Test of Science in both countries with a correlation of 0.24.

PUBLIC AND PRIVATE EXPENSES

There is huge variation in educational opportunities at the elementary-school level not widely recognized inside or outside Japan. First, although official press releases report average educational expenditures as typical of the entire country, they are not at all homogeneous. By standardizing expenditures by prefectural populations it becomes clear that gargantuan differences in elementary school spending exist. Compare 1987 figures for Tōkyō public elementary school expenses of 622,000 yen per student, which is 1.7 times that of Saitama Prefecture's 367,000 yen per student. Likewise, private expenditures for elementary schools range from 2.6% to 4.8% of family budgets in 1987.

There is a negative correlation of -0.48 between these two sources of elementary school funding. This suggests that in areas without large national spending, parents feel compelled to contribute beyond their tax dollars to support their children's educational outcomes. However, public expenditures are greatest in the narrow range of Pacific Ocean prefectures stretching from

Tōkyō to Kobe, and private spending is also greatest in those prefectures that have a disproportionate share of prestigious universities. Prefectures outside the Kantō-Kansai area contribute most of the variation to the negative correlation. Elementary school spending is greatest in the prefectures hosting the elite 45 universities in Japan. Tōkyō and Ōsaka metropolitan areas spend the most on education when combining both personal and private sources and have the greatest opportunities for entrance into the best universities. This suggests that outlying prefectures must choose between relatively small amounts of one of these two principle sources of educational funding. Financial capital has a very clear, direct linkage to educational opportunities in Japan, masked by the government PR releases of an equal chance to step up the educational ladder until high school entrance.

How have these gross inequities escaped notice for so long? I think the answer requires close attention to the myth of Japanese equality. The public has bought into the belief that they have a fair and just educational system. Japanese perceive no need to look beyond proof of sameness across graduation rates, school delinquency rates, or whatever "proof" served up by governmental authorities concerning the eradication of illiteracy, superiority of Japanese education, etc. The reason is quite simple: a student who does not live up to the model can simply be labeled as a deviant who did not try hard enough; who did not use his or her talents to go to juku or take advantage of other resources which seem open to all, even if they are not.

Government surveys confirm this picture. The adult public appears to fear change away from the status quo. Although 68 schools in Tōkyō and surrounding prefectures went on a trial five-day-school week starting April 1, 1990, government surveys of workers show that over half of them want no change from the current five-and-one-half-day system. Eighty-three percent of these respondents fear that it will lead to unfair advantages — some students spending more time in leisure activities while parents of other children enroll their children in additional cram school courses. Respondents agreeing with the shortened school week agreed under the precondition that it be used only for leisure and social activities.[9]

This precondition is unrealistic because the Japanese system is predicated on relentless extra-school studying and tutoring. Singleton (1989:11) found that Japanese view this system positively as a way to strengthen individual character and develop moral fiber, rather than the mindless exercise that Westerners believe. This belief pervades all areas of Japanese life. Whiting (1989) documents case after case of this difference between Japanese and American philosophies of building athletes. Japanese professional baseball managers have gone so far as to make a pitcher throw practice pitches until his arm goes lame; the rationale is that "proving" one

---

[9]These figures come from a Labor ministry press release to The Japan Times (May 2, 1990) of 1100 workers in factories employing 30 or more workers. Because no other identifying materials were given it is not clear how representative of Japanese these workers are in general. This is a normal problem with official surveys in Japan. The Prime Minister's Office, for example, routinely reports from an ongoing survey of 10,000 randomly sample Japanese, in spite of the fact that response rates average 75%. The attitude seems to be that size and not quality of surveys is enough to make it authoritative.

has tried his best is the more important part of playing. By definition, traditional training — either physically or mentally — in Japan assumes the ultimate superiority of repetition of fundamentals over other means of learning.

The incessant message to try harder regardless of cost applies much more to junior high schools than elementary schools. This leads to further misperceptions of the equality of elementary schools. If citizens perceive that real preparation for higher education starts in junior high school, it is easy to assume that elementary schools are relatively benign places that are not part of the educational "rat race."

These views show up in the semantic differential scores displayed in Figure 1—1. Goodness ratings deteriorate slowly from birth through junior high school as expectations for students pile up, and are always on the negative side of the scale. However, as children climb the educational ladder, adults perceive that they gain in power (or, more precisely, become less powerless) because of their increasing education. For example, more Chinese characters learned should lead to higher reading comprehension and clearer written expression. Adults expect students to become more sedentary in the pursuit of more advanced education, confirming belief in gambaru.

JUNIOR HIGH: THE APEX OF PRESSURES TO SUCCEED

Japanese perceive that the system is fair and just until entrance into high school. The reasons are similar to those already given for elementary schools. The system appears entirely fair. The junior high school system is also almost entirely publicly financed. Only 3.3% of students attended private junior high schools in 1988. All students are required to study exactly the same texts and attend the same number of hours of instruction each year in the same courses; and only minor variations in pass rates exist.

These facts provide powerful confirmation that all Japanese must be alike and the system must be successful in educating students at minimally acceptable levels. Differences between entrance prospects into the more clearly stratified high school system create the only real anomaly. As students have had eight years of time to have individually disposed of as they wish (in theory), it is easy to believe that only differences in persistence explain entrance into the highly stratified high school system. The elementary and junior high school systems, after all, appear to be benevolent, non-discriminatory systems that treat all students in exactly the same manner.

In reality, the junior high school system is just as stacked against and in favor of particular geographical areas as is the elementary system. Elementary costs correlate strongly with average junior high school expenditures per pupil. The correlation between these two variables is 0.69, confirming the strong push toward maintaining the economic-expenditure status quo. A good part of the reason that the correlation is not higher is that many junior high school students start to travel great distances to school and juku in search of the competitive edge. Some prefectures like Tōkyō become huge magnets for the aspiring students, while others such as Chiba have massive numbers of junior high students who scamper to nearby Tōkyō in search of the "best" juku or yobikō[10]. The race to enter the top high schools, already six years in the unofficial trial stage, is now officially on. Unbeknownst to most of the participants, many of their fellow competitors have the advantages of higher public-per-capita spending, better transportation infrastructures to a wider range of school and extra-curricular choices, and parents who have better ability to pay the increasing costs demanded.

Unlike the American race where one can continue to compete as one ages, the Japanese educational race is strictly limited to specific age groups. The typical college student in Japan will range in age from 18 to 22 as was true of the U.S.A. thirty years ago. Students realize that they have a very narrow window of about three years as a rōnin after high school graduation to pass into college.[11] Compare that to an average age of 28 in contemporary American universities where aspiring students have flexibility of choice in the timing of entry into universities. For the Japanese junior high school student, the race is almost purely an all-or-nothing affair at age 13 or 14: One must get out of the gate fast and never look back. For this reason, junior high school in Japan has become the focal point of student effort.

RESULTS OF INDOCTRINATION IN ITS RAWEST FORM

Students are intensely aware that their junior high years are "make it or break it" ones. The one chance to go to a university, particularly a top-ranked one, reaches its most critical juncture in junior high school when students are vying for entry into the high school system. If a junior high student succeeds in entering a high school of the quality of Nada[12] in Kōbe he or she may still have to burn the midnight candle studying. However, that student can at least rest assured that the probabilities of entry into Tōdai are grossly in his or her favor. The student who does well on high school entrance exams does so at his or her neighbor's expense creating intense personal rivalries.

---

[10]Both juku and yobikō have been part of the Japanese educational scene since the Meiji era. The yobikō originally functioned as a type of college preparatory school rather than for competitive placement on college entrance examinations (Tsukada, 1991, p. 6).
[11]Approximately one in every five male high-school graduates experiences this status.
[12]Nada consistently produces the highest number of Tōdai and Kyōdai entrants. For example, out of a graduating class of 224 in 1988, 102 members were accepted into Tōdai and 72 into Kyōdai. Admittance to Nada, hence, virtually assures entrance to the two top-choice universities in Japan.

School officials have only belatedly started to realize some of the deleterious effects of the intense pressures which reach their competitive apex in junior high school. Statistics indicate that junior high is the apex for numerous signs of educationally induced conflict. Bullying, school vandalism, "excused" school absence, and truancy have increased dramatically in recent years. These social problems fall dramatically once the educational authorities sort students into groups of similarly ranked college potential.

Bullying

Murakami (1989:151) indicates that elementary schools bore 5450 cases of bullying; junior highs yielded 3,519 cases, and high schools produced only 515 cases in the 1984—5 school year. When standardized, these figures indicate that junior highs produce roughly 25% more cases per capita than elementary schools, with high schools producing roughly 10% of the cases in junior high school suggesting the structural effects of pressures during junior high school.

Bullying appears, on the surface, to be an intensely personal act. The misperception that Japanese school violence is intensely personal is partly due to the victims' often extreme reaction of shame, occasionally pushed to the point of suicide.[13] It is a matter of deep psychological stirrings as evidenced by the very strong feelings of powerlessness (-2.84) on the part of victims shown in Table 1—1, known in Japan as higaisha ishiki (victim mentality). In some recent incidents, even after the bully publicly expressed regret over his behavior, the victim often refused to return to school, apparently less for fear than out of shame. (Hechinger 1986: 25). Missing from popular conceptions of the roots of bullying is a massive sociological literature on victimization that points to the institutionalization of all forms of violence. As in any form of victimization, most people view the bully's victim as "provoking" the bully's attack. Weaker, new, non-conformist, friendless or slower students are most likely to end up as victims of bullying.

Japanese are little different from Americans in their misplaced blame for violence on victims. The seriousness of the problem in Japan, however, heightens the extreme helplessness of the victims. What the bully's victim profile does not show is cross-cultural reference: In over 25 years of research on collecting comparable semantic-differential profiles with dictionaries in the U.S.A., Canada, Ireland, Arabia, Germany, and Japan, we have never seen a powerlessness score as low as the Japanese rating for ijimerarekko (bully's victim).

Informants tell us that the structure of the school system in Japan largely explains the victim's feelings of helplessness. Recall that in Japan education is unusually standardized. Students take the same courses with the

---

[13]Bullying and exam pressures are completely unrelated to suicide in Japan, although some researchers have made the false claim that they are related (Duke 1986). See Kurosu (1991b) for the most complete analysis to date of the actual causes of suicide in Japan.

same students six days a week, 220 days a year. Indeed, it is quite normal for 40-some students to stay together for two years or more with the same teacher. This system allows for no escaping from a bully, unlike the American one in which a student can usually transfer to a different class, or even a different school. Furthermore, the official policy of non-interventionism in student affairs by teachers and school officials guarantees a bully freedom to continue assaults with impunity. A bully can keep a watchful eye on a victim at all times. The victim cannot even escape after school because he or she is always under the watchful eye of the bully.

Bullying appears to be a reaction to Japan's brutal educational pressures. If bullying was simply a personal problem it should be randomly distributed. However, bullying is highly predictable. First, cases build up during the years of most intense competition for scarce educational advantages and then decrease dramatically after the apportionment of scarce resources. Second, girls are rarely the bully or the victim partly reflecting their exclusion from the college ladder. Boys and girls may have mixed seating arrangements during the first few years of primary school, but after primary school graduation, most schools segregate girls from boys. Authorities pressure girls to drop out of the educational opportunity race.

This sex discrimination shows clearly in Table 1—2. Although the reversal of goodness scores for female and male students takes place upon entrance into college, students become well aware of these differences much earlier. Third, victims are almost always transfer students without the security of friends and groups to protect them. The only role in Table 1—1 with better overall ratings than the classmate role as nice (0.72), slightly powerful (0.63), and slightly active (1.05) is honor student. However, because only a few students may attain honor-student status while most can attain "classmate" status, the role of classmate in Japan is indeed estimable.

This is manifest in the unusually high number of lifetime friends who come from among former classmates. It is quite common for adult Japanese to meet their former elementary school classmates for regular social events. Iwamura (1987:97) has documented the importance of school friends as sources of long-term, close relationships in Japan. Given the powerful role that former classmates have in Japan, it is easy to understand why parents are reluctant to pull their children out of schools when husbands are transferred: New schools increase the probability that their child will grow up without former classmates and will suffer victimization at the hand of bullies. The strong ties that exist between classmates are one of the strengths of the Japanese culture. However, it is also one of its Achilles heels; industrialization increasingly separates families and forces them to choose between separate households or dimmed prospects for their children's educational future.

School Vandalism

School vandalism also gives a glimpse into school-induced pressures. Compared to the United States, vandalism is rare in Japan but it is not indiscriminate. Vandalism against primary schools is so rare that the press does not even bother to report it. By contrast, one-in-three junior high schools reported vandalism of school property in 1988. Consistent with the thesis that junior high school is the focus of educational competition, the rate falls by half to one-in-six senior high schools.

Vandalism is a tangible act that should be easy to count. Although it is possible that school officials might hide acts leading to underreporting this should not affect the ratio of junior-to-senior high school rates. More suspect are the next set of official statistics: truancy and excused school absences. Both may be easily doctored or miss-reported. Particularly as Japan is a nation saddled with strong beliefs in harmony and homogeneity, there is good reason to believe that school officials must feel uncomfortable with the apparently fast-rising truancy and school absence rates.

Absenteeism

School absences appear to show signs consistent with the thesis that pre-high school demands on students are becoming unrealistic. Figures for 1988 school absences of up to 50 days tripled nationwide in only 10 years. Given the power that rests in the hands of school authorities, it is surprising that students are absent at all. For example, one of the strongest commands of obedience at the junior and senior high school teacher's disposal is the threat to give a negative evaluation on the student's naishinsho (school record). Although teacher's may rarely evaluate academic work in Japan, they are more disposed to evaluating disobedience.

Public junior high schools in Japan are notorious for imposing a wealth of military-academy-like rules to which they expect blind obedience. Hair rules have drawn increasing attention as a prime example. Local bar associations have started to document such unnecessary restrictions on student civil liberties. The Kōbe Bar Association discovered that 230 out of 1250 junior high schools they surveyed in 1989 required male students to wear crew cuts, although this rule varied greatly by prefecture.

Nearly all junior high schools surveyed in Kōbe, Fukushima and Kagoshima required crew cuts. Half of Kōbe schools planned to review the regulation. Tōkyō and 20 other cities reported no such requirement. Some school authorities commented that crew cuts encourage good study habits. Others said teachers should concentrate more on the content of the lessons rather than on school regulations. These sharp differences illustrate the divisive battles going on in Japan over doing things they way they have always been done in the past.

Mombushō mandated relaxation of dress and hair codes in 1988 in light of increasing criticism of their educational value. However, cultural pressures to stick with the tried-and-true are likely to be hard to overturn. For example, a Japan Teachers' Union survey (reported in The Japan Times, May 13, 1990, p. 2) announced that 1% of junior high schools had tightened dress restrictions while 25% had eased them, and 25% had issued stricter hair style rules while only 15% had relaxed them. Part of the reason for local school refusal to abide by national rules is parental opposition to any change that upsets the currently clear paths to higher education.

Nichibenren (the Japanese Bar Association) surveys indicate widespread serious violations of the human rights of children: How pupils must sit, stand and walk; what height and at what angle they should raise their hands to ask questions; and routes between home and school. These school rules even apply at home and during vacations. School authorities have been known to dole out heavy punishments for girls who perm or dye hair during vacations. Although Nichibenren lawyers point to a direct connection between meaningless rules and pupils who resort to violence against their teachers and others, it is difficult convincing the general public and school authorities that they are correct.

While lawyers warn of the increasing deleterious side effects of these mindless rules, schools have opted for stricter punishment of their infraction. For example, reports of school officials resorting to corporal punishment for rule infractions more than doubled between 1984 and 1988, according to the Tōkyō District Legal Affairs Bureau of the Justice Ministry (The Japan Times, May 5, 1989, p.3) Two-thirds of these cases occurred in junior high schools. The article reports the example of a 26-year old physical education teacher at a junior high school who on one occasion punched three students in the face about eight times each "because the students did not participate in the class seriously." Incredibly, school officials did not dismiss the teacher. They did no more than send him a letter of reprimand. The only disciplining given any of the Tōkyō-based teachers was a scolding.

In that report, the most common reason given for hitting students was that they had made mistakes during extracurricular club activities or skipped club meetings (22%). Other reasons were resisting and ridiculing teachers (20%); drinking, smoking and other misconduct (19%); and violation of school regulations (19%). Such physical discipline was common before World War II but was banned by Article 11 of the School Education Law following the war. Fujita (1989: 125) suggests a direct link between the increase in stricter punishment of students and school violence, citing the largest category of school violence reported to the police in 1983 (42%) was against teachers.

Truancy

Truancy provides another avenue for children to cope with school problems. The issue of truancy is highly charged in any industrialized country, but is probably a more emotional issue in Japan than the United States. For example, Fujita (1989: 125) uses comparative cross-national statistics to show stronger feelings in Japan where "85% of parents and children in Japan think 'to play truant from school should not be allowed' compared to 70% of parents and 77% of adults in the U.S.A." Semantic scores for school dropouts in Japan shown in Table 1—1 also underscore strong differences in attitudes: Americans rate a school dropout as slightly negative (-1.1), quite powerless (-1.4), and slightly active (1.1) (Heise & Lewis, 1988) while Japanese rate dropouts much more negatively (-1.67), much less powerful (-1.74) and much less active (0.53). While it is difficult to argue for complete comparability of scaling techniques across both cultures, these differences are compatible with scholarly writing on American-Japanese schooling differences. A reasonable speculation is that deviant roles are much more frowned upon, more powerless, and inactive in Japan than the United States because they are disruptive of the cultural myths of homogeneity and harmony.

The placement of blame is also of great interest for understanding deviancy of any type. It is ironic that a nation that considers itself the epitome of group-centeredness uses individualistic explanations of deviancy while those labeled as deviants themselves place the blame on social structure. Lebra (1984, p. x] points out that "the monstrous kyōiku-mama image often appears as an explanation for juvenile delinquency and the pathological refusal to attend school. Domestic violence, which in present-day Japan has come to mean a boy's abuse of his mother, is not infrequently considered a product of the mother's egocentrism."

Surveys of truants, however, give a clearer story. In 1988 the vast majority of truants were junior high school students — 86% of institutionalized truants were junior high students, 7% were elementary students, and the remaining 7% were high school students. The problem clearly is a problem in junior high schools. The Civil Liberties Bureau of the Justice Ministry conducted a survey of 3,019 persons institutionalized because they had been absent more than 50 days in 1988. Only 509 of the truants responded to their survey, suggesting high alienation and a biased sample. However, the results leave the impression that institutionalized disregard for individual civil liberties by major authority figures and organizations and economic dislocations to family life are major determinants of truancy.

Forty-seven percent of the truants traced their truancy to problems with friends: 20% could not make friends; and 19% felt isolated from classmates. Forty-four percent of the truants pointed to difficulties with their teachers; and 45% had difficulties with family members. (The numbers add up to more than 100% because the respondents sometime choose more than one response.)

Although the survey gave only individualized reasons, these problems are most likely to occur when families move to new areas where their children must start over making new friends. It is reasonable to assume that most of these individually reported troubles are due to problems children encounter when they attend new schools. We have seen that the most valued childhood role is that of "classmate." Classmates protect their friends and become lifetime commitments in Japan. The disruption of those bonds most likely is one of the most disturbing events that can occur to a Japanese student.

Reactions to truancy also illustrate the force of institutionalized patterns in Japan. Forty-three percent of the truants in the above survey said that their parents tried to forcibly return them to school while another 25% said they had been beaten or severely scolded. Truants also reported similar reactions by their teachers: 38% said their teachers came to their homes and tried to take them to school forcibly; 29% that their teachers pressured them to attend school; and 30% said that their teachers recommended that they go to educational counseling centers.

The typical reactions reported indicate that most authority figures assume that truancy is the fault of the student and has little to do with the student's environment. These reactions also indicate the strong reaction that truancy creates among the truant's significant others. The power of this negative reaction is so strong as to question the methods Mombushō uses to differentiate between students who try to escape from a hostile school system through truancy and truly physically ill students. For example, if the present system of counting physical illness as a legitimate reason for not attending school was accurate there should be little variation across the country in this reason.

However, the range of absences for reasons of physical illness ranged from 0.14% of students with excused absences of over 50 days in Okinawa to 0.52% in Saga (Mean = 0.33%) in 1985.[14] The six prefectures with the highest levels of excused long absences for reasons of illness were those in Kyūshū and Shikoku that have received the most press coverage for student-civil-rights abuses. It is difficult to accept that students in Saga Prefecture could be 3.5 times as sickly as Okinawan students. Likewise, figures for long absences due to mental illness range from 0.13% in Nara to 0.74% in Ibaraki. Again, it stretches the imagination to think that there could be a 5.7-fold difference in excusable mental problems across Japan's junior high schools, unless there were substantial (1) differences in ways of counting absences or (2) differences in school treatment of students that lead to differential mental anguish. Similarly, the rate of Japanese students absent from school for long periods increased from 9 out of 10,000 students in elementary school to 26 in junior high school in 1986. What good physical reason could explain a three-fold increase in long absences with the jump from elementary to secondary schools.[15]

These figures also encourage re-focusing on the claims that (a) Japanese students like school and that (b) Japanese schools have unusually high rates

---

[14]The data for long absences comes from tables in the 1988 Nihon Arumanakku (Japanese Almanac).

[15]An elite high school in Nada, near Kobe, refused to enroll four applicants for admission in 1990 although they had passed the entrance examinations. School records showed they had failed to attend classes for 60 to 90 days. Their parents had submitted proper excuses to their teachers as headaches, colds and other minor ailments but their pattern of absenteeism was always on Mondays. Nada has a long-term reputation passing admissions test to Tokyo University. These four students had skipped school to go to a juku cram school program although their official school years noted medical problems.

of school attendance. Official truancy rates would appear to be camouflaging much more serious problems, particularly in junior high schools. The role of truant or school dropout is so deviant, as shown in Table 1—2, that it is highly probable that children, parents, and school officials are actively masking embarrassing problems with "acceptable" excuses. Furthermore, the (1) negative labeling that attaches to truancy as well as (2) uncompromising chances for academic success outside normal channels are the more likely reasons for exceptionally low rates of truancy in Japan, rather than student liking for the system.

Cram Schools

Japanese perceive that cram schools provide opportunities to catch up if students fall behind academically in spite of the strong influence of cultural-capital influences beyond individual control. Thus, the widespread perception is that cram schools support egalitarianism and uniformity of regular schools. In actuality, cram schools are an integral part of the educational sorting machine in Japan. As with the official educational system, cram schools have clearly recognized rank order based on percentage of their students who matriculate to top high schools, or to Tōdai and other top universities.

High schools in the Kansai area that have "high success rates" for entrance into Tōdai and Kyōdai include Kyōto's Rakusei and Ōsaka's Seikō Gakuin. Such schools give their own tests that predict the probability of success in passing. In essence, there is an elite system of cram schools and high schools that sorts students out of their system that would lower their success rate, takes students who have an excellent chance of entering an elite high school or university and then "teaches" this select group the answers to questions most likely to be on high school or university entrance examinations.

The system is educationally incestuous. It succeeds in maintaining the elite status of these cram schools because the elite jukus carefully select the winners in the educational race before they enter the main event. The cram schools then go about reinforcing answers to specific test questions rather than teaching how to learn and produce new knowledge. At the same time, the myth of a homogeneous race aids the status quo because all participants in the race are of the impression that they all started out with the same life chances and that only those who kept on plugging away were the actual winners.   Because the Kantō and Kansai areas have the most highly developed cram-school systems, these areas have a distinct advantage over other areas of the country in producing students who will pass the national examinations necessary to enter the elite universities.

SUMMARY

This chapter and the next one use an educational life cycle approach to clarify and organize the relationships of students, educators, and parents in Japan. It starts with data on early child rearing and continues through junior high school in this chapter. The next chapter covers high school through graduate school and graduation from formal schooling.

Early childhood education in Japan stands in stark contrast to its American counterpart. Japanese conceptions of socialization emphasize moral education to a greater extent, yet observation suggests that Japanese preschool teachers spend little time in disciplinary actions of asocial or antisocial behavior. Rather, they allow preschoolers great freedom to devise and use peer pressure to control deviants.

The role of the Ministry of Education and the Ministry of Health and Welfare complicates the study of preschools. For years scholars have debated the role of each ministry with some arguing that there is very little difference between the Ministry of Education's yōchien and the Ministry of Health and Welfare's hoikuen, while others argue that they are quite different in function. The reason the debate has continued to simmer is due to the fact that researchers have depended on field studies using small, non-random samples of preschools. Prefectural differences reflected in correlational and multiple regression analysis help clarify differences.

Regression analysis indicates strong differences between yōchien and hoikuen. The hoikuen are primarily rural-based and serve working mothers who work out of need. Yōchien cater to urban families and professional and technical workers in prefectures with elite high schools noted for their ability to graduate large percentages of top-university-bound students. These analyses show consistent support for the function of both financial and cultural capital in the role of yōchien as bastions of privilege and status in Japan.

Another debate has centered on the effects of class size. Part of the mythology of Japanese uniqueness asserts that large classes promote traditional values of "group centeredness." However, prefectural-level data do not support this myth. Class size is extremely variable in Japan, and is consistently related to factors that are inconsistent with the "bigger is better" hypothesis. Socialization of new teachers leads to the perpetuation of this myth in spite of strong counter-evidence.

Another myth centers on the "homogeneous" nature of the entire educational experience in Japan. In spite of large amounts of superficial evidence that this is so, I show great differences in levels of spending on elementary school across prefectures that relate to levels of educational attainment. The literature on extra-school studying and tutoring personified in the kyōiku mama and juku institutions supports the thesis that all elementary school education is not equal.

The junior high school data show the darkest side of educational inequality and pressures to compete in Japan. Bullying, school vandalism, "excused" school absences, and truancy peek during junior high school yet show predicable variation across prefectures from year to year that relate to structural inequities in educational opportunities, peer group pressures, as well as unrealistic demands and strong pressures for male students to succeed in the race for limited spots in elite universities.

Chapter 3

HIGH SCHOOL AND BEYOND: THE FINAL LAPS

High school marks a major shift in governmental policy in Japan. Although the first eight years of education have at least the surface appearance of egalitarianism, high school marks an unabashed shift to an equally strong veneer of a "free-market" approach to education. High school education is still under the iron-handed guidance of Mombushō, but family savings now largely replaces tax dollars. Students are free to apply to any high school that will accept them and private and public schools openly "compete" for students. High schools choose applicants based on entrance-exam scores.

The race for entrance into the top universities has now entered the quarterfinals, with 14 years of trial heats over and students well sorted by probabilities of university-entrance success. As we have seen, these trial heats are not particularly fair. Some prefectures offer distinct financial advantages, cram school opportunities, transportation perquisites, and other privileges not easily grasped by the average citizen. Competitive exams in the ninth grade sort students into very clear career paths starting at about age 15. These exams mark some students for technical schools and they will have no chance at all of competing for the blue-blood universities and little chance of attending any college.

At worst, low exam scores in the ninth-grade relegate a student to second-class economic status for life. Children with special emotional, physical, and mental needs, if they are lucky, will attend separate schools.[1] Students who have shown promise for rote memorization will enter private and public high schools that have unambiguous rankings in terms of the probabilities of students winning the race for entry into college.

Parents whose children do not make it into one of the preeminent high schools probably believe that the system is entirely open and fair. They may express the opinion that their son or daughter simply did not try hard enough or did not take advantage of the opportunities that were clearly available to all. Some of the participants will have decided to drop out of the race all together, aided by such fairly prestigious universities as Kwansai Gakuin, Dōshisha, and Keio that offer virtual cradle-to-grave education for a few, lucky, intelligent young Japanese students whose parents want them to get the grueling testing over as early as possible.

The last lap in the race to enter prestigious universities has more clearly set obstacles to those at the bottom and more unmistakable aids to accelerate the pace of those students chosen for the final lap on the fast track. The race seems fair partly because of the sharp increases nationwide in high school enrollments since World War II. Quantitatively, Japan has made great gains in high school enrollments from only 43% in 1950 to close to 97% in 1990. To the average parent this means that their children have done better than they themselves did justifying beliefs that the system must be fair.

Graduation from high school has gone from a privilege for the upper class to being open to virtually all Japanese. What is less obvious, however, is the quality of a high school diploma. The worth of a high school degree from one school over another becomes obvious only when measured by overall success rates in entering specific universities. It is an exercise in hyperbole to suggest, as White (1987, p. 73) has, that "a high school diploma in Japan can be said to be the equivalent of a college degree in the United States." The Japanese high school system has extremes from commercial and technical high schools who excel only in producing good baseball players to private ones who produce mostly Tōdai and Kyōdai entrants who are most notable for their fact-cramming skills. However, no high school in Japan is renowned for teaching students to think independently; no Japanese school, public or private, has the intellectual stature of the cream of the top public

---

[1]Japan lags well behind the United States in admitting handicapped students to universities. I have never seen a handicapped student on the two Japanese campuses where I have taught, although both added special ramps and bathroom facilities for handicapped persons in 1989. According to a 1990 survey of universities, most freely admit to discriminating against the acceptance of handicapped students who pass their examinations. In a 1989 survey Amano (1990) looked at 517 departments at 259 four-year universities nationwide and found that 79% had received queries about entrance exams from disabled people, but only 50% of the universities surveyed had accepted more than one disable student in the previous four years. Sixty-five percent accepted less than three disabled students. Seventy-four percent did not have access for such equipment as wheelchairs, and about 35% said they would not accept the deaf, people with impaired vision and people who have no use of their hands, and 20% said they would not take people in wheelchairs. Only 3% said they had adopted a positive attitude about accepting the disabled.

American high schools such as Brooklyn Science High School in New York City or Walt Whitman in Montgomery County, Maryland. The private-public school distinction is an important one for discussing educational opportunity in Japan. Shields (1989) claims that nationally, successful applicants to Tōkyō University equally divide between free, public schools and fee-based private ones. However, this is untrue. Large metropolitan areas like Kyōto, Ōsaka, Tōkyō, and Kanagawa, with the largest and wealthiest populations, have a pattern of small public enrollments, a large private sector, and large academic track populations. For example, only 10 high schools — all private — contributed 36% of the 1988 entering class into Kyōto University; and the top-10 yielding high schools — again all private — contributed 25% of Tōkyō University's 1988 entering class. The only high school that was a member of these top-ten high schools that was not in the Kantō or Kansai area was LaSalle in Kagoshima.

Another way to look at the increasing contribution of private schools to university entrants is to observe the growing importance of the private high school market in Japan. In 1950, only 15.5% of high schools were privately operated. Between 1960 and 1965 this roughly doubled in number and has stood since at about 28% of all high schools. Only 17% of these private high schools rank in the top 400, but this 17% of the crème de la crème contributed 41% of the entering 1988 Tōdai class and 30.4% of Kyōdai's.

This dominance by a select few private high schools is relatively recent, but the change is instructive for understanding the resistance of the public to any change that might threaten the status quo. The most important threat occurred in the Tōkyō Municipal School System's experiment with reforming the elitist aspects of the system. Fear by members of the Tōkyō elite that the movement toward egalitarianism would hamper their offspring's chances for entrance into the top universities resulted in an "elite flight" to private, academically oriented high schools. A transferal of status from what had been a high-status public school system to private schools resulted.

A marked trend has occurred toward benefiting well-off families who can afford more than double the tuition charged by public high schools. Benjamin and James (1989) have given one of the best analyses of those hardest hit in the race to place students in colleges. They argue that many of the younger public academic high schools are in rural areas. They also point out that richer urban prefectures have higher proportions of private high schools and families that can afford to spend more per student. This pattern shows very clearly in the Figure 3—1 and Table 3—1 displays of the probabilities of success in entering one of the dominant 45 universities.

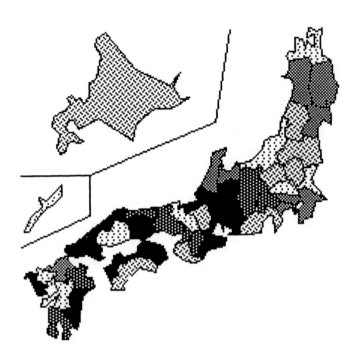

Tokushima	33.14	Ōsaka	11.88	Hokkaidō	8.17
Shimane	23.45	Hyōgo	11.85	Shizuoka	7.86
Mie	22.67	Ōita	11.57	Tochigi	7.46
Fukui	20.89	Kagoshima	11.37	Gunma	7.42
Miyazaki	20.01	Ishikawa	11.15	Kōchi	7.25
Okayama	18.69	Tōkyō	10.26	Yamagata	7.23
Ehime	17.23	Toyama	9.84	Okinawa	6.46
Nagasaki	15.50	Akita	9.60	Saga	6.20
Aichi	14.88	Miyagi	9.30	Kyōto	5.42
Gifu	14.18	Chiba	9.00	Aomori	5.16
Yamaguchi	12.78	Iwate	8.74	Ibaraki	5.10
Nara	12.69	Kanagawa	8.72	Niigata	4.97
Yamanashi	12.47	Fukuoka	8.63	Kumamoto	4.64
Nagano	12.27	Fukushima	8.58	Hiroshima	4.28
Tottori	12.19	Shiga	8.34	Saitama	4.27
Kagawa	12.18	Wakayama	8.21		

Figure 3—1   The Percent of Graduates from the Top 400 High Schools in 1988, as Defined by the *Sunday Asahi* Magazine.

Table 3—1 shows a huge divide between extremely deprived prefectures like Okinawa at the bottom with only 4.7% to the 124% in Kanagawa.[2] The four prime outliers in Table 3—1 are of particular interest: Okinawa, at the lowest end and the three highest ranked prefectures at the other. Without these four cases, the prefectural success rates distribute normally, although still with a substantial range of 80%. The three most productive prefectures are all within a normal commute of central Tōkyō, and six of the top-ten ranked universities are also within that area. This indicates both the power of the Kantō area and the relative decline of central Tōkyō, which traditionally ranked first until the "elite flight" from Tōkyō municipal to neighboring prefecture's private schools took place.

Although the pattern described by Benjamin and James is evident in this diagram, what is not evident is that actual per-capital high school expenditures have absolutely no relationship to these rates of entry into the highest status universities (r = 0.03). This is remarkable because the correlation between per capita junior and senior high school educational expenses in 1987 was 0.645, in spite of the relative stability in ranking of prefectures across all twelve years of schooling.

However, a good part of the reason for the complete lack of relationship hinges on understanding the physical (and ultimately, social) mobility afforded to some students and not to others. There is a strong -0.60 correlation between daily commuter patterns and attendance at a leading high school. The prime minister's office measures commuter patterns as a ratio of all persons ages 15 and older attending or working in the same municipality to other municipalities. The highest commuting ratios, in order, are Tōkyō, Kanagawa, Ōsaka, Saitama, Nara, Chiba, Kyōto, Hyōgo, Aichi, and Fukuoka. These prefectures contain the largest cities in Japan as well as the areas with the most accessible mass-transportation systems. At the other extreme, in order, are Aomori, Miyazaki, Kagoshima, Oita, Fukushima, Ehime, Nagasaki, Kōchi, Akita, and Yamagata.

---

[2]The reason some percentages add up to more than 100% is that it is possible to gain admitance to several universities. This does not affect the overall ranking of the prefectures in Table 9. This percentage overestimates chances of attaining admitance to one of these dream universities because the standardization is based on the assumption that a student has attended one of the top 400 high schools, which make up only 7 percent of all high schools in Japan. If I was to standardize on total high school graduation figures, the rarity of entrance into these universities might be enhanced, but I wish to demonstrate the extreme variation that exists between the so-called "top" high schools themselves in this particular table.

Table 3—1

Probabilities of Entry into the 44 Most Elite Universities
from Prefectures Containing the Top 400 High Schools Rank

Rank	Prefecture	%	Rank	Prefecture	%
47	Okinawa	4.7	23	Wakayama	50.5
46	Miyazaki	18.8	22	Hyōgo	50.8
45	Tokushima	19.3	21	Fukuoka	55.8
44	Oita	20.8	20	Nagano	56.
43	Shimane	25.6	19	Tochigi	58.1
42	Nagasaki	25.8	18	Shiga	58.9
41	Okayama	26.6	17	Niigata	59.2
40	Yamanashi	28.1	16	Kumamoto	59.8
39	Mie	32.7	15	Ishikawa	59.9
38	Akita	33.1	14	Kōchi	60.0
37	Iwate	33.8	13	Kyōto	62.7
36	Fukui	35.0	12	Kagawa	63.0
35	Ehime	35.8	11	Ōsaka	63.9
34	Tottori	36.3	10	Gunma	72.2
33	Yamagata	37.7	9	Toyama	72.6
32	Hokkaidō	38.6	8	Shizuoka	74.0
31	Saga	40.1	7	Nara	78.1
30	Kagoshima	40.2	6	Hiroshima	82.5
29	Aomori	41.0	5	Ibaraki	83.5
28	Miyagi	44.4	4	Chiba	98.0
27	Yamaguchi	46.1	3	Tōkyō	108.0
26	Gifu	46.2	2	Saitama	122.8
25	Fukushima	48.4	1	Kanagawa	124.0
24	Aichi	50.0			

*A few prefectures have probabilities higher than 100 percent because some exceptionally bright students get counted more than once if they get accepted to several universities.

The implications of ease of accessibility in traveling long distances to go to work or school has implications for contemporary attempts to reform the Tōkyō Metropolitan school system. Female enrollments in the most elite high schools, as I have previously demonstrated, are highly circumscribed. There are 156 metropolitan day high schools in Tōkyō that offer academic education, as opposed to vocational training given at technical and commercial high schools. However, only 13 of these are among the prestigious ones feeding into the elite university system. In April of 1990 the

Tōkyō Metropolitan Government, under increasing pressures to increase educational opportunities for women, raised the percentage of girls allowed to attend these 13 schools from 36.9% in 1989 to 41.1% in 1990.[3] Until 1950 Tōkyō's public high schools were all-male or all-female. Presently, the government sets a male-female ratio for all but two of the regular metropolitan high schools. The two without fixed ratios are Akikawa High School, an all-male boarding school originally set up for sons of company employees stationed overseas; and Hachiōji Koryo High School, a regular high school with specialized courses that was exempted from ratio setting when it first opened. The government is considering totally abolishing sex ratios in the near future.

Feminists fear abolishment of sex ratios as a way to keep out females. Past efforts at reform through abolition of sex-ratio limits have backfired precisely because Tōkyō's inhabitants have a huge opportunity structure to attend competing schools. The situation is no-win: Feminists want to afford their daughters equal opportunities to attend schools already available to their sons; but any attempt to increase the ratio of female students is likely to result in more male-student flight to private schools, thereby decreasing the status of the public school system even more. The irony is that Monbushō, with its stranglehold over the entire country's system, could stop the hemorrhaging. It already uses extensive central subsidies of private education to force its powers on private education at all levels. In essence, its laissez-faire policies during the post-war period have encouraged the flight to private education for sons of the elite.

Benjamin and James (1989) point out that no other advanced society has an equally large proportion of students enrolled in private high schools. They argue that Japan's public school systems have to provide diversity and choice if they are to remain competitive with the private sector. Extensive reliance on the private sector leads to major distortions in access of different socio-economic groups to higher education. In the mid-1970s government authorities decided to move toward equalizing opportunities through subsidizing established private schools and building public schools where there were no private ones.

However, educational opportunities from nursery school through high school are extremely lopsided. The system culminates in a very few high schools that operate much as "farm clubs" for "major league" universities. At every stage of the school system social factors grant distinctly better educational opportunities for some students over others. These factors go largely unrecognized because the symbols of equality of education are so powerful in Japan: It is very difficult to fight a system that has so much appearance of equality starting from the same uniforms in kindergarten to the same curriculum right down to the same high school diploma approximately 14 years later.

---

[3]Eleven of these 13 schools are among the traditional "number" schools that had only numbers instead of names before the postwar reform of the Japanese educational system.

At the end of this long road are the national university exams. Private industry has so well researched these exams that students search them out for practice. The private testing companies report the results in standard deviation values (hensachi), that superficially resemble the percentile rankings experienced by American students taking the SAT or ACT. The difference is that hensachi have no give. An American student might score only in the 75th percentile on the SAT and still get into Harvard in quite exceptional cases. A Japanese student outside a much narrower range below the 95th percentile has no chance of getting into Tōdai, regardless of less quantitative measures of aptitude — verbal skills in foreign languages, creative potential in writing, or drawing ability.

The hensachi system sorts students into the "leagues" in which they are most likely to succeed, based on the testing companies' past records. Major universities all have their own "second-stage" examinations over a weekend in February to which aspirants must travel and lodge at their own expenses, so no student or parent wants to waste chances. These preliminary evaluations have more serious consequences than those in the United States. A prospective American student need not spend great sums to visit a campus and he or she may apply to many universities with the same national test scores for a comparatively small application fee.[4]

The national test in Japan is also important because it acts as the initial sieve into university "major and minor leagues." The colorful name of rōnin (masterless samurai) attests to the importance of the national test. Tens of thousands of former high school students suffer the scornful label each year for their continued failure to make it into an elite university. These former students will often end up spending twice as much money a year as the tuition at one of the top seven former imperial universities at private cram schools for several years in pursuit of their dream.

They suffer relative to successful applicants in Table 1—1. Perception of their worth drops by roughly half a point, their powerfulness by 1 point, and their liveliness by 1.5 points in the semantic differential data. These are powerful changes in self-image, which illustrate the trade-offs huge numbers of young people and their parents are willing to make in a desperate last attempt for the benefits of credentialism from Tōdai.

The power of the desire to avoid societal scorn also explains the opposite end of the Japanese system — the increasingly downward trend in high school dropout rates to roughly 2%. Although the chances of going to a major-league university may be extremely low in Okinawa, it has an extremely low rate of drop-outs like the rest of Japan. This is because school drop-outs are among the most unfavorably rated of youth roles in Japan. A dropout's goodness rating is 1.4 points lower than a high school student's; the powerlessness score is more than 2 points lower for a male; and the activity level is about 1.3 points lower.

---

[4]Amano (1989; 1990) has documented the modern university entrance examination better than any other Japanese scholar. His work is highly critical of the unfairness of the present credentialist system.

Being branded a dropout is equal to societal rejection; much worse than becoming a rōnin. The role of rōnin at least gives the impression of continued effort and persistence. Students perceive rōnin status as much worse than eventual acceptance into a minor league university. This is part of the reason why most rōnin leave after only one year to accept entrance into a university below their original expectations.

Recommendations by school principals to elite private universities are popular in Japan as options to foregoing the college-entrance examination system and fate as a rōnin. Some 20% of private universities have application deadlines in September and October and special quotas for recommendations outside the demanding national examination system that takes place during the Winter. This system is popular because colleges can select good students, students can escape from the rigors of traditional exams early, and principals can exert their influence in the selection process. The system gives even more power to faculty over students, and it insures they do not step out of line with school discipline.

This rigorous examination system infuses bonding experiences not unlike the psychological residue left behind by military drills and fraternity hazing of students belonging to the same group, even as it forces them to compete. Partly for this reason the exam system will not likely be eliminated. The irony is that it aids the illusion to all Japanese of homogeneity and fairness of the educational process, despite the overwhelming evidence to the contrary.

YOBIKO AND RONIN STATUS

The stiff competition caused by the national examination system has given rise to a remarkable service-sector industry known as yobikō that has come to play an important role in the lives of youth. Beauchamp (1978) shows that increasing numbers of college entrants attended yobikō: 35.2% in 1953 versus 48.4% in 1957. This has increased to over half of all college entrants in 1986 (Tsukada 1991).

Tsukada (1991) has most clearly documented means by which yobikō have increasingly become an institution that "discriminates against females, the children of families of lower social status, and graduates of lower-ranked high schools" (pp. 33—34). Fathers with junior high school education have only one-fourth the percentage of children who attend yobikō while fathers who have completed college contribute four times the percentage of yobikō attendees as one would expect by chance. Similarly, men in managerial positions have almost four times the expected percentage of children attending yobikō; professionals are doubly over-represented. By contrast, father's in primary industries (those involved with extraction of raw materials such as coal mining, fisheries, lumbering) send only one-third the number of offspring to yobikō that one would expect. Males make up 84.4% of rōnin, demonstrating the bias against women.

The role of rōnin in gaining entrance to prestigious universities is so great that over half of 1984 entrants to Tōkyō and Kyōto Universities were former rōnin. The average distribution of rōnin entrants was 44.6% for all of the former imperial universities, 61.3% for the prestigious private universities, and 62.8 for the national medical colleges (Kenkyūkai 1986)

UNDERGRADUATE UNIVERSITY STRUCTURE

According to the Prime Minister's Office statistics, roughly 41% of Japanese secondary school graduates go on to post-secondary education, with 29% in four-year undergraduate programs and junior colleges. In the United States, about 55% of high school graduates continue on to the same types of programs. These statistics give the impression that Japanese college education has become relatively egalitarian. Certainly in terms of the desire for credentialism this is true. Prefectural statistics for the percentage of students going on to post-secondary education are relatively invariant. However, these statistics assume that all post-secondary institutions are equal. This is not true.

Higher education in Japan is much more highly stratified than in the United States. The apex of these strata is Tōdai's law school, because it gives the highest chance of gaining employment in the powerful Ministry of Finance or a career in the Liberal Democrat Party. The strata below are relatively unchanged in prestige, based primarily on age and the public-private dimension. Older institutions are more prestigious as are national universities.[5] This is unlike the United States where eminent universities — Chicago and Johns Hopkins — arose virtually overnight; where the "Public Ivies" such as Michigan, Wisconsin, and Cal-Berkeley challenge the old-line, private "Ivy League" institutions like Penn and Harvard; and where grades in college and outstanding ability in specialized areas can sometimes replace alumni contacts in high places for career placement.

Japanese employers use college prestige as a screening device for entry-level jobs, later jobs, and wage promotions (Sakamoto & Chen, 1992). Their regression modeling of income on human-capital and credentialing effects using SSM data for 1955, 1965, and 1975 shows clear non-trivial effects of both. Thus, although years of education makes a difference in the earnings of male Japanese workers, which university a student goes to still adds non-trivially to income growth showing the importance of the choice of universities.

---

[5]There are some notable exceptions. Two private universities in Tōkyō—Waseda and Keio—have a long tradition of supplying more than their "fair share" of the nation's politicians, journalists, and business leaders.

PUBLIC VERSUS PRIVATE UNIVERSITIES

The Japanese government has encouraged private universities because they are less costly than public universities from the standpoint of public outlays. This contrasts markedly with the U.S.A. While private universities in Japan have enjoyed an increasing share of undergraduate education in Japan, their American counterparts have lost market share. In 1950 American undergraduates chose public and private colleges in equal numbers. By 1982 78% of undergraduates attended public institutions. State and local governments had made sizable commitments to support new, low-cost institutions over the preceding three decades.

The distinction between public and private universities traces back to the founding of the imperial universities. Seven national (kokuritsu) universities claim parentage from the imperial universities, and are generally accorded the highest status due to their pre-World War II imperial status and age. These universities, in rank order are Tōkyō, Kyōto, Ōsaka, Tōhoku, Nagoya, Hiroshima, and Kyūshū Universities. In theory all of them are of equal status. From the behavior of high school aged college aspirants, however, it becomes clear that there is a huge difference in prestige between Tōkyō and Kyōto Universities versus the others. Until the 1980s Tōdai was in a class of its own, but thereafter Kyōdai gained a reputation for better science. This was due in part to students finding out that potential Nobel-level researchers were on its staff.

Monbushō's reward-and-punishment system undergirds these strata. The Ministry's national college entrance examination scores sort high school seniors and limits their range of college choices. The highest scores guarantee admittance to Tōdai, Kyōdai, and so on. The prestige of gaining first-round selection on these national tests to a high ranking university is sufficient reward for the majority of aspirants that they do not commit a "mutiny" by taking second-round tests at a less prestigious institution other than as a backup should they fail to make the second, final, on-campus examination cut. This second-round examination, if they pass, relegates them to a particular school, again with highest scores assigned to the most prestigious schools (law, engineering, medicine) and low scores to the least prestigious (religion). Within schools, departments use test scores to further classify student majors. This examination system is unyielding to exceptions: Each level shuts off certain career possibilities and leaves narrowed choices for students.

This system also has the latent function of insuring stable rank-orders of universities and academic disciplines. At the top, this assures that Tōdai, and other university, law professors gain more than the "ablest" students. Monbushō's system of annual rewards gives prima facie evidence that law, medicine, and engineering remain the crown jewels.

The price for this reward is treatment essentially as a satellite of Monbushō. University faculties within the anointed 45 out of the 455 universities can ill afford to fight Monbushō on issues of fundamental educational policy. The system more easily co-opts professors at national universities than those at private universities because they are civil servants.

Monbushō exercises its authority to prohibit professors at national universities from receiving consulting fees from industry. To move from a position at one university to another, a professor must receive formal permission from Monbushō. It controls faculty positions down to the smallest detail. For example, a department at a national university must ask Monbushō for permission to hire a replacement for a retired professor.[6] As a result, less than 2% of faculty change posts in national universities each year. In this way, the Ministry also insures its hold over rewards and punishments. However, the price it pays for this is enormous. One of the strengths of the American system of higher education is precisely its free-market ability to attract the ablest and brightest faculty members, and hence to assemble critical masses of academic specialists relatively quickly. This is a virtual impossibility under the Japanese system.

Universities also have problems of funding unknown to the American system. Monbushō dominates the national university budgets and student fees. An American-style tradition of endowments, alumni gifts, industrial consulting fees, and private grants does not exist in Japan. Most schools of business and engineering, and departments in the natural sciences in the United States have sources of funds that give them large amounts of autonomy from their universities. A Japanese professor cannot apply for grants from another ministry such as MITI or the Ministry of Health and Welfare (Kōseishō) because Monbushō forbids it.

Monbushō actively discourages any attempt at autonomy by punishing universities that step out of line. For example, a few years Monbushō tried unsuccessfully to force a president to resign at one of the national universities. He continued to resistant pressures from outside, and ultimately from the faculty injured by his unwillingness to step down. So Monbushō simply slashed university funds in a display of raw power most universities are justly afraid to test.

The Ministry also subsidizes private university education, but to a lesser extent. In 1989, average per-student subsidies at a four-year private university decreased by 3.8% to ¥179,000. Throughout the 1980s private university subsidies decreased yearly in spite of rising operating expenses and inflation. For example, they decreased from 16% in 1988 to 15% in 1989, a period with close to 3% inflation. This compares to financial contributions from the government in the United States that rose from about 30% in 1969 to some 48% in 1980. (Tonkin & Edwards 1987) Furthermore, the amount of Japanese subsidies varies depending on Ministry guidelines. The Ministry believes that some universities pay salaries that are too high and thus

---

[6]This type of decision would normally be made in an American University by the Dean of a particular college or a department at a university. The reason it is difficult to make a rational decision at a higher level is that the increasing fragmentation of specialized knowledge makes it likely that non-specialists in other fields can not make informed judgments outside their own specialties.

reduces subsidies for those institutions.[7] The Ministry does not give money to some institutions because of disagreements over school policies. For example, Towa University, in Fukuoka Prefecture, and two junior colleges did not receive any subsidies in 1989 because of administrative disagreements. The result is a highly conservative higher education system thankful for the crumbs Monbushō throws its way.

Students also rarely move between universities. Although after two years (including completion of junior college) students can change universities, few do. Student social mobility in Japan is much more constrained than in the United States. Students not only stay at one university for their entire four years; they form friendships through club memberships formed during their first weeks as freshmen. They find themselves pressured not to change clubs through their college years. As they move into their third and fourth years they spend time mostly with a small group of people in their clubs and their major field.

The result is that their lives are much more narrowly circumscribed by particular small circles of persons in their major field and university club than is true of Western universities. For example, the vast majority of American students change majors at least once, move freely between different circles of friends and acquaintances, and often change universities. The Japanese system, on the other hand, greatly aids the status quo through its resemblance to a set of tribes quite unaware of how the larger system continues to hold power over them in their fragmented state.

Cost differential also helps maintain the university pecking order. It is much cheaper to go to public universities that have the highest per-capita-student budgets and good libraries, research laboratories, and graduate programs. The range of quality and prestige at private universities is much wider; only a few compete with the national universities in breadth of quality. The average private university consists of one or two faculties — usually low-cost humanities and social science programs — without research or graduate programs. The Japanese system makes private universities virtual parasites of more prestigious public ones. They generally pay lower salaries and hire professors who have retired from national universities who wish to moonlight for a few more years. Professors who may have done meritorious work in their youth, but who have not engaged in serious scholarly activity for years often hamper the private universities.[8]

Student fees at private colleges favor the well off. One out of four families whose children entered private colleges in Tōkyō in April 1990 had an annual income of more than 10 million yen ($48.780). This is two and a half times the 1988 median annual employee's salary of 4.1 million yen ($20,000), according to the seventh annual survey of the Tōkyō branch of the

---

[7]Well-paid teaching is a myth at all levels in Japan. Teachers and professors are no better paid than their American counterparts (Schaub & Baker 1991)

[8]The average age of retirement from the national universities varies at this writing from 60 to 63 and up to age 70 at private universities. For comparative purposes, Nobel work in physics is rarely done after age 27.

Japan Federation of Private University Teachers and Employees Union. As 80% of college enrollments are at private universities, this implies an extremely heavy burden on the average family.

Average enrollment expenses for students living with their families was ¥1.3 million ($6341) including tuition and entrance examination fees. Average rental expense for those not living with their parents increased 5.9% to ¥1.87 million ($9,122) from a year previous. Considering that total expenses come to 70% of the average worker's yearly salary, it is not surprisingly that 22% of the families took out loans to cover educational expenses. Both parents were wage earners in 48.3% of the surveyed families. Half of the families expected their children in college to earn money through part-time jobs while going to school.[9]

Costs of going to a national public university are roughly half of attending a private college. This means that students blessed with the highest test scores are less likely to need loans, part-time jobs, or working mothers to complete their education. These are significant benefits of the national university system that add increased motivation to attend it. It also clarifies why few rōnin find private universities worthy goals. A rōnin is likely to spend the annual equivalent of a year's fees at a national university in preparation for entrance tests. By contrast, private universities cost twice as much at the price of lower status and less prestigious job prospects. However, the limited space in national universities forces 80% of students with college aspirations to attend private institutions.

After 1992, demographic projections show a rapid decline in the college-aged population despite the current record number of applicants. The number of applicants who failed the national college entrance exams topped 400,000 in 1990, giving rise to demands by students and parents to increase enrollment quotas temporarily. Private universities and junior colleges expect shortages of applicants to impact them first. Thus, they would like to make entrance exams even more difficult to raise the "prestige" and popularity of their schools against the current backdrop of fierce competition among private schools. Fears abound among officials of private universities that the Ministry of Education proposal will compel private universities — but not public ones — to increase admissions quotas.

SOCIAL STRATIFICATION AND CULTURAL CAPITAL

Upper-class members in any country can more easily afford elite private schooling, whether it be pre-college or college-level. Private universities prefer to have students from families who can afford their high

---

[9]Costs vary considerably between faculties within colleges. The prestigious engineering, science, and medicine faculties are much more expensive than liberal arts schools because of laboratory and equipment fees. There are also "indirect costs" which effectively bar all but the wealthiest. The 1976 Monbushō White Paper stated that 74% of private medical school admitees had paid "backdoor admissions fees" of as much as 16 million yen (over $60,000).

costs. Families with more financial means, therefore, have an obvious economic advantage over families without such means. Families with fewer economic resources, of course, may try to overcome these disadvantages through loans, employment of women, and so on. The idea that class differences exist in educational opportunity is both unpopular and not widely endorsed by the general public. Nevertheless, Fujita (1989) revealed that educational attainment has been highly related to the occupations of fathers at least since World War II. For example, in 1975 only 7.7% of fathers in agriculture sent their offspring to college versus 54% of fathers who were professionals or managers.[10] When he standardized occupations on age, the differences still ranged from 13.6% to 59.6%.

Fujita states that these data replicate in the comparable 1955 and 1965 SSM surveys. He found no evidence of fewer differences between occupational strata over time. The conclusion is that the expansion of higher education has brought more benefit to the middle strata such as white-collar and upper blue-collar workers. The differences are partly explainable in terms of economic capacity to afford direct and indirect costs of schooling. However, when Fujita controlled for ability of families to afford higher education, he still found wide differences between family income and son's attendance in college.

This is precisely what we would expect from a cultural-capital argument that some families stress values more in tune with going to college, although the SSM data do not allow a direct test of this idea. Kohn, Naoi, Schoenback, Schooler, and Stomczynski (1990) and Naoi and Schooler (1990) have worked on part of the cultural-capital problem for close to twenty years now with consistent replications across Japan, Poland and the United States. Their work suggests clear cultural-capital linkages to type of work of both men and women. They find that self-directed work increases intellectual flexibility and self-directedness — important components of success in higher education.

Conversely their cross-cultural research demonstrates that traditional occupations lead to more traditional thinking than is true of more modern occupations. Their findings should generalize to the differences in educational attainment that I have discussed. Farming and fishing, for example, are traditional occupations with little need for high intellectual flexibility. Parents with occupations requiring high intellectual flexibility (medicine, law, engineering, etc.) are likely to give their offspring a distinct advantage in dealing with major social decisions.

Thus, Rohlen (1985/86) is inaccurate in suggesting the Japanese educational system is a "true meritocracy" that allows a "broad cross section of the population to attend college with little relationship between income and success." Although Rohlen believes this "meritocracy" has only broken down since the rise of the juku in the 1980s, the data do not bear him out. Japan has a long history of marked social stratification effects on education that do not appear to have changed significantly from World War II until

[10]His figures come from the decennial Social Stratification and Mobility (SSM) surveys.

the mid-1980s. Bauer and Mason (1992) suggest that there is no convincing evidence that income distribution in Japan is more equal than in other OECD countries. They also point out that the rapid appreciation of the Japanese stock market and land prices during the late 1980s led to greater inequality in the distribution of wealth.

Sociologists who study education cross-culturally refer to such phenomena as the juku and yobikō as part of shadow-education systems. They are not peculiar to Japan. Taiwan, Hong Kong, and Greece are among the countries with similar informal, or shadow-education systems and clear, rigid hierarchies of educational opportunities. An analysis of a random sample of 7,240 high school seniors who graduated in 1980 by Stevenson and Baker (1992) provides the clearest evidence for the cultural-capital advantage offered by juku and yobikō. Their regression analysis demonstrated that even after controlling for student and school differences, high family SES (parents' educational attainment and family income) increases the chances that children will undertake various types of shadow education such as juku, practice examinations, and rōnin life by 10 to 15 percent.

Shadow education has become so pervasive that Stevenson and Baker found that the high schools with successful university placement programs (e.g., read "top" high schools in this study's analysis) have co-opted the shadow education system by offering their own examination preparation activities as after-school programs. Another clear indicator of differential cultural capital in this study was urbanization. Students from urban areas had a clear advantage in access to the resources offered by the shadow-education industry, with the natural exception of correspondence-school course work.

Stevenson and Baker (1992) also assessed factors that contributed to becoming a rōnin, and advantages accruing to students who used the shadow educational system. The same factors that contribute to shadow education during high school are also at work during the rōnin period. Wealthier parents, more well-educated parents, and urban residence modestly contributed to increased changes of students taking on the role of rōnin. Most importantly for the thesis of a tight linkage between shadow education and educational attainment, however, was the finding that (pp. 1653-1654):

> "[t]he direct effects of practice examinations and correspondence courses . . . [add] 16% and 25% respectively to the probability of entering a university after high school. Using a tutor decreases one's chances of attendance, which most likely reflects the remedial character of most tutoring. . . . After-school classes (juku) have only a small and non-significant effect on attendance, probably because students in better high schools (who tend to do better on examinations) use their high school's after-school program instead of juku . . . . [and] the effect of being a rōnin is dramatic because it increases university attendance by 80%.

INSTITUTIONALIZED SEX DISCRIMINATION

Higher-education enrollments reached 2.4 million, but women made up only 33% of student enrollments in 1988. After factoring out junior-college attendees, this proportion dropped to 25.5%, and it plunged to roughly 10% in the top-three universities. Benjamin and James (1989) note that the higher education of women is a consumption, not a production, good in Japan. The Stevenson and Baker study (1992) demonstrates the sex discrimination inherent in the shadow-education system as a family investment in sons rather than daughters. Their findings demonstrate a significant male-bias in which girls are denied the advantages of shadow education for entrance into four-year institutions of higher education. Japanese junior colleges are the epitome of such sexist attitudes toward higher education for women. Women made up 91% of junior-college enrollments in 1988. The curriculum is reminiscent of finishing schools of a by-gone era. Courses are geared for raising children and being a good housewife.

The budding feminist movement in Japan has created sensitivity within the government toward portraying action toward correcting sex discrimination in higher education, but action has only led to surface reforms (Fujimura-Fanselow 1989). Roughly 30% of women enroll in institutions with exclusively female student populations with traditional family and household-oriented curriculum.

Part of the reason for sex discrimination in higher education is due to discrimination in the job market. The National Personnel Authority's 1989 White Paper on national public servants emphasized the record-high 150 women who passed the national exam for high-ranking government employees in 1988, although this was only 8% of total hires. The Class I Exam, which is the gateway to high-ranking posts into government bodies, has long been dominated by males. There has been a fourfold increase in women taking this exam since 1975 when only 15 of 678 new hires were women. However, 84% of the 1814 who passed this exam were graduates of national universities, with another 13% who were graduates of private colleges, underscoring the structural impediments to women's entry into the public-service sector.

These figures illustrate the gross inequities based on sex and prestige of university. An optimist might say that there has been a threefold jump in women hires and a fourfold surge in private university hires over a 13-year period. However, these increases are based on small bases. Furthermore, modern governments play a role as the employers of last resort. Private business barriers to female employment are even greater. Women's roles are largely relegated to the less prestigious secondary sector of the economy and part-time work (Brinton 1988). In spite of anti-discrimination laws, industry continues to hire women just out of college into temporary, non-career track positions meant to last until the women reach age 25 or get married, whichever comes first. Knowledge of such discrimination serves as an effective barrier to increased aspirations among young women. There is no purpose in attaining a high-caliber education if a women realizes she will be effectively barred from using it.

Ironically, the industrial competition for male college graduates was a buyer's market during the late 1980s, with an average of three job offers per male graduate. Industry had no comprehensive hiring-practice plan to deal with such manpower shortages. By fiat, less prestigious companies found it necessary to hire foreigners and Japanese women to deal with their work place shortages.[11] To date deep-rooted male antipathy to women in career-path positions effectively bars considering hiring well-educated Japanese women. For example, Kyōto University has produced many of Japan's Nobel Prize winners but had no women Assistant Professors or Professors on its staff as late as 1991.

STRUCTURE OF THE SELECT FORTY-FIVE UNIVERSITIES

The university stratification system in Japan appears quite straightforwardly ranked from every citation I have given in previous parts of this chapter. This section analyzes student populations to show some features of the universities that are not apparent from, and even contradict, many of the assumptions current in popular and academic writing.

The National Universities. At the apex of universities are the former seven imperial universities. Japanese often point with pride to these as "national" universities because they are open to anyone with satisfactory test scores. However, Table 3—2 illustrates the huge disparity in chances of gaining admittance from the 400 nation-wide high schools that form the cream of the high school feeder system. The distribution is not highly skewed — it is close to zero (0.5%). Nevertheless, the range of graduating seniors who attain admittance to a national university is extremely large, from Okinawa with only 0.43% to Toyama at 20.60%. All of the three lowest scoring prefectures are in the far western part of Japan. Part of the reason is that students in the far west have only Kyūshū University relatively close to their homes. All of the three highest scoring prefectures are in the Kansai area, which is the area with the most national universities.

The top universities fairly well serve 33 prefectures — those within one standard deviation of the mean. Nevertheless, there are huge differences in life chances implicit in these figures. The fact, for example, that no high school senior from Okinawa was admitted to five of the seven elite universities implies considerable bias in the system, as does the knowledge that a student attending a high school in Toyama has 48 times the chance of attending one of these elite universities as does an Okinawan.

---

[11]The recession of the early 1990s found these same companies laying off women and foreigners.

Table 3—2

Basic Univariate Measures of Average and Distribution for the National
Universities, Standardized per 10,000 high school graduates in 1988

University	Min	Max	Mean	S.D.	Skew	Outliers
1. Tōkyō University	0	615	158	132	1.7	7
2. Kyōto University	0	1102	154	191	3.4	6
3. Hokkaidō University	0	1452	99	207	6.1	2
4. Tōhoku University	6	1223	191	245	2.5	11
5. Nagoya University	9	736	122	138	3.1	6
6. Ōsaka University	0	657	135	146	1.8	10
7. Kyūshū University	0	1635	157	321	3.0	10
OVERALL	43	2060	962	472	0.5	6

The above argument assumes that all degrees from these universities
are equal, which is decidedly not the case. Choice jobs and professions in
both private and public sectors go first to graduates of Tōdai and Kyōdai,
and then to other universities, according to alumni power. As Rohlen
(1985/86) notes, Tōkyō University produces less than 3% of all university
graduates, but it produces nearly one-quarter of the presidents of Japan's
leading companies. Also, one in four members of the lower house in the Diet
is a Tōdai graduate. Nine of the last 16 Japanese prime ministers, 11 out of
16 sitting Supreme Court justices, six out of 21 cabinet officials and 150
members of the current Japanese parliament graduated from Tōkyō. A sixth of
all seats on the Tōkyō Stock Exchange are occupied by Tōdai graduates. The
all-powerful ministries of trade, finance, and foreign affairs are controlled by
Tōdai alumni. The most powerful government agencies simply do not bother
to go far beyond Tōdai in their recruiting. This means that Tōkyō University
indirectly has extraordinary influence on everything from the price of rice to
the revamping of Japan's taxation system.[12]
    All of the top seven universities have relatively lopsided and wide
distributions, reflecting the fact that each attracts students primarily from
their immediate regions. In each case the prefecture with the highest outlier
is one which is within easy commute. This puts students from poorer
prefectures, on the periphery of the national rail infrastructure, or outside of
the metropolitan areas hosting these universities, at a distinct

---

[12]Miyahara (1988) used 1975 SSM data to argue that the differences between advantages of going to
elite universities in Japan are small. However, those differences must be small because only a few
graduates of the elite universities may become Diet members, prime ministers, or industrial captains.

disadvantage. Interestingly, Tōdai has the lowest level of skewness and smallest range reflecting its position at the apex. However, given the national mania for admission, its admissions range and skewness are gargantuan. In the entire post-World War II period, Tōdai has not accepted one Okinawan high school graduate.

Tōdai is the national symbol of the pinnacle of higher education, so it would seem that a government that cared strongly about equality of education would create at least some prefecturally allotted national scholarships and prefectural quotas for entrance. Such a system would bring truly underrepresented prefectures closer to educational equality and would help stem the Kantō-area overrepresentation created by the present system.

Public versus Private Universities. Inequities in the higher educational system spring partly from the national government's history of low financial support for public higher education. The post-war baby boom response was to encourage the expansion of private universities to handle the increasing demand for a college degree. This is precisely the opposite of the United States where a surge in new public institutions during the late 1960s relieved a similar bulge in college-bound youth. The result is that 80% of college-bound Japanese students must attend a private university. The post-war baby boom and the trend toward credentialism created a buyer's market which has greatly aided the private universities because it has created increasingly larger pools of competitive aspirants. The Ministry of Education encourages this trend through its policy of curbing educational outlays from government coffers.

However, the demographic trends for the 1990s are clear. A sharply decreasing pool of 18-year-olds forebodes an acute drop in private university status and funding sources. Many of these universities, under pressure from Monbushō, greatly expanded their physical facilities to accommodate more baby boomers. They will now experience declining enrollments and applicants with lower entrance test scores. With little more than student tuition to work with, market forces will pressure private universities with low rankings (1) to close or (2) to search for non-traditional student populations, as has occurred in the United States in recent decades.

To better understand status relationships among the 45 dominant universities, Figure 3—2 displays the results of a statistical analysis called cluster analysis.[13] This form of analysis sorts objects (in this case, universities) by degree of similarity according to the type of data (here, high school background of entering freshmen). This technique clarifies the social ecology of student populations in Japanese universities. For readers

---

[13]There are different methods of cluster analysis which can give considerably different results. Although I ran cluster analysis using a variety of assumptions (i.e., distances between universities based on percentages, gamma, Pearson, and Euclidean; linkages which were either single or complete) the results were remarkably robust. Also, because the university data is highly skewed, Euclidean distances seem the most reasonable as they normalize statistical differences. The single linkage method highlights nearest neighbors (socially, not physically) better than the complete-linkage method.

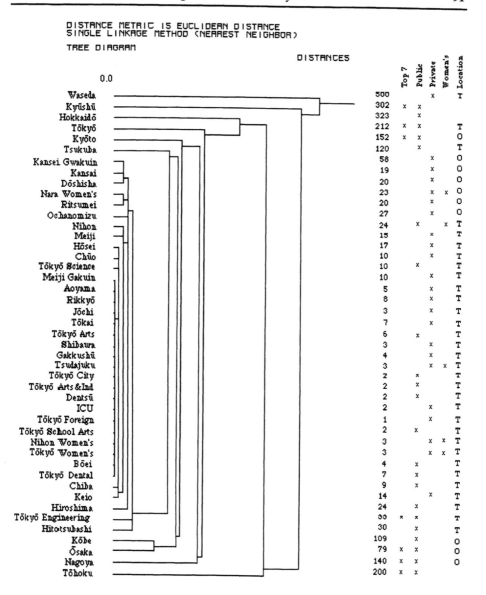

DISTANCE METRIC IS EUCLIDEAN DISTANCE
SINGLE LINKAGE METHOD (NEAREST NEIGHBOR)
TREE DIAGRAM

Figure 3—2   Tree Diagram Linkages for the Top 45 Universities in Japan, including Status as a Member of the Top 7 (Imperial), Public, Private, Women's and Tōkyō (T)—Osaka (O) Area

who are unfamiliar with Japan, I have added some identifying information to the right of the tree-diagram display. This information displays social distances from other universities and useful identifiers (top 7, public, private, women's, and geographic location).

The most unusual universities are at the top and bottom extremes of Figure 3—2. Waseda is the most distinctive university, at a relative Euclidean distance of 500 from the norm. It is located in Tōkyō, and Japanese consider it to be among the top private universities. Although Figure 3—2 indicates that Waseda is the most unique university among the 45 top picks, its correlations with all of the other choice private universities in the Tōkyō area are above 0.6, and even its correlation with Tōkyō University is 0.42, suggesting that it does not differ greatly in terms of student admissions.

What does make Waseda distinctive is its size. It has close to 80,000 students, nearly double the size of its closest competitor. Waseda's size gives it greater variation in student admissions than any other university, accounting for part of its singularity. Also, its size gives it such high visibility, that quality and quantity of students and alumni are easily confused. For example, Waseda is "well known" for the sheer number of its graduates who have become journalists, implying that one of its fortes is mass communications. However, a plausible alternative hypothesis is that its visibility is a simple function of its massive alumni roster. Larger graduating classes may produce larger numbers of journalists who, in turn, aid future alumni to find jobs in the same field.

Disregarding Waseda, Figure 3—2 bears out Japanese beliefs that the most distinctive universities in Japan are the former imperial universities. All of the seven former imperial universities are at the extreme top and bottom of this figure. However, the nearest neighbors in this figure are social rather than physical. For example, Tōhoku is geographically closer to Tōkyō than other former imperial universities, yet its student populations resemble more those of Nagoya and Ōsaka. Similarly, the student populations at Kyūshū are socially closest to Hokkaidō and Tōdai. On the other hand, the universities at each extreme have more in common (shown by the connecting lines in the tree diagram) than to those platooned in the middle of the pack.

A perusal of the public university positions indicates that, with few exceptions, the diagram locates them at the two extremities. This bifurcation would be interesting to explore at faculty levels to see whether or not it also exists there. Because Japanese universities incestuously hire faculty primarily from among their own graduates this bifurcation probably would replicate for faculty.

The 22 private universities, excepting Waseda, have little to distinguish themselves from one another. They primarily clump in the middle — particularly those which are within the greater Tōkyō metropolitan area. Their distance scores indicate this: 16 of the universities have Euclidean distances within 24 points of each other. This bodes ill for their future given the present pressures created by a shrinking market for quality applicants.

One other finding clearly emerges from the right-most column. Universities in the non-Tōkyō area are — with the exceptions of Waseda and Tōdai — at the extremes in terms of student populations. Student populations at most public and private Tōkyō universities are relatively interchangeable with each other. These universities draw from a much more homogeneous population than the other universities. Although this point may seem obvious, it is apparently lost on the private universities, each of which requires its own entrance examination in addition to the national one, as a way of distinguishing college-bound material. The national tests have already clearly marked college-bound statuses. As Reischauer (1988) notes in his critique of Japanese higher education, the private universities use their own exams mostly as a lucrative source of income. There are numerous would-be students who continue to retake their exams with little hope of passing in spite of the fact that their <u>hensachi</u> and national exam scores give them little hope of succeeding.

Another important technique for exploring the structure of a large number of variables is factor analysis. This statistical method is useful for searching for underlying dimensions. Table 3—3 displays the results of a factor analysis of student populations in the 45 universities. The first factor can be labeled Tōkyō Metropolitan Area universities. All of the loadings in bold are metropolitan Tōkyō universities and all have high factor scores.

The second factor highlights Kansai, or Ōsaka-area, universities. Although this second factor has a clear set of high loadings, it has only one-third of the power of explanation of the first factor. It explains only 15% of the variation among the 45 universities versus 43% for the first factor. This confirms the overpowering influence of Tōkyō on higher education. The other three factors do not parsimoniously discriminate among the remaining universities. Only a few universities load highly on any of them. In essence, this analysis suggests a Kansai-Kantō (Tōkyō-Ōsaka) split in academia, in line with popular beliefs.

However, other popular Japanese beliefs do not hold up, either by the results shown in Table 3—3 or Figure 3—2. First, neither analysis shows evidence that the four women's universities are of lower status than the other universities. Second, outside the seven prime national universities, neither method clearly rank orders public over private universities. This suggests that after former imperial universities cream off the top-scoring students from a very small number of high schools, that the national tests do not distinguish among the remaining population of applicants.

The other surprising feature not distinguished between these analyses is between general universities and specialized technical schools. The <u>Sunday Mainichi</u> list includes a number of technological schools — Tōkyō Science, Tōkyō Engineering, Tōkyō Arts, and Dentsū — that attract students with unusual skills. In the United States, for example, technological schools like the Massachusetts Institute of Technology or the California Institute of Technology normally attract students with extremely high mathematics abilities. Neither of these techniques indicate that similarly high-ranked technical schools in Japan draw particularly distinct bodies of students.

Table 3—3
Factor Analysis Results using Varimax Rotation of the Top-Ranked 45 Universities, Sorted by Factor 1 Loadings

University	Rotated Factor Loadings				
	1	2	3	4	5
JOCHI	0.954	-0.079	-0.080	0.072	0.148
CHUO	0.944	0.146	0.085	-0.042	0.108
GAKUSHU	0.941	0.038	0.030	0.086	0.120
AOYAMA	0.941	0.026	0.049	0.010	0.102
RIKKYO	0.934	0.060	0.063	0.073	0.145
TOKYO SCIENCE	0.928	-0.003	0.056	-0.073	0.097
MEIJI	0.925	0.112	0.123	0.037	0.111
TOKYO ENGINEERING	0.905	0.013	-0.276	-0.085	0.085
TOKYO WOMEN'S	0.896	-0.033	-0.187	-0.054	-0.180
KEIO	0.891	-0.186	-0.245	0.017	0.142
MEIJI GAKUIN	0.878	0.142	0.218	0.039	0.151
NIHON WOMEN	0.866	-0.016	-0.057	-0.156	-0.199
WASEDA	0.861	-0.006	0.144	0.064	0.137
HOSEI	0.855	0.235	0.287	-0.100	0.073
NIHON	0.833	0.236	0.300	-0.020	0.108
TOKYO CITY	0.833	0.062	-0.021	0.218	-0.202
ICU	0.794	-0.015	-0.199	-0.137	0.063
TOKYO FOREIGN	0.787	0.103	-0.299	0.015	-0.150
TOKYO AG & IND	0.763	0.052	0.116	0.099	-0.207
TOKAI	0.702	0.316	0.361	-0.071	0.096
TOKYO SCHOOL ARTS	0.696	0.241	0.078	0.148	-0.388
HITOTSU	0.685	-0.050	-0.545	0.027	0.180
SHIBAURA	0.666	0.197	0.081	-0.460	-0.046
CHIBA	0.663	0.212	0.325	-0.102	0.047
DENTSU	0.641	0.177	0.003	0.009	-0.239
TSUDAJUKU	0.636	-0.024	-0.530	-0.348	-0.153
TOKYO	0.596	-0.305	-0.550	-0.051	-0.217
ŌSAKA	-0.220	-0.931	-0.119	-0.038	-0.069
DOSHISHA	-0.243	-0.915	0.064	0.004	0.084
KOBE	-0.264	-0.903	0.027	0.080	0.006
KANSAI	-0.286	-0.897	0.133	0.035	0.081
KANSEI GWAKUIN	-0.265	-0.867	0.072	0.081	0.065
KYOTO	-0.118	-0.822	-0.065	0.075	0.074
NARA WOMEN'S	-0.154	-0.738	-0.089	-0.327	-0.259
RITSUMEI	-0.232	-0.693	0.019	-0.453	-0.014
HIROSHIMA	-0.164	-0.051	-0.751	-0.207	0.152
KYUSHU	-0.141	0.171	-0.661	0.319	-0.005
NAGOYA	0.118	-0.028	0.038	-0.728	0.055
TOKYO ARTS	0.387	0.109	0.037	-0.119	0.670
OCHANOMIZU	0.488	-0.009	-0.461	-0.389	-0.427
TOHOKU	0.093	0.255	0.366	-0.187	-0.347
BOEI (Self Defense)	-0.147	0.270	-0.471	0.484	-0.224
TOKYO DENTAL	0.485	-0.465	-0.337	0.263	-0.153
HOKKAIDO	0.010	0.083	0.082	0.133	-0.126
TSUKUBA	0.304	0.124	0.015	-0.332	-0.120

VARIANCE EXPLAINED BY ROTATED COMPONENTS

1	2	3	4	5
19.5%	6.8%	3.5%	2.2%	1.7%

PERCENT OF TOTAL VARIANCE EXPLAINED

1	2	3	4	5
43.4%	15.1%	7.7%	4.8%	3.7%

Ehara (1984) provides some interesting comparative data on the factor structure of a much larger set of universities (N = 137) in 1965. He used a broad set of 25 variables on university environments (type of institution, financial structure, instructor characteristics, student population, features of student life, and other characteristics). Three factors stood out in differentiating among his sample of universities. The first was institutional scale. Institutional scale included such features as diversity of curriculum, academic calendar, number of research facilities, integration of departments, number of Ph.D.s, and the level of participation in university associations. The second factor was academics, as measured by an emphasis on medical studies, the ratio of graduate to undergraduate students, and competitiveness of examinations. The third factor emphasized the difference between national and non-national universities and included such variables as costs of university fees, the emphasis on staff benefits, and the existence of self-governing associations.

Ehara's work employs data over 20 years old, and he uses a quite different sample and variables, so it is difficult to make comparisons. Nevertheless, his work roughly underscores the previous factor analysis. First, his analysis stressed the uniqueness of the mammoth private universities such as Waseda, Keio, and Dōshisha. Second, location in the central (Kansai-Kantō) versus peripheral areas greatly differentiated universities. Third, factor scores greatly differentiated between public and private universities.

Features Peculiar to Japanese Universities - In spite of the great differences between institutions of higher learning there are some strong features they all share that work against any of them ever attaining the world-class status of Oxford, Heidelberg, Harvard, or other eminent institutions. This section focuses upon some of these features and indicates how they work against higher learning and scholarship. There are certainly individual scientists of international repute, and many fine students, at Japanese universities. However, this section argues that the present educational system seriously curtails the chances that Japanese universities can attaining international eminence.

The real new year in Japan starts April 1 for government, business, and education. This is the day that schools enter into session and business induct their new salaried employees. From the standpoint of weather it is often a very pleasant time with cherry blossoms out over much of the country suggesting the blooming of Spring and fresh beginnings. However, from the standpoint of integration into the larger international community it clearly sets Japan apart. All other industrialized nations start their school years near the end of Summer. A 1978 UNESCO survey found that out of 213 countries only 9 (4.2%) started their school years in April, with 98 (46%) commencing their school years in September (Nihon Zaigai Kigyō Kyōkai 1981).

This difference in social calendars holds numerous dire consequences for teachers and students who might consider transferal between Japanese and non-Japanese schools. Japanese students who accompany their fathers to overseas employment must adjust to a nearly completed school year elsewhere and typically have to return before completion of another year. Elsewise they may simply stay out of school nearly five months that further postpones their integration into host-culture schools and peer groups.

Western professors and researchers considering work or research collaboration in Japan normally do not come at or before the start of the new academic calendar year because they do not appreciate the fact that it is more than a simple inconvenience of scheduling. Typically they arrive during the summer vacation months well after graduate and undergraduate students have started research projects under the supervision of Japanese faculty leaving them without apprentices under their own tutelage. The scientists and engineers from the United States who have made the mistake of a late start doing research under the auspices of Japanese universities have lived to regret it. Invariably they find themselves left out in the cold with a poor choice, if any, of graduate students to work with unless they have an academic host who personally arranges such important matters beforehand. Also, although summer vacation separates the school year into two "semesters," summer vacation is simply a long break of two months between the continuation of the same courses so that students are already half way through their course work when most Westerner scholars arrive.[14]

Undergraduate student culture in Japan is also comparatively anti-intellectual in orientation. Although the charge that colleges are little more than four-year playgrounds for resting between the end of the marathon to get into college and the start of adult life with a salaried job is an overstatement, student priorities place class attendance and performance much lower than in the United States. Part of the reason is the high cost of attending colleges in Japan that forces the majority of students to take on part-time employment.

University club activities in Japanese universities also contribute to the problem. Club functions resemble American fraternities and Ivy League schools when they were little more than finishing schools for the sons of the rich. Senior classmates apply pressures on freshmen to join one (and only one) club for the entire undergraduate experience during the early weeks of April each year. The manifest function of clubs revolves around some activity (sports, English conversation, or the like). However, significant latent purposes include the formation of social bonds that will continue for life and the provision of potential contacts in the job market through alumni relationships.

Clubs are at their most time-consuming during the first two years of college. The "choice" between attending class or doing an upperclassman-dictated club activity for freshmen and sophomores is no contest. After all,

---

[14]There is a small movement in the direction of a true semester system in the science and engineering schools which, if it becomes widespread, will certainly aid closer integration of Japanese higher education into the international mainstream. Nevertheless, entering between semesters will still produce a competitive disadvantage because year-long project assignments will already be well under way.

those upperclassmen will graduate soon and then they will form an important bridge to the salaried world. Furthermore, in one or two years, freshman and sophomores will also be in a position to control future inductees. Hence, the rewards and punishments under senior member's control make them a powerful force in the daily lives of students.

An on-line literature search of NSF's Japanese database for academic studies of club activities at universities in Japan turned up no studies of these important institutions. From personal observations at a top-seven national university and an elite private university I would judge that they play only a minor role for the science and engineering majors who make up one-fourth of all undergraduates. In my experience, these students have the greatest commitment to attending classes, learning English, and doing assignments. The structure of science departments and engineering schools encourages more serious study through extensive laboratory work, formal mentor-apprentice bonds, and stiffer than average regulations and requirements.[15]

The structure of university-wide academic requirements also works against serious student scholarship. Typically students enroll in from 14 to 20 courses each year. Each course meets one and one-half hours a week. This system encourages only very superficial learning because of the irregularity of class meetings and course overload. Because students do not officially have to declare a course until the final exams, the instructor has little idea who is, or how many students are, enrolled in a class until the first or second "semester" exam periods.

This system naturally discourages students from committing themselves to courses. With little responsibility for attending classes, doing homework, or taking exams, the system encourages procrastination and high dropout rates from courses with serious academic content. The effect is akin to allowing horse-race spectators to place their bets as the horses are entering the final home stretch. Students wait until late in the school year when it becomes obvious that they have fallen too far behind to catch up and then quietly drop more demanding courses by simply not showing up. Pressures from administration officials not to flunk students who chose club activities over school attendance also send students the signal that school work is of low value.

Scholars often comment on the lack of a concept of "community" in Japan (Iwamura 1987). Pressures to climb the educational and work place ladders have often been suggested as reasons for the lack of community in Japanese life. Students and adults may have so many pressing commitments that they have little time to devote to community activities. Whatever the case, universities mirror the larger society. Universities are not integrated into their surrounding areas and do not attract students to large campus-sponsored events as is true in the United States. The high cost of land in

---

[15]These demands are starting to have their toll. In 1987 the number of science applicants to universities reach a peak with 133,000 majoring in engineering and 11,300 in the physical sciences. By 1990 this had dropped 11% to 118,000 choosing engineering and declined 15% to 9,600 electing physical-science majors.

Japan has contributed to this fragmentation. Dormitories are often many kilometers distant from university campuses. Large areas for baseball diamonds, soccer fields, or auditoriums are a true luxury in central cities. The result is that many of the unifying elements of American universities (campus-based dormitories, theaters, and sports arena) are rare in Japan.

Administrators also show little commitment to surrounding community use of campus facilities so distinctive of American universities. There is a very clear cultural separation in Japan between "us" and "them" that extends to walling off universities from the local area inhabitants and which inhibits close "town-gown" relationships from blossoming. Westerners find living near universities particularly gratifying places because they exude intellect and culture beyond their immediate walls: There is no Japanese equivalent of an Ann Arbor, Madison, or Berkeley with their intellectually unbounded atmospheres. The reason is largely due to Japanese educational policy that draws a clear dividing line for who may and may not "benefit" from their institution, and which does not recognize the benefits of closer relationships to the larger intellectual community. The Japanese conception of education is something best passed down from superiors to inferiors, not something to be wrestled out through open discussion among relative equals.[16]

Another factor that discourages the development of world-class Japanese universities is the faculty system. Monbushō, not individual universities, has final say over the appointment of all full-time national university faculty positions. This control extends from appointments and promotions within national universities to faculty movements between all universities. This policy assures little competition between universities for outstanding or renowned faculty or for universities to engage in long-term planning for future academic needs. The most prestigious universities — all national — have no direct control over their own institutional needs.

The Ministry could not possibly have the expertise to judge the ranking of scientifically meritorious work in an age of specialization so it falls back on what it can judge: prestige of institutions and age of applicants. Watanabe (1991) points out that such traditional Japanese attitudes have made it impossible for Japanese scientists to "make a creative contribution to the development of modern science." (p. 109) Thus, the system functions to protect the Ministry's control over academia and it encourages age stratification. Reward comes from not bucking the system over long periods of time. Only with the retirement or death of one's direct senior professor does one get promoted within a national university.

Monbushō uses these criteria for judging the recipients of national science and engineering academy honors. The average age of these men is over 65 — decades past the time they did their most creative work.

---

[16]There are many cases in the United States where a professor without special competence in a particular area will send a graduate student to take courses in that area with explicit instructions to take good notes for instructing the professor in new developments of interest. This bi-directional learning scenario is improbable in Japan where mentor-student relationships are conceived as unidirectional.

Furthermore, the Ministry uses these same criteria for judging which Western scientists ought to be brought to Japan for special grants and awards. It is a bet on horses that have already won the race and allows for no dark-horse candidates. This system misjudges the state of American (and European) higher education where there is no one university that excels in all fields. A healthy system for aiding creative, state-of-the-art science requires more decentralized control of administrative decision-making.

The typical career pattern for Japanese academics encourages doing "safe" work: typically, a translation of a major work by some Western academic in the same field. This leads to what Mouer and Sugimoto (Mouer & Sugimoto 1985) aptly term "shadow academics" in which Japanese academics will, unknown to their Western counterpart, follow the career of renowned Western academics through a long series of translations rather than doing pioneering studies of their own.

Finally, in order to neutralize fellow academics from increasing power and upsetting the status quo, lengthy faculty meetings become a necessary burden on professorial time. College faculty meetings at the top seven universities, for example, may occur at least once bi-weekly and last from three to seven hours. This system directly mimics the national government's own version of "democracy" without a helmsman as von Wolferen (1989) describes it. College presidents and deans in Japan have no real power beyond their networks of relationships. They, like the Prime Minister, have no real authority to make or carry out institutional policy. Their status is lower, and power only slightly higher, than that of other important roles in higher education as illustrated in Table 1—2. A university president averages 1.22 in goodness (a measure of status) compared to 1.52 for a full professor, 1.52 for a scholar, and 1.36 for a researcher. By contrast, a university president has an average 2.2 power ranking compared to 1.86 for full professors, 1.56 for scholars and 0.58 for researchers. Full professors are clearly forces that university presidents must reckon with. They are a full three-quarters of a point higher in status while only a quarter of a point lower in power.

Jinmyaku ("old boy" networks) are a necessary evil of the Monbushō-created system at its worst (Watanabe 1991). Power emerges from a widespread network among one's fellow colleagues within the university rather than from the influence of one's research in one's discipline. The time spent on building jinmyaku and attending faculty meetings is necessary to gain power but is valuable research time lost.[17]

Regional Patterns of Recruitment of College Graduates - Officially, the legal recruiting season for new employees starts during the Summer vacation of one's senior year although, surreptitiously, many seniors

---

[17]"Old boy" networks in academia are important sources of power in the United States, but intellectual "fiefdoms" in the United States would be difficult to maintain by university-based social networks alone. They also require the status of recognition of scientific merit bestowed from one's profession. Recognition of merit by one's discipline gives academics a potent weapon in turf fights within their home institutions for pay increases, promotions, and job offers lacking in Japan.

have already taken class time off to travel to Tōkyō at least once to search for a job. Blue-chip corporations have already signed on seniors from the elite universities in the Tōkyō area. These system infractions are reminiscent of professional sports violations in their rush to sign up hot amateur college prospects. This is likely to be the case as long as the Japanese economy resembles the present buyer's market.

Universities in the Tōkyō area have another advantage beyond those already mentioned. They are closest to the home offices of major corporations. One of the peculiar features of the Japanese college-recruitment process is that corporations expect seniors to travel to Tōkyō at their own expense. It should come as no surprise, then, that Tōkyō residents have the highest percentage of college graduates who remain after finishing college with 69.6% of science and engineering graduates, and 70.8% of all college graduates. This compares with an average of 19.7% of engineering and science graduates, and 36.9% of all graduates, who find work in the same prefecture where they attended college. Almost all prefectures are exporters of college talent. Only four prefectures keep the majority of their science and engineering majors and only six retain the majority of their non-engineering graduates. There is a strong 0.82 correlation between these two measures suggesting that similar forces operate toward recruiting of general and science-engineering graduates.

The strong attraction of Tōkyō and Ōsaka stands out. Saitama, Chiba, Kanagawa, and Yamanashi essentially provide bedroom communities for Tōkyō workers and thus keep only 12.3, 12.5, 18.3, and 18.6% of their college graduates in their local economies. Similarly, Nara, Kyōto and Hyōgo serve a similar role for Ōsaka by enjoying only 16.6, 17.7, and 24.3% of their college graduates in local employment, compared to 52.1% of Ōsaka-based college graduates. On the main island of Honshū only Tokyo, Nagoya, and Ōsaka retain a majority of their college graduates; Shikoku's Matsuyama, Hokkaidō's Sapporo, and Okinawa's Naha cities perform the same functions on the other islands.

These figures also suggest strong regional-market segmentation for college graduates. Okinawa, which has the poorest record for placing students in the prestigious universities on the mainland employs primarily its own college graduates. Nevertheless, almost half of Okinawan engineering and science graduates leave for jobs elsewhere, indicating the serious brain-drain problem that continually faces Okinawa.

Similarly, although the Japanese government touted a new policy during the 1980s of turning Kyūshū into a Japanese version of California's Silicon Valley, Kyūshū-trained engineering majors leave for more fertile areas. Fukuoka manages to keep only one-fourth of its engineering graduates with the other Kyūshū prefectures keeping only half that amount. Not only are the brightest and best of the high school students attracted to Tōkyō, but those remaining students who finish college — particularly those with science and engineering degrees — in their own prefecture have a high probability of joining the brain drain upon graduation, reconfirming the powerful effect of the Kansai and Kantō regions on impoverishing the rest of Japan.

More interesting is the employment pattern for educators that is unrelated to engineering and scientific employment. For example, the correlation between education and science-engineering majors who remain in the prefecture of their college training is a non-existent -0.02. Contrary to the employment of other students, education majors are most likely to stay in the same prefecture after finishing college. The median percentage is 75.1% staying, with 38 prefectures keeping more education majors than they export. Thus, education majors have quite different employment patterns from non-education majors. Educators are more locally oriented; non-education majors more cosmopolitan. The conservatism reflected in educational employment patterns offers even more support for the status quo mechanisms that maintain the educational stratification system. Industry and the major cities benefit from higher education, with highly skilled workers gravitating in their direction, but statistics show no similar benefit for other areas with prestigious universities. The ecology of prefectural education reflects home-grown education for the vast majority of educators.

These figures are consistent with Benjamin's and James' (1989) conclusion that only "average" university students become teachers in Japan. The best and brightest students have little incentive to become teachers. Physical facilities are Spartan, teachers are paid no better than in the United States, and Japanese teachers and professors are employed on a year-long basis with pay and promotion based on seniority rather than merit. These features discourage excellence in education.

Overemphasize on similarities among Japan's schools, salient differences from the United States, and a robust Japanese economy lead to the false conclusion that the end-product of Japan's education is a high—quality learning experience with relatively homogeneous life chances. Schools in Japan operate five and one-half days a weeks and some 210 days average instruction compared to 180 in the United States. Yet none of these features entail additional expenditures on education. It would also be a mistake to assume that number of days is equivalent to, or better than, quality of instruction. Even with considerably less instructional time, schools in the United States still produce significantly higher as well as lower mathematics scores because of wider variation in quality of instruction (Schaub & Baker 1991).

POST-BACCALAUREATE EDUCATION

In 1982, Japan had one-fifth as many undergraduates and one-twentieth as many graduate students as the United States. According to the Ministry of Education's 1989 White Paper on Education, only six of 10,000 Japanese in 1987 had attended graduate school, versus 69 Americans in 1985, 28 in France, and 9 in Great Britain. Graduate programs enroll only 3% of all university students compared to 11% in the United States. The Japanese figures are mostly for master's level graduates in engineering and the basic sciences. The demand for doctoral work is even lower in Japan. The role of Japanese universities essentially stops with undergraduate attendance, leaving graduate education an underdeveloped component. There are at least ten reasons for this.

First, the large corporations that dominate the Japanese economy bestow few rewards and many costs for education beyond the baccalaureate. The typical college-educated worker has a career dominated by seniority. Any deviation from the normal seniority system (Dore & Sako 1989; Rohlen 1974) is fraught with penalties. A college senior who enters graduate school for several years extra study and then enters corporate life is likely to start at the same salary he would have had he entered straight into the corporation after graduation, essentially putting him several years behind his graduate class who have now had salary increments yearly, based upon seniority. His compatriots who took the normal route will also be several years ahead in terms of the seniority necessary for career promotion. The more typically career-oriented Japanese worker who works several years and then decides to return to graduate school would find himself at a similar disadvantage upon returning to the same corporation (assuming they would want him back).[18]

Second, major industries prefer to give their own on-the-job training to career-oriented personnel rather than send them to graduate schools. Corporations reward employees who take corporate-sponsored, on-the-job training by not stopping the clock on seniority benefits while granting continued salary increases and up-to-date research-and-development equipment on site. The cooperative employee never feels threatened of losing ground to his competition. Moreover, corporations award on-the-job training to employees with the most promise of promotion, giving them further incentive to acquiesce to authority.

Third, the job market in Japan is a lopsided buyer's market that discourages college graduates from continuing their studies. In 1990, small- and medium-sized enterprises offered an estimated 550,000 jobs, but only 100,000 males graduate each year. The job ratio was 10 offers for every computer science graduate, with a 30-to-1 ratio in electrical engineering at the time. With new college graduates relatively free to select among numerous offers, there is little incentive to spend even more years in delayed gratification. Furthermore, the best students have traditionally shunned doctoral work in favor of the lucrative professional undergraduate majors of law, engineering, and business.

Fourth, Japanese universities do not have a tradition of industry-university cooperation on research and development projects (Bartholomew

---

[18]Career promotions are based less on merit than seniority in Japan. Bureaucrats normally assume the role of kachō (section chief) at about age 40 to 45; Kyokuchō (division chief) at age 50, and jimujikan (administrative vice-minister) at about 52 to 53 years-of-age in the government. Both private and public career paths in Japan resemble American military promotion systems to a great extent.

1989; Morse & Samuels 1986; Watanabe 1991). The Ministry of Education discourages cooperation through prohibitions on professors taking consulting fees from private industry, giving them effective control over academic research. Many American university professors — particularly in the sciences, education, and business — have active private consulting practices that lead to strong private industry-university relationships. These relationships give them a relative autonomy from their own institutions that is unheard of in Japan.

Similarly, national education policy in Japan is a top-down affair unlike the United States that operates according to consensus among many actors. The United States operates according to consortium arrangements among the very institutions of education themselves. Quality control in the United States is in the hands of accreditation agents of higher education, and there is virtually no government regulation of the quality of degrees or the adequacy of instruction. The highly specialized nature of higher education at upperclassman- and graduate-levels requires decisions beyond the purvey of non-specialists. It is unreasonable to assume that any government can adequately control higher education without dependence on university self-regulation.

Fifth, prestigious universities and research and development corporations in the United States have increasingly attracted and sought out partnerships. American corporations receive tax breaks for donations to non-profit organizations, so they often donate scientific equipment and funds. This is a foreign idea in Japan. The Japanese government has attempted to seed several "science city" areas — most notably, Tsukuba and Kansai — in an effort to promote similar corporate-university partnerships. Still, these efforts have shown little promise to date.

Part of the reason is undoubtedly due to the lack of tradition with philanthropy, but a large part is due to the lack of incentives that corporations and individuals have for forming those partnerships in the first place. Another part is due to the imposition of the federal government in local affairs. Tsukuba was, and continues to reflect, a hodgepodge of competing hamlets. Still another part of the problem is the mislabeling of these as cities for "science" (basic research) cities. Industry pays for 79% of the research, and expects "practical" applications in return. Government and industrial policy discourages Japanese universities from engaging in basic research.

It is also interesting to compare philanthropy in the United States with Japan. While philanthropy is virtually unknown in Japan, private universities in the United States could not survive without it. In 1981 private gifts to Japanese universities accounted for only 9.3% of current revenue, and endowment income accounted for 55.1% in the U.S.A. (Tonkin & Edwards 1987).

Sixth, universities in Japan offer few incentives for going to graduate school. Government funds for university-sponsored research account for about one-tenth of the funds available in the United States. Prestigious American universities offer fellowships and teaching assistantships to graduate students drawn from such funds, while Japanese graduate students depend primarily on their personal and family resources. Thus, Japanese students find it necessary to work at part-time jobs outside of their specialty, creating conflicts of interest between basic needs and time for study.

Seventh, the top universities are poorly structured for graduate-level research. The prestigious national universities are based on a modification of the old Germanic "chair" system. A science or engineering department is authorized to have six positions. Two of those are equivalent to Full Professor positions. Under the direct authority of each Full Professor are two Assistant Professor positions.[19] An assistant professor cannot be promoted until "his" full professor dies. The direct command of full professors over assistant professors stifles junior faculty. This system also discourages "critical masses" of scholars needed to carry out specialized academic research and variety of course offerings. Because of the plethora of professors in each specialty, most university course offerings from junior year in undergraduate school upward focus on general "seminars" under the direction of each professor rather than actual specialized courses.

Similarly, under each assistant professor is one or two poorly paid "assistants" (joshu) who are considered the most promising among the graduate students. These assistants serve as "gofers" for the professors: doing secretarial work (as there are no secretaries in most departments), library research, laboratory supervision, and even teaching of courses assigned to the professors. The system, in other words, inhibits individual researchers below the level of Full Professor from doing their own, creative research. Scarce job and promotion prospects essentially hamper individually motivated studies at ages considered optimal for creative contributions in the West. The fact that professors receive tenure upon hire and are paid almost entirely according to their seniority means they have little external incentive to upgrade their skills, perform research, or work at classroom performance.

This system of strict hierarchy extends all the way down through the system, so that seniors have clear authority over juniors in the same department. Customs reinforce this system throughout all of Japanese life. Strict hierarchical position earmarks eating arrangements at banquets, with the most senior faculty member seated in the guest of honor's place down to the youngest person seated at the far end of the room; seniority determines names on rosters; and name-calling suffixes and general patterns of communication with regards to research follow the same strict customs of senior-junior statuses. This strict pecking order inhibits the free exchange of ideas which is so central to the concept of higher education. Teaching methods place memorization and obedience above originality. Classroom norms consider the raising of questions impolite. The result is intellectual anemia.

Eighth, university services also hamper the free exchange of information found in American universities. They offer research facilities which are inferior to those in private industries. Library budgets are

---

[19]One position is allocated to the lower-status liberal arts departments.

assigned to individual faculty. In practice this means that each member of the department can (and often does) order the same books or journals from university operating funds. Although books and journals ordered by individual faculty are the property of the university, this system is highly inefficient. From the standpoint of graduate students and researchers who often have trouble tracking down particular research materials, and who may find the professor holding a particular material of interest using its loan. It is one more tool for control of junior scholars. From the standpoint of the entire system it wastes valuable resources by encouraging multiple copies of the same rarely used materials. This system may work to the advantage of full professors as a symbol of their personal status and power, but clearly dampens creativity on the part of aspiring talent at lower levels. Also, archives are primitive by comparison to those in the West. Archivists are without legal, professional status, and have no centralized authority to aid accumulation, management, or dissemination of historic materials (Ogawa 1991).

Ninth, Japanese industry indirectly maintains the low status of Japanese graduate schools through its reliance on overseas training of employees. Corporations are willing to send selected employees to study English, business management, and other fields abroad for up to three years. In effect, they give in-house grants for graduate education abroad at the expense of supporting similar programs at home. Rather than support the creation of a world-class graduate education system at home, these grants continue to recognize the low status of their own system.

Tenth, Japanese universities have no tradition of hiring internationally acclaimed faculty.[20] Berkeley, Princeton, Oxford, Cambridge, and other world-class Western universities have long-standing policies of acquiring the best and brightest researchers and graduate students, regardless of nationality. Discriminatory university regulations limit tenured positions to Japanese nationals in all of the elite national universities, save Tōdai where six of eight foreign faculty members hold tenure (Geller 1992). The rare non-Japanese on university faculties are virtually all on "renewable" contracts. This policy discourages most serious Western scholars from joining Japanese university faculties. The result is that Japanese universities suffer a huge disadvantage in the international marketplace of ideas. They end up playing a role more of science consumers than producers.

Some universities attempt to partially overcome these limitations by sending graduate students and professors to the West for advanced training. The number of Japanese receiving post-secondary education in the United States grew by 527% between 1960 and 1983; or from 2,168 to 13,610 individuals. About one-third of those persons were graduate students.[21]

---

[20]For comprehensive reviews of scientific and technological cooperation see Mowlana (1986) and Wallerstein (1984).

[21]The Japanese are not unique in this regard. The United States hosts 32% of all documented foreign students worldwide. The closest contenders are France with 13.7%, followed by Germany, the USSR, and the United Kingdom (Tonkin & Edwards 1987). The large number of foreign graduate students

However, the reward system does not encourage large numbers of internationally trained university professors and graduate students because there are few grants available which offer the necessary outside support. Worse yet, national prejudice against Japanese who spend lengthy amounts of time overseas works as a discouraging factor.

Not surprisingly, the internationalization of academia in Japan is very spotty and one-side. Trips abroad for educational purposes are almost nonexistent: Only 2.3 out of every 10,000 Japanese were out of the country in 1988 for studies at foreign institutions. Even this number is misleading, because the Greater Tōkyō and Ōsaka Metropolitan Areas account for the vast bulk of these trips. For example, the highest figures were for Tōkyō (7.6), Kyōto (6.5), Kanagawa (6.0) Nara (6.0), Ōsaka (4.9), Hyōgo (4.8) and Chiba (4.5). These seven prefectures contain all of the nationally renowned universities in the Kantō and Kansai areas listed in Figure 2—9. These prefectures also contain one-third of the Japanese population yet supply fully two-thirds of all residents studying abroad.

Furthermore, data on foreign residents in Japan precisely mirrors this distribution. A correlation of 0.63 indicates that prefectures that have more foreign residents also send more Japanese nationals overseas for educational study, clearly reflecting the educational advantages that exist in the Ōsaka and Tōkyō areas. In essence, these figures are consistent with the major thesis of these chapters that educational benefits are highly skewed toward residents living in an area comprising barely 6% of the total area of Japan.

THE ROLE OF WOMEN

Although I demonstrated severe social barriers to women's introduction to higher education earlier in this chapter, there are strong macroeconomic pressures to widen their role in the labor force. Women now account for 36% of the work force, and one out of four domestic firms claims to promote women. Nevertheless, 90% of the companies polled in 1990 by the Labor Ministry report that women represent less than 1% of their managers. Foreign-affiliated firms report figures that are substantially higher; 4.8% of division managers, and section chiefs are women in such firms.

Pressures for credentialism and a buyer's market have aided women. The average level of education attained by secretaries has increased markedly in recent years giving them more of the qualifications and leverage needed for promotion. For example, the average secretary in 1970 had gone no further than high school, yet ten years later a four-year college degree had become the norm for secretarial positions. The result is that employment rates among female university graduates rose from about 60% in the latter part of the 1970s to 68% in 1981 (Fujimura-Fanselow 1989).

---

in the United States gives it a tremendous intellectual network advantage so it continues to be the major worldwide supplier of higher education as a commodity.

In spite of this rise, Brinton (1988) has documented that women continue in jobs peripheral to the main economy due to a system of human capital development that encourages the maintenance of greater gender stratification than the American system. The job market in Japan is highly segmented along lines of primary and secondary labor markets, mirroring the firmly entrenched oyabun-kobun (parent-child) industries. Major industries dominate subsidiary ones (Mosk & Johansson 1986) in a very one-sided arrangement in which the principal industries dictate terms of their relationships with subsidiary "child" companies. The result is that subsidiary companies pay lower wages, offer less job security, locate in the less prestigious areas away from Tōkyō, are the first to feel the effects of economic problems, and so on. Economic conditions give subsidiary firms little choice beyond hiring more men with less prestigious and fewer educational credentials, and women.

Women also rarely gain full-time university faculty positions. In 1981, the Ministry (Mombushō 1990) estimated that roughly 14% of the 37,000 master's degree candidates, and 10% of the 18,000 doctoral candidates, were women. Women who try to break into academia find that members of all-male laboratory groups do not accept them. Discrimination takes the form of being the last informed of social functions, and exclusion from sports activities and annual retreats. Women in academia find great disadvantages in their ability to develop smooth human relations in the face of strong male bonding.

Nevertheless, the Japanese economy continued to create more jobs than male applicants in the 1970s and 1980s, leading to better employment opportunities for women. From 1975 to 1980 the number of women employed in the following types of work increased by 50% or more: architecture, real estate, advertising, information processing, newspaper reporting and editing, civil administration, and technical jobs in scientific fields (Tōkeikyoku 1990).

ADULT EDUCATION

Adult education is a relatively new idea in Japan compared to the United States. Japanese university students are highly age-stratified. It is rare for students outside the traditional range of 18 to 22 to attend college classes. In spite of its rarity, adult-education is expanding and is likely, given the rapid aging of the Japanese population, to continue multiplying. In 1989 only 3 of every 1000 Japanese were attending adult-education classes at universities, but this was three times the figure of ten years earlier. Although the number of adult-education courses offered expanded by two and one-half times during the same period, the average class size was 120 students; much too large for serious study by American standards.

The large average class size suggests a huge market for adult education and insufficient staffing. Part of the problem is Monbushō control. For example, it scheduled 686 adult-education courses in 1989 with 50,800 attendees in 90 of the 96 national universities. This means it allowed an average class attendance of 74 attendees per class in national universities, but even private universities averaged over twice that number of attendees. Clearly, these adult programs are built on mass lectures for passive audiences. It would appear that educational authorities have found a new, highly lucrative source of income which will increase rapidly with the graying of Japan. However, the overly large class sizes indicate the construction of yet another educational tier of suspect quality. Monbushō's figures show that 59% of the attendees were taking liberal arts courses, 11% studied professional skills in vocational classes, and 6% took foreign languages. Such large class sizes are too large for more than superficial surveys of academic materials.

The relatively low position of adult education in Japan is partly due to the dominant role in the training of workers and the content of public education taken by private industry. Dore and Sako (1989) have most clearly depicted the reasons. Industry expects to give specific on-the-job training and grueling days at the firm. Thus, the dominant ideology considers school the place where students learn the work ethic and their places within the larger hierarchy rather than specific skills. Unlike Great Britain and the United States where workers seek additional vocational training and certification of skills that lead to promotion and pay increases, such behavior is rare in Japan. Learning is done on the job and initially involves frequent rotations. Older workers help younger workers build competence with supervisors writing up job specifications and procedure manuals for workers. Japanese firms make do with a minimum of formal in-house training and do not rely on expensive consulting firms to come in and seminar their workers to death, nor do they underwrite expensive university tuition.

The system Dore and Sako describe works well as long as workers have little power. However, the growing shortage of technologically adept workers, the horizontal diversification of industries, the mushrooming of an international economy, and the necessity for highly specialized skills learned in graduate school constitute trends that seem to be gaining momentum in all of the industrial countries. Japan is not immune to these trends. For example, engineering school applicants have been decreasing over the last several years, and new engineering baccalaureates are finding well-paying non-engineering positions more attractive than engineering positions, similar to the experiences of other advanced industrial countries. As long as employee alternatives to the traditional system continue to expand, Japan will need to offer higher quality public alternatives in adult education to meet the needs of its aging population.

Monbushō does not release adult-education figures by prefectures, but it would be surprising if they did not reflect the current stratification system. Most probably the Tōkyō and Ōsaka areas benefit the most from opportunities for adult education. Adult education is clearly a low priority and of low status. Thus, it is likely that attendees are women, senior citizens, and men without college education or from less prestigious colleges and universities who are not on the salaried staffs of the primary-sector industries most likely to offer quality on-the-job training already. In other words, the system probably maintains the illusion of increased educational and work opportunities for the masses.

SUMMARY

This chapter focuses upon the last stages in the competition for educational credentials. Entrance into Japanese high schools has been influenced by numerous inequities in financial and cultural capital. The sorting of students into different high schools marks an important rite de passage. It hardens the options for students interested in going to universities that count. Prefectural differences in results of students in the national entrance examination process gives much insight. Student chances depend largely upon entrance into the "right" high schools, well developed transportation systems which open up opportunities to attend those same high schools, and government policies which have long aided and abetted a set of elite high schools which specialize in opening college opportunities to a select few. In spite of the myth of the homogenizing effects of gambaru (giving it the old college try), structural factors greatly determine who goes to the top universities.

The universities themselves are also highly stratified. However, whereas the top high schools are disproportionately expensive private schools, the elite universities are mostly national. Ministry of Education policies and funding support a relatively rigid system based primarily upon age of institutions. Entrance requirements to universities aid perpetuation of a strong pecking order. Few students or faculties change universities during their careers. Social mobility is narrowly limited to relationships established during one's first weeks in college. Sex discrimination is strongly institutionalized, further restricting college markets to particular groups of males.

The national universities deserve the modifier "national" only to the extent that they are funded by the national government. They recruit their students primarily from surrounding prefectures. Tōkyō and Kyōto Universities, serving the Tōkyō and Ōsaka metropolitan areas, respectively, are the first among equals in career outcomes. The national government has encourage further division between these national universities and a select number of private elite universities. Although government policy encourages a clearly demarcated stratification of universities, cluster and factor analyses suggest a more complex picture in which high school location (Tōkyō or Ōsaka) makes a great deal of difference. In fact, although the popular press makes Todai appear as if it should have the most distinctive student population, other national universities (Tōhoku, Nagoya, Ōsaka, and Kyūshū Universities are more distinctive, and one private university (Waseda) is the most distinctive of all. Because faculty are primarily recruited from among undergraduates from the same institutions, it is likely that the same patterns would hold at other levels of universities (faculty and administration).

There are other features that make Japanese peculiar compared to other advanced industrial nations. Japanese higher education outcomes, like industry, are based more on seniority (age) and ascribed characteristics (sex, ethnic background) than on merit. The ascriptive nature of Japanese higher education is not the only feature of that keeps Japanese universities from reaching their highest potential. Employment practices and patterns also discourage post-baccalaureate education. The results clearly show in relatively low attendance figures in graduate schools and an impoverished sense of adult education outside the narrow confines of company in-house training programs.

Chapter 4

SOCIALIZATION, MARITAL IDEALS, AND THE MARRIAGE SQUEEZE

A major assumption underlying the preceding chapters on education concerns the effects of cultural capital investments. Those chapters suggest that cultural-capital investments in Japan differ significantly across prefectures. This chapter proposes that such differences greatly affect the participation of young men and women in the marriage market in Japan. The thesis turns on a well-developed sociological literature on marriage markets, sex-age ratios, and the "marriage squeeze" for the purpose of making sense of prefectural-level differences concerning the transition from youth to adulthood.

In 1983, Schoen published a much cited article on age as an important criterion in spouse selection. Schoen's work has spawned a large number of studies on scarcities of males and females in various societies. He argued that these scarcities create "marriage squeezes" due to the resulting asymmetries in the availability of potential spouses. Suzuki (1989) replicated Schoen's methods for the prefectures of Japan, and discussed some of the problems with measuring the "marriage squeeze" in the Japanese context. In the process, Suzuki produced a series of important alternative measures of the Japanese marriage squeeze that form the backbone of this chapter.

On the other hand, Billig (1991) points out that Schoen's method gives a too-narrow understanding of the marriage squeeze in terms of age. Schoen conceived of the marriage squeeze in purely demographic terms: that is, the relative availability of spouses at appropriate ages. He viewed age as the sole criterion of spouse selection. Billig demonstrated how status hypergamy, where women marry men of higher status, serves to perpetuate marriage squeezes against women. Age-based marriage squeezes are only one special case of a more general cultural capital, including distribution of wealth, power, status, levels of education, and religious purity.

Thus, there are other ways of limiting female choice and ensuring that males still have the stronger position in the marriage market despite their demographic disadvantage. Billig showed that (1) if women ideally find their husbands in families that have higher status than their own and (2) if the status distribution is hierarchical, then larger numbers of women seek spouses among smaller numbers of men. This brings the issue back full circle to the role of cultural capital in mate selection. This chapter expands upon the theses of both Billig and Suzuki by reference to discrepancies between Japanese men and women's ideal mate and the influence of both age and other important demographic and ecological factors on marriage rates.

The public in both the United States and Japan have a propensity to focus on the marriage problem at the individual level. A translation of a year's worth of the equivalent of "Dear Abbey" letters to the Mainichi Shinbun (McKinstry & McKinstry 1991) gives numerous examples of individually directed complaints concerning marriage. The irony is that both Japanese and Americans perceived Japan as a group-oriented nation yet both sets of citizens see the trees (individuals) and not the forests (groups) causing national problems. For example, Japanese newspaper and magazine columnists criticize trends toward "selfishness" among young women and young men raised as "pampered momma's boys." See, for example, the article by Wakao Fujioka, The Japan Times, April 2, 1990). Fujioka's discourse is all psychological, with charges that young men have mother's complexes, are self-centered Peter Pans, and are slovenly and stingy by nature because their mother's overprotect them. This debate assumes individual traits cause the current problems this chapter addresses. By so doing it indicates little comprehension of the power of forces external to young people.

As Edwards (1989) has pointed out, marriage is not "purely a private matter of the heart." It is, indeed, a public articulation of social values and social life. The determination of a life-long mate is a fundamental building block of society. A maxim of family sociology is that norms strongly influence mate selection. Familial and kinship structures are highly conservative institutions that induce the status quo and the conservation of traditional values and beliefs. Normally this translates into strong pressures toward homogamous marriage as expressed in similar values, background, and social class.

There is also a strain of anti-intellectual thought current in Japan known as Nihonjinron, often translated as "theories of the uniqueness of the Japanese race" that argues for racial differences separating Japanese from outsiders. Nihonjinron finds wide expression in both the popular press and academia. Essentially, it attributes any and all differences that do exist between Japanese and other humans to racial uniqueness (Hamaguchi 1985, provides a recent example). By contrast, this chapter suggests that the American and Japanese marriage markets are almost polar opposites, not due to racial or individual explanations, but because of different (a) sex-role ratios in interaction with (b) cultural norms concerning work and marriage. Japanese-American differences in norms are entirely explainable in normal social structural terms. There is no need for unparsimonious racial uniqueness postulates.

As is true of other modern industrial peoples, the Japanese have become obsessed with public opinion polls. The social survey has reached a state of high public regard for taking the national pulse of everything from abortion attitudes to xenophonia. However, polls assume that groups, organizations, and nations are nothing more than the sum of individual opinions. This section highlights the results of a high-quality, series of quintennial public opinion polls taken among young, marriageable Japanese (Kōseishō 1989) concerning their conceptions of the ideal mate.[1] These surveys originated from concerns over the increasing delays in marriage that have led Japan to become the oldest marrying industrial nation. However, this series of surveys leads to the mistaken conclusion that simply polling individuals over their marital ideals is an accurate reflection of the forces that lead toward or away from marriage. To the contrary, the demographic evidence indicates a widening gap between the cultural norms that reflect the ideals of cultural capital and a Japanese social structure that produces not-so-evident external social constraints on attaining individual expression of those cultural ideals.

Consider first the normatively ideal woman that young men imagine. Some 70% of single men suggest that they want to marry women about four to five years younger than themselves. This desire matches the historical norm in Japan although the present demographic impossibility of attaining this goal is causing grief for both unmarried Japanese men and women. By contrast, the American ideal and outcome among never-married men has long been wives who are two years their junior. For the population below the age of 30, U.S. Census estimates of the number of men to women two years their junior is nearly equivalent to the ideal (Government Printing Office 1980).

SEX RATIOS AND MARRIAGE MARKETS

Cultural norms are certainly an important part of the decision to marry. However, students of the family believe that they are only part of the story. Sociologists assert that there are social structural factors beyond individuals that are highly influential in society. Besides the structural factors I've already shown, one other very important structural factor that the average lay person ignores is the sex ratio. After all, individuals want a boy or a girl, and do not normally think in terms of such structural factors as the ratio of boys to girls born.

---

[1]The annual survey, which has been conducted every year since 1980, includes over 30 closed-ended questions given to a nationally representative sample of 5,447 never-married youth from ages 18 to 34. The result is an extremely rich source of sociological data that has barely been tapped by Japanese, much less non-Japanese, scholars. For example, question 31 in the 1989 survey asks whether the respondents would prefer a love-based (ren'ai) or arranged (miai) marriage, yet these statistics go unreported in the non-Japanese press while scholars report the results of much more unsystematically collected data.

Sociologists define the sex ratio quite simply as the number of males per 100 females. In most societies, the newborn infant sex ratio is 106. A sex ratio of 106 may seem a little high, but it is not high enough over the human life cycle to offset the inherent biological weaknesses of males. Around age 21 when most young adults are starting to think about marriage in most societies, including Japan and the United States, the sex ratio is a near "perfect" 100; that is, there is almost exactly one man for every woman of age 21. However, after age 21, it is normally all "down hill" from the male point of view. Increasingly, more men die off than women for a variety of reasons. Women naturally live much longer, men often have more dangerous jobs that lead to death, men engage in warfare, and so on. By age 65, in most industrial societies, the sex ratio is so highly skewed that it is increasingly common to find areas where there is only one man over age 65 per 100 women over that age. Japan is the fastest aging society in the world implying increasingly lopsided numbers of female senior citizens without mates.

As long as the sex ratio is not "close" to 100 (roughly between 90 and 110), sex-ratio problems crop up in any society (Guttentag & Secord 1983; Ireland 1982). For example, if we find sex ratios over 110, we also note higher-than-average incidences of crime. Larger proportions of men to women highly correlate with such social dislocations as more crime, violence, and disease in any society.

According to Becker (1973), the marital marketplace shares similarities to economic ones. Individual characteristics (e.g., race, class, education, earning potential, etc.) may be treated as "goods" that potential spouses use to assess the members of the opposite sex. However, Guttentag and Secord (1983) noted that such characteristics usually vary over time and place because of differences in sex ratios. Lower sex ratios (oversupplies of women) ought to lead to lower market value for women. This situation should encourage sexual permissiveness, female civil liberties, high illegitimacy rates, high divorce rates, and greater economic independence for women. High sex ratios (oversupplies of men), by contrast, should elevate the valuation of women. High sex ratios strengthen traditional sex roles (double-standards, homemakers, virginity), low illegitimacy, low abortion rates, low divorce rates, and higher economic mobility for women.

Technically, I speak of the crude sex ratio; the sex ratio for an entire society. However, within any society, the distribution of men and women occurs unevenly. Men are typically more over-represented in rural farming and frontier areas. Sometimes, norms may lead to differential sex ratios. In households which have lacked male offspring for generations, the desire for a male child strongly articulates into high sex ratios (Lebra, 1984, Pp. 159).

In the United States, farming areas in the upper Midwestern states of North and South Dakota sex ratios are very high--over 130 marriageable young men may occur per 100 marriageable young women because women flock to the large cities (ironically, recall, in search of marriageable young men). By contrast, it is not uncommon to find very low sex ratios in major cities like New York (e.g., the 1990 sex ratio for the Bronx was 83.1) or Washington, D.C. where women pursue their search of marriageable men. The sex ratio in some Japanese rural areas now reaches 233, as bachelors over 35-years-old have quadrupled over the last half of the 1980s.

High-sex ratios in areas like the American Dakotas or the Japanese Sea rural communities of Tōhoku force young men with a strong desire to marry to import brides. Thus, some rural areas in Japan have become famous for importing brides from such places as the Philippine Islands. Sawauchi Township in Iwate Prefecture tried to induce young Japanese women through improved housing and health programs without success. City officials finally resorted to inviting Chinese women to work as agricultural trainees to attract marriageable ones. In the Dakotas, similarly, young farmers may place personal advertisements for brides in urban newspapers, usually to no avail.

Given the basics of sex ratios, let us return to Japan first, and America second, to consider the influence of sex ratios on the attainment of culturally imbedded norms. If Japanese youth disregarded their cultural values, the crude sex ratios would not present much of an issue. The crude sex ratio for all male and female 28-year-olds is well within the 90 to 110 range. It was about 106 during the late 1980s. However, we know that the average 28-year-old Japanese single male desires a mate who is 23-years-old, and women's ideals match those of men's.

Herein lies the rub. Since World War II the Japanese birth rate has been steadily declining so that each year there are fewer babies born. For example, in 1988 the average Japanese couple had 1.57 children and by 1991 that figure had dropped to a world low of 1.54 children. This drop of 0.01 children per couple per year seems insignificant on the surface. However, in terms of millions of people it translates into a significantly smaller pool of 23-year-old women than 28-year-old men each year. Currently it translates into half a million excess young men in their late twenties and early thirties.

The 1990 census indicated 8,318,000 single men aged 20 through 39 and 5,263,000 single women of the same ages. At birth, as in most nations, boys outnumber girls by five percent, but because men seek to marry younger women from smaller cohorts than their own, the odds become worse as the birthrate has declined. For instance, there were 550,000 more single men aged 23 through 35 than single women age 20 through 32 in 1990. Although men aged 30 through 35 are a group with no shortage of potential partners, 28 percent have remained single, triple the number 15 years ago.

Figure 4—1 visualizes the age-specific sex ratio problem for each prefecture. This formula assumes that (a) Japanese men and women will marry only once, (b) never get divorced, and (c) 28-year-old men will marry only 23-year-old women (Suzuki 1989). The 1989 crude divorce rate in Japan was stable at only 1.37 per 1000 population compared to 3.6 times as much in the United States so the first assumption is highly realistic. The second assumption, as we shall see, is much less realistic. However, Suzuki's 1988 figures for the proportion of Japanese males who will never marry illustrates the huge sex-ratio gap that declining birth rates have encouraged. The highly unrealistic ideals currently held by youth probably more than offset any sex-ratio overestimates.

The major cities of Tōkyō and Ōsaka are the worst places for men to find mates. Suzuki's measure suggests that over one-fourth of 28-year-old men in Tōkyō will not find 23-year-old mates. By contrast, the best chances for men occur in such rural prefectures as Wakayama, Yamacata, and Nara where roughly 12% can not find a 23-year-old mate. This is contrary to periodic newspaper accounts that decry the particular dirth of marriageable women in the countryside and that depict a foreign bridal market for farmers. The real problem is an urban phenomenon.

This apparent urban-rural contradiction fades away when one focuses on the particularly low status that farmers have in the Japanese marriage market. More than a paucity of young women forces farmers to import brides. What is more important, single Japanese women say they have no desire to marry farmers. The normative undesirability of farm life is one of Japan's most serious problems.

Although the government of Japan has a long standing platform to keep agriculture (and particularly rice) free of international competition, the Liberal Democratic Party is well aware that this is becoming impossible due to the disaffection of the young from farm life. By the year 2000, the Japanese government estimates that there will be only 75% of the farm labor necessary to keep its present agricultural policy viable. Young Japanese men and women rank farming extremely low as an occupational choice. The young men do not want to farm and the young women do not want to marry farmers.

Note that the sex-ratio estimates in Figure 4—1 paint a picture quite the opposite of the United States where big cities attract women in search of jobs and mates causing huge sex-ratio problems for women. Eighty-five single men per 100 single women is a typical ratio for the largest American cities. In Japan, by contrast, first-rate jobs cluster in such large metropolitan areas as Tōkyō and Ōsaka, and occupational sex discrimination works against female entry into high-status occupations (Brinton 1988). Thus, Japanese cities are much more attractive to single males than females leading to sex-ratio problems more unfavorable for single men than women.

Ignoring Japanese sex-ratio realities for the moment, consider the educational level of the ideal wife among young, never-married Japanese men. Some 98% say they desire women who are either junior college graduates (if they themselves are college graduates) or who have less than a high school education (if the men are high school graduates). Even more telling is the fact that few male college graduates indicate they desire women who graduated from four-year colleges or universities. Figure 4—2, which lists the number of males per 100 female high school students advancing on to college in 1984, illustrates the totally unrealistic nature of this strong educational norm.

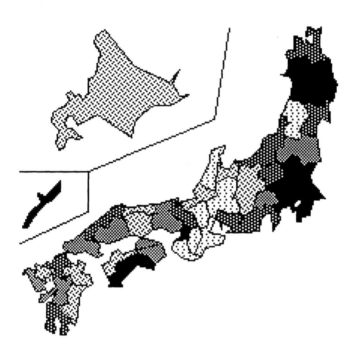

Tōkyō	27.3	Niigata	17.9	Ehime	15.8
Kanagawa	22.6	Fukuoka	17.4	Miyazaki	15.8
Saitama	20.9	Aomori	17.2	Toyama	15.5
Okinawa	20.5	Kagoshima	17.0	Ōita	15.3
Ibaraki	20.3	Shimane	17.0	Fukui	15.1
Chiba	20.2	Tokushima	16.9	Nagano	15.0
Kōchi	19.5	Yamanashi	16.7	Okayama	15.0
Iwate	19.0	Nagasaki	16.6	Saga	15.0
Ōsaka	18.9	Hyōgo	16.3	Ishikawa	14.9
Tochigi	18.7	Kumamoto	16.3	Gifu	14.8
Akita	18.6	Yamaguchi	16.2	Mie	14.1
Gunma	18.4	Kagawa	16.1	Shiga	13.9
Shizuoka	18.4	Hiroshima	16.0	Wakayama	13.7
Kyōto	18.2	Fukushima	16.0	Yamagata	13.0
Miyagi	18.1	Hokkaidō	15.9	Nara	12.8
Aichi	18.0	Tottori	15.9		

Figure 4—1 The Percentage of the Male Population Who Can Be Expected Never to Marry Based on 1985 Data.

In all but four (the essentially rural prefectures of Tottori, Hokkaidō, Yamagata, and Ishikawa) of the 47 prefectures, the number of young women going on to college equals or exceeds that of young men. This leaves the men with little choice but to consider marrying women with at least as much education as themselves, or breaking the age-bracket norms.

Although Chapter 3 demonstrated that the vast majority of those female college entrants went to junior colleges, this figure visualizes the problem facing young, unmarried Japanese men. The most advantageous scenario is that of Tottori where for 100 women who advance on to college there are 114 high school males who do the same. At the most disadvantageous extreme is Kōchi where, for 100 female college entrants, only 61 young men enter college. Assume for a moment a demographic equality in the number of marriageable men and women (which is certainly not the case in Japan). This implies that some 40 young men per 100 women in Kōchi must marry women with more education than themselves. However, the reality is even worse if we consider the fact that 20% of the men in Kōchi can never expect to marry simply because the pool of young men age 28 is that much larger than the pool of 23-year-old women.

This implies a worst-case scenario in which either roughly half of the young men in Kōchi may never get married or they will have to drastically change the standards for their ideal mates. Note that Tōkyō has roughly the same worst-case scenario of close to 50% of young marriageable men who should have trouble finding mates 5 years their junior and who also have less education than themselves. If there was a no overlap of worst-case instances, Tōkyō would end up having the dimmest prospects of 27% of its young men trying to find a mate.

The best-case scenario is Yamagata with the most advantageous combination of a low ratio of men who can never get married to a high ratio of men to women who go to college. Still, nearly 13%, or one of every eight, of all Yamagata men are never likely to marry without seriously bending their age and educational standards. Note that the most urbanized areas such as the greater Tōkyō and Ōsaka metropolitan areas present particularly great challenges for young men who wish to find women with less education than themselves.

The irony is that there is a weak inverse relationship between the marriage squeeze and the male-to-female ratio for college attendance ($r = -0.29$) across the 47 prefectures. Thus, the fewer men per 100 women who matriculate into college, the more exacerbated the marriage-squeeze problem. Earlier chapters noted that Japanese parents consider college education a male prerogative, and hence they push their sons more than their daughters to go to college. Hodge and Ogawa (1991, pp. 74—75) point out that the gap between the educational levels of wives and husbands has been shrinking over the past three decades. Their time-series data agree with the basic thesis of this chapter: Prospective wives, by catching up with (and surpassing) prospective husbands in educational attainment, have unwittingly created more of a marriage squeeze problem for men over time.

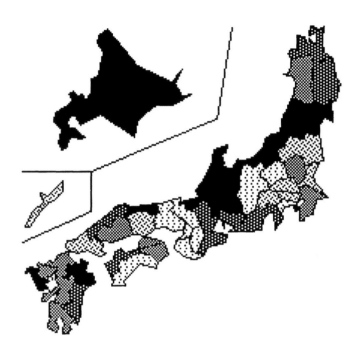

Tottori	113.92	Mie	89.97	Yamanashi	79.04
Hokkaidō	108.90	Shiga	88.43	Tōkyō	79.01
Yamagata	107.18	Iwate	88.21	Fukushima	78.54
Ishikawa	102.30	Miyazaki	88.15	Ibaraki	76.89
Fukui	100.64	Akita	86.18	Kagawa	75.90
Toyama	100.62	Hiroshima	85.48	Yamaguchi	75.52
Niigata	100.54	Kagoshima	85.25	Kanagawa	75.28
Gifu	100.00	Saga	84.39	Gunma	75.21
Miyagi	100.00	Tochigi	83.46	Wakayama	73.01
Nagasaki	98.88	Fukuoka	83.09	Nara	72.79
Ōita	95.41	Chiba	81.51	Hyōgo	70.09
Shimane	95.19	Kumamoto	81.16	Nagano	65.99
Aomori	95.65	Tokushima	80.45	Ōsaka	65.66
Aichi	93.44	Okayama	79.49	Kyōto	65.54
Ehime	91.43	Okinawa	79.24	Kōchi	60.93
Shizuoka	90.61	Saitama	79.15		

Figure 4—2   Males per 100 Female High School Students Matriculating to College in 1984

There is essentially no relationship (r = 0.08) between the male-to-female ratios of high school graduates and college matriculates. This suggests that high school graduates ought to be analyzed separately from college matriculates. Men who complete only high school desire wives without high school diplomas; college-educated men desire women with high school or junior college degrees. So it is wise to consider the plight of high-school-educated men separately from college-educated men.

Figure 4—3 demonstrates that there are only 17 prefectures in which there are more male than female graduates from high schools. This data indicates how slim the male high school graduate pickings are. At best, graduating seniors in Yamanashi have a surplus of only 13 male high-school graduates per 100 female high-school graduates with the luxury of marrying women without high-school degrees of the same age in Yamanashi. The remaining 30 Prefectures are inhospitable to the typical Japanese man's dream wife.

A comparison with the United States is informative. In the United States, young men desire women with roughly the same educational background. (Anderson, Bagarozzi, & Giddings 1986; Cahn 1989; Pursell, Banikiotes, & Sebastian 1981). The reason is that American college graduates say they prefer a woman who will be an intellectual companion: that is, a woman who will have roughly equal education as themselves and thus, with whom they can share experiences. Thus, American men, unlike their Japanese counterparts, rank such individual traits as perceived understanding, similarity in intelligence, and sense of humor as important mate-qualities. American men also rank dyadic similarities such as trust and social, physical, and task attraction as important.

Still, educational and age homophily remain strong components of actual mate and friendship selection in the United States (Liedka 1991, pp. 463—464) although not as strong as these more qualitative indicators of ideal mates. Anderson and his colleagues (1986) report the results of constructing an ideal mate scale using American college students that provide interesting cross-cultural reference. The six dimensions, in rank order of importance, in this scale are (1) emotional gratification and support (e.g., My spouse is caring); (2) sex-role orientation and physical attraction items (e.g., My spouse is sexually attractive); (3) spousal satisfaction (e.g., My spouse satisfies me intellectually); (4) emotional maturity (e.g., My spouse is emotionally healthy); (5) intelligence (e.g., My spouse is as intelligent as I am); and lastly (6) homogamy (e.g., My spouse is approximately the same age as I am). Data split by the sex of American respondents shows similar ideals while the Japanese data suggest gender differences for ideal mates.

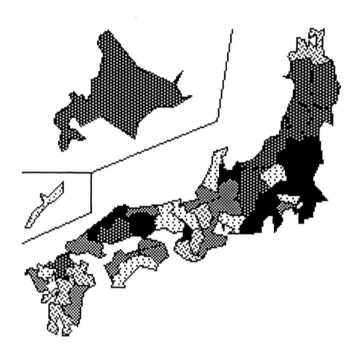

Yamanashi	113.21	Yamagata	100.09	Aomori	98.04
Tochigi	108.45	Fukuoka	99.94	Kagoshima	97.95
Saitama	107.76	Miyagi	99.68	Shiga	97.50
Ōsaka	105.53	Niigata	99.51	Kagawa	97.47
Shimane	104.83	Tottori	99.49	Nara	97.40
Toyama	102.58	Miyazaki	99.44	Ōita	97.37
Chiba	102.25	Gifu	99.22	Saga	97.13
Shizuoka	101.66	Kanagawa	99.13	Kōchi	96.81
Ibaraki	101.56	Fukui	99.10	Aichi	95.99
Fukushima	101.26	Mie	99.00	Ishikawa	95.62
Okayama	101.24	Tokushima	98.71	Kyōto	95.53
Hokkaidō	101.23	Nagasaki	98.69	Gunma	94.51
Iwate	101.05	Ehime	98.60	Okinawa	94.37
Hiroshima	100.62	Yamaguchi	98.60	Tōkyō	90.89
Nagano	100.58	Kumamoto	98.59	Hyōgo	89.06
Akita	100.53	Wakayama	98.07		

Figure 4—3   The Number of Males per 100 Female High School Graduates in 1988.

Although Americans are presently much less restrictive in what they say are their educational and age restrictions than Japanese, this was not always the case. It is worth noting that demographic trends in the United States show a long-term rise in age-homogamy. The average American female was 4.1 years younger than her husband at first marriage in 1890. However, only 1.8 years separated men and women entering their first marriage by 1978 (Government Printing Office 1965, p. 45; Government Printing Office 1980, p. 83). American youths do not rank age as important, but their behavior implies that it makes quite a difference. By contrast, growing American gender differences in educational attainment have become a problem. Women are more likely than men to graduate from high school in the United States. Also, for all races, women surpassed men in college attendance during the early 1980s (Cheatham 1986).

Table 4—1

Results of a Regression of the Male-to-Female Ratio for College Matriculation and Suzuki's Marriage Squeeze index on the Age-Specific Marriage Rate for Men ages 25—29.

Variable	Betas
M/F College Matriculation	0.22
Marriage Squeeze Index	-0.59*

$r^2 = 0.48$

*at least twice the standard error of the beta

Table 4—1 presents a test of the marriage prospects of single Japanese men based on the discussion in this chapter section. Recall that regression analysis provides a pseudo-experimental way of separating the effects of alleged independent variables on some dependent variable. In this case, we focus on variation in the age-specific marriage rate for men ages 25 through 29. The educational background of women stands out prominently in men's answers. Thus, this table demonstrates the influence of the ratios of men per 100 women who go to college versus a measure of the proportion of single men who can never get married due to the decreasing Japanese birth rate (Suzuki 1989) .

Table 4—1 suggests that the independent effects of the ratio of males per 100 females matriculating into college (Beta = 0.22) and of the marriage-squeeze index (Beta = -0.59) are in the predicted directions. However, the net effect of the marriage squeeze is almost three times as strong in depressing young men from marrying as the male-to-female ratio of college matriculation is in easing the task of men to find women with less education than themselves.

In total, these two predictors account for close to half of the variation in the marriage rate among men ages 25 to 28 across the 47 prefectures (r^2 = 0.48). The greater the proportion of men in their late twenties to women in their early twenties, the lower the chances that those men will marry. Those chances for marriage drop in prefectures where relatively more men than women enter college. One reason why this effect is only approximately one-third the size of the marriage squeeze effect is most probably because there are only four prefectures in which more men than women go to college.

THE STRENGTH OF THE JAPANESE (FEMALE) YEN

American women of all races have ideals that, in conjunction with their own increasing educational aspirations, have precipitated a decreasing pool of marriageable men. The reason appears to have less to do with perceptions of intellectual compatibility than with bread-winning security. Men of any nationality with less education are more likely to be laid off or fired. From this standpoint, women's preferences for husbands with college education are entirely rational.

The relationship of the Japanese educational system and economy parallels the American relation as we saw in Chapter Three. More education translates into more secure and better paying jobs. The infamous "lifetime" job security system (nenkō jōretsu) in Japan functions only for approximately one-fourth of all Japanese workers. This system has traditionally favored men who have attended one of the elite colleges or who have entered into a white-collar career-track in one of the largest and most prestigious industries. These industries depend upon sub-contracting to a huge temporary labor force composed largely of women, non-college educated men, and foreign laborers who suffer the consequences of part-time work, piece work, low wages, and layoffs (Gordon 1985; Hanami 1989; Imai & Itami 1988). Thus, if Japanese women are rational, we would expect them to make their future spouses' educational attainment, job security, and wage potential of the highest priority.

As expected, Japanese female norms mirror their American female counterparts. Ninety-one percent of Japanese women in the aforementioned national survey (Kōseishō 1989), regardless of education, indicated that they want a husband who is a university graduate. Because university graduation is a necessary condition for entry into the life-time, job-security system in Japan, this norm is a natural reflection of rational aspirations. Nevertheless, reality shortchanges women's aspirations. In 1988, the percentage of male high school graduates entering college ranged from 15% in Okinawa to 37% in Ehime with a prefectural median of 27%. At best, only one of 2.5 women in

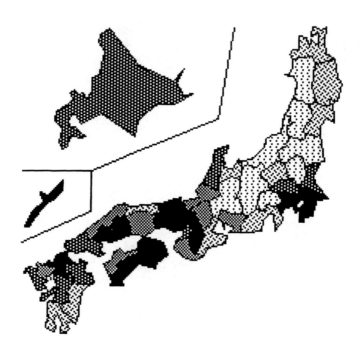

Tōkyō	11.3	Hokkaidō	8.4	Miyagi	7.8
Nara	10.8	Saitama	8.4	Kagoshima	7.7
Kanagawa	10.4	Okayama	8.4	Iwate	7.6
Okinawa	10.3	Yamaguchi	8.2	Aomori	7.5
Kyōto	10.0	Wakayama	8.2	Gifu	7.3
Fukuoka	9.3	Kagawa	8.2	Fukui	7.3
Kōchi	9.2	Ehime	8.1	Akita	7.2
Hyōgo	9.0	Saga	8.1	Ibaraki	7.2
Tokushima	8.9	Miyazaki	8.1	Niigata	7.1
Nagasaki	8.8	Shimane	8.0	Shizuoka	7.1
Chiba	8.8	Tottori	8.0	Gunma	7.1
Hiroshima	8.7	Shiga	7.9	Nagano	6.9
Kumamoto	8.6`	Yamanashi	7.8	Yamagata	6.8
Ōita	8.6	Aichi	7.8	Fukushima	6.8
Ōsaka	8.5	Mie	7.8	Tochigi	6.7
Ishikawa	8.5	Toyama	7.8		

Figure 4—4   The Percentage of Employed Persons Age 15 and Older Who Were Engineers in 1988

Ehime can marry a college graduate; at worst, one in six Okinawan women. Northern Japan presents slimmer picking grounds educationally than western Japan by this measure.

Of course, college education is only a necessary and not a sufficient condition to enter the elite fourth of Japanese men with lifetime job security. Some occupations are more likely than others to secure the good life women desire of their ideal husbands. In recognition of such security, 69% of unmarried women in the above-mentioned poll said they prefer a husband who is an engineer, but 54% "would accept" a public servant or office worker as a second-best choice. American men and women typically react in disbelief to such preferences. They often ask why Japanese women do not rank physicians or lawyers at the top. First, recall from Chapter 3 that male high school seniors with the highest national college-entrance scores are routed into engineering schools in the most prestigious universities. In essence, engineering majors reflect the cream of the cream of college matriculates. Second, although medicine and law are close to the top in prestige of major (as reflected in college-entrance test scores) medical and legal job prospects do not match engineering in job security and pay. Industry rewards engineers with the highest starting pay. What is more important, it bestows the highest prospects of gaining lifetime employment upon engineers. Young, unmarried women's desires for a husband with high job security and pay perfectly replicate in marriage to engineers.

One of the distinctive features of Japan that American admirers often point to is the high proportion of college graduates with engineering expertise compared to the United States. In the United States engineering embraces about 1% of university degrees compared to roughly 10% in Japan. Thus, Japanese women have nearly 10 times an American women's chance of marrying an engineer. Of course, the chance of marrying an engineer still greatly mismatches the desire in Japan.

Figure 4—4 shows how chimerical the young women's marry-an-engineer ideal is. I double all of the figures to reflect the fact that only half of the population are males. The prefectures with few engineers are in rural areas such as Tochigi, Yamagata, and Fukushima where, at most, 13% of adult men work as engineers. The prefecture with the highest chance, not surprisingly, is Tōkyō with approximately a 22% chance. This clarifies part of the obvious attraction of Tōkyō for both men and women. It is the Mecca for high-prestige occupations. Yet even in Tōkyō less than one of three women can fulfill the dream of marrying an engineer (69%/22% = 31.4%).

Figure 4—5 displays the percentage of persons age 15 years old and over with professional and technical occupations by prefecture. This figure aids visualization of the obstacles to marrying an engineer among the 54% of young women who said a public servant or office worker would be an acceptable spouse. The range is from 13.6% in Tōkyō to 7.5% in Yamagata. Doubling these figures accounts for the fact that Japanese men fill virtually 100% of such occupations. It, thus, gives a crude idea of the actual percentage of men with professional or technical employment. The correlation between

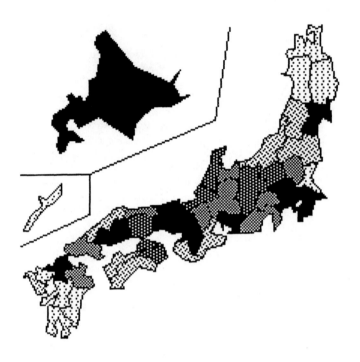

Tōkyō	13.6	Ibaraki	10.1	Aomori	9.1
Kanagawa	13.3	Hokkaidō	10.0	Tottori	9.0
Nara	12.2	Yamaguchi	9.9	Kagoshima	8.9
Okinawa	11.9	Kumamoto	9.9	Saga	8.9
Fukuoka	11.7	Kagawa	9.8	Mie	8.6
Kyōto	11.6	Okayama	9.8	Iwate	8.6
Hiroshima	11.1	Wakayama	9.7	Toyama	8.6
Tokushima	11.1	Ehime	9.7	Niigata	8.5
Chiba	11.0	Aichi	9.4	Tochigi	8.3
Kōchi	10.9	Shiga	9.4	Nagano	8.2
Hyōgo	10.8	Fukui	9.4	Yamanashi	8.1
Ōsaka	10.7	Shimane	9.4	Akita	8.1
Ōita	10.7	Miyazaki	9.3	Gifu	8.1
Ishikawa	10.5	Gunma	9.2	Fukushima	7.7
Nagasaki	10.4	Shizuoka	9.1	Yamagata	7.5
Saitama	10.3	Miyagi	9.1		

Figure 4—5 The Percentage of Employed Persons Age 15 and Older Who Were Employed in Professional or Technical Occupations in 1988

the data in Figures 4—4 and 4—5 is 0.93, confirming how the careers of choice occur only in particular prefectures. The large urban areas are clearly more attractive than rural areas as hunting grounds when it comes to prestigious careers. A woman's chance would be roughly fifty-fifty of meeting an engineer, government official, or office worker in Tōkyō but drops to one-in-four in such rural prefectures as Yamagata and Tochigi.

So far I have made the oversimplified assumption that effects outside those I have been illustrating are equal. However, this is not true. For example, the 0.36 correlation between the college-entrance sex ratio and the percentage of jobs that are professional or technical further illustrates the dilemma. Schools of higher education in urban areas disproportionately attract women because engineers occur there in the greatest numbers. Paradoxically, the worst chances of meeting a man with such qualifications are in those urban areas. This paradox of women's attraction to urban areas is well known in the United States as well. Ireland (1982) has shown that large urban cities such as New York and Washington, D.C. attract American women in search of eligible bachelors, creating intensified competition among women from the resulting narrowed pool of men.

To understand why, consider a hypothetical situation in which a city has one million male and 1.1 million female adults, or a sex ratio of 90.9. If 90% of the men marry, only 50% (200,000 women to 100,000 men) of the remaining single women can find any spousal prospects. The dilemma is: the higher the rate of marriage in a society, the poorer the marriage prospects for the larger group among the remaining pool of unmarried persons. Now assume that this hypothetical city is the center for extremely attractive jobs that attract 5,000 new male applicants and 15,000 women in search of a spouse. The new chance of an unmarried woman finding a husband drops to an even poorer 48.8%.

Recall that over half of single women say they would accept an office worker or public servant as a second-best solution. Figure 4—5 gives a good approximation for the problems single women face because the correlations between professional-technical occupations and such jobs are very strong. The correlations range from 0.64 with managerial jobs to 0.75 with employment in sales. The percentage of Japanese over age 14 employed in managerial positions ranges from 3.0 in Aomori to 7.0 in Tōkyō. For sales and related positions, the comparable rates are from 11.1% in Nagano to 18.4% in Ōsaka. One can easily see once again why women from rural areas relocate to cities where the chances are up to twice as good as back home for finding an ideal mate. Indeed, closer inspection of all of the associated maps indicates that the male-dominated occupations that are most attractive to single women in search of a mate proliferate chiefly in the Greater Tōkyō and Ōsaka areas.

By contrast, American women are much less restrictive in educational and occupational restrictions for potential mates. As with American men, they prefer a spouse with similar educational and family background to their own. Americans rarely mention specific occupational requirements. The next chapter section suggests social structural reasons why they are much less fussy than Japanese women.

Table 4—2 presents the results of correlational analyses of male occupational categories with marriage rates of women in their early twenties. Regression analysis is not a recommended method in this case because of high associations between many of the occupational categories. For example, the correlation between percentages of managers and clerks is 0.93. Such powerful correlations can cause misleading results in regression analysis.

Table 4—2

Correlations for Types of Occupations with the Age-Specific Marriage Rate for Women ages 20—24 and the Mean Average Age at Marriage for Women

Variable	Marriage Rate	Mean Age
% Scientists/Engineers	-0.13	0.04
% Professional/Technical	-0.63	0.39
% Managers	-0.58	0.30
% Clerks	-0.60	0.30
% Sales	-0.69	0.31
% Farmers	0.47	-0.05
% Craftmen	0.27	-0.49
% Self-Employed	0.33	-0.10
% Workers at Home	0.44	-0.12

A comparison of correlations across columns suggests consistent support for the effects of young, single women's desires to marry into the more prestigious occupations. All of the negative correlations in column two suggest that the higher the ratio of women in their early twenties who marry, the lower the probabilities that they will marry a man with a relatively prestigious occupation. By contrast, the longer they wait, as reflected in higher mean average ages at marriage, the more chance they have of marrying a man who is in a more prestigious occupation. The main exception is for marriage to scientists and engineers. However, these two correlations are not inconsistent with the sex-ratio thesis because I have already demonstrated the great impracticality of limiting one's choice to such a narrow pool of men. Clearly the lack of correlations in the scientist-engineer row suggests that women have little chance of marrying such men.

On the other hand, the last four rows of data in Table 4—2 suggest the value to young women of waiting as long as possible. Column two indicates that the earlier women marry the more chances that they will marry men with undesirable occupations. Families with self-employed men and family-owned businesses are particularly undesirable to young women. Lebra (1984, Pp. 84) suggests that young women turn down marriage proposals primarily when the groom-to-be is atotori (a successor to a family business) Japanese women because of the difficulties posed by "too many relatives." By contrast, the third column suggests that the longer women wait, the more chance they have of minimizing marriages to men with such undesirable occupations.

Consider the sum-total dilemma first from the standpoint of the average Japanese single woman's dreams. If 91% of Japanese men were university graduates, 69% were engineers, and the number of 28-year-old men was exactly equal to the number of women age 23, there would be many fewer problems for either sex in Japan. However, only about 25% of Japanese men are college graduates, 5% of whom are engineering graduates, and there are on average 15% more men age 28 than women age 23. These structural features impede women from finding the ideal mate in a society where marriage is extremely important for male career advancement.

The most interesting part of the Guttentag and Secord (1983) thesis concerns the effects of extreme sex-ratios on individual behavior. The reason is that sex-ratios reflect relative supply and demand of men and women. A sex-ratio that favors women as it does in Japan should allow women more individual independence because their relatively lower supply makes them more valuable. By contrast, the overabundance of marriageable young Japanese men makes them into less valuable "commodities." The Japanese press blames the growing independence of single women on their familial upbringing, but the sex-ratio thesis suggests that the relative scarcity of women is a more parsimonious explanation for the changing roles of women and men in Japanese society because other societies with similar ratios during other historical periods have produced similar behaviors.

Figure 4—6 visualizes the results of another regression analysis that summarizes the main threads of the argument expressed so far. This analysis suggests that the higher the ratio of men to women, the higher the rate at which women marry near the ideal age of 23. Population density also affects the marriage rate, although negatively. Higher population densities would seem, on the surface, to increase marriage prospects because they increase the size of the pool. However, population density reflects the worst marriage squeeze ratios. That is, the most urbanized areas of Japan have the highest ratios of young men age 28 to women age 23. Such areas give women the correct impression that the "fishing" is better and so women in such areas may feel that they can well wait until the right "fish" comes along. Still, there are other characteristics of high-density areas that probably add to the low marriage rate among women ages 20 through 24. For instance, higher density areas require longer commutes, have higher proportions of jobs that require longer working hours, and allow for greater anonymity. All of these characteristics reduce the chances of finding a mate.

Interestingly, the negative correlation between the Suzuki marriage-squeeze index and the age-specific marriage rate for females age 20-25 reduces to statistical non-significance in the regression analysis. All other statistical associations remain significant at beyond the 0.001 level. The unfavorable effects of population density outweigh the effects of larger ratios of males to females in college. This also helps explain why fewer women have been marrying at ideal ages in recent years. Thus, this regression supports the rationality of later over early marriage that we saw in Table 4—2 earlier. Women gain significantly more chance of finding a good prospect by waiting.

Adding to the power of women in Japan is the trend toward greater female work-force participation. This has increased their economic independence which in turn has allowed them greater options to postpone marriage, further reducing the number of women of age 23 who want to marry at that age. In 1990, the average age of Japanese grooms had increased only slightly to 0.4 years above the cultural ideal of 28 years of age, while the average bride was 2.7 years older than the ideal age of 23. Men are finding it necessary to marry women 2.3 years younger than themselves rather than the 5 years they would prefer. Also, the age of marriage in Japan has become the highest in world, after surpassing Sweden in 1990. There is every reason to believe that the demand created by unfavorable sex-ratios and unrealistic norms will further reduce the differences in ages of Japanese men and women and increase the age at first marriage.

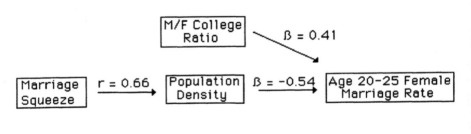

Figure 4—6   Path Diagram of the Major Determinants of Marriage for Women Age 20-24

To understand why, consider the breakdown of the mean 1985 age at first marriage by prefecture for men. As one would expect from the above theory, Tōkyō has the highest mean age of 29.0, and all of the remaining highest ages are in prefectures within commuting distance, following by the prefectures in the Kansai area surrounding, and including, Ōsaka. In essence, the two metropolitan areas that include nearly two-thirds of the total Japanese population already had mean ages at marriage in 1985 that were 0.6 years above the 1990 country average. The lowest mean average ages at marriage were in rural prefectures such as Kagawa (27.6) and Okayama (27.6). The correlation between mean age at first marriage of Japanese women and men is 0.75 reflecting the desires of both sexes to marry as close as possible to their ideal. However, the square of that correlation, 0.57, which gives the amount of one variable predictable from the other, illustrates how poorly this desire matches reality. If every Japanese could marry the person of at least the ideal age then we would expect a perfect 1.0 correlation. The large amount of unpredictability in this correlation suggests looking at the age differences at first marriage across prefectures.

Figure 4—7 shows the mean spousal difference in age at first marriage for 1985. The range is from 2.1 years in Miyazaki to 3.1 in Shiga. A larger difference is closer to the ideal, suggesting that the central part of Japan surrounding Ōsaka with its superb transportation system gives young people an advantage in marrying closer to the national ideal. By contrast, more rural regions of Japan appear to have more homogamous age-based marriages due to their less-than-ideal marriage markets. Tōkyō is relatively well off on this measure, but individuals living or working in the Tōkyō area have a mass transportation system that at least partially offsets the disadvantages of its particular age-specific marriage sex-ratio. One of those disadvantages is the sheer size of Tōkyō. As one of the world's largest cities, size creates a great likelihood that unmarried Tōkyō residents know individuals who are having a difficult time finding a suitable marriage prospect. The result is a psychological intensification of the actual social problem. Hodge and Ogawa (1991, p. 112) corroborate this viewpoint with the observation that "[t]he numerous choices available in metropolitan areas probably increase the difficulty in making a final commitment." Signs of the individual-level experience of desperation occur throughout the popular press. Many single men who reach the ages 30 to 35 without marrying have become __desperate__ in looking for wives in part because they look at single life as preventing them from job promotion. Some run photographs and vital statistics in women's magazines listing their age, interests, desirable mate traits, etc.

These ads suggest that most young Japanese men remain unaware of (a) actual sex-ratio prospects and (b) changing expectations among single women. Young women in Japan have long been quite choosy about their marriage partner's educational background, economic situation, appearance, and status. However, unknown to most men here, the quintennial National Fertility Surveys of the 1980s (Kōseishō 1989) indicate that young unmarried women are becoming even more choosy.

This chapter posits that women's rising expectations are a function of changing age-specific sex ratios that have made them into an increasingly valuable commodity. Guttentag and Secord's (1983) thesis suggests that whichever sex is the relative minority enjoys comparative power and freedom. Thus, it is no accident that young, unmarried Japanese women continue to make up a larger portion of the high-school graduation, college-matriculation, and the full-time labor pools in spite of cries by politicians

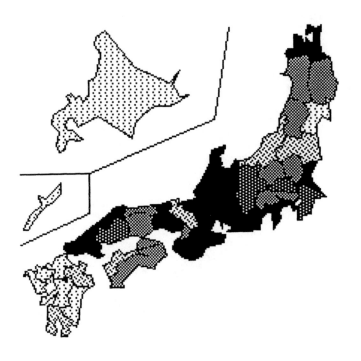

Shiga	3.1	Hiroshima	2.8	Iwate	2.6
Ishikawa	3.1	Nagano	2.8	Kyōto	2.6
Gifu	3.0	Chiba	2.8	Niigata	2.5
Mie	3.0	Saitama	2.8	Kagoshima	2.5
Wakayama	3.0	Ōsaka	2.7	Ōita	2.5
Aichi	3.0	Okayama	2.7	Ehime	2.5
Fukui	2.9	Tottori	2.7	Fukushima	2.5
Toyama	2.9	Kagawa	2.7	Saga	2.4
Shizuoka	2.9	Tochigi	2.7	Miyagi	2.4
Kanagawa	2.8	Tokushima	2.7	Hokkaidō	2.3
Ibaraki	2.8	Yamanashi	2.7	Fukuoka	2.3
Aomori	2.8	Tōkyō	2.7	Nagasaki	2.2
Yamaguchi	2.8	Kōchi	2.6	Kumamoto	2.2
Shimane	2.8	Yamagata	2.6	Okinawa	2.1
Nara	2.8	Akita	2.6	Miyazaki	2.1
Hyōgo	2.8	Gunma	2.6		

Figure 4—7 The Difference in Mean Age at First Marriage in 1985

that a woman's place is in the home. The Japanese labor market experienced decades of labor shortages from 1960 until 1990 because employers discriminated in favor of men. As the shortage reached critical proportions, the educational and work-force markets opened up to women, however reluctantly.

The result is that single women became a powerful force in the Japanese economy during its expansionary period. Women gained a measure of relative economic stability that allowed them the largest disposable income of any Japanese group because they largely lived with their parents freeing them to save large portions of their money for such things as clothes and travel. This large group of single women naturally desires a mate who will provide the economic stability to maintain the high quality of life they enjoy as singles.

Thus, it should not be surprising that single women say they want a husband who can provide them with the economic stability to maintain the high quality of life they enjoy as a single (Kōseishō 1989). Of course, this desire is unrealistic because the salary necessary for this good life is well beyond the means of virtually any single man in Japan. For example, according to Altmann, Inc., one of the largest computerized matchmaking services in Japan, many women specify on their applications that they are looking for a man with an annual income of over ¥10 million ($48,780).[2] When Altmann personnel tell them that is unrealistic they simply check off the next highest category of ¥6 million ($29,268), while only 13.3% of all male Altmann applicants claim an annual income of over ¥6 million. Ironically, the choice of an annual salary of ¥10 million is highly realistic for the type of life the typical single woman wishes to continue. Her parents are likely to have bought their present dwelling at a time when land prices were relatively reasonable and, in any case, she doesn't have to worry about paying for expensive housing. However, a young couple starting out in Japan must face a housing market that has become out-of-reach for all but the very rich.

Single women in the Ministry of Health and Welfare polls (Kōseishō 1989) also say they want to have two children and that they do not expect to have careers after marriage. Yet both of these desires are impossible dreams for the average Japanese woman as evidenced by the decreasing average number of children per couple and the increasing numbers of married women among the ranks of the employed. Single women confuse their relatively favorable age-specific chance of marriage compared to men with the chance of marrying their ideal mate. The outcome is postponement of marriage by masses of single women in search of a non-existent "Mr. Right."

Adding to the dilemma is the increasing relative personal freedom experienced by single women today as a fruit of their advantageous sex-ratio status. Because Japanese families are much smaller than in the past, boys

---

[2]Altmann, Inc.pioneered the growing marriage information service (kekkon jōhō sābisu) industry. From a zero-base, this industry grew to over 5000 businesses with more than 250,000 registered persons during the 1980s.

whose families own small businesses experience great pressures to take over these businesses when their parents retire. Young women are extremely reluctant to marry a young man whose parents run a small business, even if their husband-to-be is not currently working for his family. They fear the future pressures to have sons and their families return to inherit the relative insecurity of such businesses. Another fear is the great lack of freedom they would experience as a member of the households of their husbands' parents. This automatically eliminates about 12% of Japanese families from consideration. The percentage of households with 6 or more members gives a good approximation to such three-generation situations. In 1985 this variable ranged from 4% in Tōkyō to 20% in Yamagata. Households with six or more inhabitants are most prevalent in rural prefectures. Thus, even though the more urban prefectures have very small portions of such households, the large prevalence of three-generation households in rural areas probably puts further strains on marriage prospects because young women "red-line" rural areas as sources of husbands, further reducing the pool of eligible bachelors.

Comparisons of the Institute of Population Problems (Kōseishō 1989) survey results over time confirm this trend. Although the trend in number of young people willing to live with either set of parents in 1988 dropped for both men and women compared to the survey done five years previously, it fell most drastically for young women (pp. 53-54). Furthermore, young women are much more reluctant than young men to accept living quarters with parents; 62% of men would accept such circumstances compared to only 41% of women. These differences become clearer still when broken down by urban-rural location of respondents. When broken down by rural area, urban area of 200,000 or less, and urban area of greater than 200,000 population, there are no demonstrable differences between male respondents. Women, by contrast, show increasing reluctance to live with the parents of their spouse after marriage, in more urban areas.

A maxim of sociology is that modernization creates great pressures toward democratization. Democratization of the sexes is no exception. The studies by Anderson (1986) and others indicate the normative pressures toward physical, social, and psychological homogamy in American marriages. Analysis of Detroit area survey data (Thornton & Freedman 1979) shows that among women, younger ones, those with more education, those with better-educated husbands, and those who have work experience show the greatest movement toward egalitarian marital and familial roles. That is, it is precisely younger, more educated, working American women who desire husbands with whom they can share their life.

Thus, it should come as no surprise that the Ministry of Health and Welfare survey results (Kōseishō 1989) confirm similar trends among single women in Japan. Young Japanese women say they wish closer intellectual and emotional companionship with their spouses than previous generations. They are less willing to marry men who would limit their personal freedom. And they want more sharing of familial responsibilities. These are all signs of change that perfectly match Guttentag and Secord's theoretical expectations. The relative lack of autonomy on the part of women in responding to marriage proposals of the past has given way to more options over the past two or three decades (Lebra, 1984, Pp. 113). Women of marriageable age do not present themselves as helpless about their marital destiny, as pressured into marriage by the "surrounding" situation, or as devoid of self-interest and conjugal love as their mothers' generation.

As single Japanese women gain the power to more easily express their personal choices, single men should lose such power. Hence, young Japanese men view marriage not as a personal right but as a social obligation — an obligation to meet their parents' expectations and to obtain trust and promotion at their companies. There are numerous ways that single men show the most interest (and, hence, less power) in spousal choice. One is in their use of personal want ads in the search for a wife. As examples, look at a local American alternative newspaper. It is likely to contain personals such as the following ones from single males gleaned from the St. Louis The Riverfront Times (February 12-18, 1992):

> . . .caring, cuddly, kindly disrespectful, cynical. If a special look while in a crowd, a gentle touch just for contact, relaxed times, and freedom to do your own thing are important, contact F-12397.

> What complicated winds blow through the climate of the female mind? Fill my sails with: Nostalgia, intelligence, honesty, sensitivity, passion, fun, sensuousness and love. . . F-12383

> Searching for a great lover. No sleazy affairs. Must be available for a regular, physical relationship of unlimited surroundings. Not looking for a commitment. . . Please send letter stating what makes you a great lover with revealing photo. F-12397

It is difficult to imagine such letters in a Japanese publication. The letters in McKinstry (1991) are much more innocent and resemble the America of the 1950s. The above letters illustrate the relative power low-sex ratios give to American single men compared to Japanese bachelors.

Another difference is the disproportionate male registrations with marriage bureaus that can cost ¥300,000 ($1,463) for a two-year membership. The advertisements used by these marriage bureaus appear mostly targeted at men.[3] Personnel who work at these marriage bureaus invariably note that the men display characteristic signs of powerlessness — lack of social skills, passion, and assertiveness — that Guttentag and Secord's theory predicts given the huge oversupply of bachelors in Japan. The matchmaking fees charged for men also reflect the oversupply of men; women pay about half of the $60 to $110 fee charged to men to attend computerized matchmaking parties.

---

[3]The interested reader may wish to look at the special article on computerized matchmaking that ran in issue #11 of Mangajin (Ito, Murray, & Loveless 1991) in which various advertisements are displayed and translated into English.

According to U.S. Census figures, there are roughly 94 single men per 100 single women at age 25. This implies that men are a scarce resource in the United States compared to women who are in oversupply. By age 35 the ratio of unmarried men to women leaves about 70 unmarried men per 100 unmarried women. This creates pressures on American women to accept less than women in Japan. Part of the problem America has with illegitimate children, and abortions may be blamed on the demographic pressures women experience to find a mate from a too-small pool of eligible men. Single women, as they age become more likely to accept a man's demands for sex on first dates because they are desperate to find a spouse (Ireland 1982). Likewise, in Japan, men must accept less than they prefer if they are to find women to marry.

Before World War I, many young American men felt pressure to carry on the family business or farm and women often moved into their spouses' parents homes much like in Japan. Until this century there were matchmakers similar to the traditional nakōdo in Japan. Such films as Citizen's Kane or the musical The Matchmaker remind us of the remnants of this old Western custom. However, the high mobility required by industrialization eroded this tradition (Goode 1963). The Institute of Population Problems surveys also suggest the erosion of the nakōdo tradition, although not as fast as sociologists of the family predicted (Goode 1987). As many as 40% of young married persons claim to have met their mate through miai.[4] Nevertheless,Kojima (1991, p. 4) points out that the large majority of miai marriages are not really arranged in the traditional sense. Instead, young people use the term to refer to any formally arranged meeting by members of the older generation (e.g., bosses, relatives, teachers, and even matrimonial agencies). By contrast, youths conceive of ren'ai matches as informal introductions by persons of the same or younger generation (e.g., siblings, colleagues, and friends).

Lebra (1984: pp. 87-92) also delineates how ren'ai and miai marriages are not mutually exclusive. She found few cases of "unquestioned compliance" among her female respondents; only five women, all in their 70s stated that they had accepted the proposal of a nakōdo without question. The second type was "coercive compliance." Four other women who were a little younger accepted the nakōdo's proposal but felt coerced to marry the mediator's choice. Thus, Lebra classified these women into a "coercive compliance" pattern. The third pattern was "rationalized consent" which usually implied acceptance of the mediator's proposal without mediation based on feelings of personal liability such as timing of age and tekireiki (ideal or appropriate timing for marriage), or senior-sib rank, or socioeconomic status and prestige of the proposal. All of these reasons are extrinsic to the person of the groom. A final pattern was one of "controlled choice" that embodied more intrinsic

---

[4]Lebra (1984, P. 103) describes miai as a series of precautionary measures used to minimize the risk of a marriage that would prove embarrassing to the families of the proposed union. Typically each family secretly collects information regarding family background, including the kōseki, or house register.

acceptance of the woman's fate. The mediator introduced the two principles, and in course of interaction they came to like each other. By the time of the wedding both informants believed they had met through miai. Lebra concluded that two orthogonal continuums of compliance-autonomy and unmediated-mediated underlies these four types   (p. 98).

Appropriateness of the age of marriage is also an interesting indicator of cultural norms. Japanese refer to the "appropriate" time of marriage with the term tekireiki. The idea is firmly entrenched that remaining single is odd and marriage is inevitable. This type of idea existed in the United States in the not-so-distant past. Before World War I, American women who were not married by age 23 were often referred to as "old maids" or "spinsters," again suggesting historic similarities shared by the United States and Japan. However, American women no longer feel such intense pressures to marry at young ages as in the past.

Similarly, American companies no longer intensely pressure young male employees to marry. For example, in the 1950s, William F. Whyte wrote a classic book called The Organization Man (1956). Whyte wrote about how necessary it was to marry "the right sort of woman" to advance up the corporate ladder. Corporate mogul expects junior men on the move up the ladder of organizational advancement to marry a women who would do all the "right" things to help her husband advance: have children, raise those children properly, entertain her husband's business associates at home, keep the house clean and beautiful, belong to the "right" clubs and women's organizations (those that would advance her husband's career).

Because of the strong institutionalization of a marriageable age in Japan, one might well expect higher marriage rates in Japan. However, this is not true; as we shall see in the next chapter, higher divorce rates cause higher marriage rates. On the other hand, Figure 4—8 suggests that the marriage squeeze in Japan may very well be reducing crude marriage rates in spite of strong cultural norms favoring marriage by certain ages. This figure indicates that Japanese rates paralleled changes in American ones from 1925 until 1960. Throughout the 1960s and early half of the 1970s, the rates were virtually the same. However, since 1975, Japanese rates have steadily dropped. Of course, there are many possible influences upon such trends, but the drop is consistent with the thesis of a Japanese marriage squeeze.

Tekireiki involves social pressures on single men and women to marry at normatively appropriate ages. Salaried workers who are young and unmarried feel very strong pressures from their companies to marry. Businesses do not like to send single men abroad. Unattached males are regarded as less stable and reliable, loose cannons as it were. The organization-man syndrome of the American 1950s was very similar to the "Salariman" (actually the correct English word is "white-collar worker") phenomena of contemporary Japan. The Salariman phenomena will pass the way of the organization man. The reasons are several-fold. First, more women in Japan, as in the United States, are working after they get married and for the same reasons: To have enough money to buy a house and to educate their children. Although much higher percentages of Japanese than American women say they will not work after marriage, the actual rate of working in Japan for women is now similar to Western countries (Brinton 1988). Second, according to government survey results, more men in Japan, like in the United States, indicate that they would prefer to spend more time with their families. Young, married men are starting to question the post-World War II-imposed tradeoff of company loyalty for family time. Third, small, but increasing, numbers of young women in Japan now tell pollsters that they want an intellectual and emotional relationship with their husbands (Kōseishō 1989). The higher the level of education a woman attains in either the United States or Japan, the more likely she wants to have such an intimate relationship with her spouse. Ironically, most men in both countries would prefer their spouse to be a housewife and mother; but more educated women have other ideas in both countries.

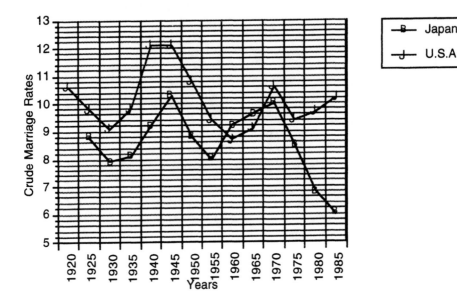

Figure 4—8.   Crude Marriage Rates for the United States and Japan from 1920-1985

Sources: Japan Statistical Yearbook, 1988; U.S. Department of Health and Human Services, Vital Statistics of the United States, 1985.

SUMMARY

This chapter demonstrates that the marriage-squeeze issue in Japan is much more complex and serious in consequences than early formulation using traditional sex-ratio measures based on age. It also shows consistent evidence that universal social structural factors provide superior explanations to popular individualistic explanations offered by the mass media.

National fertility poll results of ideal mates drawn from large random samples of Japanese youth underscore the social constraints imposed by demographic and ecological realities. They highlight the problems facing young men and women who wish to marry. The gap between ideals and reality forebodes longer investments of time necessary to search for a satisfactory mate and the role of the declining birth rates that continue to drive the present system.

Two of the most serious threats to the traditional male conception of an ideal mate are increases in the number of young women with more education than men and the oversupply of young men. These problems are greatest in the most populated regions of Tōkyō and Ōsaka. From a woman's perspective, a future husband's job security and earnings potential appear to be the driving forces underlying her expectations. However, there are neither enough single, male college graduates nor enough lifetime-security jobs available to satisfy the demand, even in urban areas such as Tōkyō. The data suggest that young women are entirely rational in delaying marriage. The longer young women delay marriage the greater the chance they have of escaping marriage to a man with low occupational status and the greater the chance of marrying a man of high occupational status.

These social forces, in conjunction with current oversupplies of young marriageable men, converge to give young women an unprecedented intoxication of power concerning marriage-market choice. The irony is that young women are correct in perceiving that they have relatively great choice in choice of spouse while their choices are not as good as they perceive. This over-perception of power leads them to delay marriage in their searches for suitable prospects. The increasing delay in marriage of young women in turn has unintended, ill-effects. It creates great anxiety among young men who must spend greater financial and temporal resources in their efforts to get married. It gives women an illusion that they can ask for totally unrealistic things like exceptionally high living standards. And it automatically eliminates significant portions of young men from the pool of eligible bachelors because of the low status of their family background, further increasing the desperation of such men. In a sense, the irony is that the benefits of empowerment of females, while good at an individual level, clash with societal expectations which, at least in the short term, have serious consequences for such problems as how to increase the national birth rate and what to do about the fast graying of Japan.

Chapter 5

FAMILIAL CHANGE AND STABILITY

Japanese families achieved a replacement level of fertility at a rate unmatched in history. Within the decade following the war Japan achieved a spectacular 50% reduction in its crude birth rate. This feat is even more remarkable when set in the context of the general state of disorganization Japan found itself in 1946. The end of World War II left Japan with a shattered economy without raw materials or overseas markets (Taeuber, 1962). The 1991 crude birth rate of 1.53 continues the pattern of dropping births that demographers at the Ministry of Health and Welfare opine may bottom out at 1.38 by 1996, well below replacement level.

Although Japanese families have experienced social change with unprecedented rapidity, they have shown few such signs of stresses as high divorce and juvenile delinquency rates that sociologists normally equate with accelerated social change. This chapter employs the family life cycle to understand some major features of change and stability in the modern Japanese family. As in Chapter 4, this chapter offers reasons why official Japanese explanations of family change are less plausible than ones grounded in variations in social structure.

Japan has shown remarkable familial continuity in spite of extraordinary social change. As one example, the crude divorce rate was only 1.46 per 1000 population in 1900, dropped slightly to 1.04 in 1973, and yet was still only a minuscule 1.26 in 1988. This evidence of a generally stable divorce rate over nearly a century is unmatched among industrial societies. Sociological prognosticators have also had a particularly poor record in predicting the institutional demise of the three-generation household and the arranged marriage system in Japan (Goode, 1963; 1987). In essence, the structure of the Japanese family life cycle continues to delight researchers with the challenge of its complexity. In some respects it shows spectacular change unlike that of other countries. In other ways it demonstrates an ordinary constancy.

The typical Japanese family life cycle is highly predictable. Cohort analysis suggests clear generational change associated with the increasing urbanization and growing affluence of Japanese. Hodge and Ogawa (1991, p. 111) demonstrate that younger cohorts of Japanese women are becoming "more likely to work before marriage, to contract marriages in the free market, and to establish neolocal households after marriage." Chapter 4 considered a few of the major dynamics of marriage markets in Japan and showed consistent evidence that the dynamics underlying the Japanese marriage market are remarkably similar to those driving the American market, in spite of numerous superficial differences. It discusses popular Japanese explanations of why Japanese men and women have increasingly postponed marriage, and offers more likely reasons. The present chapter turns to a consideration of married Japanese.

Because women typically enter marriage as workers but quickly drop out to have children, the relationship of women to the worlds of work and everyday family life presents a natural starting point. The remarkable shrinking size of birth cohorts has led to profound changes in educational institutions and marriage markets. The nature of family formation also turns on the continued decreasing family size. This chapter ends with a consideration of the relationship of marriage and divorce in Japan. This has been one of the starkest examples of differences between Japan and the rest of the industrialized world. Thus, it provides a particularly good test of whether Japan is really different culturally, or whether the differences are superficial or due to institutional factors.

ALIEN WORLDS OF WORK AND FAMILY

Coser (1974) coined the expression "greedy institutions" to refer to the family and the workplace because of the commitment of time and energy that each demands during the peak years of family formation and career mobility. Employed American mothers find it difficult to obtain jobs that reduce stress and job-family tension because they are usually reduced to marginal "women's jobs" outside central lines of authority (Glass & Camarigg, 1992). In essence, Glass and Camarigg demonstrate that gender segregation worsens the position of American working mothers. Companies overwhelming assign women to work that has less flexibility, less rest time, more outside supervision, and less autonomy than men. Although comparable studies do not yet exist, all of the evidence suggests that Japanese institutions of the family and workplace are equally as greedy. From the standpoint of women in either country the only viable solution is either to forgo marriage or work during marriage.

Neither Japanese nor American women appear willing to forgo marriage. Japan rivals the United States in the primacy of marital status.

Although Americans are among the most marrying of peoples, Japanese are even more likely to get married. According to the Prime Minister's Office statistics for 1983, only 2% of Japanese were never-married women age fifty or older. National Opinion Research Center polls for the same period suggest that roughly 5% of American women had never married by the same age.

However, the primacy of work differs for married American and Japanese women. Until the 1960s, the Japanese life course was uncomplicated. Japanese women entered the labor force after completing junior high or secondary education, and they worked, with few exceptions, in primary industry. Women left the work force permanently to marry by age 25, resolving the potential conflict between marriage and work. By the 1980s, Ministry of Labor surveys (Nihon Rōdō Kenkyūsho, 1981) indicate that the pattern of labor-force participation of Japanese women had changed dramatically. The pattern of the 1980s came to resemble the American "M" with peaks at ages 20-24 and 35-50. Japanese women ages 25 to 34 elevate family responsibilities over work during their child-rearing years, after which they return to work. This M-like pattern correlates with higher rates of educational attainment, fewer children, longer life spans, and the declining farm population. These patterns follow world-wide trends in modernization, urbanization, and industrialization. The result is that the typical female worker of the early 1990s is middle-aged, married, works in the service sector, and is closer to her male counterpart in age and years of service than was true twenty years earlier.

Longer life spans have also contributed to the propensity of Japanese women to enter the work force. Before WW II, Japanese women lived only an average 7.6 years after empty-nesting. The average has more than quadrupled to 43.8 years in the intervening half-century. Additionally, over 96% of Japanese women now graduate from senior high schools compared to 37% in 1950. The implication is that more young women have been delaying work in favor of more schooling raising the level of work they are qualified to enter.

As in other industrial countries, wage differentials highly correlate with type of work. Japanese women earned 54% of men's wages in 1980 compared to only 43% in 1960. Nevertheless, after controlling for education, length of service, age, and employment status the 1980 earnings' differential compares quite favorably. Upham points out that "Female high school graduates receive over 90% of parity initially—over 95% for college and university graduates — and, although the degree of parity immediately begins to decline, it never dips below 70 percent (1987, p. 126)."

A major problem, of course, is acquiring work equal to men's. Once women stop work for marriage they lose seniority and "regular" or "permanent" status. "'Part-time' workers in Japan often work the same hours as regular employees but receive only 45% of average male salaries. . . . As of the mid-eighties, 70 to 80% of Japanese companies refused to hire female graduates of four-year universities. (Upham, 1987, p. 127)" Thus, the problem facing young women is to get their feet in the door of the permanent job market. The extraordinary health of the Japanese economy of the 1980s aided women greatly because major corporations found insufficient numbers of young men to fill entry-level jobs that require a college education. The peak in labor-force participation among 20 to 25 year-old women is also due in part to the rising age at first marriage and cohort (generational) effects (Hodge & Ogawa, 1991, p. 38). However, Hodge and Ogawa used regression analysis in a convincing demonstration that economics has little to do with female labor-force participation. They show that the ratio of university tuition to GNP per capita has had no effect over the last several decades on women's work patterns, nor has the rapid economic expansion of the last three decades (Hodge & Ogawa, 1991, p. 38—39). This demonstrates — in spite of the apparent growing similarity of Japanese-American M-like patterns of women's employment — that the basic career patterns of women in each country are different. Japanese women show a continued clear preference for family roles over work roles. The typical life-course pattern is: education, job, quitting the work force for marriage and children, and more time in the labor force after empty nesting. By contrast, American women increasingly combine work, marriage, and family leading to a weaker trough in the "M" during the child-rearing years (Masnick & Bane, 1980).

The top of the second peak has also changed because of generational effects. Some 49.4% of women were in the labor force in 1980 according to the Prime Minister's Office; of these, 66.7% were married. However, since the 1960s increasing numbers of Japanese women have gone back to work as their childbearing years near their end. Thus, the peak of working women in their forties has grown over the past several decades. Still, because the majority of women do not work after marriage and the birth of their first child, the trough has remained at nearly the same level throughout the same period.

Of those women who continue to work during their child-rearing years, over half engage in work that is relatively easy to fit into a subservient role to their child-rearing roles. Nearly 20% engage in family businesses attached to their living areas, 20% in naishoku (part-time piecework that women can work around their household chores and family responsibilities), and 15% in part-time work outside the home. Iwamura (1987, p. 36) corroborates this pattern in more detail: "In almost every case. . . the housewife related her (work activities) to her housewife's role. . . . [P]iecework at home (naishoku) is an alternative." Women usually told her that they need the money earned from such labor to buy a new home or educate their children.

The reason for the first peak in the "M" pattern of Japanese women's employment is not due to changes in marital rates of labor-force participation even though the gross number of working married women in 1985 was double the 1965 figures. It is due to the significant shift in employment among unmarried women. Among the cohort of women aged 25—29 in 1981, 90% of those who were married had premarital work experience. However, this dropped to just over 50% among the cohort aged 45—49 in the 1981 Mainichi survey (Hodge & Ogawa, 1991, p. 76). Nearly 56% of married women under age 35, 46% of those aged 35 to 45, and 26% of those over age 45 said they planned to work in the future in another survey (Iwamura, 1987, p. 49). In the same survey, younger women were more likely to ask someone to look after their children while they worked whereas older women never considered handing their children over to outside help (p. 50).

Japanese society has the most strongly institutionalized gender differentiation of any industrialized country (Brinton, 1988). The comparatively rigid nature of the Japanese social structure works against women. As I have demonstrated in the first three chapters, the educational system pushes each sex into different tracks that leads to competitive advantages for men over women. Numerous institutional structures give males a human-capital advantage: (1) parental perceptions of marked differences in the practicality of investing in the future of their sons versus daughters due to limited resources, (2) perceptions of labor-market discrimination against women; (3) the availability of private and extra-curricular schooling options for males; (4) the sex-stratified tracking of men and women; and (5) actual employment discrimination in hiring and development of employees based upon sex.

However, Brinton (1988) suggests that the household and the labor market make competing demands on women unknown in other industrialized countries. Japan is the only industrial country in which "never-married women have an occupational wage-rate advantage over married women" (p. 309). This acts to attract young women away from marriage to labor-force participation. At the same time, Japan "has the most pronounced 'double peak' age pattern of female labor-force participation" (p. 308—309) reflecting the attraction of marriage and child rearing over labor-force participation. This tension resolves through norms concerning life-cycle timing that rigidly schedule the appropriate ages that men and women must pass through various rites de passage. One's sex and age-cohort largely determine one's schooling, marriage, child bearing, and job-hunting statuses. Each has relatively narrow windows of acceptability: marriage between the ages of 23 and 27 for women; job hunting in the Fall of one's senior year, entrance into the corporate world during the first week of April each year for graduating college seniors, and so on.

Norms play an important part in maintaining this gender-stratified world for men and women. Norms and behavior are relatively tightly linked in Japan. Educators and employers rationalize gender differentiation on the basis of the low percentages of women who believe in combining marriage and work. Supervisors point to the inefficiency inherent in investing in training for female employees who are likely to quit work within three to five years of graduation from school. Older colleagues question the wisdom of career promotions and the risks of promotion of newlywedded women who will most probably give birth to their first children within two years of marriage.

Normlessness also may play a role in maintaining gender stratification. The lack of norms supporting baby-sitting probably depresses positive attitudes toward work among younger women. Iwamura (1987, pp. 70—71) observed that Japanese experience much greater difficulty than

Americans in arranging for private child care because Japanese are uncomfortable with using outsiders as baby-sitters. While 69% of Iwamura's respondents admitted to having left their children with a baby-sitter in an emergency, 39% had while the mother studied, and only 26% had while the mother worked. Younger, more highly educated women with white-collar husbands were the most likely to champion baby-sitting by strangers in their homes in Iwamura's study.

Although younger cohorts of women clearly show less resistance to baby-sitting as an aid to entering the work world, Upham (1987, p. 128) suggests that strong ideological resistance continues to limit opportunities for women to join the gainfully employed. First, ideological pressures from the government equate family with the three-generation household and place the burden of care for the elderly and young upon the shoulders of married women. Second, male authorities instill the fear that equal opportunity for working women would deprive men of their bread-winning role through increased competition for jobs. Third, conservatives assert that career women have no place in corporations with their long hours of overtime and single-minded commitment to work over family. Upham's study suggests almost universal agreement among Japanese men and women upholding strong ideological beliefs in the superiority of men. Japan is a world in which women are perceived as superior at child rearing and homemaking (p. 67). Iwamura (1987) corroborates this view with independent data.

Lack of child-care provisions in Japanese companies reinforces these ideological beliefs. Yokakaihatsu Center (1987), a private survey institute, released figures based on a poll of 511 companies in which 90% stated that it was not possible to give child-care leave to their male employees. Just over 10% of these companies said that they had, or would soon have, provisions of child-care leave for their female employees, but 63% said it was not possible to provide such services. Finally, 42% said that it was not possible to re-employ female employees 3 to 5 years after they gave birth.

Large-scale probability surveys carried out under the auspices of the Prime Minister's office indicate that housekeeping is almost the sole responsibility of housewives. These studies (Sōrifu [Prime Minister's Office], 1983) confirm that husbands and sons rarely do cooking, dish washing, or laundry while daughters help in such tasks only about half the time. Self-inflicted discrimination may be part of the problem. A 1975 opinion poll on working women's attitudes in 10 countries sponsored by the Japan Broadcasting Corporation indicated that the percentage of women in favor of having husbands help with the housework, including working in the kitchen, cleaning house, and doing laundry was lowest in Japan at 51%. The next lowest country was Thailand with 69%. At the other extreme, all of the respondents in Sweden indicated favorable attitudes towards help offered by their husbands (Sodei, 1982). Thus, although Japanese women are clearly victims of discrimination, their attitudes show that they help perpetuate the system.

Self-discrimination also continues to plague improvements in the status of Japanese women. Wives report (Iwamura 1987, p. 78) embarrassment if outsiders see their husbands doing such things as sweeping the walk. They feel they will be thought of as derelict in their own "wifely" duties by others. These women report that they want their sons to be self-sufficient and help their future spouses. Still, there is little evidence that they teach them how to do so. Home takes priority for women while work does for men, even though younger women may state that they should be able to engage in activities unrelated to the roles of wife and mother. The inherent conflict between work and home pressures women to desire work activities that provide modest incomes without interfering unduly with family responsibilities.

Sodei (1982) cited a comparative survey of 11 countries by the Japan Economic Planning Agency. This study reported that Japanese husbands with wives working in full-time jobs spent approximately 18 minutes per day on domestic chores; ones whose wives had a part-time job admitted to 36 minutes of help; and ones whose wives were a full-time homemaker, only 12 minutes. These statistics give Japan the dubious distinction of being lowest among all of the 11 surveyed countries in contributions of husbands to domestic chores. They also reaffirm the unusually great separation of men's world of work from women's world of home in Japan.

Women's attitudes toward these separate spheres are more complex than is generally understood in the West. Relative to their position in 1953 survey data, Japanese women gained a much more positive image toward the position of women over the proceeding 20 years (Iwao, 1976). This gain in image was no doubt in part due to fundamental reforms instituted during the post-war occupation giving women basic rights that have taken firm hold. Nevertheless, it would be a mistake to assume that Japanese have caught up in power with women in other industrialized countries. Saso (1990, p. 900) cites from an international survey that suggests two-thirds of British wives think either they make the final economic decisions in the household or they do it jointly with their husbands. The same survey found only one-third of Japanese wives felt similarly, although 80% Japanese wives traditionally hand over pocket money to their husbands from his pay check compared to 30% of British wives.

Still, the sharp Japanese distinction between the worlds of work and hearth gives certain advantages to women. Iwamura (1987, p. 21) points out that "too much involvement of the husband may undermine both the wife's authority and her ability to maintain an escape route from onerous duties." Suzanne Vogel (1986), likewise, found that wives feel hampered if their husbands are around too much, making it difficult to use the excuse that they must consult their husband if they are present. Upham (1987, p. 151) observes that the Japanese conception of sex differentiation does not have the Western connotation of inferior and superior, but rather of a need for mutual cooperation.

This debate over the connotations of inferiority-superiority versus mutual cooperation has sparked much debate. Numerous Japanese scholars (Hamaguchi, 1985; Murakami, 1984; Nakane, 1970) argue that Japanese social relationships are unique. Their arguments suggest that Japanese society functions as a tightly knit fabric of hierarchical relationships that perpetuate the collectivity rather than the individual. The orientation of norms is towards others, not self. Thus, the normative structure "resolves" the dangers underlying any superior-inferior relationship through mutual expectations of reciprocity. Lower-status members may give up pecuniary returns for protection by higher-status persons. Or higher-status persons may invest time in training lower-status persons with the expectation of elevation in status through expressions of gratitude.

Proponents of the hierarchical-society thesis suggest that horizontal relationships (friend, colleague, companion) dominate Western societies, while vertical ones (father-son, master-apprentice, mentor-student, supervisor-subordinate) epitomize Japanese society. Both horizontal and vertical relationships exist in both countries, so the debatable question is the extent to which each plays a role in each society. Japanese academics who espouse the Japan-as-a-vertical-society thesis usually take their belief a step further and suggest that this characteristic makes Japan uniquely unqualified for Western examination. Nevertheless, many Japanese social structures invite comparison. One in particular — lifetime employment (shūshin koyō) — is often the subject of great debate as a uniquely Japanese institution.

The shūshin koyō system is a post-World War II phenomenon with remnants dating back to the 1942 Ordinance on Labor Management in Essential Industries (Garon, 1987, p. 225) . It is difficult to pinpoint the exact percentage of Japanese workers under lifetime employment. Estimates of about one-fifth to one-fourth of the work force provide generally acceptable estimates. Workers covered under the lifetime-employment system are male, full-time white-collar employees with college degrees who work for the largest corporations. The system does not generally include women, subsidiaries of large corporations, union workers, or low-skill jobs. Lifetime employment is certainly overstated. While Japanese male workers change jobs less frequently than their American counterparts they do change. Cheng (1991) used the 1975 Social Stratification and Mobility survey data to estimate 5 inter-firm job shifts by age 65 compared to 11 for American men.

The lifetime-employment system operates within what economists call a dual structure of enterprises. Dual structures produce occupational inequities in all industrialized countries. The primary sector in dual structures consists of large-scale, capital-intensive, and high-wage firms. The secondary sector, by contrast, includes small-to-medium scale, labor-intensive, and low-wage industries. In the case of Japan, Dore (1986, p. 50) documented the trend during the 1980s for large-scale enterprises "to expand in both employment and output at the expense of the small-scale (ones)." In any industrial economy, small firms have difficulty competing with large ones in range of differentiation in productivity, level of capitalization, and capacity to export.

Dual structures create significant advantages for large-scale enterprises that, in the case of Japan, have a significant impact on workers. For one, they give large corporations the ability to manufacture products and provide services cheaply and to guarantee lifetime employment to a substantial portion of their regular employees. Smaller subsidiaries of the major corporations (Toyota, Mitsubishi, Mitsui, etc.) cannot afford such luxuries. They find themselves at the mercy of their parent corporations in hard times because the large conglomerates, rather than cut their own work forces, simply cut orders from their subsidiaries. Should times become even harder, large industries can cut surplus foreign and female workers next. The subsidiaries and sub-contractors, in turn, have little recourse outside reducing their own work forces, reducing pay, or other measures that are likely to include their regular, male employees. Indeed, even in the best of times Saso (1990, p. 77) points out that Japanese companies with less than 30 employees pay wages that average only 60% of the wages in companies employing 1000 or more persons. Because women comprise more than 50% of the employees in these small firms, this dual structure clearly depresses women's pay relative to men's.

Saso (1990, p. 83) points out that, in spite of low wages and cavalier treatment by small companies, women "on average stay continuously with the same company for almost as long as the men." Still, the myth persists that they are only weakly attached to labor. Core industries systematically exclude women from participation in full-time work. Still, women persist in contributing to the Japanese economy through small companies, family businesses, and self-employment.

Upham (1987, p. 138) traces employment discrimination against women back to the mid-1960s where he noted increases in overt and explicit discrimination in wages, retirement, and reduction-in-force policies. He states that such practices gradually disappeared during the late 1970s, but reappeared in the 1980s. During the 1980s, women actively challenged a broad range of employer practices such as discriminatory promotion, job rotation, and tracking. Because of the success of those lawsuits, companies changed their hiring patterns and refused to ". . . hire highly educated women or hire women only as part-time or temporary employees (P. 138)."

A comparative survey of 11 nations underscores differences between Japanese and Western attitudes toward women. While only 6.9% of Japanese agreed that it was better for women not to have occupations, less than one-sixth as many Americans, Swedes, West Germans, and British answered affirmatively to the same question. In answer to whether it was better for a woman to work until marriage and then quit 14.2 % of Japanese agreed compared to from 0.6% among Swedes to 3.3% among Americans. Finally, another question asked whether or not it was better for women to quit work on the occasion of a birth and not to resume until after all their children had grown up. Forty-three percent of Japanese answered affirmatively compared to from 35% in Sweden to 61.8% in Britain. Clearly, Japanese show highly conservative attitudes toward the role of women in the home versus the workplace.

Nevertheless, surveys sponsored by the Prime Minister's Office do show a decline in conservatism over time. In 1972 over 83% of both men and women agreed with the statement that "Men should work; women should stay home" compared to 49% of women and 63% of men in 1984. By 1987, affirmative responses had fallen to 37% of women and 52% of men (Saso, 1990, p. 97)). Although men's opinions lag behind women's, this is a remarkable 59% decline for women and an equally impressive 39% drop for men over a 15-year period. So, although Japanese may show more conservative attitudes towards men and women's roles, they certainly show marked change.

We can get a rough estimate of the geographical distribution of lifetime employment from adding up the percentage of Japanese over 14 years old engaged in professional, technical, managerial, or sales jobs (see Figures 4—2 and 4—4 for all but sales figures). This method certainly produces greater overestimates for the lowest ranked prefectures because (a) most head offices of major corporations are in Tōkyō with a few in Ōsaka and Nagoya, and (b) women hold some 37.7% of sales jobs, according to a 1987 Japanese Management and Coordination Agency survey of labor. Nevertheless, the results are consistent with expectations and with Cheng's (1991) analysis of the 1975 Social Stratification and Mobility survey data.

Those male workers blessed with lifetime employment, in turn, pay a heavy price for the benefits. First, industry guarantees their jobs only until sometime between ages 55 and 60 when companies expected them to retire or take another job at considerable financial loss. Second, employers expect them to pledge unfailing loyalty to their companies. This means that large corporations demand that lifetime employees put the corporation above family and kinship. Co-workers bring strong pressures to bear on regular employees to work outside normal business hours without extra pay, not to take vacation time, to socialize with co-workers after work hours, and so on. The result is clear pressures toward great separation of the male world of work and the female world of home. The husband's friends come from among his work mates. Peer pressures push colleagues toward such group activities as bar and restaurant hopping after work, and playing golf on weekends.

Tōkyō leads with 36.0% and Nara, Ōsaka, and Kyōto follow with 33.2%, 32.4%, and 31.5% of jobs that have the minimal qualifications for lifetime-employment status. With the exceptions of Hokkaidō and Miyagi Prefectures, areas north of Tōkyō comprise the lowest number of high-status jobs with between 22 and 23%, depending on the prefecture. Despite having lifetime-job security, these jobs are not as valued as similar ones in Tōkyō or Ōsaka because Japanese usually consider assignment to such areas a demotion.

Workers assigned to successive stints in provincial branches or offices of a major corporation or the civil service have a special expression, senmon wa dosa-mawari, in which dosa is a kind of "pig-Latin" reversal of the syllables for "Sado" Island to which criminals were sent to serve sentence of forced labor without hope of ever returning to the mainland alive. While it is true that companies rarely dismiss white-collar workers, they quite commonly assign them to the provinces to convey the message that their career courses are no longer on an upward track.

The major cities in Japan hold the best jobs, but have become notoriously expensive places to live. It is not unusual for new home buyers to have from two to three-hour commutes from outside Tōkyō. Figure 5—1 reflects this problem. It shows that all of the prefectures with major cities in Japan are outliers. All of the major cities have less than half the median percentage home ownership. Thus, it is not by accident that the correlation between high-status jobs and the chance of owning one's own home near to where one works is negative (r = -0.86). Workers with premium jobs pay a heavy price in travel time for their work status.

Home ownership is an indicator of high living standards. Because non-disposable income (taxes, social security payments, mortgage payments) rose faster in Japan than discretionary disposal income during the 1980s, Japanese families have found themselves squeezed to make ends meet. Saso (1990, p. 95) cites from Ministry of Labor survey data in 1987 showing that close to 70% of married women who work do so to maintain a reasonable household income, in spite of the fact that they have no other option than parttime, low-paying work.

Japanese have little sense of community compared to the United States where persons with higher status occupations are more likely to own their own homes. One solution is to offer subsidized company housing called danchi. Danchi resemble ghetto high-rise tenements of American cities without the encumbent dangers of crime. Any sense of community comes from the sharing of a common workplace among the men. Company-ownership creates a homogeneity that sets each housing complex apart from its surrounding neighborhood. The families in these apartments aspire to moving out as quickly as they can save enough to buy their own place. Thus, expectations of short-term stays produce low commitments to the housing complex.

Occupational status grossly affects the opportunity for lifetime employment. Blue-collar workers have less job security and are more likely to change places of employment than white-collar employees in all industrial countries. Thus, Dore and Sako (1989) suggest that Japan is not particularly unique in job stability. They acknowledge that western Europe's blue-collar workers are more mobile than Japan's, but point out that European white-collar workers are as likely to stay with the same company. Companies generally promote middle managers from within the lower ranks in both Europe and Japan.

Scrutiny of prefectural patterns of female labor-force participation confirm the dual-track nature of the employment of men and women. In 1988, the percentage of women engaged in the labor force ranged from 59.% to 35.4%. Prefectures with low rates were in the most densely populated areas such as Nara, Kanagawa, Ōsaka, Tōkyō, Chiba, and Kyotō. Such low-density, rural prefectures as Fukui, Tottori, and Toyama were at the top in female labor-force participation. Primary-sector industries such as agriculture, forestry, and fishing serve as the major employers in rural areas, suggesting the crucial role that female employment plays there.

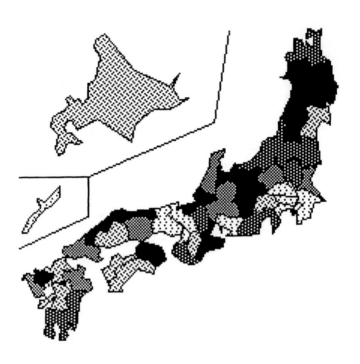

Toyama	63.95	Tochigi	53.92	Nara	42.03
Yamagata	63.68	Kagoshima	53.77	Kōchi	41.24
Akita	62.31	Aomori	53.20	Miyagi	39.80
Iwate	61.19	Shizuoka	52.83	Fukuoka	34.90
Shimane	60.87	Ibaraki	52.43	Hokkaidō	34.33
Saga	60.31	Gifu	51.88	Hiroshima	34.15
Tottori	58.79	Okayama	50.92	Aichi	33.26
Fukui	57.24	Nagasaki	49.54	Hyōgo	32.25
Nagano	56.61	Yamaguchi	47.89	Chiba	31.34
Mie	56.14	Gunma	47.82	Saitama	31.03
Tokushima	55.98	Kagawa	47.82	Kyōto	30.24
Miyazaki	55.56	Ōita	44.88	Okinawa	28.71
Shiga	55.07	Ishikawa	44.34	Kanagawa	23.20
Niigata	55.05	Kumamoto	44.04	Ōsaka	20.60
Wakayama	54.80	Yamanashi	43.68	Tōkyō	15.87
Fukushima	54.78	Ehime	42.65		

Figure 5—1   The Percent of Home Owners in 1986

The correlation of 0.52 (p < 0.05) between percentage of farmers, fishers and lumber workers with the percentage of female labor-force participation confirms this strong relationship. By contrast, male labor-force participation is negatively associated with those same occupations (r = -.0.38; p < 0.05). A regression analysis of the employment of farmers, fishers, and lumber workers on female and male labor-force participation confirms the gendered bifurcation of occupation. The standardized beta for females is 0.57 (p < 0.01) and for males is 0.43 (p < 0.01). These two variables explain 46% of the variation in the percentage of farmers, fishers, and lumber workers, showing the irony in such labels as fisher<u>men</u> and lumber<u>men</u>. Indeed, according to Prime Minister's Office statistics for 1992 (Sōrifu, 1983) women make up 48% of the work force employed in the agricultural and forestry industries, compared to 40% in non-agricultural work.

A Japanese woman interested in combining work with the rearing of children must find ways to juggle the demands of each type of greedy institution. In 1992, over 90% of the 3.75 million jobs classified as agriculturally or forestry-related were family-owned. The attraction for women must evidently be the high overlap between job and family duties. The irony is that the strengthening economy, modernization, and mechanization of all sectors of the rural economy have forced both husbands an wives to seek employment in the cities. In the three expansionist decades of the 1960s through 1980s, primary-sector employment contracted drastically. In 1960, 43.1% of women worked in the primary-sector, but by 1990, less than 10% did. Only 5.9% of the 64-million strong labor force found employment in the primary sector by 1990. As in other advanced industrial nations, service-related jobs in the tertiary sector have replaced the primary sector as major sources of employment. From 1960 to 1990, the tertiary sector nearly doubled from 36.7% to 62.7% of all employment of women.

Not surprisingly, educational attainment is a key factor in job stability in Japan. The more schooling, the less chance of job change. According to 1989 statistics from the Ministry of Labor's annual Survey of Employment Trends (Rōdōshō Staff, 1991), 7.9% of all working-aged men and 9.5% of working-aged women changed places of employment during 1989. The service industry (particularly eating and drinking establishments and retail stores) and construction industry showed the most change, consistent with jobs requiring little education and low prestige. The exceptionally low-rankings of Tōkyō (39th ranked with 7.2%) and Ōsaka (44th ranked with 6.4%) was almost assuredly due to high concentrations of lifetime employment. At the other extreme, prefectures most remote from Tōkyō and Ōsaka had nearly double the national average change in jobs — Aomori was first with 15.3%, followed by Okinawa and Hokkaidō with 13.6% each. The economies of other prefectures at the high end such as Yamaguchi Yamagata, Miyazaki, and Kōchi function through fishing, farming, and other primary industries requiring little schooling.

Chapter 4 showed that young unmarried Japanese women want nothing to do with young men who come from families with such low-status occupations. They prefer the job security and affluence of the white-collar world, even it comes at the price of losing their husbands to the corporation. Although numerous students of Japan have suggested that the corporation has replaced the extended family and village society for Japanese men, this is really most apparent only in the largest metropolitan areas. Japanese in areas less blessed with large corporations may covet such trade-offs, but they lack the educational base to produce youthful aspirants and the economic attractions to draw back the few home-grown products who attain the necessary educational qualifications.

Sociologists of the Japanese family system have often pointed to the ie as the prototypic social unit. Although often translated as "household" or "family," ie really refers to a legal institution for transmission of property rights. During the Tokugawa and early Meiji eras, a patriarch without a "suitable" male heir, or no male heir, might legally adopt a son-in-law to succeed him. Households engaged in business were ie by legal definition, regardless of blood ties. The family has always had historic ties as an economically, integrated, and publicly recognized social unit. A complex of paternalistic relations tied individuals through the ie.

The ie is an anachronism in the corporate world of modern Japan. Corporations demand loyalty and commitment from their employees that the ie of the pre-capitalist era used to command. The ie combined kinship with economics, whereas the corporate world demands separation of the worlds of family and job. Nevertheless, the corporate world cleverly borrows the language of the ie to cement its sense of legitimacy. It is not by accident that industries refer to head office-subsidiary firms as parent-child (oyako) relationships, that one's office superiors take up the serious role of nakōdo to help find promising young workers a suitable mate, or that workers might refer to their "boss" with the term oyakata (father-figure). At the same time that the corporate world demands priority over family life, it has borrowed family terminology to justify its own existence and to symbolize its own paternalistic base of authority.

The problem, of course, is that most work that is available to married women is low-paying and part-time, contributing to low bargaining power at home and work. Blumberg (1991) provides a comprehensive, cross-cultural theory of gender-stratified power that explains many of the apparent differences between Japanese and non-Japanese women. Specifically, great relative contributions to household income (the less the gap between a wife's and husband's income contribution) give women "greater voice and leverage in family decisions, somewhat greater say in the overall relationship, and only a little more help from their husbands in housework." (p.8)

Even more important is the power of giving over receiving. The income normally available to women to spend is subsistence income, giving them very little control. The greater surplus (disposable) income available to give, the more leverage the giver has. Blumberg also notes (p. 23) that greater macro-level gender inequality imposed by the political, economic, legal, and ideological systems gives women less return on their surplus giving compared to men. For example, she cites from American research demonstrating that a wife must match her husband's surplus giving of $10,000 with $12,700 to get the same return in power. Presumably it would take even more surplus giving in an even more gender-differentiated society such as Japan to match a husband's disposable spending. This inherent "triple whammy" also explains why Japanese men contribute less than men in other industrial nations to domestic labor. Women who experience fewer disposable household-income-contribution gaps and less institutionalized gender discrimination at the societal level also experience less differentiation in contributions to household labor. Working full-time does not relieve a woman of doing the most monotonous, dirtiest, or most pressing household labor. The greater the triple-whammy gaps in gender stratification, the stronger the likelihood that the husband will contribute only to the "nicest" chores leaving the wife with the "nastier" ones.

STATUS AND POWER INHERENT IN FAMILY VERSUS WORK IDENTITIES

Chapter One introduced the semantic differential (SD) technique as a procedure for studying three universal dimensions of micro-interaction — status (goodness), power (powerfulness), and activity (liveliness). This chapter section returns to the same data set (Umino, Matsuno, & Smith, 1991), and compares the Japanese data with a comparable set of American data. The SD is a standard psychometric technique for measuring the connotations of stimuli. I use it here to demonstrate important differences in connotations between Japanese and Americans in their images of family and work roles, and to emphasize the inherent power of work over family identities in Japan.

Table 5—1 reports direct American-Japanese comparisons of 11 common family-kinship terms. Americans consistently rate these common kinship identities as having higher status (Evaluation) and being more active (Activity) than Japanese. American fathers are 0.7 points higher in status than Japanese fathers. Husbands show a status advantage of over 1.1 points. I have not computed t-tests for significant differences. The reason is that neither the American nor the Japanese data set uses random samples from the general population. Nevertheless, a difference of 0.5 or greater on a 7-point scale is statistically significant with these data because of their small standard deviations. Virtually every one of the 11 status comparisons is significantly different by this standard. All of the differences suggest that Americans derive more status than do Japanese from familial identity.

Table 5—1

Comparison of Average Family and Kinship Identities
from American and Japanese SD Lexicons

IDENTITY	Evaluation		Potency		Activity	
	USA	Japan	USA	JAPAN	USA	JAPAN
Father	2.34	1.64	1.89	2.08	-0.34	-1.80
Mother	2.33	1.80	1.90	1.48	0.04	-0.72
Husband	2.27	1.12	1.36	1.40	0.93	-1.00
Wife	1.67	0.96	0.88	0.20	0.97	-0.52
Son	1.55	0.56	0.57	0.00	1.79	1.00
Daughter	1.19	0.48	-0.09	-0.72	0.88	1.40
Grandfather	2.28	1.76	1.36	1.36	-1.59	-2.24
Grandmother	2.40	1.48	0.41	-0.08	-1.35	-2.16
Uncle	1.11	0.68	0.66	1.04	-0.34	-1.16
Aunt	1.30	0.44	0.16	0.64	-0.18	-0.16
Widow	1.02	0.00	-0.70	-1.24	-1.08	-1.68

SOURCE: American data come from Heise (1988) and Umino, Matsuno, and Smith (1991) present all Japanese data.

A comparison of a larger set of 40 familial identities shared across the two lexicons gives an even better test of the differences in familial status across both countries. For this more complete set, the median difference is -1.08, and 37 of the 40 identities show 0.5 or greater differences in status for Americans, when rated by women. Male raters display a similar pattern: a median difference of -1.06. There are only 5 identities with status ratings less than 0.5 among American familial identities.[1]

Power differences between Americans and Japanese show less clear order. The middle columns of Table 5—1 suggests that Japanese fathers have insignificantly (0.19) more power than American fathers, but that American mothers have significantly more power (0.52) than Japanese mothers. The power differential between the identities of husbands and wives mirrors those of fathers and mothers. The SD data suggest that the debate over the relative power of father-mother and husband-wife dyads in Japan versus the United States favors male roles. These data support the arguments of Iwamura (1987), Vogel (1986), and Upham (1987) that the relative powerlessness of Japanese women creates the need for protective barriers, rather than the arguments of Murakami (1984), Nakane (1970), and

[1]The formula subtracts American scores from American values, so a negative value implies the Americans score higher, and a positive value implies the Japanese score higher.

Hamaguchi (1985) that superiority-inferiority relationships are unimportant in Japanese male-female relationships.

The data on sons and daughters also support an interpretation of male power. American sons are 0.57 more powerful than Japanese sons. Japanese daughters are 0.63 weaker in the eyes of Japanese than American daughters are to Americans. Within each culture, likewise, sons — not surprisingly — are more powerful than daughters in the SD results; 0.66 higher for Americans and 0.72 higher for Japanese. Table 5—1 also demonstrates the consistent male power advantage for grandfathers and uncles over grandmothers and aunts.

The SD data also suggest that Japan is a culture that is quieter or less active than the United States. Thirty-one out of 40 comparable familial identities have lower activity scores among both the Japanese male and female samples. The mean difference in activity score is -0.7 for both sexes, demonstrating the general agreement across both sexes on appropriate gender roles.

On the other hand, Table 5—1 also reflects similar universal stereotypes. Widows are lowest in status among ratings of kin in both cultures. There is a clear status increase related to generation in both cultures with grandparents accorded the highest esteem. Furthermore, men's kinship identities are quieter than women's, regardless of culture. Power shows clear similarities. Widows, followed by daughters, have the least power; parents have the most power (with Americans more egalitarian). Men have more power than women within generations (again, with the American father-mother exception). The parent roles have more power than spousal roles, within each sex.

These rating similarities and differences seem to reflect the American and Japanese cultures credibly. There are many other Japanese-American consistencies in spite of difficulties of giving precise one-for-one translations for all identities and behaviors. The current Japanese and American SD files are skimpy on commercial identities. The Japanese SD file includes only 29 commercial identities of which 12 have American equivalents.[2] Thus, analysis of Japanese-American differences in the connotative meaning of commercial and other occupational identities can only be suggestive.

The correlations for evaluation ratings between Japanese and Americans, using the common commercial identities are 0.3 for men and 0.2 for women, suggesting very little communality in the production of status. Similarly, activity correlations are both only 0.3 for men and women. But the sources of power are extremely similar — 0.9 for both men and women. These results indicate some of the reasons for confusion over Japan as a special case culturally. Power appears to have much the same underpinnings in each culture, although status and activity do not.

---

[2]Those identifities are janitor, civil servant, clerk, trainee, secretary, work superior, lawyer, boss, subordinate, receptionist, and authority.

One way to show the relative power of family versus work identities using the semantic differential lexical rankings is to contrast the relative amounts of status and power each gives to particular individuals. Table 5—2 lists important life-stage identities that Japanese women are likely to go through and the three most likely occupations open to them. Note that the highest status derives from motherhood. Being a mother is 1.53 points higher in status and 1.47 higher in power than being single on a 7-point scale — suggesting overconcern about whether single women want to marry and have children. Indeed, becoming an old maid (o-rudomisu) implies loss of status. To stay unmarried lowers a women's status by 1.83 point over her best scenario of marrying and having children. The best case is the expected life-course of marriage on schedule, motherhood, completed by grand-motherhood, bringing the greatest amount of respect. Deviations from the expected life course — late or no marriage, marriage without children, divorce, remarriage, and widowhood — lead to significantly lower status and power than staying on the expected upward track.

Table 5—2

Comparison of Japanese Women's Fundamental Sentiments concerning Selected Marital and Work-Related Roles

IDENTITY	Goodness	Powerfulness	Liveliness
Single	-0.18	-.036	0.60
Old maid	-0.48	0.18	-0.24
Bride	0.36	-.060	0.39
Wife	0.66	0.60	-0.24
Housewife	0.24	0.36	0.33
Mother	1.35	1.11	-0.54
Mother-in-law	-0.63	0.90	0.48
Divorcee	-0.30	-0.57	-0.06
Remarried	-0.09	-0.18	-0.21
Grandmother	1.11	-0.06	-1.62
Widow	0.00	-0.93	-1.26
Receptionist	0.09	-0.66	-0.33
Secretary	0.66	0.03	-1.08
Nursery aide	1.14	0.57	0.03

SOURCE: Umino, Matsuno, and Smith (1991).

Allowing oneself to become stuck in a typical female occupation also is an unprofitable act. Becoming a bride gives greater status and power than becoming a receptionist or secretary. Nursery school aides fair well, in part, because this work connotes particularly feminine traits and denotes a job mostly occupied by women who will marry and have children on schedule and then quit work with very useful child-rearing skills.

FAMILY FORMATION AND PROCESS

The official pre-war slogan of Japan was "Give birth, build Japan." The purpose was to increase the population for the government's own imperialistic ends. The Japanese have no trust for politicians who urge young women to bear more children. Many citizens believe that the government promotes population increases as a panacea for protracted labor shortages that attract young women and foreign guest workers to the job market. Yet the government continues to criticize young women for the increasingly record-low birth rates. It foists blame on women who go to college and who want to work. It does not recognize such structural problems as lack of maternity leave, few child-care facilities, expensive housing, few playgrounds, pressures on children to pass the national university exam, and low subsidies for child support (currently ¥5000 ($24) per month for the first-born for 3 years).

Gary Becker (1973) offers a more social-structural approach. He stresses the importance of sex-specific roles. Becker views unmarried men and women as trading partners who decide to marry if each partner has more to gain by marrying than by remaining single. As in all trading relationships, the gains from marriage hinge on each partner having something different to offer to the other. In most societies women traditionally rely on men for provision of food and shelter as well as protection. Men rely on women for the bearing and rearing of children as well as for the maintenance of the home. Bloosfeld and Huinink (1991, pp. 145—146) extend Becker's theory by suggesting that women extend their participation in schooling that delays their transition to adulthood. The normative expectations that young women in school are "not ready" for marriage and motherhood is further under-girded by the increased career resources that further education brings postponement and avoidance of having children.

The other side of the sex-specific-role equation recognizes the plight of Japanese men. A Japanese man who marries at the age of 28 can expect a steep decline in income in 27 years. This is because companies expect men to retire at age 55. This leaves a narrow window of about 7 years for childbearing as children born after the father reaches age 34 "would still be in college and economically dependent when their father's income drops" (Coleman 1983, pp. 119—120). Hodge and Ogawa (1991, p. 29) point out that the opportunity costs of raising children have risen steadily since the mid-1970s when measured by university tuition as a percentage of GNP per capita.

IDEAL FAMILY SIZE

Numerous fertility surveys support the position that Japanese women would like much larger families than they now have. Hodge and Ogawa (1991, p. 143) used the Mainichi Survey of Fertility and Family Planning to show that 60% of Japanese women of childbearing age view three children as the ideal, and that 30% consider two children ideal. In essence, there are few differences in values concerning the ideal size of families. Still, politicians blame the current low-birth situation on young women with more education.

Hodge and Ogawa found only a slightly lower number of ideal number of children among younger, well-educated women living in urban areas compared to the overall mean ideal (p. 123). In essence, wife's education, age, and husband's occupation makes virtually no difference in the ideal number of children. Contrary to government propaganda, the Mainichi survey data suggest that "better-educated women and women with better-educated husbands want more, not fewer, children." (p. 153) That such Japanese have one to two children less than they think is ideal indicates that social structural impediments must thwart their aspirations.

DESIRED FAMILY SIZE

Desired family size provides a useful measure of family planning that is more sensitive to the realities of social structural impediments. Hodge and Ogawa (1991, p. 82—83) demonstrate that both ideal and desired numbers of children have decreased slightly for younger cohorts. For example, 20-24 year olds in a 1981 Mainichi survey said the ideal number was 2.5 compared to 2.8 among 45-49 year olds. The desired numbers were 2.4 children for the 20-24 year olds and 2.5 for the 45-49 year olds, respectively. This is still roughly one more child that Japanese would like to have than they have.

Two factors — living space and patri-locality of residence — proved important predictors of desired number of children in Hodge and Ogawa's Mainichi analyses. When there was more than 1.0 persons per room, women wanted fewer children than when there was at least one room per person. Women in patrilocal situations appeared more likely to desire larger families, presumably because they are more susceptible to day-to-day influence from their in-laws.

ACTUAL FAMILY SIZE

As early as 1971 demographers warned that Japan would face a labor shortage in the 1990s so the government started to give financial inducements to mothers. The ratio of children 14 or younger to Japan's overall population in 1990 hit its lowest level since the end of World War II, in spite of such inducements. For example, there were only 22.83 million children under 15 in 1990; down 760,000 from the year before. Broken down by sex, 11.7 million were boys and 11.13 million were girls. The under-age-15 population accounted for 18.5% of Japan's population, a drop of 0.7 percent in one year. Demographers expect this ratio to continue to decline until at least 1995 when it should bottom out at 17.6 %. In 1990 there were 8.1 million children 5 or younger, 9.36 million ages 6 to 11, and 5.38 million ages 12 through 14. There were 1.87 million 14-year-olds and declining numbers for each descending age.

The rank-order of prefectures with high and low percentages of their population under age 15 has remained stable over the last several decades. For example, the prefecture with the highest rate in 1980 was Okinawa with 30.4% and the lowest was Tōkyō with 20.6%. In 1990, the respective figures were 25% for Okinawa and 15.5% for Tōkyō. The lowest percentages remain in the dense Tōkyō-Nagoya-Ōsaka corridor, with the highest percentages in the more distant rural prefectures. Government officials have become increasingly alarmed at the lower quantities of children born to women in Japan. Hodge and Ogawa (1991) demonstrate that Japan's fertility and family planning are remarkably similar to other countries. Out of 120 correlates expected from theory and research on the socioeconomic differences in fertility, they found only 14 that differed from expectation, all of which were trivial differences (p. 41).

Sociological theorists recognize the substitution of quantity for quality of children in the decision to have a child (Becker, 1973). In Japan, like other countries, prospective parents make decisions about how to improve the quality of the children they have that require trade-offs with the number of children they can afford. These decisions end in fertility differentials like those shown in the crude birth rates in Figure 5—2.

Not surprisingly, the data in Figure 5—2 provide a near mirror-image of the percentage of population under age 15. Tōkyō ties with Toyama for the lowest crude birth rate at 11.4 per 1000 population. Okinawa is highest with 17.6. A regression analysis of crude birth rate on the percentage of females in the labor force, percent of students enrolled in high school, and gross prefectural domestic product per capita supports Hodge and Ogawa's results. All three correlates of the birth rate are negative, as expected. The beta for gross prefectural domestic product per capita, is -0.37 which is more than twice as large as its standard deviation. Similarly, the beta (-0.47) for percentage high school enrollment is also significantly larger than its standard deviation. Interestingly, the effect of the percentage of females in the labor force is small (-0.15) and non-significant, suggesting that female labor-force participation has no relationship to the birth rate. The total explained variance is 30%. Substituting the percentage of persons living in densely inhabited areas for the percentage of females in the labor force does not change the results significantly. The best predictor is still high school enrollment followed by prefectural affluence. Density is unrelated, consistent with Hodge and Ogawa's (1991, p. 180) finding that urban and rural differences have declined to a paltry one-tenth of a child less for urbanites compared to residences of rural areas.

I noted in the last chapter that Japanese have become the oldest marrying people. Late marriage patterns imply lower numbers of children that couples will conceive. In another test of robustness, I regressed crude birth rate on female high school enrollment rates, gross prefectural product, and mean ages at marriage by prefecture. Although the Pearson's product correlation between mean age at marriage and the crude birth rate is only -0.19, the beta drops to a statistically insignificant -0.08, and the other two predictors continue to have statistically significant betas of nearly the same weights as in the previous regressions, with 29% variance explained. We can conclude that economic and educational conditions continue to have great influence on the birth rate in Japan, but that age of marriage has no real influence. The reason is mostly likely that the mean number of children is now so low (1.5) that, unless the mean age at marriage continues to increase, attainment of the 1.5 child norm is quite practical within the first two or three years of marriage.

CONTRACEPTION AND ABORTIONS

The Japanese have clearly become highly efficient at limiting their population growth. This raises the question: How did they do it? Less than one-quarter of Japanese married women of childbearing age used any form of contraceptives at the beginning of the 1950s (Tsuya, 1986). The birth-control pill has only recently become legally available in Japan and women do not use it widely because the medical community has not received it well. Similarly, medical professionals do not warmly support the IUD or sterilization. Instead, the most preferred methods of contraception since World War II are, ironically, the least reliable: rhythm, condoms, or a combination of the two (Coleman, 1983; Tsuya, 1986). Part of the reason for the condom-based preference is that the Japanese family-planning groups developed the condom distribution after World War II as a means of supporting their efforts to bring down family size. Now those agencies are loathe to develop more effective methods of birth control out of fear they would not be as profitable as condom sales.

Contraception in Japan correlates with reaching family-size goals. Hodge and Ogawa(1991, P. 230) used the Mainichi newspaper's fertility and family planning survey data to show that the husband's education continues to be more important than the wife's in the decision to practice contraception. Coleman's survey data corroborates the male-dominance thesis (1983, pp. 97-98) . Japanese women in his study said that their husbands were the single most important personal source of information on contraception. Among men, male schoolmate friends provided the primary source of contraceptive information.

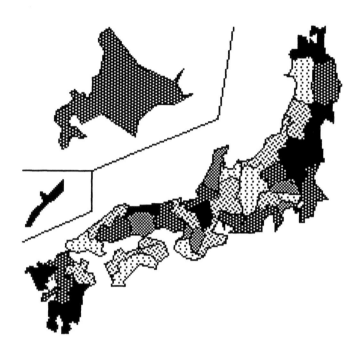

Okinawa	17.6	Iwate	13.0	Ōita	12.4
Miyagi	14.0	Chiba	12.9	Niigata	12.4
Shiga	14.0	Hiroshima	12.7	Ehime	12.3
Fukushima	13.9	Fukui	12.7	Yamanashi	12.2
Miyazaki	13.8	Hyōgo	12.7	Mie	12.2
Saga	13.7	Hokkaidō	12.7	Shimane	12.1
Nagasaki	13.6	Gunma	12.7	Kyōto	12.1
Tottori	13.5	Nara	12.6	Nagano	12.0
Kagoshima	13.5	Okayama	12.6	Kagawa	12.0
Tochigi	13.5	Kanagawa	12.6	Wakayama	11.9
Aomori	13.4	Ōsaka	12.5	Akita	11.9
Aichi	13.3	Saitama	12.5	Kōchi	11.8
Ibaraki	13.3	Ishikawa	12.5	Yamaguchi	11.7
Fukuoka	13.3	Tokushima	12.4	Tōkyō	11.4
Kumamoto	13.2	Yamagata	12.4	Toyama	11.4
Shizuoka	13.1	Gifu	12.4		

Figure 5—2   The Crude Birth Rate per 1,000 Population in 1983

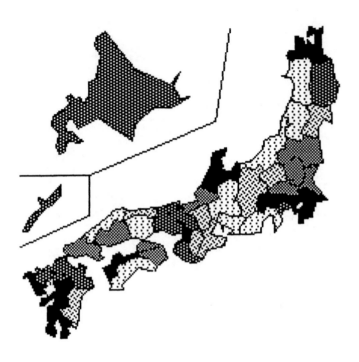

Kagoshima	29.7	Okinawa	21.5	Tottori	19.7
Ishikawa	26.5	Ōita	21.5	Nagano	19.6
Chiba	25.2	Kanagawa	21.3	Miyagi	18.8
Yamanashi	24.5	Saga	21.1	Shiga	18.6
Kumamoto	24.5	Hyōgo	21.1	Mie	18.4
Aomori	24.3	Yamaguchi	21.0	Gunma	18.4
Ehime	23.8	Fukushima	20.9	Gifu	18.2
Toyama	23.5	Kagawa	20.8	Kōchi	17.9
Ōsaka	23.4	Hiroshima	20.8	Okayama	17.7
Tōkyō	23.3	Ibaraki	20.8	Niigata	17.2
Nagasaki	23.3	Fukui	20.4	Shizuoka	17.2
Fukuoka	22.7	Tochigi	20.4	Aichi	17.1
Hokkaidō	22.4	Saitama	20.1	Akita	16.5
Iwate	22.2	Tokushima	20.0	Shimane	16.5
Kyōto	22.0	Miyazaki	19.9	Yamagata	15.2
Wakayama	21.9	Nara	19.7		

Figure 5—3   Abortions per 1000 Live Births in 1987

Hodge and Ogawa (1991, p. 60) used trend analysis to show that Japanese couples chose more effective contraceptives with increasing GNP per capita. Nevertheless, roughly one-quarter of all pregnancies are still terminated by abortions (Coleman, 1983). The most likely reason that wives give for postponement of their first birth is that they want to stay in the work force for a longer period of time (Coleman, 1983, p. 117).

Japanese have enjoyed effective legalized abortion since the 1948 passage of the Eugenic Protection Law which, in practice, granted abortion on demand. This law permitted Japanese greater access to legal abortion than any other nation in the world as reflected in its comparatively high rate of abortion. The revised Eugenic Protection Law of 1949 required spousal consent. However, Coleman (1983, p. 22) points out that there are few complaints of lack of consultation among stable married couples. The profound social cleavage found in the United States over abortion rights does not exist in Japan (Coleman, 1983, p. 70-72; Hodge & Ogawa, 1991, p. 134). Japanese are much less restrictive than Americans in their attitudes and beliefs concerning women's rights to abort.

Although most ob-gyns require an unmarried woman's parents to validate the consent form, relatively few unmarried women have abortions. In 1987, teenage abortions accounted for only 6% of the total, or 27,542 abortions. Still, teen abortions have doubled over the past decade. Kenji Hayashi of the Institute of Public Health (1989) believes teen-age pregnancies have increased due to pressures of "examination hell" as more women marry later and pursue higher education. Hayashi also notes that sex education is non-existent in Japan, yet premarital sex is on the rise. Seventy percent of female students that he surveyed said that they predicted that schools will have courses on pregnancy, marriage and contraception in 10 years while 80% of teachers said they did not offer or have plans to offer such a course. However, Hodge and Ogawa (1991, p. 59) believe that better-educated women are likely to be more careful and effective users of their contraceptive of choice, and hence less likely to abort.

Figure 5—3 gives the official abortion rate per 1000 live births in 1987. Muramatsu (1978) suggests that the number of actual abortions is much higher than the number reported — perhaps as much as 70% higher. The reason is that physicians have large incentives to under-report abortions they perform for both insurance and tax reasons. There is no reason to believe that the discrepancy between actual and reported abortions is unevenly distributed across prefectures. Physicians licensed to perform abortions in Kumamoto claim to have performed almost three times the number in Yamanashi in 1988. Thus, the rank ordering of abortion rates in Figure 5—3 should be treated with caution. It appears as if physicians in the Kantō and Kansai area may underreport abortions to a greater extent than in more rural areas. Or it may be that women in rural areas simply have less control over their bodies. This last thesis is certainly consistent with the idea that more education and urbanization negatively relate with the abortion rate.

The discussion of previous findings on family planning in Japan suggests that gross prefectural product, percentage of females employed in the labor force, percentage of women enrolled in high school, percent urban, percentage of dense areas inhabited, and mean age ought to be positively related, and that the mean age at first marriage ought to be negatively related, to the abortion rate.

Table 5—3 reports zero-order correlations as first tests of these expectations. Only 4 of the 6 correlations have the expected sign and none of the correlations is significant statistically. Regression analysis changes the relationship of each independent variable very little. None of the betas are statistically significant, and the regression explains a meager 15% of the difference in the abortion rate across prefectures.[3]

These findings are perfectly consistent with the main contention of Hodge and Ogawa (1991). Post-industrial nations like Japan should have very weak and inconsistent predictors of family planning. Figure 5—3 shows marked differences across prefectures in the abortion rate — Kagoshima's 29.7 rate is nearly twice than of Yamagata's 15.2. Nevertheless, explaining such ecological differences with traditional predictors is highly unsuccessful. Other "obvious" correlates of family planning also do poorly in predicting the abortion rates. A reasonable proxy for the extended family in Japan is households with six or more persons. We would expect the conservative, patriarchal influence of such relationships to increase pressures upon women to have more children yet the correlation of -0.36 is in the wrong direction. Similarly, we ought to expect that families that are more well off in terms of area available for raising children and job security ought to contribute to larger families.

After introducing controls for the percentage of females in the labor force, tatami-area per person, and the percentage of jobs that are high SES, the beta for household sizes of six or more is still negative, although it is not significant statistically. This regression has no statistically significant predictors and only explains 8% of the variation in the abortion rate. Even the percentage of females in the labor force is spurious as a predictor of the abortion rate. Again, these negative results suggest that Japan is well into the post-industrial period of family planning.

Government critics of young women are simply wrong in their persistent attacks. The low birth rates and high abortion rates among the Japanese appear to have nothing to do with more highly educated females and women in the labor force. Nor do they have any significant relationship to other popular explanations such as overcrowding, standard of living, and so on.

---

[3]There is an autocorrelation between GPP and dense/hab, and between %dense/hab and %urban, so I left both the percent urban and the ratio of density to habitable land out of the regression.

Table 5—3

Zero-Order Correlates of the Abortion Rate per 1000 Live Births

Correlate	Expected	Actual
GPP	+	0.13
% FemLF	+	-0.24
%HSenroll	+	0.18
%Urban	+	0.08
%density/hab	+	0.17
Xmarryage	-	0.20

CHILD REARING AND JUVENILE DELINQUENCY

Japanese youths are much more under the supervision of family members and school officials than their American counterparts. Japan has lower divorce rates, levels of poverty, school absenteeism and dropout rates than the United States, so that many of the factors that allow opportunities for youth crime and delinquency in the United States have low efficacy in Japan. Furthermore, when the police apprehend a juvenile, both his or her teachers as well as parents are expect to discuss the problem with the police and to accompany the youth when he or she apologizes to the arresting officers and juvenile section-officials of the police department. Thus, it should come as no surprise that delinquency rates in Japan, depending on the crime, are roughly one-twelfth (for violent crimes) to one-twentieth (for larceny) that of the United States, even when we consider differences in reporting and accounting methods (Bayley, 1991).

One of the assumptions underlying much of criminology is that crime should decrease in an aging society because youth commit crime in disproportionately high numbers. Japan is the most rapidly aging industrial society, so we might expect its already low crime rates to decrease even further. However, annual white papers on crime in Japan suggest quite the opposite.

While birth rates continue to decrease the annual white papers on crime indicate increasing numbers of children arrested. In 1981 the total number of criminal arrests was 416,672 excluding traffic accidents, and juveniles made up 52.2% of these arrests. The police arrested a total of 67,906 children under age 14 during the same year. For felonies, known to police there were 1,266,658 cases in 1977 and 1,462,010 in 1981. However, the juvenile ratio of felonies hovered between 26 and 27% for the years from 1971 to 1981. By contrast, juvenile arrest ratios for violent offenses increased rapidly from 19,448 to 25,078 cases versus 100,408 to 169,711 total arrests over the ten years from 1971 to 1981. Juvenile delinquency increased even more dramatically after 1982 (Keisatsu Chōhen, 1990, p. 164) in comparison to the general population. By 1989, total juvenile arrests had blossomed to 193,206 cases, of which 74.7% were for theft.

As with any official crime statistics, these figures surely under-estimate actual crime. The negative attitudes of victims and witnesses and the fear of having too many unsolved crime cases on file lead to low reporting of crimes (Bayley, 1991). There is some question as to whether these increases are due to changes in children's behaviors, police behaviors, public-reported behaviors, or some combination.

The annual white papers on crime suggest that the most of the crimes associated with juvenile delinquency are property crimes (stealing, fraud, embezzlement), but these reports only hint at the possible causes. For example, Japanese crime reports indicate that the juvenile perpetrators come from normal, economically middle-class families, although the mass-media shows increasing concern with the effects of latch-key children without proper adult supervision. There is also impressionistic concern over (a) the pressures of a too competitive educational system and (b) the deleterious effects of broken homes. Yet no serious analysis of these possible hypotheses exists, and there is little use of sociological theory to tease out the possible causal links.

This section uses the rate of juvenile delinquency reported to the police for youth ages 14 through 18 because this is the age of greatest saliency. For example, the range for youth ages 14 to 18 is from 13 to 27 arrests per 1000 population, but for all youth under age 20, the rate is from 4 to 10 arrests per 1000 population. Also, the correlation between the two measures is 0.85, suggesting highly similar geographic incidence. As one should expect, Figure 5—4 indicates that the dense, central Honshū area from Tōkyō to Ōsaka has the highest juvenile arrest rates.

The three-generational household gives greater social control and is a much more conservative institution than the nuclear family, which should translate into lower juvenile delinquency rates. There is a low, but theory-consistent, correlation of -0.19 between number of persons in the household and the over-age-14 juvenile delinquency rate.

Miyazaki (1982; 1977) contends that youths with affluent parents commit a large part of delinquent acts. However, a number of indicators of affluence have low, and even inconsistent correlations, with the official delinquency rates. The percentage of profession and technical workers has a correlation of 0.19; the percentage of managers has a Pearson's r equal to 0.11 and gross prefectural product per capita has an r= 0.17. Nevertheless, the higher the percentage of home owners, the lower the rate of juvenile delinquency. Also, the number of household rooms per capita also does not correlate with the juvenile delinquency rate, and has the wrong sign (r = -0.07).

Also, affluence is most probably entangled with numerous other variables such as urbanization and density for which Miyazaki and others have not properly controlled. After adding population density to gross prefectural product per capita, the percentage of professional and technical workers, and the percentage of managers, as predictors in a regression analysis none of these variables is statistically significant in explaining the juvenile delinquency rate. Thus, the evidence does not support a role for familial affluence.

Miyazaki also hypothesizes that juveniles commit crimes to relieve the stress and frustration of their school life because of long school days, cram schools, and study hardships. He points out that roughly three-fourths of larceny cases are created by junior or senior high school students. In the case of abuses of organic solvents like adhesive thinner and bond, close to 60% are committed by children not in school. Also, he believes children who come from schools labeled "poor," "second-class," or "low-grade" leads to inferiority complexes that result in such students turning to crime and delinquent acts. Rohlen (1983, p. 298-299) also states that "[d]elinquency is obviously correlated with school rank" based upon an analysis of 5 schools in the Kōbe City area.

Note the dangers of using small, or non-representative samples. There is no correlation between official juvenile delinquency rates and the known use of stimulants or glue sniffing. This suggests that different sets of individuals engage in each type of behavior. There is also no correlation between delinquency and any available indicator of school pressures at the prefectural level — the percentage of (a) high school students matriculating in college; (b) junior high students who play hooky; (c) students going on to the top 400 high schools; (d) population without at least a sixth grade education; (e) or students accepted at the top 40 universities.

Only one of Miyazaki's claims receives modest support: the deleterious effect of latchkey environments. Both the percentage of females in the labor force and divorce rates correlate positively with juvenile delinquency rates. After regressing official juvenile delinquency rates on female labor force and divorce rates, both regression weights are positive and the divorce-rate beta is more than twice its standard error. Even so, these two independent variables explain only 10% of the variation in official delinquency rates.

In sum, juvenile delinquency appears to be much more complex than previously assumed. Delinquency appears to have no relationship to the educational rat race, family affluence, or the three-generation households. The only empirical relationship that does receive support is the deleterious effects of lack of adult supervision as measured by divorce and female labor-force employment.

Japanese adolescents have very little opportunity to use illegal drugs compared to Americans. Because Japan is an island nation without the porous borders of the United States, it is much easier for the authorities to minimize drug imports and, thus, drug use. American statistics compare percentages of youth who use marihuana, Japanese use the base of millions. In 1988 the police reported only 11 cannibis-related drug offenses per million population. The major port city of Yokohama and neighboring Tōkyō, were at the high extreme with only 50 cases per million population. Yet national surveys of American adolescents report average percentages of marihuana users of 15 to 20% between 1971 and 1988 (Johnson and Kaplan 1991).

Alcohol abuse is a major issue in the United States where as many as 20% of teenagers report drunkenness at least once a week (Calhoun, Grotberg, & Rickley, 1980). However, teenage alcohol use is vitally non-existent in Japan. Stimulant drug-related offenses known to the Japanese police are likewise paltry. The national mean was only 22 per 100,000 population in 1988. The closest equivalent to American marihuana or alcohol abuse is glue-sniffing. Glue-sniffing, including paint thinner and solvent, and related offenses known to the police are measured per 10,000 population in Japan, with a prefectural range of .4 to 5.5, and a mean of 2 offenses in 1988. Approximately 25% of each society are adolescents, so it is clear that drug abuse is a minor problem in Japan even if the Japanese press and public perceive it is a growing threat.

Glue sniffing is a quite different type of deviancy from larceny and other crimes, as evidenced by the 0.28 correlation between the two. Sniffing glue is a much more retreatist activity. It can be much more easily hidden from discovery than missing property. However, like delinquency-related crimes, the correlates of drug abuse are very weak or nil. Out of 21 correlations based upon the preceding delinquent crime analysis, only one is significantly different from zero. The percentage of students entering the top 40 universities has a correlation of -0.51 (p <.01) with glue sniffing which makes intuitive sense, Glue sniffing can lead to serious, permanent brain damage, so we would expect successful college aspirants to have lower than normal drug use.

Only a few, weak correlates of glue sniffing manifest themselves. The percentage of people moving during the past five years had a weak, positive correlation (r = 0.15). Traditionally, places with higher population change are more susceptible to social pathologies of various types. Police make great efforts in Japan to know the residents of the areas they are responsible for patrolling and to keep updated lists of residents (Bayley, 1991). Every owner-occupied community has highly conspicuous maps showing the locations of all buildings and the surnames of their owners. These types of social control mechanisms assure much less of the anonymity and anomie conducive to high crime and delinquency areas in the United States.

Furthermore, Japan has very little sub-cultural support for deviant and criminal roles by comparison to the United States. Table 1—1 lists important connotative information on a number of youth identities. One of those identities is important to the present analysis: juvenile delinquent (furyō). Our Japanese respondents view juvenile delinquents as 0.6 less powerful (-1.4) than does Heise's American sample (-0.8). As a more general test, I compared 14 deviant crime-related identities for which data exists on both American and Japanese. In all cases, the Japanese identities were lower in status and power. The Japanese socialization system may inculcate a more futile sense of the role of deviant criminal identities than the American one.

Table 5—4

Correlations between Delinquency Rates for Persons age 14 to 18 and Glue Sniffing and Some Possible Causes (N=47 Prefectures)

Variable Name	Delinquency	Glue Sniffing
Gross Prefectural Profit per Capita	0.18	0.05
%Professional/Technical Workers	0.19	-0.12
%Managerial Workers	0.11	0.13
%Unemployed	0.25	-0.23
%Females in Labor Force	0.08	- 0.05
%Urbanization	0.23	0.07
Population Density	0.18	0.03
Divorce Rate	0.25	-0.11
Divorce Rate for Males 40-44	-0.08	-0.07
Tatami per capita	0.00	-0.13
Industrialization Index	0.06	0.11
Sex Ratio for Persons under Age 15	0.07	0.05
Persons per Household	-0.19	0.00
% of Households with 6 or More Persons	-0.07	-0.11
Dependency Ratiio % Children	-0.29	-0.10
%Movers	0.08	- 0.07
%Newcomers	-0.09	0.15
%High School Seniors going to College	-0.05	0.00
% Jr. High School Students Playing Hooky	0.18	0.21
%H..S. Seniors from Top 400 High Schools	0.03	-0.09
%Illiterate	0.03	-0.22
%H.S. Seniors going to Top 40 Universities	0.05	- 0.51**

**significance level > 0.01

DIVORCE JAPANESE STYLE

The Family Bureau of the Japanese court system reported only 43,000 petitions for divorce during 1988, down from a record high 49,000 in 1983, and lower than the 45,000 in 1979. The 1983 high translates into a trifling 1.5 divorces per 1,000 persons when compared to the 4.03 American rate.

Kumagai (1984) appears to have correctly argued at the time that the divorce rate would abate. While the American rate climbed to 4.8 per 1000 Americans by 1988, the crude Japanese rate fell to 1.26 during the same period.

However, the reason that Kumagai gave may be wrong. She argued that the 1983 rate was a demographic artifact of the baby-boom cohort. The fastest growing component of the overall Japanese divorce rate is for spouses in their 60s, which rose from 2.9% of the total divorces granted in 1979 to 4.6% in 1988 — an increase of 83.5% over a decade. Similarly, petitions from wives over age 60 doubled from 1.4% to 2.8% of the cases during the same period. Because the Japanese divorce system generally awards significantly greater monetary settlements the longer the marriage, the rise in husband's petitions among senior citizens indicates much pent-up demand for divorce. For example, the family courts settle about 90% of divorces in favor of wives. While the average settlement was ¥3.87 million ($18,878) in 1988, this divorce-settlement payment nearly doubled to ¥6.95 million ($33,902) for marriages of more than 20 years.

In spite of the increase in divorces during the 1980s, Hodge and Ogawa's (1991, p. 81) cohort analyses of Mainichi survey data indicate no erosion of basic conservative family values during the post-World War II period. Comparisons of American and Japanese semantic differential data support the much more conservative Japanese attitudes towards divorce-related identities. Four identities (stepfather, stepmother, stepchild, and divorcee) for which there is comparative Japanese-American data suggest that Japanese divorce-statuses are consistently lower in status and power. By contrast, recall from Table 5—1 that Americans gain more in status from marital identities, even ones involving divorce (e.g., remarriage). These connotative data indicate that marriage is more attractive to Americans, while Japanese have greater incentive to avoid divorce.

The data presented suggest that divorce and marriage rates should be related in the United States but not in Japan. It is not by chance than the United States leads Japan (and the rest of the world) in both divorce and marriage rates. As strange as it may seem at first, high divorce rates very much determine high marriage rates. The only viable reason for getting a divorce in a society in which marriage has relatively high status is to get remarried. In turn, remarriages among divorced individuals drive up the marriage rate because, in essence, remarried individuals get recounted. The 1988 American divorce rate was 3.8 times as high as the Japanese rate while the American marriage rate was only 1.7 times as high as the Japanese rate. Yet the correlation between the crude divorce and marriage rates is positive and as strong in Japan (0.63) as it is in the United States.

Japanese like to imagine themselves as part of a homogeneous culture with low conflict that their relatively low divorce rates reflect, but there are more compelling reasons for the divorce rate differences that do exist. First, Japan has only recently become a mobile nation, while the United States has a long history of geographical mobility propelled by industrialization. Sociologists of the family have long argued that divorce is partly a function of geographical mobility (Corley & Woods, 1991; Glenn & Shelton, 1985; Zimmerman, 1991). When families move, individuals find it easier to act independent of kinship pressures to remain married when the marriage goes sour. The primary assumption is that as physical distance increases, opportunities for monitoring relatives and applying social pressures to conform decreases. As Japanese businesses move employees to new locations in Japan and send more employees overseas these sorts of sociological influences ought to loosen group controls over individuals. The correlation of 0.72 between Japanese who made intra-prefectural moves from 1975 to 1980 and the divorce rate in 1980 supports this hypothesis. It is significantly different from zero at the 0.001 level.[4] The total intra- and inter-prefectural movement correlation with divorce also is significant statistically and has the predicted direction (r = 0.55; p < .001)

The great migration from rural to urban areas — particularly to Tōkyō — that has taken place since World War II has caused great social dislocations, and divorce appears to continue as one of them. The areas around Tōkyō show the greatest amount of immigration with 8.23% of metropolitan Tōkyō area residents changing location between 1975 and 1980 while more rural areas along the northern Japan Sea coast having less than half that amount of migration.

Another problem of migration not captured by the above variables is the "dekasegi", or migrant worker, problem.[5] The dekasegi are young farm men who search for work in the big cities during the long northern winters. Their absences create strains upon their families and communities, who are left with temporarily larger dependency ratios of senior citizens and lower sex ratios of marriageable young men to women. The problem is one that particularly affects the Tōhoku region. In 1980, 4.4% of workers in Akita sought seasonal work outside their prefecture, Aomori was second with 3.5%, Yamagata was third with 2.4%, and Iwate fourth with 2.2%. Other prefectures had virtually no migrant workers. Thirty-one of the prefectures had less than 1 in 1000 workers engaged in seasonal, migrant work. If we leave in just those 40 prefectures that are not outliers, there is a correlation of 0.38 (p < 0.01), supporting the idea that migrant work, like other forms of migration, does contribute to divorce in Japan.

The problem of dislocation of men (and their families) to overseas business offices has also caused great alarm in the popular press. Note that it is particularly a problem for precisely those cities with the types of men women claim as ideal mates: the Kantō, Nagoya, Ōsaka, and Hiroshima where the bulk of head offices are. The increasing "solution" has been for companies to send their male employees overseas for 3 years while the wife fends for the family back home causing one sort of problem. Another solution to take the kids along to an alien school system causing another sort of

[4]I deleted Kyoto's 346 per 1000 score because it is an outlier, almost 5 times as large as the 63.9 score for the next highest case, Hokkaidô.

[5]A request of the National Science Foundations National Science Information System's Japanese database turned up 62 publications on the dekasegi problem, indicating a substantial literature.

problem. Here again, there is a correlation with the correct sign of 0.25. In sum, all of the migration data is consistent with expectations: the more, the higher the divorce rate.

Conservatives in all industrialized nations are fond of charging, on the other hand, that divorce is a positive function of female participation in the labor force. The idea is that independent sources of money give women independence of marital choice. The issue became a major one in Japan during the 1980s because the economic climate was so favorable to men that there were more good jobs available than eligible young men to fill them. Industry felt pressured to fill vacancies with either Japanese women or foreigners during that period. Conservatives charged that filling vacancies with women would undermine the family system.

However, recall that Hodge and Ogawa (1991) found no generational change in conservative familial values among men or women during the post-war period. International survey data strongly supports women's work as a means to providing supplementary income for housing, education, and other necessities rather than as a means of gaining independence from their husbands (Saso, 1990). Furthermore, Japanese women have been highly consistent in quitting full-time work to raise a family within one or two years of marriage. Thus, we should expect no relationship between the divorce rate and female labor-force participation, and this is precisely what we find in Japan (r = 0.03).

A simple regression of the crude divorce rate on total population change from 1975 to 1980, the percentage of workers who were dekasegi, and the sex ratio underscores the unexceptional nature of the causes of Japanese divorce. Intra- and inter-prefectural movements of population have the strongest beta equal to 0.71, which is significant at the 0.01 level. The sex-ratio beta of -0.29 is statistically significant at the 0.05 level. Together, these two variables explain 40% of the variation in prefectural divorce rates. Emigrant-work status has an insignificant beta of 0.14. This low beta is perfectly reasonable given the small number of prefectures affected.

This leaves us then with the question: If the causes of divorce in Japan are ordinary, why then are divorce rates so infrequent? Although there are undoubtedly multiple reasons for the exceptionally low divorce rate in Japan, sex-ratio theory suggests one of the most reasonable and parsimonious explanations. High sex-ratios, as explained in Chapter Four, have given Japanese women more power to control their lives than they used to have. Women's liberation is not possible anywhere without the aid of structural changes that shift power away from men. In the United States, World War II created strong impetus for sex-role changes. Industries temporarily opened such traditional male occupations as welding and ship building to women to prove their capabilities. In Japan, sex-role imbalances have shifted in favor of women. According to Guttentag and Secord's theory (1983), high sex ratios ought to make men less valuable, and women more valuable, commodities. Such structural changes ought to make it easier for women to control their own destinies. The initial impetus for Guttentag and Secord's sex-ratio thesis came from the her curiosity over why the lyrics of

Mozart's age (a period of high sex-ratios) emphasized exclusive life-long commitment for marriage among men, while contemporary American songs (during a period of low sex-ratios) praise brief liaisons and casual relationships (p. 10—11).

The correlations between age-specific sex ratios and divorce rates for men and women over age 55 are -0.47 and -0.46, both of which are statistically significant at beyond the 0.001 level. Tōkyō and neighboring Kanagawa are outliers that, when removed, raise those correlations slightly to -0.53 and 0-.50, respectively. This is precisely as Guttentag and Secord predict. High sex ratios associate with more conservative familial and sex roles. The "unique" situation of Japan's low divorce rates is not unique by historical and international standards. Rather, Japan's high sex ratios encourage a number of institutions that seem remarkable to Americans only because we presently are a low sex-ratio society. Thus, high-ratio indicators in Japan seem strange to us: obsession with virginity for unmarried girls; wifely chastity; unprovocative dress for women; stable, traditional occupations; male eagerness to make marital commitments; and low illegitimacy rates.

Guttentag and Secord never proposed a simple relationship between sex-ratios and other variables. They made an important distinction between structural power and dyadic power, and pointed out that structural controls may easily overwhelm dyadic power (pp. 25—26, 29). As is true of most societies, men hold enormous structural power in Japan. The legislative, judicial, and administrative systems in Japan are highly paternalistic. Although Japanese law includes irretrievable breakdown of the marriage, regardless of fault, as grounds for divorce, Upham (1987, pp. 12—13) argues that the judiciary effectively nullifies divorce statutes through its hostility toward divorce. He points out that family-court judges go so far as to deny divorce in the face of clear evidence of fault on the respondent's side. Conservative social values — no doubt reinforced by the high Japanese sex ratio — work against divorce in Japan.

The swamping of legal statute by conservative social values may be more understandable to Americans who recall how difficult it was to get a divorce in the United States until the 1970s. The barriers to no-fault divorce in the United States first came down in the State of New York because of the hypocrisy foisted by the need to "prove" adultery or cruelty — the only acceptable reasons at the time. A highly lucrative business arose around private detective agencies and photographers. Namely, a husband and wife would go to a private detective agency and "set up" a false adultery charge against the husband (usually). A woman worker at the private detective agency would go to a hotel with the husband. The detective would "break in" on the couple and take pictures as "proof" that the man was cheating on his wife. Of course, the court was fully aware of the false pretenses, but would grant a divorce. The lawyers and private detective agencies made huge sums of money out of this gray market until the State of New York liberalized divorce laws to more reasonable grounds for divorce. Most other states followed New York's lead by 1980 in accepting "no fault" divorce on grounds of incompatibility.

The main point of this anecdote is to illustrate why a low divorce rate does not imply a low amount of familial conflict or a high amount of family happiness where people have relatively little freedom to divorce. A true test of family conflict and happiness would be a "free marketplace" to divorce and get married — a state that does not exist either in the United States or Japan, although the United States is infinitely closer to such a free marketplace. One reason already stated is that the family courts, and related mediation services, in Japan often deny couples the right to divorce. Second, the work place and kinship pressures to get married and stay married exist in the United States also, but to a much lesser extent than in Japan. This is partly because we have a longer tradition of geographical movement. Third, Japanese law imposes greater disincentives to divorce on persons who are married longer through stiffer alimony payments. Nevertheless, Japan is becoming increasingly vulnerable to industrial needs for a more mobile work force. This will undoubtedly create pressures for change in Japanese divorce laws and individual requests for divorce. Already we can see some of this in current divorce ratios.

Whether or not divorce, or change in divorce laws, is good or bad is less relevant than the trade-offs that people are willing to make. The real trade-off is not between individualism and marriage but industrialization and familism. In Japan, like other Western countries, industry has demanded great commitment. So far the Japanese have consistently chosen work commitment over marriage. However, there is an inherent conflict built into work commitment in that sociologists believe it creates individualism in the long run. In the United States, increasing numbers of people have tried to turn from work commitment to a marriage commitment, but the post-industrial work place emphasis on individualism is a powerful force that rather easily displaces any attempts to build and maintain groups of any type.

This creates a strong challenge and dilemma for nations like Japan who would try to maintain group goals over individual desires. In the longer run, industrialization wins. This shows up clearly in tests of differential divorce rates. Furukai and Alston (1990) tested both human-capital factors such as those already discussed versus social integration variables (rates of industrialization, urbanization) in explaining prefectural variation in divorce rates. Their results confirm that urbanization, modernization, and industrialization promote the disintegration of traditional norms and values.

Producers in the family economy have more power and prestige than consumers. The more power and prestige accrue to those who control the distribution of valued goods beyond the family. Women's increased productivity has eroded legal and customary restraints on their behavior. For example, marriage has declined as an institution in Japan as elsewhere. There is greater postponement of marriage, fewer persons ever marrying, a lower ratio of time spent in wedlock, and shorter marital duration.

SUMMARY

This chapter focuses on a few selective, but important, indicators of change and stability in the familial life course in Japan. The first is the tension caused by the greedy institutional conflict of work versus family. Work and familial roles are more strongly gendered in Japan compared to the United States. This shows up in the much more M-like pattern of married women's work patterns in Japan. Married Japanese women with children have a lower propensity to continue work after having their first child. Part of the reason is normative resistance to alternative child-care arrangements although the younger generations are showing some willingness to use baby-sitting. Corporate ideology also reinforces more traditional housekeeping and mothering roles. International surveys continue to place Japan at the more conservative end of sex-role attitudes and behaviors.

Primary-sector industries that give guarantees of lifetime employment to select male employees are particularly noteworthy as greedy institutions. Demographic data corroborates the pattern as less unique of Japan as a whole than select regions in major cities; in particular, Tōkyō. The regional nature of lifetime employment encourages discrimination against women, and aids maintenance of the present status quo that keeps women out of mainstream work. It also favors men with higher education. I suggest that the structural power inherent in the life-time employment system vests the traditional paternalistic base of authority in the corporate world.

Semantic differential data suggests that status and power have quite different bases in Japan versus the United States. In support of the corporate replacement of family-centered life in Japan, the connotations of American familial identities have higher status. The SD data also support greater structural power differentials between husbands and wives in Japan than the United States. In spite of these differences, both cultures grant greater status to persons who assume older, male, and married roles.

Japanese women appear to gain much more esteem from child-oriented roles than work roles. Attitudinal data underscores the willingness of Japanese women to leave work for child-rearing roles early in their marriages. Although the behavior of women does not seem to be pronatalist because of the increasingly fewer children considered ideal and the decreasing birth rates, the SD data corroborates other survey data that Japanese women prefer motherhood to work.

Regression analysis of the likely causes of variations in the crude birth rate supports Hodge and Ogawa's thesis that Japan is a post-modern society with low and inconsistent relationships among family planning variables. Although late marriage correlates with small family size, the relationship is spurious. Higher female educational attainment and affluence does appear to negatively affect actual family size in Japan, but the relationships are weak and leave the largest portion of the variance still unexplained by variables that work in less advanced countries.

Contraception and abortion practices in Japan since World War II have diverged greatly from the United States. The pill has not reached wide acceptance, and abortion is available on demand for all practical purposes. In spite of such differences, variation in prefectural abortion data is also highly consistent with family planning theory. The regression and correlation data suggest that the Japanese government is wrong in assuming higher education females and working women are most likely to resort to such techniques. In fact, the low correlations and regression results suggest that virtually all Japanese women resort to similar family-planning styles. In fact, the ecological data suggest that abortion is more prevalent among rural women with less education.

Crime and delinquency are extremely low in Japan lending support to the myth of uniqueness. Ironically, Japanese criminologists who have tried to explain recent increases in juvenile delinquency usually blame it on the "Americanization" or "Westernization" of Japan. Correlation and regression of prefectural variations in delinquency cases known to the police and glue sniffing do not support such ideas. For example, although the popular press blames much of the problem of increases in latch-key children, neither the percentage of females in the labor force nor the divorce rate can explain more than 10% of the variation in official juvenile delinquency rates. There is also no support for causative effects of educational rat-race pressures, affluence, or the demise of the three-generation household on juvenile crimes. Similarly, out of over 20 correlation tests, only one — the percentage of high school senior going to top 40 universities is statistical significant. I interpret these weak correlations as evidence of much lower sub-cultural support for deviant and criminal behavior because of semantic differential data from this chapter and early ones that shows that Japanese crime-related identities are much lower in esteem and power than their American counterparts.

The final test of Japanese uniqueness is the remarkably low divorce rate. Once again, however, the uniqueness disappears in the face of standard sociological theory and analysis. Japanese divorce-statuses are consistently lower in status and power than comparable American identities. The American system rewards marriage, even re-marriage, over singlehood, while the Japanese system has greater disincentives to divorce once married. Even so, divorced Japanese are better off remarrying than staying single, leading to a high positive correlation between crude divorce and marriage rates in both cases.

The causes of divorce also are remarkably similar. Migration in its various forms — household relocation in Japan, seasonal migrant work, and international moves — all have the predicted positive relationship. Although conservatives often charge that the women gain power through work statuses that increase their propensity to seek work, the Japanese data — like its Western counterparts — do not support this contention.

This still leaves one nagging question: Why are Japanese divorce rates so low? The distinctions between structural power and dyadic power aid the analysis. Japan is a high-sex ratio society that mirrors other such societies across the centuries. That is, the high number of marriageable men to women has all the classic indicators of conservative familial and sex roles. At the dyadic level this gives women power over the men in their lives to keep their promises of commitments. At the same time, structural power in Japan is still very much in the hands of a male government that has consistently used its conservative social values to deny divorces in the face of relatively liberal divorce statutes instituted during the post-war Occupation.

Chapter 6

PREHISTORIC AND HISTORIC ROOTS OF ETHNIC PLURALISM

The previous chapters have each, in their own way, shown that Japan is neither as homogeneous nor as inexplicable a society as many ideologues would have us believe. Wiener (1989) has documented that the "unique aspects of Japanese culture" thesis is relatively new, taking root only after the Meiji Restoration. This chapter tackles what is perhaps the most ideological debate in modern Japan: the myth of racial and cultural homogeneity.

The myth has deep roots in history. It goes back at least as far as the Tokugawa Era (1615-1868) debate over whether Japan should be "open" (kaikoku) or "close" (sakoku). The popular press displays much ambivalence over the value of "internationalization" (kokusaika) versus its concomitant "problems." Some demagogues still warn of the "invasion" of hordes of foreign workers (gaijin rōdōsha).

Another mirror for understanding how the myth is maintained is the categorization of Korean-Japanese and Chinese-Japanese. The law categorizes these populations — most of whom were born and brought up in Japan since World War II — as permanent residents (teichaku ijūsha) who can be deported at will, rather than as citizens of Japan. They are permanent outsiders.

A more interesting example of the insider-outsider discrimination is the treatment of returnees and their children (kikokushijo). Many Japanese treat these people as if they have lost their Japanese identity through exposure to foreign cultures.

In essence, these types of practices and attitudes provide a Rorschach test for studying geographic, racial, and ethnic variation in Japan because each of these concepts is unevenly distributed across the Japanese archipelago, even as they have predictable patterns. This chapter deconstructs the internationalization of Japan. First, it provides a short introduction to pre-historic and historic evidence underlying the multi-ethnic origins of the Japanese. Then, it outlines the current multi-ethnic group make-up of Japan as a precursor for an excursion in the final chapter into variations in internationalization and ethnicity in modern Japan.

DE-CONSTRUCTING "INTERNATIONALIZATION"

The current tendency to view foreign interchange as a problem seems strange in light of Japan's long history of borrowing from other cultures. Even more strange is the peculiar tendency of many Japanese to deny — even to try to cover up — the long history of foreign influence on Japan. All cultures engage in myth making, but the Japanese seems more bent than most peoples on covering up their past for the dubious purpose of promulgating the "myth-istory" of the uniqueness of their culture. It is as if there was no non-Japanese answer to the question: Where did the Japanese come from?

PREHISTORIC TRAILS

Like the mythic brothers, Romulus and Remus of the legendary founding of Rome, Japanese myth places the founding of Japan on the shoulders of the brother and sister deities, Izanagi and Izanami. The myth was first written out in Chinese during the eighth century in two famous Japanese chronicles: the kojiki and the Nihongi. The average Japanese probably thinks of them as indigenously borne. However, almost assuredly, these myths were adaptations from the Asian continent because they were written in Chinese and are remarkably similar to Asian myths.

Modern archeological and historical methods suggest that the origin of the Japanese was not spontaneously borne out of a vacuum. Cultural artifacts, blood, genes, and language have all left consistently clear trails for the origins of the Japanese. Unlike mysteries over the migrations of some populations, the geographic proximity of Japan to the Asian continent makes it easy to surmise the natural points of cultural contact that must have taken place over thousands of years. From the South, it would have been easy for fishing villages from Taiwan to establish trade throughout the lower archipelago. In the North, the Japanese archipelago extends beyond Hokkaidō up through the Sakhalin Islands, making easy passage by small boats or rafts to and from Siberia. The main island of Honshū itself is less than 100 miles by boat from the closest point of the Korean Peninsula.

Thus, it should come as no surprise that recent archeology connects the peopling of the Japanese Archipelago through these natural points of immigration and trade. Hanihara (1991) uses dental characteristics that are relatively invariant over centuries, to demonstrate physical affinities between the Paleolithic (circa 17,000 B.C.) Minatogawa people of Okinawa, the Jōmonese of the Neolithic period (circa 6,000 to 8,000 B.C.), and modern Japanese. Turner (1987) and Dodo and Ishida (1990) show that even ethnic groups considered by lay persons to be non-Japanese (e.g. Okinawans, Ainu, and Tokunoshimans) are clearly descended from the Jōmonese.

Suzuki and Takahama (1992) factor analyzed tooth samples from modern Akita, Okinawa, Tanegashima, and Tsushima populations as well as Jōmon and Yayoi samples. They confirm and extend Dodo and Ishida's work. Tanegashima (off the southwestern coast of Kyūshū) and Taiwan samples closely approximate ancient Jōmon samples. The Tsushima (midway between Pusan and the Honshū coast) affiliates with the ancient Yayoi population. Their Okinawan and Akita samples end up midway between the Jōmon and Yayoi poles.

These researchers conjecture that the most plausible peopling of Japan followed two primary routes. First, the Nansei (Southwest) Island chain must have provided the route for the spread of physical traits from generalized Asiatic populations into Kyūshū. This would include Southeast Asian migrants such as the Negritos of the Philippines, the Dajaks of Borneo, and some of the Lesser Sunda Islanders. All of these groups share cranial and dental features similar to the ancient Jōmonese and the present-day Okinawans. The strong Black Current — an essentially powerful river in the Pacific Ocean that moves up past the Philippines, past Taiwan, through the Ryūkyūs, and on by the main islands of Japan — surely provided a constant voluntary and involuntary source of migration. Second, the physical traits of the Japanese of Kyūshū and Honshū share close affinity with northeast Asians, including the Chinese and Koreans. This two-pronged peopling theory can explain 84% of the variation in dental and cranial records. Third, they point out that modern scholars agree that the language of the Ryūkyuan (Okinawan) Islands branched off as a Japanese dialect during the prehistoric period.

Archaeological records of distinct, ancient northern and southern cultural groups of ceramic works also fit a two-pronged peopling theory (Chinen 1990). The archaeological, medical, and cultural sources I have cited are relatively inaccessible to the average Japanese, but the national broadcasting system (NHK) has produced numerous documentaries that explain these findings in lay terms with clear displays of important artifacts and records from sites in Saga and Nara prefectures. These publicly broadcast documentaries have traced the clear prehistoric spread of Chinese culture (e.g., swords, ceramics,) and blood lines from the area around present-day Hong Kong up through Korea and then across into Kyūshū and Honshū.

In this way, much of Japan's civilization and culture jumped the narrow straits between the Korean peninsula and the Japanese archipelago between the Prehistoric Age and the early nineteenth century, including pottery making, metal work, weaving, printing, medicine, religion and literature. For example, archeologists now believe that rice cultivation entered northern Kyushu from the southern Korean Peninsula between 300 B.C. and 200 B.C. Bronze and iron tools appear to have entered by the same route during the same period. Researchers have discovered similar metal tools and stone tombs in many areas facing the 200-km long channel between Korea and Japan. Thus, archeologists and historians agree that the first agricultural age in Japan (the Yayoi Age) indicates the strong influence of continental culture brought over from the Korean peninsula about 3000 years ago.

Linguists have also demonstrated strong affinities of the pre-Kanji (Yamato) Japanese language to Ainu, Atayal (from Indonesia), Taiwanese, Cambodian, Korean, and Nepalese. Given the archaeological record, we should expect such linguistic ties. Yasumoto (1989) has used the same quantitative methods as in Chapter 3 to show the relationships of Japanese universities in a convincing demonstration that the Ural/Altai (Mongolian, Tungusic, Japanese, Korean, etc.) languages are as well connected as the European romance languages are.

The Northern Urasian languages all have common grammatical structures such as subject particles, adjectives that come before nouns, and sentence structures (Yasumoto 1989). They also share numerous words. Yasumoto's research suggests that the earliest roots of Japanese were Korean and Ainu, with southern Asian language influencing vocabulary at much later dates. Work by Shibatani (1990, p. 6) also points to remarkable similarity between various Old Japanese words and various Ural/Altai languages. For example, the Japanese word for dark (kurashi) shares strong resemblances to the Ainu word for shadow; the Korean words for cloud and soot; the Tungusic, Turkic, and Hungarian words for soot; and the Mongol word for black that are unlikely to have occurred by chance.

More impressive are the shared characteristics of Japanese and Ural-Altaic languages. Fujioka (1908 [1985]) notes some 14 characteristics supporting an Old Japanese—Altaic connection. These include vowel harmony, lack of articles, non-gendered grammar, suffixed verb inflections, postpositions instead of prepositions, a question particle attached to the final position of interrogative expressions, and no native words with an initial r sound.

Shibatani (1990) also undermines the myth of the uniqueness of the Japanese language. He shows that it has strong affinities to the most common characteristics in world languages. Agglutinative affixation is common to morphology throughout the world. He also notes that Subject-Object-Verb grammar exists in half of all languages (Shibutani 1990, p. 91). Likewise, Martin (1966) reconstructed the proto-forms of Japanese to Korean for 320 cognates in a strong demonstration of the close affinity between the two languages. Later (1975), he established beyond reasonable doubt the strong historic dependence of Old Japanese on Turkish, Mongol, and Tungus. Thus, strong evidence suggests genetic links of Japanese to other languages. Indeed,

Japanese resembles a creole — a language born of the intersection of numerous other languages, not unlike the origins of modern English.

HISTORIC TRACES

The historic records of systematic international contact with the Japanese started soon after the birth of Jesus in the West. Buswell (1990) argues that the history of religion in Asia — especially in China, Korea, and Japan — should be investigated as a whole because there has been a great deal of mutual influence and cross-fertilization over the centuries. After all, these countries shared a common writing system and written language. Chinese was the lingua franca of educated discourse through this region. Even Tibet and Vietnam had an influence on Japan through literary Chinese.

The first recorded Japanese missions overseas entered China in AD 57. From the fifth through the thirteenth century, Japanese emissaries went to both China and Korea. Bennett, Passin, and McKnight (1958) point out that as early as the seventh century AD that the word ryūgakusei had entered the Japanese language with the meaning of "overseas scholar" while enjoying the positive connotation of "bearer of enlightenment from the lands beyond the sea."

Chinese records document extensive travel to Japan from A.D. 147 to 190. They refer to widespread civil war and anarchy until the rise of a woman ruler, Pimiku (the Sun Princess). There were also frequent travelers to Japan during China's Wei Dynasty (220—265 A.D.) who made reports on the frequency of female rule and polygamy. About A.D. 600, Chinese influence in Japan strengthened with the introduction of Chinese methods of government and written histories, as recorded in the Kojiki and the Nihongi. In the Eighth Century other Chinese influences became institutionalized in Japan with the Taihō Code of 702 and the Yōrō Code of 718, establishing a patriarchal system and the subjection of women in the Confucian manner.

The Heian period (794—1185) saw the modeling of Kyōto based on Chinese plans with wide boulevards and grid-like streets. Throughout this period there are ample records of Japanese going to China and Korea to study Buddhism and Confucianism; and learn the Chinese writing system, which they brought back to Japan. Many of the unusually complex features of the present-day Japanese language are due to the fact that Japanese traveled to different areas of China over hundreds of years. Those early travelers brought back the kanji readings they learned. Thus, kanji that had different regional reading (say, in Cantonese and Peking-style Chinese) became incorporated into the Japanese language. The point is that extensive international trade and travel, as serious scholars have long known, occurred among the learned classes through the first 1500 years A.D.

Apparent literary cross-fertilization between Korea and Japan occurred during the three ancient Korean kingdom periods of Koguryo (37 BC-AD 668), Paekche (mid-fourth century-660) and Silla (57 BC to AD 935). Ancient Korean of the seventh and ninth century occurs in many parts of the literary classic Man'yōshū (A Collection of a Myriad Leaves). Miller (1981) points out that familiarity with Chinese poetic anthologies such as the Wen Hsüan during the eighth century influenced the Man'yōshū.

There is also a substantial unpublished literature on Korean origins that exists in the grants-in-aid applications and reports of Japanese archeologists. For example, the National Science Foundation's National Center for Science Information Systems retrieval service lists scores of scholarly reports that curiously never get published. As a sample, one report by Hayao Nishinakagawa of Kagoshima University traces the introduction of horses and cows in Japan to Korea during the sixth century. Another by Yoshikazu Takaya of Kyōto University indicates that certain strains of rice were introduced from Korea during the same period. Still others by Hatsushige Otsuka indicate the discovery of numerous artifacts of clear sixth-century Korean origin from the tumulus in Ikaruga of two people believed to have been members of the Japanese ruling elite in Nara's Yamato Court at the time.

Around the fifth century the Yamato Imperial Court in Nara learned Chinese characters (kanji) from Koreans to record their history. The kanji themselves are one of the best examples of past internationalization in Japan. What would the Japanese language be without the influence of the Chinese characters? Even the Japanese syllabary, or kana, owe their development to a simplification of Chinese characters.

Envoys from dynasties on the Korean peninsula brought Confucianism and Buddhism to Japan during the same period. They also imported religious scripture and statues of Buddha. The surnames of many illustrious Japanese families traces back to Korea via these envoys — Toyoda, Hiramatsu, Fuwa, Matsusaki, Wada, Takemi, Shimizu, Uno, Inoue, Kono, and Yamaguchi. (Most ordinary Japanese did not have a family name until the Meiji Restoration.) Japanese archeologists have long known that many influential families, including the Japanese royal family, had strong ties with those in ancient Korea. As Sanson (1951) pointed out long ago, "The degree of Japan's isolation may easily be overestimated if we think only in terms of the sakoku period; and if we exclude that period, we find that Japan shows a tendency to expand rather than to withdraw, from the earliest days of expeditions to Korean kingdoms in almost prehistoric times to the (Korean) campaigns of Hideyoshi in 1592 an 1597" (p. 5).

Abu-Lughod (1989, p. 306) provides an impressive set of maps and commentary documenting the overlapping inter-regional circuits of world trade from at least 748 A.D. through the sixteenth century. Japan had clear ties to the West even at this early period. Japanese sources in 748 A.D. wrote of the presence of Arab and Persian sea traders in Chinese ports (Di Meglio 1970). Chinese and Middle Eastern sources corroborate the Japanese texts in demonstrating a roughly three-month passage between the Persian Gulf to China by way of the Palk Strait north of Ceylon, the Bay of Bengal, the Malay Strait, and the Indochinese peninsula. Both Chinese and Arab ships passed back and forth.

By the fifteenth century international trade had become so routine that the port of Malacca had four harbor masters, each of whom handled different trading partners. One handled the Middle East, Persia, India, and Ceylon. A second handled local Malayan trade. The third's responsibility was Java, Borneo, Makasser and other islands. The fourth harbor master specialized in trade with Siam, Cambodia, the Ryūkyū islands, and China. In this way, Japan proper became indirectly, but firmly, linked to world trade. Abu Lughod points out (1989, p. 317) that the official records of shipping trade must only tap the tip of the iceberg. A huge amount of unofficial shipping trade between private parties surely passed unrecorded during this period. We can surmise this from the spread of China's superior technologies of paper making, silk production, business practices, and production passed westward as far as Europe by way of the Silk Road of Marco Polo fame, and eastward to Japan. Hsieh (1992) and Hamashita (1986) document the interpenetration of southeast Asian port cities, European colonies, Islamic states, and maritime regions as far south as Siam (Thailand). The Mediterranean world-system of the same age paled by comparison to this so-called Nanyang world-system. Through it, China spread its foreign influence into Japan; an influence that is still recognizable in archaeological finds. Hamashita goes so far as to charge that Asian history is the history of a unified system characterized by internal tribute/tribute-trade relations, with China at the center, and that Japan chose its course so as to cope with the tribute-trade system.

Ceramic remains aid the study of the spread of foreign influence in Japan (Barnes 1990; Mellott 1990; Pearson 1990; Underhill 1990). The native pottery of Kyūshū did not advance far beyond the unglazed pottery of the Yayoi Period (circa 200 B.C. - 200 A.D.) until the sixteenth century. By contrast, China and Korea had produced beautiful celadons for over 600 years and historic records show that great numbers were imported and sold to finance construction of temples during the Kamakura Period (1185-1391 AD).

The period of the thirteenth through the sixteenth centuries saw both the Kamakura and Muromachi bakufu (military governments) engage in diplomacy and official trade with the Sung, Yüan, and Ming dynasties in China and the Koryō and Yi dynasties in Korea (Shōji 1990). It was Chinese Ming, rather than Japanese, policy to forbid contact with foreigners during this period. Ironically, the unintended consequences of Ming policy lead to the Ryūkyū kingdom's ascendance as an intermediary in trade. According to Shōji (p. 401), numerous Sung Chinese worked as outside laborers and shrine dependents in the great Japanese temples and shrines. This led to intensive import and trade of Chinese goods such as saddles and silk cloth, and ownership of Japanese land by Chinese. In this way, the establishment of Buddhism strongly affected the adoption of Chinese culture in Japan.

Shōji (p. 408) claims that no less than forty to fifty ships each year traded between Sung and Japan. Indeed, so many Sung copper coins entered Japan that the Sung officials banned their export due to the shortage of money created. The Kamakura bakufu, in turn, stopped the practice of barter in favor of the handiness of copper coins for trade of all kinds. In time, the outflow of Japanese rice in chase of Sung coins led to famine in Japan and excessive inflation in Sung China. This suggests that the clamorings for closing off Japan may have been less in response to chauvinism than to rational economic perceptions.

In the case of the Koreans, pirate attacks on Japanese ships and shipwrecked sailors gave common reasons for the establishment of full diplomatic and trading relationships between the two countries. Although diplomacy and trade with the Koryō dynasty was spotty at times, the need for suppression of piracy and exchange of shipwrecked sailors kept open limited Koryō-Japan relationships.

During the fifteenth and sixteenth centuries, Okinawa became a crossroads for imports and transshipments from countries in both Africa and Asia. Both Chinese and Korean interpreters accompanied Okinawan ships that returned with exotic spices, jewels, textiles, and rare woods. Okinawa established at least 44 official embassies to kingdoms in Southeast Asia including Siam (present-day Thailand) during the fifteenth century. Official records show that Okinawans sent out hundreds of official missions to Java and Siam during this period that established Okinawa as a city-state not dissimilar in status to that of the European city-states that flourished at the same time (Kerr 1958).

In 1592, Toyotomi Hideyoshi organized those clans under his control for eight years, sending an army of 170,000 men in 1590 to invade the Korean peninsula. A second attempt in 1597 failed with the death of Toyotomi in battle after fierce resistance by Koreans. Ironically, these conflicts benefited the development of the ceramic industry in Japan's western regions. Toyotomi's armies brought captive Korean potters to Arita and Kagoshima in Kyūshū, establishing the ceramic arts there between 1592 and 1598. This signified the start of the most dynamic period of glazed pottery production for the kilns of Kyūshū. This pottery eventually became most famous because the master of the Japanese tea ceremony, Sen no Ryū, prized it.

The Tokugawa family replaced the Toyotomi family in 1603 and sent a series of missions to Korea to restore damaged cultural and economic ties with the Yi Dynasty while banning trade with all European nations except the Netherlands between 1641 and 1853. However, internationalization was not a one-way street during this period. Tani (1985) documents the rise of Nihon-machi (Japanese towns) during the fifteenth century in various parts of southeastern Asia. He estimates that 100,000 Japanese traveled overseas during this period.

Furthermore, Otsubo (1992) provides an excellent deconstruction of the myth that the Tokugawa bakufu ruled with much central power and little local autonomy. She gives evidence that the rulers of Tsushima mediated between the Tokugawa rulers and Korea. The bakufu granted special privileges to Tsushima officials for their commercial, trading, diplomatic, and interpreting skills and services. Similarly, she points out that the bakufu allowed Date Masamune, a feudal lord in northeastern Japan, to establish direct commercial relationships with Spain and Mexico during the early years of the seventeenth century.

Shortly thereafter in 1635, the Dutch gained control of Japanese trade by default. The Tokugawa shogunate gave the Dutch monopolistic rights that effectively excluded other European traders because of their efforts to promote Christianity. The zenith of Pax Neerlandica lasted from 1647 to 1672. Rising winds of protectionism throughout Europe in the early 1700s brought Dutch influence to an end. From the middle of the sixteenth century Japanese officials allowed the Portuguese to import their firearms, medicine, astronomy, clocks, and most significantly, their religion (Israel 1989).

This influence extended to Japanese syntax and vocabulary. Earns (1993) traces the influence of Dutch on Japanese from 1600 until 1868. Many scholars have noted the large number of loan words in Japanese, starting with Dutch words like pan for bread. However, Earns illustrates how Japanese translators created linguistic innovations such as pronouns (kare, kanojo), inanimate things as subjects of transitive or causative verbs, a new copula (de aru) for literary usage, and relative pronouns (tokoro no).

By the end of the sixteenth century Portuguese Jesuits and other missionaries threatened the traditional order through the conversion of nearly one million Japanese to Christianity, before being ruthlessly eradicated (Sansom 1962, p. 173). This was the start of the factional debates over sakoku and kaikoku (open country) that still reverberate. Nevertheless, there are records of 12 diplomatic missions from the Korean Yi dynasty to the Tokugawa shogunate between 1607 and 1811, even though this was the height of the era of seclusion.

The closed-country period did not effectively cut off all interchange with the outside world. Keene (1952) notes that Japanese intellectuals continued to do Dutch studies (Rangaku) from 1720 until 1798. Goodman (1990, p. 194) suggests that the Matsumae fiefdom (located in what is now Hokkaidō) had considerable leeway to challenge the official xenophobia. Indeed, the extremities of Japan were relatively porous because of their long histories of fishing and trade with the mainland and Taiwan. Katherine Plummer (1984) documents the role of Japanese fishermen who ended up in places such as Kamchatka, Alaska, Hawaii, and the west coast of the United States during this period. As one example, the Russian government ordered Japanese fishermen stranded in Vladivostok, Irkutsk, and eighteenth-century St. Petersburg to teach Japanese to generations of Russian interpreters.

Similarly, Jansen (1992) argues that the Japanese actively pursued Chinese and Korean contacts throughout the Tokugawa Period. He notes that Nagasaki, in particular, saw an explosion of Asian trade during the sixteenth century. For example, Jansen claims that thirty to forty percent of the world silver output during 1615 and 1625 passed through the Nagasaki port. Chinese goods, expatriate scholars, religious leaders, artists, and artisans were important vehicles of the day for the dissemination of Chinese ideas and technology throughout Tokugawa Japan.

OPENING OF JAPAN DURING THE MEIJI ERA

The official re-opening of Japan traces back to 1868, ending the unusually xenophobic period known as the <u>sakoku jidai</u> that had started in 1637. The Meiji Restoration of 1868 promoted the import of practically anything their official missions to the United States and Europe considered useful for a new Japan. Maeyama (1984) colorfully summarizes the Japanese history of internationalism that followed as one in which Japanese went to Europe and the United States to learn, to North and South America to emigrate, and to Asia to invade during the early part of the twentieth century.

Learning. Bartholomew's (1989, p. 45) history of Japanese science supports Maeyama's thesis. In the waning years of the Tokugawa shogunate, officials allowed eight shogunal delegations to travel abroad. These delegations returned with 200 books, and opened up technical study opportunities in Europe during the early 1860s. But the Meiji Period allowed for even freer exchange.

Bartholomew (p. 64) notes that the Meiji government played catch-up with the West partly through the hiring of 8,000 foreign scientists and engineers whom they treated with great respect. He notes (p. 65) that "By 1870, it was common for medical men to be chosen in Germany, whereas British subjects and to a lesser extent Americans reigned in physical science." Not surprisingly, these foreign mentors affected the decisions of their Japanese students to study overseas.

The world-respected predominance of German science during the 1880s provided the natural model for the Japanese to restructure their own national university system. The greater part of the present Japanese system of higher education originated with the experimentation with European higher education that fit the needs of the Japanese bureaucracy for practical, applied knowledge. Bartholomew well summarizes this influence: ". . . the Meiji government was reluctant to accept autonomy or equality for science. It tried to co-opt almost every interest, and to make science the servant of the state." (p. 125) Indeed, the same could be said for modern Japanese governments.

The importance of the internationalization of science and education during first years of the Meiji government should not be underestimated. The government allotted almost a sixth of the annual national education budget to sending officially designated <u>ryūgakusei</u> abroad and to supporting them while they were there (Kashioka 1982) .

Another sign of the internationalization of Japan was the standardization of the Japanese written language after the 1850s. Twine (1991) points out that the beginning of the Meiji Era saw a confusing multiplicity of written styles ranging from Classical Chinese over diluted forms of Sino-Japanese to Classical Japanese. She notes that Japanese elites were well aware that Europe's ascent to world dominance came partly from the standardization and nationwide spread of the modern European languages. Mass education can not develop when only the highly educated can understand a written language. The genbun'itchi (unification of spoken and written language) movement of the Meiji Era successfully reformed style and script in large part due to Western encroachment.

Emigration. Out-migration can take one of two forms. In the least radical case one may move to a different part of one's country. Americans have a long history of movement westward in search of space and cheap land. Likewise, the historical population pressures and high cost of living in central Honshū proved particularly enticing for many Japanese to emigrate westward and northward from the start of the Meiji Era through World War II.

Although biological research has shown that the aboriginal Ainu peoples of Northern Japan are relatives of the modern-day Japanese, their physical characteristics, customs and language fool most people into thinking they are a separate race. The people of Edo (an earlier name for Tōkyō) set up barriers against attacks from the Ainu, much as the Romans who invaded England set up Hadrian's wall in the north to protect themselves from the "barbarians," or the American settlers set up fortresses in the case of the American Indians.

Around the start of Meiji, about a million Ainu lived in Hokkaidō, and before that time they existed throughout the northern half of Honshū. Over the years, mainstream culture has co-opted the culture and language of the Ainu. Numerous cities north of Tōkyō bear Ainu names such as Sapporo, Tomakomai, and Hachinohe. Many of the summer festivals of the north salute the impact of inter-cultural contact between mainstream and Ainu cultures; for example, the Nebuta and Neputa mix Chinese, Japanese, and Ainu mythologies. In any event, the Meiji government encouraged the settlement of the Northern frontier much as did the American government in our western expansion. Land was cheap and plentiful in the north. The government subsidized agricultural science in part to aid settlers farm more efficiently in the North with its harsh climate and short growing season. The most northerly border was always amorphous and ill-defined until the end of World War II when the former Soviets effectively cut off their newly captured northern territories. Yet various northern groups of people had prehistorically and historically shared the Okhotsk Sea.

Recall that the Southwestern part of Japan also has ancient roots for the exchange of goods, information, and peoples as I have already stated. Okinawa is actually part of the 650-mile long Ryūkyū archipelago. Okinawa Island was the capital of an independent kingdom until the seventh century when the Chinese forced it to pay tribute. Later, in the seventeenth century, both China and Japan forced it to pay tribute. Japan did not incorporate the territory until 1879. Thus, the Japanese generally neglected their newly conquered territory, leaving the Okinawans to their old habits of interchange with Taiwan. Thus, Okinawa and Suo Village in Taiwan have long shared common fishing grounds and intermarriage.

Wherever the Japanese emigrated, they have concerned themselves with setting up Japanese schools. One of the best ways to trace emigration outside Japan, therefore, is through Monbushō's records of nihonjingakkō (Japanese schools). It should come as no surprise that the first recorded school was in Pusan, the closest Korean port city to Japan, in 1877. By 1897, enough Japanese resided in Shanghai that the government established a nihonjingakkō there also. New nihonjingakkō were established throughout Korea and Manchuria during the second decade of the twentieth century reflecting the growing influence of the Japanese throughout northeastern Asia. In the Philippines, Manila also had a Japanese school established in 1919. The great Japanese emigration to South America, likewise, led to the first school on that continent in 1920. The out-migration of Japanese became so strong prior to the end of World War II that by 1935, there were 206 nihonjingakkō, and 751 by the end of the war (Okubo 1983, pp. 46—47)

Huge populations of Okinawans and other Japanese migrated to Hawaii during the early part of the twentieth century. By 1924, nearly half of the Japanese population in Hawaii (circa 125,000) came from Hiroshima and Yamaguchi prefectures. Great differences in language and customs created clear-cut divisions within the Japanese expatriate communities. Natives of Okinawa and Fukushima who followed, were subject to ridicule and discrimination as a result of their strange speech and customs (Moriyama 1985). This provides an interesting sidelight on the alleged homogeneity of Japanese society in the late nineteenth and early twentieth century. By 1980, nearly 300,000 first-generation Japanese had migrated to Hawaii, and another 300,000 to the U.S. mainland. The total population of Japanese descents reaches to 600,000 in the United States.

South America also has received huge numbers of Japanese migrants during the past century — approximately 44% of all Japanese emigrants. Brazil accounted for 800,000 of the 1.5 million emigrants of Japanese origin and their dependents by 1990. The flood began in 1897 when poor farmers abandoned their homeland in search of more productive, and larger, plots of farm land. By 1990 there were also 56,000 Japanese immigrants living in Peru, 32,000 in Argentina, and 12,000 in Mexico. If one counts their descendants, there may be 1.15 million persons of Japanese descent in Brazil, and 80,000 in Peru. There is a 0.96 correlation between the size of the emigration rate in Japan and the health of the Japanese economy since World War II. Thus, as economic times improved, emigration rates dropped until only 2,446 Japanese emigrated in 1984, 60% of whom left for the United States.

The irony is that the Japanese economy of the 1980s was so healthy that it created a serious labor shortage in small firms in Japan pulling back former emigrants and their offspring from Latin American nations, while the woeful economic plight of those nations has had a pushing effect. About 40,000 Latin American-Japanese have returned, mostly from Brazil, to work in Japan. Although Japan does not normally admit unskilled foreign workers, the government makes exceptions for descendants of Japanese emigrants who no longer hold Japanese nationally. They can obtain visas for up to two years to visit relatives, and many have used those visas to obtain work.

Invasion. At the end of the nineteenth century, China and Japan vied for control of the Korean peninsula. Both countries conspired through the Li-Ito Convention of 1885 that had established each country as "co-protectors" of Korea as an excuse to put down a Korean revolt in 1894. After the suppression of the insurrection, Japan refused to withdraw its troops and pressured a Korean court to abrogate its agreement with China. This led to the First Sino-Japanese War between Chinese and Japanese troops in which the better-equipped Japanese easily won. The humiliated Chinese signed the treaty of Shimonoseki in 1895 in which they ceded Taiwan, the Pescadores, and the Liaotung peninsula to Japan,[1] and approved nominal independence for Korea. The Chinese also opened up their trade ports to Japan, and granted them the rights to open factories and engage in manufacturing in China.

The colonialist government policies in Japan promoted an impoverished and landless class in southern Korea, giving incentive to Koreans to immigrate to Japan. A critical labor shortage made the relatively cheap Korean labor attractive to Japanese factory and mine owners. Neither the post-war depression nor attempts at official regulation significantly stemmed the flow of Korean workers to Japan. In 1917 slightly more than 10,000 Koreans resided in Japan proper, but by July of 1923, the number had ballooned to 120,000. Part of the resulting Japanese-Korean conflict resulted from the Koreans' status as immigrant workers who took jobs at the bottom of the economic and social pecking order. Many Japanese, thus, came to regard the immigrants as culturally and socially inferior because the Koreans took dirty, degrading jobs. The stereotype of Koreans as indolent, dirty, and of low moral character easily took root in this atmosphere. Labor exploitation led to Korean involvement with leftist political movements, Japanese anarchists, and Communist, only increasing Japanese hostility and prejudice.

The Great Depression in the West brought on the Showa depression of 1930-1935. Some eight Japanese conglomerates built the South Manchurian Railroad (Mantetsu) during this period of colonization and exploitation of mainland Asians. By 1932 the Japanese Kwantung army occupied Manchuria and had established the puppet state of Manchukuo. China, of course, did not take all of this passively. From 1937 until 1945, the Japanese and Chinese clashed in the Second Sino-Japanese War.

Two days after war's end 275 Japanese-Manchurian immigrants committed mass suicide in a Manchuria colony out of fear of Chinese retaliation. Members from Kutami in Kumamoto Prefecture chose to kill themselves over being slaughtered by others. One man lived to tell what happened. These were among 220,000 frontier settlers sent to Manchuria to secure the Manchurian border against the Soviet Union and solve the

---

[1]Russia, France and Germany forced the Japanese to give back the Liaotung peninsula within a week.

economic crisis. The majority of immigrants made it back home in spite of repeated attacks by liberated Chinese (Jones 1949; Umemoto 1975). The government encouraged the immigration of Buraku to Manchuria during this period as a means of solving the Buraku problem. About 70% of Kutami migrants were Buraku. The Buraku Museum of Liberty in Ōsaka features these emigrants' lives in the colonies. The majority were poor farmers who left hometowns with the hopes of owning land and avoiding the military draft. Most people do not realize that it was the children of these migrants who have become today's Chinese orphans trying to repatriate.

The government drafted Koreans to fight in this war as well as World War II. It also dragooned Koreans into various types of forced labor. Japanese companies paid 60% of the wages of regular Japanese miners, and regularly worked the Korean laborers from 6 AM until 10 PM or midnight (The Japan Times, Friday June 15, 1990, p.3) Documents indicate that at least 26 Japanese companies used Koreans as forced labor during that period. By the end of World War II an estimated 2.5 million Koreans had been brought to Japan against their will to engage in hard labor at coal mines and construction sites for military facilities. In sum, 10% of the Korean labor force was forcibly sent to Japan as slave-labor. An uncountable number of Korean women were permanently marred emotionally through dragooning into prostitution as "comfort women" for Japanese troops. The lack of official recognition of Japanese responsibility for atrocities committed during this period has long been a major sore point in Korean-Japanese relations.

Japanese history virtually ignores this period. A junior high school history textbook, published by Kyōiku Shuppan in 1969, allocated just nine lines to Japan's annexation (an euphemism) of Korea in 1910 and never used the word "colonization". It reads "With the signing of the treaty, Japan had Russia (in the ending of the Russo-Japanese War) acknowledge its rights to guide and protect Korea. Following the Russo-Japanese war, Japan made Korea a protected nation, and internal policy, diplomacy and military affairs were entirely controlled by the Japanese resident general."

Likewise the same explanation appears with some additions such as the assassination of the first Japanese governor general, Hirobumi Ito, amid anti-Japanese feelings and concludes that "Such situations gave rise to opinions in Japan for annexing Korea", in a 1970 senior high textbook published by Shimizu Shōin. Only in 1975 — years after Japan normalized diplomatic relations with South Korea — did the word "colony" appeared in a Japanese high school history textbook.

The 1975 Tōkyō Shoseki textbook devoted a total of 18 lines on the colonial rule of Korea. It reads

In 1910, Japan forced Korea to sign an annexation treaty and made it a colony. Following the colonization, Japan carried out land surveys, and many Korean farmers lost their land ownership. Those landless farmers became tenant farmers or vagabonds, and the number of those later compelled to emigrate to Japan rose. The teaching of Korean history was banned and Japanese was taught to assimilate (the Koreans). However, sentiments of discrimination against the Koreans intensified.[2]

Throughout the 1980s, China and South Korea accused Japan of whitewashing its military activities in Asia before and during World War II, referring to high school textbook references to the 1937 aggression against China as an "advance into China" and the enforced relocation of Koreans out of their homeland for forced labor as "the implementation of the national mobilization order to Korea."

A junior high school history textbook published in 1990 by Shimizu Shōin clearly mentions Japan's "invasion of the continent." The same company's 1981 textbook described the same activities as an "advance into the continent." Not until the 1990 edition were "sufferings of Koreans" mentioned. That edition stated that

Later, the use of Japanese at school was made compulsory and Korean names were forced to be changed to Japanese names. Furthermore, Shintō shrines were built and Koreans were forced to visit the shrines, Japan carried out such policies with the backing of Japanese troops and police. Against such discrimination and oppression, movements for (Korea's) independence died hard.

Again, although the 1969 Kyōiku Shuppan edition did not touch upon the plight of Koreans during the colonial rule, the 1990 editions states that

. . .(Japan) taught Japanese history and geography in Japanese instead of Korean history and geography at schools. (Japan) intended to deprive the Koreans of their national identity and pride through such education. The development of Korea's own industries was also deterred because (Japan's) permission was required to run (Korean) corporations.

Strong social pressures to cover up the facts make obtaining accounts at odds with the official chronicle more difficult. Recent years have witnessed Korean survivors who endangered their own lives by keeping lists of the real names of Koreans forced into hard labor, the names the Koreans were given in Japan, their Korean addresses before placed into servitude, their dates of birth and death, and the cause of their death. Future historians will no doubt find these lists useful in deconstructing the official accounts.

A Japanese farmer in Iwaki, Fukushima, compiled such a list of 411 Koreans who died after being forced into coal mining before and during World War II. The farmer collected personal data on 292 Korean workers placed at the Joban Mine, 55 at the Yoshima Mine and 64 other Koreans. All

---

[2]The New York Times (November 11, 1992) published English translations of other samples of Monbushō's political editing of textbooks in an article by David E. Sanger

lost their lives due to malnutrition and accidents at the mines between October 1939 and January 1946, according to his account. The farmer pointed out that conducting this kind of research was extremely dangerous at the time because the authorities did not want any kind of a paper trail that might later incriminate them (The Japan Times, June 2, 1990, p. 2).

The authorities' fears were well justified. South Koreans drafted to fight for Japan during World War II and the surviving families of others who died while engaged in forced labor periodically gather in Seoul to demand compensation. They continue to protest a 1965 South Korean pact that relinquished individual damage claims and provided only limited compensation to some 9,000 claimants. They also demand an official statement of apology from Tōkyō, release of secret lists of war victims, and exhumation and return of victims remains.

According to lists kept by the political police through the end of World War II, some 243,000 Koreans were forced laborers during the war. The National Archives in Tokyo's Chiyoda Ward lists 56,808 in Hokkaidō with the largest portion; Fukuoka second with 47,806; and Nagasaki third with 20,474. Those prefectures had numerous coal mines where many of the forced laborers worked. As many as 300 South Korean survivors of the Hiroshima and Nagasaki bombings continue to press for reparations for their sufferings (The Japan Times, March 28, 1990, p. 3).

An estimated 43,000 Koreans worked on Sahkalin Island as forced labor when the island was Japanese territory. About 3,000 who want to return to South Korean still live on the island. A key unresolved issue is reparation for Koreans who died while serving in the Japanese military or as forced labor. There are also questions about the sovereignty of Takeshima Island, an islet in the Sea of Japan, because of contested fishing rights. Not surprisingly — considering the unresolved, sordid history of Japanese-Korean relations throughout the past 100 years — half of Korean and Japanese survey respondents in both countries say they dislike the other country.

Fukurai and Alston (1990) blame much of inaccurate perceptions of Japanese history upon Monbushō-sponsored re-writing of school history and social studies texts. They cite textbooks, class instructions, teachers' attitudes, and general school policies as remaining biases against minorities as late as 1985. Fukurai and Alston suggest that the educational system preserves the structure of oppression and discrimination against minorities through treating ethnic issues as taboo. Nevertheless, numerous ethnic problems exist in Japan, starting with the caste-like Burakumin.

BURAKUMIN: THE INVISIBLE "RACE"

The myth of Japanese homogeneity also requires denial of the history of the Burakumin, whose plight probably arose out of Buddhist beliefs imported from China and Korea from the eighth through the tenth centuries (DeVos and Wagatsuma 1966). Buddhist dogma merged with Shintō beliefs to generate justifications for occupational segregation of certain "polluting" occupations associated with blood and death (skinners, butchers, leather workers, cremators, tomb watchers, and so forth) into an untouchable class known originally as the eta. It came to include other degrading roles such as beggars, actors, and jugglers (Upham 1987, p. 79).

Buddhism strictures against the taking of life in any form combined with Shintō notions of ritual impurity during the Nara era (710-784 AD). Ancient Shintō beliefs record that the association of certain ritual impurities inherent in one's occupation changed the very nature of the person to become defiled and polluted. This pollution was believed to be hereditary and communicable. Thus, the government forced these people to live separately in ghettos, called buraku, or villages. Officials struck all official references to them, as if they didn't exist. Maps did not show buraku. Authorities even shortened distances on maps to emphasize the non-humanness of being an outcast. Official registers of the Japanese kōseki did not list their births, deaths, or marriages.

During the Tokugawa Period (1603-1867) the Shogunate formulated a four-tier system of caste, consisting of — from top to bottom — warrior, farmer, artisan and merchant. Two outcast groups called the eta (the Great Filth) and hinin (non-humans) were outside that system. Because the eta and hinin were physically indistinguishable from other people, the authorities often forced members of the two groups to wear special clothes or shoes and made to live in ghettos or on marginal farm lands.

Neary (1989) argues that there was no sense of group identity among the eta or hinin, and that they regarded themselves as less than human, as impure and not deserving of better treatment. This view meshes with the ways in which Tokugawa authorities used these untouchables to suppress peasant rebellions. However, research also indicates that they constantly struggled against discrimination, particularly from the latter half of the eighteenth century (Upham 1987, p. 79).

After the Meiji Restoration and the opening of Japan in 1868, the government officially eliminated caste restrictions in 1871. This was just eight years after the Emancipation Proclamation freed slaves in the United States. However, the Meiji government also began a system of family registers that listed each citizen's family background. This kōseki system still records each person's address at the time of birth, thereby potentially allowing companies or prospective spouses to determine whether a family is from a buraku area. Cynics have interpreted the emancipation declaration of August 28, 1871, that gave Burakumin full citizenship, as a government response to a practical need to integrate all groups in order to ensure support for state policies. Farmers remained fearful that they would be reduced to similarly low status and government officials also remained hostile to opening family registers to anyone who paid a fee.

The first organization formed by and for Burakumin was the Fukken Dō mei (Restoration of Rights League) in Kyūshū in 1881. Such political activity was not unnoticed by the government. It formulated social policy planned to contain the expansion of potentially subversive organizations. The government researched the numbers and living conditions of Burakumin, but made no real efforts to change their life situations. Government authorities, including the courts, upheld continued discrimination, even to the extent of attempts to exterminate the Burakumin through pogroms (Upham 1987, p. 80).

The government also tried unsuccessfully to stop the formation of self-improvement movements such as the Suiheisha (Equality Society) formed in March of 1922. Authorities tried giving money to impoverished outcast communities in the hope that would pacify the discontented and prevent the spread of radicalism (Neary 1989). Finally, authorities split the movement through imprisonment of major leaders by 1930.

Post-World War I social unrest and inflation led to major riots over rice, contributing to growing militancy among the Burakumin. Violent confrontations occurred between Burakumin and groups of commoners. The Burakumin tactics shifted toward carefully orchestrated campaigns of denunciating and publicly humiliating their discriminators. The goals were to obtain public apologies and promises not to continue the discrimination. However, as the Burakumin became increasingly allied with socialist, communist, and other leftist groups, their plight became sharply polarized. Battles with rightists and ultra-nationalists often ensued. The courts did not help matters because they tended to give the Burakumin harsh sentences, leading to further alienation and radicalization.

In theory, the new Constitution of 1947 allowed greater freedom of movement and the Burakumin Liberation League (an outgrowth from the Suiheisha) quickly forged close alliances with the Japanese Communist Party and the Japanese Socialist Party. This representation allowed wider recognition and legitimacy to their claims. This led to a four-year study of the Burakumin social conditions (Deliberative Council for Buraku Assimilation 1965).

This report showed that discrimination was deeply rooted throughout the society, in spite of common ancestry. Ghettos were consistently located in the worst topographical locations and were often subject to periodic flooding. Public services like fire protection, sewers, water lines, streets, street lights, public offices were often absent. Employment opportunities were similarly limited. More than twice the national average of households were on relief. The offspring of Burakumin found particularly limited educational opportunities.

Over three decades have passed with little evidence of change. Although socialist and communist politicians continue to argue that special programs should be generated to assist Burakumin, the invisible minority still faces difficulties in finding employment, discrimination in marriage, trouble in finding adequate housing, and barriers to forming social contacts outside of their ghettos (DeVos and Wagatsuma 1966; Hawkins 1989).

When the first edition of Edwin Reischauer's book The Japanese Today: Continuity and Change was translated into Japanese during the 1970s, almost all references to Burakumin were edited out without his permission. This anecdote personifies the official response. The Japanese government still maintains that they have no minorities as defined by United Nations

Covenant on Human Rights. Technically they are right, as the Burakumin are not genetically differentiable from non-Burakumin Japanese. Still, many Japanese believe Burakumin to be somehow genetically different more than 100 years after outcast status was abolished.

Government figures officially counted 1,162,372 Burakumin and 4603 Buraku areas in 1985, but the Buraku Liberation League (BLL) estimates 3 million Burakumin, or about 2.5 percent of Japan's 121 million population live in some 6,000 neighborhoods euphemistically known as dōwa chiku (integration districts). Even if BLL figures are high, official figures are surely low. According to government surveys (Yagi 1980) there are Burakumin in Yamagata, for example, but the numbers used in Figure 6—1 show none. Also there are at least 22 areas in Tōkyō where discrimination is not officially reported because people in the area had to agree that it was a discriminated area for inclusion. Furthermore, the Buraku Liberation League has confirmed more than 50 such locales in the Tōhoku region. Thus, the definition of Buraku is a difficult one to pin down due to the resulting stigma.

If we accept the Buraku Liberation League's estimates as more complete than official counts, Figure 6—1 suggests that substantial areas of the Greater Ōsaka metropolitan area, in particular, are of Burakumin status — over 10% of the residents of Ōsaka, Hyōgo, and Fukuoka prefectures. Adjoining Kyōto and Nara prefectures also have substantial Burakumin minorities with approximately 5% of their population of invisible status. Thus, contemporary Burakumin areas are a feature mostly of the area from Ōsaka westward across Honshū, and southward through Shikoku. There appear to be no Burakumin north of Tōkyō, nor on the island of Okinawa in Figure 6—1, although this also is surely due to under-reporting.

Since 1953, national, prefectural, and local governments have allocated over 2.6 trillion yen ($13 billion) for housing, community improvement and other projects directly affecting the Burakumin. Upham (1987, p. 106-107) suggests that such gross improvements in Buraku housing, medical care, police and fire protection, and community facilities is directly attributable to the BLL's postwar campaign of "administrative denunciation."

Government contributions to Buraku improvements are not given out of altruism or guilt. Rather, they are part of a systematic attempt to keep grievances particularized, "so the BLL's actions and demands seem so idiosyncratic that the fundamental issue of equal treatment is obscured and substantial political appeal lost (Upham 1987, p. 121)." Thus, it is not surprising that fundamental changes in education and employment are not a serious component of the governmental agenda. The Buraku unemployment rate is 10 times higher than the general population rate, while admissions into colleges are less than half the national average, according to BLL figures.

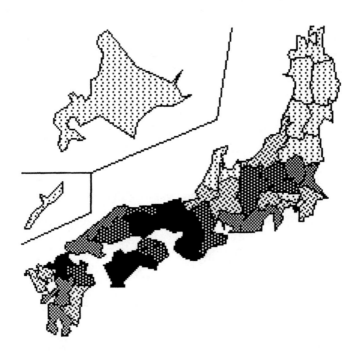

Hyōgo	13.17	Ōita	1.95	Saga	0.14
Ōsaka	12.32	Nagano	1.92	Niigata	0.09
Fukuoka	11.69	Tochigi	1.87	Yamanashi	0.03
Nara	5.34	Yamaguchi	1.75	Nagasaki	0.03
Okayama	4.87	Kumamoto	1.09	Toyama	0.00
Kyōto	4.46	Shizuoka	0.95	Ishikawa	0.00
Wakayama	4.07	Aichi	0.88	Okinawa	0.00
Ehime	3.87	Kagawa	0.73	Tōkyō	0.00
Kōchi	3.80	Kagoshima	0.71	Yamagata	0.00
Hiroshima	3.70	Ibaraki	0.53	Akita	0.00
Mie	3.69	Shimane	0.52	Fukushima	0.00
Saitama	3.47	Miyazaki	0.43	Miyagi	0.00
Shiga	3.11	Gifu	0.37	Iwate	0.00
Tokushima	2.85	Fukui	0.30	Aomori	0.00
Gunma	2.69	Chiba	0.26	Hokkaidō	0.00
Tottori	2.16	Kanagawa	0.16		

Figure 6—1   Percent Burakumin in 1987

Table 6—1 helps clarify the janus-faced response of the Japanese officials toward the Buraku. Official measures of health and housing do not indicate any effects of Buraku discrimination. Rates of infant mortality and low-weight babies are excellent measures of inequity. High rates on either measure indicates generally poor health of both parents and grandparents (Knowles 1980; Weeks and Rumbaut 1991). Yet these measures have no correlation with being a Burakumin. Likewise, Burakumin children are no more likely to be absent from elementary school than other children due to serious, long illnesses. The Japanese health-care system appears to be completely blind to Burakumin status, by these three measures.

The BLL has vigorously campaigned local governments for better housing and living conditions. The lack of correlations between Burakumin status and locally-financed or Housing Loan Corporation-financed housing supports the success of the BLL in procuring access to government-sponsored housing loans. On the other hand, subsidized private-company housing, an area in which governments have no real authority, shows a moderately negative correlation (-0.31).

The implication is that private corporations continue to discriminate against Burakumin as employees. However, this correlation should be interpreted with considerable caution because Burakumin have higher unemployment rates than average (r = 0.26; and r = 0.38 with Ōsaka removed as an outlier). Also, as a society based on educational credentials, employment and unemployment are directly related to one's educational background.

On the other hand, the block of educational indicators is entirely consistent with the continued discrimination thesis. The prefectural government of Ōsaka, where the highest percentage of Burakumin are, spends much less than the average prefecture on elementary school education, in spite of the fact that it has the highest percent of Burakumin, and sustains the greatest brunt of BLL pressure to reform its educational funding. Thus, although other prefectures with high percentages of Burakumin are likely to receive greater educational spending per capita than the average (r = 0.26), Ōsaka's much-less-than-average spending reduces the correlation to near zero. One wonders if Ōsaka's outlier status reflects a covert backlash against Buraku denunciations.

Burakumin are also less likely than other Japanese to live in prefectures with better-than-average support of junior high school education and continuing education programs during the evening, although numerous investigators have indicated that the high dropout rates of Burakumin implies greater need. The other educational correlations paint a similarly dismal picture of discrimination. Burakumin youth are much more likely than other Japanese students to miss school for economic and social reasons.[3]

---

[3]Because public support for education ends after the eighth grade in Japan, there are no official statistics on per capita spending for senior high schools at the prefectural level. However, the data presented in Chapter 3 implies that Burakumin, as a disadvantaged class, must have much lower possibilities for affording the high costs of the private high schools that feed into the elite universities.

Table 6—1

Correlations between the Percent Burakumin and Various Measures
Indicative of their Social Status

VARIABLE	PERCENT BURAKUMIN
HEALTH	
Infant mortality rate	0.03
Rate of babies born under 3700 grams	0.07
Percent of elementary school students absent with long illness	0.08
HOUSING	
Percent of locally financed housing	-0.01
Percent Housing Loan Corporation financed	-0.11
Percent of company-issued housing	**-0.31
COMMUNITY SERVICES	
Building fires/ per 1000 population	0.01
Percent with urban sewage systems	-0.22
Grievances over air quality per 100,000 population	**0.42
Grievances over noise per 100,000 population	0.23
Grievances over vibration per 100,000 population	0.21
Sports facilities per capita	**-0.38
UNEMPLOYMENT	
Percent unemployed	*0.26
% Unemployed (Okinawa removed as outlier)	**0.39
EDUCATION	
Percent elementary school students absent for economic reasons	**0.31
Percent elementary school students absent without good reason	**0.30
Per capita spending on elementary school education	0.07
Per capita spending on elementary school education (with Ōsaka removed as outlier)	*0.26
Percent of jr. high school students absent for economic reasons	**0.22
Per capita spending on jr. high school education	**-0.30
Per capita spending on evening educational programs	**-0.34
HOUSEHOLD COMPOSITION	
Percent of extended families of 6 or more in same household	**-0.44
Percent of nuclear families	**0.41
CRIME/DELINQUENCY	
Delinquency rates	*0.25
Yakuza per 10,000 population	0.21

One asterisk (*) denotes significance at the 0.05 level; two asterisks (**) at 0.01 level.

Shimahara (1971) and others (Fujimura-Fanselow 1989; Sueo and Miwa 1986) have given overviews of the educational problems of the Burakumin consistent with these correlations.

Being a Burakumin also implies that one is more likely to live in an undesirable area. Buraku areas continue to have less chance of urban sewage systems that meet modern standards. They also have less sports facilities per capita — playgrounds, gymnasiums, ball fields, and dōjō (traditional martial arts centers) — than average. By contrast, they are more likely to live in areas plagued by higher than average air, noise, and vibration pollution. Because Burakumin live predominantly in urban prefectures in the Kansai area, all indicators but the percent with urban sewage systems should be interpreted with caution, although they are again consistent with the scant published data (Kaneko 1978).

Burakumin are much more likely than average to be unemployed or under-employed. The BLL has long fought to limit access to lists of place names in which Burakumin live (chimei sōkan); but employers and university registrars find it easy to obtain lists of Buraku areas (Upham 1987, pp. 114—117, 122—123). Thus, Burakumin find it almost impossible to gain entry into universities or jobs that would give them the so much prized economic security of lifetime employment. The average salaries of university graduates in firms with over 1,000 employees are 26% higher than those of graduates in firms with under 100 employees. The overall difference, regardless of educational level, between employees in the biggest and the smallest firms is 58% (Benjamin and James 1989, pp. 79—80).

The positive correlation between high unemployment and Burakumin status attests to the continuation of this problem. This is in spite of the fact that BLL litigation effectively led to restriction of the family-registration system in the mid-1970s. With Okinawa removed as an ethnic outlier in its own right, the correlation is 0.39, which is statistically significant at the 0.01 level. This is consistent with BLL figures showing that 10.5% receive welfare benefits that are 9 times the national average and nearly twice the average for all other minority groups combined. More than 20% of Buraku households are either on relief or exempted from all taxes for reasons of poverty, whereas the figure for the majority is somewhere below 7 percent. The government exempts almost half (46%) of Buraku households from all but the uniform basic household tax while the national figure is about 20 percent (Upham 1987, p. 116).

The ie household system — standardized and legalized through Meiji Civil Code — also is lacking in Buraku areas. The ie ideology emphasized family continuity, ancestor worship, and the family as an economic unit, in the service of industrialization (Smith 1972). Households of six or more persons suffice as a crude measure of the ie today. However, Buraku have a strong propensity to consist of nuclear families rather than extended kin. Smaller families provide signs of residential and economic insecurity in Japan as elsewhere. This implies that Buraku organization is outside the traditional Japanese model for transferring both authority and property from generation to generation. Discrimination against Burakumin as marriage partners among the general population reinforces these barriers (Lebra, 1984, Pp. 87).

Outcast status also correlates with higher-than-average delinquency and organized crime (yakuza) rates. Von Wolferen (1989, p. 104) notes that the yakuza are among the few Japanese groups that welcome Burakumin as members. There is a long tradition in criminology that traces the roots of crime and deviancy back to poverty (Hirschi 1969; Merton 1938, provide classic statements). Sociologists have repeatedly demonstrated that it is an oversimplification to posit poverty as a cause of crime or delinquency. Nevertheless, at the ecological level poverty is quite commonly associated with deviancy and crime. The correlations between yakuza membership, delinquency rates, and playing hooky in both elementary and junior high schools with the percentage of Burakumin bear this out. Areas with Burakumin associate highly with all three measures of crime and delinquency.

After regressing the percentage of Burakumin and unemployed on the rate of yakuza, the standardized beta for unemployment status remains robust and positive while the Burakumin beta drops by half to an insignificant 0.13. The relationship between the percentage of Burakumin and delinquency rates also disappears after controlling for per capita income while per capita income continues to have a positive (beta = 0.26) relationship to delinquency rates. The betas for unemployment rates and per capita income are more than twice their standard errors. The association between rates of playing hooky and percentage of burakumin are spurious. Controls for high-status jobs (professional, technical, managerial, and sales) reduce the relationships to statistical non-significance.

Each of the simple regression analyses described above suggest that it is the low social statuses of Burakumin (high unemployment, low family income, low SES) that contributes to their social problems. In other words, being Burakumin does not contribute to crime and delinquency. Onuki-Tierney (1987) points out that Japanese government officials have long exploited the Burakumin by co-opting them into deviant and criminal roles. Pre-Meiji era governments deliberately elevated their numbers in order to create rivalries. Some officials went so far as to employ the outcasts in the hated roles of executioner and torturer. Van Wolferen (1989, p. 101) goes so far as to suggest that Japanese governments have long used out-groups like the Burakumin as a means of controlling unorganized crime. The Machiavellian assumption is that since it is impossible to stamp out unorganized crime that it is better to encourage organized crime. Organized crime can more easily be watched, controlled, and co-opted by the authorities. But co-optation simply leads to self-fulfilling prophesy and perpetuation of discrimination.

Certainly all of the correlations in Figure 6—1 are consistent with past documentation of Buraku discrimination, but then past Buraku researchers have not attempted to properly separate out Buraku influences from other variables that are known to be highly correlated with them. The prefectural-level data has over one-fourth of its cases with essentially no official Buraku populations, so proper controls are difficult to institute with this level of data. Still, the earlier use of simple regression analysis demonstrates a technique that ought to be employed more frequently in Buraku studies to specify hypothesized relationships.

OKINAWANS

In 1988, the population of the Okinawan islands was just over 1.2 million, close to the median prefectural population of 1.7 million. There are 13 prefectures that have smaller populations. It is virtually impossible to separate those who speak Okinawan, or identify themselves as Okinawans from other Japanese. Official government policy simply discourages making such distinctions. There is relatively little in-migration to Okinawa; it averages about 5 main-island emigrants per 1000 population each year. This aids keeping the historical mix of Okinawans and non-Okinawans and cultures low.

By contrast, Okinawa has suffered greatly from depopulation of its island population toward the capital of Naha, and a brain drain of its brightest to the main islands. The Okinawan rate of intra-prefectural movement (43.3 per 1000 population) between five-year censuses is almost twice the median rate of 24. The smaller islands do not have sufficient fresh water or means of subsistence. These factors push their populations toward the prefectural capital.

The economy of Naha is highly dependent on the American military and Japanese tourism. It has the highest percentage of persons in protective (self-defense force, police, fire fighters) occupations: 2.8% compared to the prefectural median of 1.2%. It also has a much higher percentage of service-based employment than average; 8.9% versus 6.% on average throughout Japan. These factors probably serve to attract Okinawans from the less-blessed smaller, neighboring islands.

However, military bases and tourism do not provide a strong socioeconomic base. This is reflected in Okinawa's unemployment rate, which runs close to 3 times the national average. The isolation of Okinawa's educational system from the main islands is a major contributor to maintenance of the economic status quo. Chapter 3 demonstrated the poor chances that persons from the Ryūkyū Islands have of gaining admittance to the top universities. It ranks dead last with only 0.4% of students attending one of the top 400 high schools admitted to one of the top seven public universities (all of them going to Kyūshū University) in 1988, versus a national median of 9%. No Okinawan senior high school has ever had a student admitted to either of the top two universities. Even if we broaden the base, Okinawa is an outlier with 4.7% versus a national median of 50% of top high school graduates who matriculate to one of the top 44 universities.

Chapter 5 has already demonstrated the tight linkage between education and occupation in Japan. The most prestigious universities provide the bulk of the coveted life-time employment occupations that are sheltered from unemployment. But there is a more pernicious side to the isolation. For the Tōkyō and Ōsaka areas that hold the bulk of the prestigious universities, the high ratios of college graduates who find employment within the same prefecture as the university of graduation is a sign of strength. For Okinawa, which is at the bottom in prestige of high schools and universities, however, this has the opposite implication. The prefectural median for the number of college graduates who find employment outside the prefecture of their university is 36%. Okinawa has a ratio exactly double that rate, reflecting thae high loss of its brightest minds.

Similarly, only 48% of Okinawan science and engineering college graduates find employment outside the prefecture compared to 80% of comparable graduates from other prefectural science and engineering programs. It has less of a brain drain to the major urban centers than the average prefecture. On the other hand, this suggests the difficulties faced by Okinawan graduates in competing for the best jobs.

The ratio for science and engineering jobs underlines this problem. Fifty-two percent of Okinawans who graduated from a university in the same prefecture found employment in the Ryūkyūs, or two and a half times the national median of 20%. Thus, although the brightest of the bright have an even greater chance of finding employment outside their prefecture than the average college graduate, this drain of nearly half of its graduates surely hurts Okinawa more than average because of its low rates of in-migration from the main islands to replace those who leave.

AINU

Archeologists are in agreement that the Neolithic Jōmon population gave rise to both the Ainu and Ryūkyūans (Kozintsev 1992). Modern Ainu, unlike the Okinawans, however, have had high rates of intermarriage with Honshū immigrants to Hokkaidō. The result is that only about 25,000 aboriginal Ainu exist today. Once a hunting and gathering people, many of them have been reduced to living off seasonal tourism.

Assimilationist policy that forces all Japanese to have "Japanese" names has not deterred prejudices to flourish among majority Japanese. For example, a popular myth implies that syphilis is peculiar to the Ainu people and passes into the "purer" Japanese population via them as a vehicle (Hokkaidō Shuppan Kikaku Center 1980). Part of the problem is that the aboriginal (Jōmonese) genetic complex appears to be quite unique on a worldwide scale at the same time that modern Japanese traits are virtually indistinguishable from those of modern Chinese (Kozintsev 1992). It is almost impossible for Ainu to pass into mainstream society given their distinctly non-Mongoloid characteristics.

Mizuno (1987) described their plight. Only 78% of their youth continue to high school, compared to a national average of 95%. While 35% of Japanese youth matriculate into college, only 8.1% of Ainu youth do. The

Ainu population receiving welfare benefits is 6 times higher than the national average.

SUMMARY

There are many other long-term international influences in Japan's history. This short, incomplete history of Japan only tells a part of the story. Internationalization of Japan did not really start in the Meiji period as some persons have suggested, although it certainly has blossomed since. And, except for an extremely short period during the Tokugawa period, Japan has always been a nation like others — bound to all humans through trade. Even during the Tokugawa period, areas furthest from Tokyo were difficult to manage and contain. The point is that the anti-internationalist sentiments of the bafuku were clearly not shared by all Japanese.

Neither are the Japanese a "pure" racial stock, unlike other peoples. Prehistoric traces and early historic records both show consistent intermixing of Mongoloid populations throughout the Japanese archipelago. The irony is that the Ainu may truly be the purely unique race while modern Japanese are close cousins to Koreans and Chinese. Further compounding the irony is the fact that outcast Burakumin are ethnically the same as other Japanese but are treated as if they are different. The concluding chapter will consider how and why the myths of homogeneity and uniqueness operate in modern Japan. It ends by exploring the nexus between Japanese social structure and the ongoing debate over internationalization.

Chapter 7

INSIDERS AND OUTSIDERS: BOUNDARIES TO "INTERNATIONALIZATION"

One of the most overworked words in the Japanese language of the 1980s and 1990s is <u>kokusaika</u>. This word, although translated as "internationalization", defies easy translation. Even native Japanese are usually puzzled by its definition. Newspapers reported in 1989 that the Foreign Minister, a person who should have an expert's view on international affairs, said that kokusaika was a "little vague" in meaning.

Ask a Japanese person what the meaning of kokusaika is and you are likely to receive a blank stare. The problem is partly due to the fact that the word has become a cliché; a stock bit of rhetoric devoid of content. Goodman (1990), states that <u>kokusaijin</u> (international person) is a buzz-word pointing to someone who can "bridge the gap between Japan and the outside world, but without clear meaning (p. 137). "

White (1988) uses the metaphor of overseas returnee as a photographic negative of the Japanese ideal to express the ambivalence. The returnee muddies the clear line between civilization and barbarianism; the ideal of homogeneity and plurality; insider and outsider (yosomono). The word kokusaika, thus, inspires ambivalence in the hearts of Japanese. Internationalization has a positive connotation to Americans and Europeans, but it more typically carries both negative and positive implications for Japanese.

It is difficult for many non-Japanese to understand the deep-seated xenophobia that rests underneath the guise of the Japanese need to internationalize. Nationalism, chauvinism, and racism color any definition of kokusaika. Kesavan (1989, p. 114) states the problem more bluntly: "A call for internationalism on the basis of an awareness of superiority of the Japanese race goes against the spirit of internationalism." A typical Japanese might vocalize the need to learn English for the purpose of selling Japanese goods overseas, but refuse to take business English lessons from an Indian or Jamaican who spoke perfect Queen's English because of his or her color. The same person might adamantly hold the view that Japan must sell to the outside world, but fear living overseas because the experience might leave his whole family tainted as no longer "really" Japanese.

Companies have difficulty finding employees to work overseas because the employees are afraid to take their male offspring off the Japanese "fast track" to a good university. Thus, they often leave their families back in Japan. At best employees rarely accept more than a three-year overseas assignment for fear of the influence this might have on their children's or their own future.

INDICATORS OF INTERNATIONALIZATION

The exchange of goods, services, people, technology, and information underlies any true definition of internationalization. Some Japanese critics believe their country is like a black hole in space, receiving culture but not transmitting any. This chapter will demonstrate that idea as oversimplified. Japan meets all of those standards to varying degrees. The large number of Japanese who have received overseas experience challenges the image of Japanese as only "export-oriented." After the 1960s some 3000 Japanese companies opened offices and branches overseas. By 1982 there were 5,000 to 6,000 businessmen and their families in New York area alone.

According to a Ministry of Post and Communications White Paper in 1988, Japanese information transfers rose spectacularly during the three previous years, up 40.8% over the 1985 figure to 134.61 million calls. Cross-border flows of books also reflect Japan's increasing international role. In 1978, Japan was the fourth largest publisher of book titles following the United States, the former Soviet Union, and the United Kingdom. In that year, as the dominant book publisher in Asian, it exported "635 million copies of 43,973 books" at the same time that 63% of its imported books came from the United States (Mowlana 1986, p. 79). While it is very difficult to keep track of transnational information flows, the Japanese Post and Communications has tracked various types of data (credit and medical histories, criminal records, travel reservations, financial transactions) by industry (trading firms, banking, and air transport) demonstrating the increasing interdependence of Japanese with other nations (Japanese Post and Communications 1982).

Similarly, during the 1980s, Japan found itself faced with a challenge to its traditional identity from a growing number of international issues, including the status of unskilled foreign labor, refugees and foreign students. It tried to increase the number of foreign students studying in Japan in the

1980s, but also to limit the number of refugees and unskilled foreign laborers who came to take advantage of economic opportunities. In 1988, Japan accepted 8,854 refugees and increased that number by 3,498 in 1989. But during the last two decades the Japanese government has considered accepting unskilled foreign workers on four occasions, and each time it has opted to keep its door closed.

Some top businessmen proposed that Japan accept a small number of unskilled foreign workers as trainees in industries suffering from acute labor shortages during the bubble years of the late 1980s, with the assurance they return home once they completed their jobs. However, the government opted in June, 1988 to keep out such unskilled labor. Even with the ban, the number of illegal workers — mostly construction workers, factory hands, and prostitutes from poor nations — swelled to 100,000 by government estimates.

At the beginning of the 1980s there were 10,428 foreign students in Japan. That number increased to 25,643 by 1989 with Mombushō aiming to top 100,000 by the year 2000. More important has been the increasing placement of foreign students attending universities or vocational schools in Japanese companies. Before 1987 only about 100 placements took place each year. However, placements really took off in 1988 with 520, and the 1989 figures were again nearly double that figure, according to Yochiro Koshibe, the publisher of Career Information, a Japanese job-placement magazine for foreign students.

Especially small and medium-size companies which are not attractive to Japanese students accepted these new workers. A work-force shortage accounted for this change of employment policy. More interesting was the fact that major Japanese corporations have started to place advertisements in Career Information, a magazine oriented toward job placement of foreigners. Ten blue-chip companies placed advertisements in the first-ever issue and 32 in the second issue including Nippon Telegraph and Telephone Corporation, Seiko Epson Corporation, Suntory Ltd., Toshiba Corporation and Mitsukoshi Department Store demonstrating inroads into the major corporate world.

Returnees from abroad are also a bridge to the outside world. Japan, as Chapter 6 demonstrated, is a multicultural society composed of numerous clans based on geographical or social association. There are historically accented differences in their population. This is why the political system has found it necessary to force a sense of identity and homogeneity. There are many invisible minority groups in Japan — women, Korean-Japanese, Burakumin, and Chinese-Japanese — who are eroding barriers to internationalization. Returnees from overseas symbolize another source of confrontation with national character and identity, total obedience and conformity.

Complicating the issue, parts of Japan are highly internationalized while other regions are not. The most internationalized prefectures in Japan receive benefits paralleling Goodman's (1990) findings that Japanese children who have lived overseas gain an elitist, rather than a stigmatized, status effect. Taylor and Yamamura (1990) point out that the international trade system is crucial for determining Japan's technological future. The flows of information, goods, and people referred to above mostly benefit those who live in the Kantō and Kansai areas. Nevertheless, the strong ambivalence surrounding internationalization suggests that many Japanese remain unconvinced of the its importance.

The controversy over an elitist versus a stigmatizing effect of internationalization is also complicated by Japanese culture. Lebra (1992a) notes the unusually strong connection between time and space in the Japanese concept of ba. She points out that "If the Western way of thinking and acting presumes the structural opposition of mind and body, subject and object, transcendental and mundane, true and false, it appears that Japanese are more guided by the social binary of uchi (inside) and soto (outside) or ura (rear) and omote (front) (p. 5)." Lebra goes on to assert that "It seems that the uchi-soto boundary is sharpest . . . at the national level." (p. 8) Traditionally anything non-Japanese was automatically defined as of Lebra's lower, outside status. During the brief Tokugawa period of unilateral sakoku (closed country) policies it was possible to isolate Japanese from non-Japanese culture. But this is no longer the case. Japan now reaps the benefits of participating in the larger multi-lateral world.

Herein lies the irony. During the prehistoric and historic periods discussed in Chapter 6, it was ura-nippon (the Japan Sea side) and "soto-Japan" (the fringes farthest from Tōkyō and Ōsaka) that promoted, and benefited the most from, international exchange and trade. The Tokugawa rulers used vassals in the hinterlands as buffers between themselves and foreigners. The elites hung onto power by controlling the inflow of foreign culture. The present demonstrates a historic inversion. The Kantō-to-Kansai center of insiders now aggressively seeks, and accrues the most profit from, international exchanges of all types.

According to the soto-uchi thesis, a select few perform international work to protect the mainstream of Japanese society from disruption or contamination by unpredictable contacts from outside. These people have the important brokerage task of protecting the core of citizens by handling its external relations leading to their inevitably marginalization through their individual contacts with non-Japanese. The sharp distinctions between uchi and soto should lead to treatment of returnees as "nearly pariah-like brokers." (p. 114) Part of the problem, however is that much of this research was carried out decades ago raising the question: Has the nature of the crisis subtly shifted in the intervening years?

Japanese commerce, for all its modernity, is still patterned after traditional cultural dichotomies. Meaning normally comes from traditional statuses. A person's own household or business clearly and automatically defines one as an insider and those not members as outsiders. Overriding these statuses, however, is the status of Japanese national. Unlike most other nations, birth in Japan does not automatically give a right to citizenship. Government policy since the Meiji Era has recognized official kinship registry (kōseki) as the only legitimate claim to Japanese citizenship. Thus, proof of birth in Japan (even for one's parents, grandparents, etc.) is not sufficient for Japanese citizenship. Not being able to trace one's ancestry through the kōseki automatically makes one non-Japanese except under extremely rare circumstances.

Elite, insider statuses in Japan originate from relatively narrowly ascribed statuses based on ancestry, yet achieved statuses based on one's education and overseas experience have gain ascendancy in the post-World War II era and have increasing power to supplant and supersede traditional statuses. The tension between traditional ascribed and modern achieved statuses, thus, becomes one likely reason for institutionalized ambivalence toward internationalization.

In this century the non-Japanese group with the lowest ascribed status are permanent residents (teichaku ijūsha) of Korean and Chinese heritage. There were about 680,000 Korean-Japanese with this status in 1990.[1] Chinese-Japanese add another 130,000 to registered foreigners. Spouses of Japanese citizens contribute another 48,000 to Hōmushō reports. Lie and Fujieda (1992) estimate that about 150,000 illegal aliens (visa overstays, deportees, abusers of student visa, etc.), can be added to legal visas issued to 25,000 students and 25,000 workers from foreign countries. In total, then, less than 1% of the Japanese population consists of foreigners who are permanent residents, legal workers, students, or illegal aliens.

The first part of this chapter will consider the current status of each of these major non-Japanese groups. The second part focuses on Japanese abroad with long-term visas who presently number about 600,000 (Kurashima 1990) and those who have been abroad and returned. They and their children are often presented through the mass media as forever tainted by their long-term stays. This leads into the final section in which I discuss contemporary signs of internationalization that undermine attempts to maintain the myth of Japanese homogeneity.

KOREAN-JAPANESE

As birth on Japanese soil does not grant the right to citizenship, children born to Korean-Japanese parents who were brought forcibly to Japan cannot easily take Japanese citizenship. Over 80% of Korean-Japanese were born in Japan, yet nationality is based on "bloodlines" legitimized through the kōseki system. Persons of Korean ancestry must carry alien registration cards (gaikokujin tōroku shōmeisho). Adding insult to injury, many speak no Korean which acts as an effective barrier to their "return" to Korea. Thus, a large portion of the Korean-Japanese population carry the burden of a virtually country-less status.

One of the sorest points of discrimination is the requirement that all Korean-Japanese be fingerprinted. The South Korean government has long pushed the Japanese for broadening the rights of Korean-Japanese. Thus, the

---

[1]Because Japan is an island-nation with an efficient system of surveillance and visa-tracking system, the number of illegal foreigners cannot be much higher than the total of foreigners with visa "overstay" status.

Japanese government has toyed with less controversial systems of discrimination such as a family-based registry of Korean-Japanese. Still, resistance to change is strong. Foreign Ministry authorities promised in 1990 to exempt third-generation Korean-Japanese residents from the controversial fingerprinting requirement, and to refrain from deporting them unless they committed extremely serious offenses such as sedition, subversion, assaults on diplomatic establishments or their personnel, drug-law violations and crimes carrying prison sentences of seven or more years.

By contrast, other foreigners with permanent residence status are currently subject to extradition under 20 categories of crime. The agreement gave Korean-Japanese the right to re-entry permits valid for up to five years, but only four children qualified as of 1990. Naturally, Korean-Japanese feel that the right to live in Japan permanently should not be a contested point. Re-entry permits do not solve basic problems of housing, job, and cultural education. Neither do they solve the problem of fingerprinting requirements for the third-generation[2]

Korean-Japanese, who have essentially no memory of their grandparents' fatherland or language, do not understand why they are singled out. Nevertheless, a 25-year-old Korean-Japanese treaty expired in 1991 leaving discrimination unaddressed. This treaty of 1965 granted permanent residency to Koreans who came to Japan before the end of World War II or who were born in Japan on or before January 16, 1971, and their children born on or after January 17, 1971. It apparently never occurred to the treaty drafters that those Koreans would want to stay in Japan indefinitely so the treaty gave no recognition to their ethnic identity. Or, perhaps, the treaty did not recognize Korean naturalization precisely as a stimulus to leave. Whatever the case, hundreds of thousands of Japan-born Korean residents remain disaffected by systematic discrimination that the constitution legitimizes.

Korean-Japanese are not allowed to work in many educational and government jobs, let alone run for higher public offices. Voting rights exist only for naturalized citizens. This issue most affects Korean-Japanese who make up close to 75% of foreign residents. Article 15 of the Constitution stipulates that kokumin (nationals) have the right to choose their public officials. Article 93 states that local officials will be elected by jūmin (residents). Because an increasing number of western countries allow foreign residents to vote in local elections (Sweden, Denmark, Norway, Canada, the Netherlands, Switzerland, Germany, and parts of the United States), questions arise as to whether Article 93 may be interpreted to include foreigners. The ruling Liberal Democratic Party has never discussed changing voting rights. The second largest party, the Japanese Socialist Party, has also never taken up this sensitive issue.

Ōsaka prefecture, which accounts for more than 30% of Korean-Japanese residents, is most affected by this, and other forms, of

---

[2]Under the Alien Registration Law, all foreign residents age 16 and over are required to register their fingerprints and carry identity cards.

discrimination. Figure 7—1 demonstrates the concentration of Korean-Japanese in the Ōsaka-Kyōto area where they make up roughly 2% of the total population. It is worth noting that when combined with the relatively disenfranchised burakumin and other out-groups, Osaka prefecture has a greater percentage of residents of minority status than the average black population of the United States.

The lack of legitimate political representation gives Korean-Japanese no real recourse to change their life situations. Adult Korean-Japanese male unemployment hovers around 30% — over ten times the official Japanese figure. Those who do find employment are found mostly in occupations despised because they are dirty, dangerous, or poor-paying: factory work, manual labor, and the service industries.

Part of the reason Korean-Japanese accept jobs with low status traces back to their low amounts of educational capital. Korean-Japanese students have half the chance of Japanese students of entering the most desirable public academic high schools. Compared to other students, they are twice as likely to attend night schools (the lowest status academic environment), and they are more likely to attend vocational high schools of lower status (Rohlen 1983, p. 197). Due to opposition from Monbushō less than 10% of municipal and private colleges and universities have been willing to accept graduates of Chōsoren (Federation of [North] Korean Residents) or Mindan (Association of [South] Korean Residents) high schools, and none of the prestigious national universities presently accept such students.

In spite of educational discrimination, only 13.6% of Korean-Japanese children attended Korean-oriented schools in 1988. These schools are neither governmentally approved nor supported (Umakoshi 1991, p. 283). While Korean-oriented education aids third and later-generation Korean-Japanese to keep in closer contact with Korean culture and language, it ultimately reinforces barriers to integration. It also effectively bars graduates from entry into the all-important university system and higher status occupations (Yamamoto 1984). Also, Korean-Japanese who decide on Korean education must decide whether to send their children to Mindan or Chōsoren schools, adding complexity to the political and cultural status quo (Umakoshi 1991). The reason is that the Liberal Democratic Party supports South Korea and the Socialist Party supports North Korea. Thus, chauvinistic politics encourage splits in the Korean-Japanese community mirrored in education.

Thus, roughly two-thirds of Korean-Japanese residents identify with South Korea, yet only 8% of Korean-Japanese children attend their schools. Part of the problem is that the North Korean-affiliated schools have a much stronger commitment to ethnic education and identity as well as funding from the North Korean government. Thus, Chōsoren runs schools in 29 prefectures while Mindan can only support schools in Tōkyō, Ōsaka, and Kyōto.

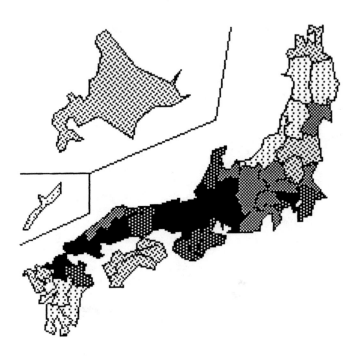

Ōsaka	219.8	Ishikawa	28.7	Tochigi	12.5
Kyōto	187.9	Tottori	28.0	Hokkaidō	11.9
Hyōgo	134.6	Chiba	23.3	Kagawa	11.8
Yamaguchi	92.7	Ōita	23.0	Aomori	11.1
Aichi	87.1	Shizuoka	21.8	Kōchi	10.8
Tōkyō	70.4	Nagano	21.5	Fukushima	10.6
Shiga	65.6	Saitama	19.8	Niigata	10.4
Fukui	61.7	Shimane	18.2	Iwate	9.5
Hiroshima	59.7	Miyagi	17.9	Miyazaki	7.9
Fukuoka	57.2	Yamanashi	16.8	Akita	7.8
Gifu	51.0	Toyama	16.7	Kumamoto	7.6
Nara	48.1	Ibaraki	16.4	Tokushima	5.2
Mie	47.7	Gunma	15.8	Yamagata	4.8
Okayama	45.6	Saga	15.0	Kagoshima	2.6
Wakayama	43.5	Ehime	13.5	Okinawa	2.2
Kanagawa	40.0	Nagasaki	13.2		

Figure 7—1   Korean-Japanese per 10,000 Population in 1988

Institutionalized racism also exists in the job market. Even in Ōsaka, which has the largest Korean-Japanese minority population, some Korean-Japanese feel compelled to sue for job discrimination. A third-generation Korean-Japanese resident as a senior at Ōsaka City University unsuccessfully petitioned the Ōsaka District Court in 1990 to cancel the municipal government's refusal of his employment application on racial grounds (The Japan Times, June 21, 1990). Mintoren (The National Council for Combating Discrimination Against Ethnic Peoples in Japan) has documented systematic housing discrimination against Korean-Japanese residents as well as barriers to government positions and corporate occupations justified through the present system of ascribed exclusion from citizenship rights.

Discrimination has led to various forms of "passing" into mainstream society. War-time laws forbade the use of Korean names by those forced to work in Japan. Some Korean-Japanese have continued the use of Japanese names in an attempt to evade discrimination. About 90% of Korean-Japanese use their Japanese names (Umakoshi 1991, p. 288) because it is easier to pass as Japanese than suffer the stigmatization as a Korean. Others have tried to "pass" as Japanese by marrying into Japanese families. Kōseishō statistics indicate the increasing intermarriage rates between persons of Korean and Japanese ancestry. In the ten-year period from 1976 through 1985 intermarriage rates increased by 50% to a record high of 71.6% of Korean-Japanese married to Japanese. Children of these marriages are allowed as of 1984 to chose between the nationality of either parent. However, the strong pressures for children to assimilate runs counter to the goals of internationalization through respect for ethnic diversity.

Other Korean-Japanese have tried a form of reverse passing by becoming mitsu'nyūkokusha (hidden immigrants). As a result, the Justice Ministry and Mindan both agree that there are between 20,000 and 30,000 "hidden" Koreans living in Japan. These are Koreans who returned to their homeland at war's end, where disappointment with economic opportunities led them to return illegally. Most used brokers to arrange passage in Korean boats and then transferred to Japanese vessels. Subsequently, relatives in Japan took them in. Their position as illegal immigrants makes them particularly vulnerable to blackmail by employers who may threaten to turn them into the police if they show dissatisfaction with substandard salaries or working conditions.

The revised immigration act that went into effect June 1, 1990 considerably stiffened the penalties for aiding and abetting illegal foreign workers. Employers who hire illegal foreign workers may be subject to fines of up to ¥2 million ($9756) and prison sentences of up to 3 years. Any illegal foreign worker who acts as a broker for other illegal workers faces similar fines and sentences.

One other sign of discrimination worth mentioning is the experience of Koreans caught in the Hiroshima or Nagasaki atomic-bombings. The South Korean Atomic Bomb Victims Association, based in Seoul, has spent nearly a half-century demanding recognition and compensation for suffering as victims (The Japan Times, April 16, 1989). Forty-five years after the atomic bombing, the City of Hiroshima had still refused to allow a cenotaph dedicated to Korean victims to be placed within the Peace Memorial Park along with the cenotaph for Japanese victims (The Japan Times, May 19, 1990, p. 2). Under pressure from the Korean association, city officials placed a cenotaph in the park at the annual August 5 memorial service for the deceased. However, vandals torched the cenotaph on May 23, 1991, sending outrage throughout the Korean-Japanese community over this overt sign of discrimination in death as well as life (The Japan Times, May 24, 1990).

Min (1993) has contrasted the situation of the 1.8 million Koreans living in China with the Japanese case. She points out that radically different governmental responses have led to different Korean responses in both countries. Specifically, she notes that the Chinese government has long encouraged the full ethnic expression of Koreans through such policies as issuance of all official documents in both Chinese and Korean; government funding of ethnic schools; and establishment of ethnically autonomous areas for Koreans. The outcome has been that Koreans grossly outperform Chinese in college attendance. Thus, the pluralistic minority policy of China has led to radically different living conditions for Korean-Chinese, than the colonized-minority policies of Japan.

CHINESE-JAPANESE

The second largest group of foreigners in Japan are the Chinese-Japanese permanent residents who number about 130,000 (Nyūkankyoku 1988). Like the Korean-Japanese, many (or their offspring) are the victims of Japanese imperialist expansion during the first half of this century. Although Korean-Japanese complaints of discrimination have found some outlets through the mass media, Chinese-Japanese grievances are more invisible to the public — perhaps due to their smaller population size. Nevertheless, Chinese-Japanese are subject to the same forms of discrimination as the larger Korean-Japanese community.

The strong sense of hierarchy in Japan may also give higher status to Chinese-Japanese than Korean-Japanese. The Japanese, after all, owe a great debt to Chinese language and culture that may create a greater emotional ambivalence toward the Chinese than Koreans. Further, Chinese have a longer history of unforced residence in, and trade with, Japan. Iwakabe (1989; 1990) and Ichikawa (1991) document the long association between Nagasaki and China and Taiwan. Ichikawa uncovered over 40,000 documents left by a Taisho-Era Chinese merchant named Tai Eki Go who did business in Nagasaki that demonstrate extensive maritime trade between Nagasaki businesses and cities in the Taiwan-Strait area. His research also uses archival records from the Chinese Cemetery and Goshin temple in Nagasaki to buttress this long association.

Iwakabe points out (1989; 1990) that by 1867, the Tokugawa government found it useful to establish treaties regulating Chinese registration in the Nagasaki area. According to Iwakabe, treaties laid the foundation for control of all foreigners in Japan. From the standpoint of the Chinese, these treaties during the last days of the Edo government opened up the possibilities of Chinatowns in port-cities such as Yokohama, Kōbe, and Nagasaki. Research by Yamashita (1990) clarifies how the special regional characteristics of the Chinese-Japanese in modern Japan developed from these treaties. Chinese — mainly from Taiwan, Guangdong, and Fujian provinces — settled Chinatowns near major ports. These Chinese distinguished themselves in three businesses prior to World War II—Chinese restaurants, hair-dressing, and tailoring. Since the war, however, their major economic activity has become Chinese restaurants.

The distinctive differences between Korean-Japanese and Chinese-Japanese minorities in Japan, thus, probably explain much of the relative lack of friction between Chinese and Japanese. Chinese came largely willingly and early. Japan is an age-stratified society that gave Chinese an advantage in the pecking order among the minority statuses. They also stayed in mostly relatively cosmopolitan areas around major ports where they formed unique commercialized ethnic towns that were not in direct competition with Japanese. The Koreans, by contrast, were more likely to have been brought to Japan as forced labor. Koreans found themselves without the social-support systems available to the Chinese to continue their former lives. The result has been that the Chinese-Japanese have not been radicalized or discriminated against to the extend that the Korean-Japanese have.

RESIDENT ALIENS

During the red-hot economy of the 1980s, one of the most-discussed topics was the problem of foreign workers (gaijin rōdōsha). The Mainichi Shinbun (1990) inaccurately describes an invasion of foreign workers during this period in terms similar to American fears over cheap, Mexican labor. The current Immigration Law favors foreigners who possess particular skills for jobs that cannot be filled by Japanese nationals (Spencer 1993).

As it is very difficult to enter Japan without a proper visa, immigration authority reports of deportees, overstays, and legal foreign workers must give an accurate account of the actual number of foreigners living in Japan. In 1987, the Hōmusho counted about 25,000 foreigners with legal work visas, about 70,000 "overstays", and close to 15,000 deportees. Additionally, another 65,000 foreigners were residing in Japan on studies-related visas. An unknown percentage of these students actually provided low-wage labor for small firms. The 21,000 visa-holders for internships (4-1-6-2) and vocational training (4-1-16-3) are the most likely abusers of the system. Of those on legal work visas, the most likely problem arises among the 13,000 kōgyō (entertainment) visas. Thus, the true number of illegal foreign workers could not easily have exceeded 171,000.

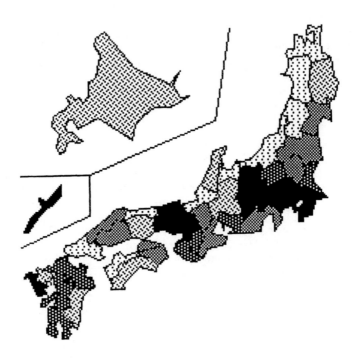

Tōkyō	260.8	Aichi	32.0	Gifu	18.7
Hyōgo	178.0	Wakayama	31.5	Kōchi	18.3
Ōsaka	110.2	Kumamoto	31.3	Miyazaki	17.9
Kanagawa	101.9	Ōita	30.0	Saga	16.1
Okinawa	82.9	Tochigi	29.3	Tokushima	15.5
Kyōto	71.3	Miyagi	29.3	Ishikawa	15.4
Chiba	52.3	Hiroshima	28.6	Ehime	15.0
Yamanashi	50.2	Shimane	25.5	Yamagata	13.9
Nagasaki	49.8	Shiga	23.2	Toyama	13.5
Nagano	44.0	Fukushima	21.6	Fukui	13.0
Saitama	43.7	Shizuoka	21.4	Akita	13.0
Nara	39.8	Mie	21.4	Aomori	12.8
Ibaraki	39.6	Kagawa	20.5	Yamaguchi	11.6
Fukuoka	36.9	Okayama	20.0	Niigata	11.5
Gunma	35.6	Iwate	19.8	Tottori	9.8
Kagoshima	32.3	Hokkaidō	18.8		

Figure 7—2   Chinese-Japanese per 100,000 Population in 1988

The real problem appears to arise from several structural sources rather than actual numbers of foreigners. First, the majority of illegal workers are dark-skinned Asians from third-world economies. They are attracted to Japan because they can earn more in one day than they could back home in months or years. Second, they are willing to take on the dirty, dangerous, and difficult work spurned by Japanese. This creates ambivalence for those who would like to deport all foreigners but who recognize how difficult it is to find job replacements for foreign workers. Third, like other minorities, they are concentrated in major metropolitan areas. This makes their numbers seem larger than they actually are which increases the perception of threat. Fourth, the high percentage of women workers deported for work as prostitutes, strippers, and bar hostesses and men as manual workers easily reinforces stereotypes (Keizai Kikakucho Sōgō Keikakukyoku Economic Planning Department of the General Planning Bureau, 1989). Fifth, the numbers, while minuscule by European or American standards, increased exponentially throughout the 1980s. For example, the number of vocational visas issued from 1985 until 1988 increased five-fold. Thus, many Japanese fears concern future increases in foreigners.

The number of legal resident aliens per 10,000 population in 1988 also proves enlightening information. Not surprisingly, the rural areas show almost no foreign residents with Yamagata the lowest at 7.8 per 10,000 population. Foreign residents concentrate in the largest cities with Ōsaka containing the highest concentration of 2.3%. The median foreign-resident population is quite low at 29 per 10,000 population, but all of the major cities are outliers with over 1% of their populations consisting of foreign residents. As foreign residents within cities with more foreigners cluster in particular areas (like Roppongi in Tōkyō) it is easy to see how Japanese in those areas with high concentrations might feel particularly threatened. One of the problems with current surveys is that they do not distinguish such types of contextual effects in their tabular breakdowns.

One soaring source of immigration is foreign brides. In 1970 there were only 2,108. By 1980, the number had doubled to 4,386. 1990 figures show a decade quadrupling to 17,800 foreign brides. No complete breakdown exists, but about 60% of those are Korean-Japanese and Chinese-Japanese, and most of the remainder come from countries like Thailand and the Philippines. The phenomenon began as a result of the perceived shortage of marriageable young women in rural areas. It has since spread to urban areas where matchmaking fees as high as $20,000 have been reported. Again, it would be helpful if national surveys broke down attitudinal questions dealing with foreign brides by areas known to have larger and small percentages of foreigners. That type of analysis would give much better indicators of the acceptance or rejection of foreigners than survey researchers now employ.

Working and living conditions are extremely substandard for most foreign laborers. As Japan has not yet signed the United Nations International Convention on the Protection of the Rights of All Migrant Workers and Members of Their Families, the status of illegal foreign workers is precarious. The Ministry of Labor reported that illegal alien workers received 60% less in wages than Japanese workers. Illegal aliens live in fear of discovery so they are easy prey by labor brokers and employers. Their illegal status excludes them from the health-care system. Many are forced to subsist in substandard housing with inadequate lighting, food, safety, and sanitation (Spencer, 1993, pp. 764—766).

THE UNEVENNESS OF INTERNATIONALIZATION

Internationalization in Japan has a variable history. Some parts have a much longer history, and acceptance, of internationalization than other parts. This section pieces together some current data on internationalization to show more concretely where internationalization is most prevalent in Japan. Sister city ties, Japanese passport holders, Japanese who take trips abroad and the reasons they take those trips, and the locations of foreigners in Japan operationalize different aspects of internationalization upon which this section capitalizes.

SISTER CITY TIES

One of the most popular means of promoting international cooperation, friendship, and exchange are sister ties between various governmental units such as cities and states (or prefectures in the Japanese case). Sister Cities International, Inc., based in Arlington, Virginia, has seen an escalation in the establishment of ties of formal exchange in recent years. For example, in Japan alone, during the fiscal year starting in April 1988 through March 1989, 18 towns, 37 cities, and 3 prefectures formed new sister relationships.

Many of these sister ties develop out of personal relationships. For example, Montana's relationship with Kumamoto Prefecture started in 1982 because then-Ambassador Mike Mansfield came from the state. By 1984 Kumamoto prefectural and Montana state officials had established strong liaisons and public relationships. Typically these sister relationships have lead to festive exchanges and commemorative gift-giving of a substantial nature: tours of folk-dance groups; gifts of stained glass, dishes, bronze statues; and other exchanges are common. As an example, the Tōkyō metropolitan government spent close to a quarter of a million dollars to send sumo wrestlers to New York in 1985 to celebrate a quarter-century link.

As of 1990, 109 cities in Japan each had more than two sister cities abroad. American cities had sister relationships with 213 Japanese cities, followed by the Chinese with 93, the Brazilians with 42, and the Australians with 33. Thus, Japanese sister ties appears to match closely diplomatic and political interests of the national government.

The raw number of sister ties reported by Sister Cities International is not a particularly interesting variable because it does not control for size of population. For example, Tōkyō has 22 ties while Yamagata and Miyagi have 15. Because Tokyo is obviously much larger than either of the other prefectures, it is helpful to standardize ties by population size, as shown in Figure 7—3. There is only a correlation of 0.18 between the raw and the population-standardized number of sister ties, suggesting how misleading the raw figures are. The correlation between raw number of sister ties and population size is a healthy 0.79. As one instance, Tōkyō appears to have the most sister ties in the raw data, but falls to the second-to-last position after taking its large population into account.

The average prefecture has a mean of 6.9 sister ties per million population. Shiga and Ishikawa are outliers with extremely high numbers of sister ties per million population; 19.5 and 14.7, respectively. Tottori and Tōkyō, by contrast, have extremely low numbers of sister ties. With the exception of Kyōto, all of the major population centers have sister ties that fall below the median of 6.2.

On the other hand, one might wonder what the main cause of sister ties is. Although it is clear that a few individuals or some government officials like former Ambassador Mike Mansfield have worked hard on behalf of such internationalization, population size is a major necessary, but not sufficient, condition. Larger populations are most likely to have a few people who want to have such ties and who work actively for them.

Still, a large metropolis such as Tōkyō does not need sister ties to promote internationalization because it is the major Japanese center of world trade and finance. Until the new airport was opened in Ōsaka virtually all air flights into and out of the country went through Tōkyō making it the primary center of tourism as well. Other prefectures with export-oriented industries and ports — Fukuoka, Aichi (Nagoya), Ōsaka, and Hiroshima — also have less-than-average number of sister ties as do prefectures that serve as bedrooms for Tōkyō's labor force (Kanagawa, Chiba, Fukushima, Ibaraki, Tochigi, and Saitama)

The main influence on sister city ties turns out to be size of population most probably because the larger the population the more chance that some few members will have a vision of the importance of such ties. However, larger populations do not produce larger numbers of sister ties. To the contrary, there is an extremely robust negative relationship between the size of prefectural population and sister ties.

Table 7—1 summarizes the results of the best predictors of sister ties. Although they are not shown, additional regression analyses show population size is the best predictor. In this table a decrease of one standard unit of population size lead to almost one standard unit drop in sister ties. In numerous other tests, this relationship is robust, never dropping below a beta of -0.7.[3] Thus, large population size discourages internationalization as measured by sister ties.

---

[3]After dropping multi-collinearly related variables.

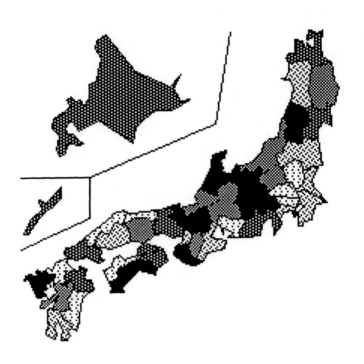

Shiga	19.5	Aomori	7.2	Kagoshima	4.4
Ishikawa	14.7	Ōita	7.2	Ōsaka	4.4
Yamanashi	14.2	Hyōgo	7.0	Fukushima	4.3
Wakayama	12.8	Miyagi	6.8	Chiba	4.3
Yamagata	11.9	Nara	6.7	Kanagawa	4.2
Kyōto	11.4	Kumamoto	6.5	Akita	4.0
Kōchi	10.7	Gifu	6.4	Shimane	3.8
Toyama	10.7	Gunma	6.2	Tochigi	3.7
Nagano	9.8	Niigata	6.1	Saitama	3.6
Saga	9.0	Fukui	6.1	Aichi	3.4
Nagasaki	8.8	Kagawa	5.8	Miyazaki	3.4
Hokkaidō	8.3	Iwate	5.6	Fukuoka	3.2
Tokushima	8.3	Okayama	5.2	Ehime	2.0
Shizuoka	7.7	Mie	5.1	Tokyo	1.9
Yamaguchi	7.6	Ibaraki	5.0	Tottori	1.6
Okinawa	7.4	Hiroshima	4.6		

Figure 7—3   Sister Ties per Million Population in 1989

Not surprising, taking tours overseas encourages the formation of sister-city ties. This predictor is also quite robust throughout various regression analysis not shown. The strength and sign of this beta suggest that Japanese who have taken trips abroad are most likely to support sister ties with foreign governments. Throughout the 1980s record-breaking numbers of Japanese took foreign vacations most likely due to their growing affluence and increasing disposable income. Numerous critics have suggested that such tours have superficial effects because they normally are short-term tours done in groups. However, this predictor supports the positive influence of overseas travel on international outlook. It exists under all forms of overseas travel, regardless of purpose. For example, the beta weights are roughly the same for overseas travel for educational purposes, business trips, long-term stays, or short-term vacations. The reason is due to the extremely high correlations between various purposes for overseas travel, none of which are below 0.9.

Table 7—1

Results of a Regression of Population Size, Japanese Overseas Tourists per 1000 population, and the Number of Library Books Lent per 100 Population on Sister Ties per Million Population

Variable	Betas
Population Size	** - 0.96
Overseas Tourist per 1000	*0.38
Library Books Lent/100	*0.42

$r^2 = 0.34$

*Significant at 0.05 level
** Significant at 0.01 level

One other strong predictor stands out as significant and robust. Persons who check out library books also have a strong propensity to support municipal and prefectural sister ties with comparable overseas governments. This indicator appears to measure cosmopolitan outlook. Newspaper readership is not a significant predictor, by contrast, probably because Japanese newspapers rarely act as a force independent of the government. Foreign correspondents often complain of the strong filtering of information by government officials. The result is a propensity for competing newspapers to print highly uniform reports of a parochial nature. Book publishers, being less centralized, are less subject to governmental control. Readers probably find much more diversity of opinion in books than newspapers.

The three predictors in Table 7—1 account for a total of 34% of the variation in sister ties. The results of this regression are significant statistically at beyond the 0.001 level. Thus, even though roughly two-thirds of the variation remains unexplained, the results suggest that both public libraries and overseas travel broaden the prospects for Japanese citizens to participate in international affairs.

The American government stopped publishing data on American overseas travel in 1983 making direct comparisons of the factors responsible for variations in overseas-human flows for the United States difficult. However, the use of 1983 data on American passport holders with 1990 data on American sister ties is quite enlightening and even surprising. First, although Japanese think of Americans as much more internationally minded than themselves, the sister-ties data do not support such a view. The median number of sister ties for Japanese prefectures is 6.2 per million population compared to 7.1 for American states. The 0.9 difference is due to 4 American outlier states — Oregon, California, Hawaii, and Alaska — that have unusually large numbers of sister ties. Each of these outlier states has more sister ties than the highest ranked Japanese prefecture; Alaska has twice as many as the next highest state or the highest prefecture.

However, the explanations for sister ties differ somewhat for the United States. Population size and book readership appear not to have any influence unlike in the Japanese case. The most robust predictor of American sister ties is the rate of Japanese factory establishments in Table 2—3. (The causal order here is not completely clear. It may be that sister ties lead to the establishment of Japanese factories as well as vice versa.) However, as in Japan, passport holding has a significant influence. Persons with passports are most likely more internationally minded than the average citizen.

The most interesting difference between the American and Japanese case, however, is the influence of college-student culture on internationalization. The liberal influence of American universities, which attract large percentages of both faculty and students from abroad on sister ties, is not surprising, but probably not well appreciated by the American public. By contrast, Japan has far fewer foreign students than other major industrial nations. Although Monbushō plans to more than triple that number to more than 100,000 by the end of the century, the high costs of living, lack of scholarship aid, and other barriers make that a highly unrealistic goal.

Table 2—3

Results of a Regression of Passport Ownership, Japanese Factories
per Million Population, and the % of Adults in College
on American Sister Ties per Million Population

Variable	Betas
% with Passports	* 0.25
Japanese Factories per million	**0.56
% in College	*0.29

$r^2 = 0.58$
*Significant at 0.05 level
** Significant at 0.01 level

JAPANESE OVERSEAS VOLUNTEERS CORPS

One if the most visible marks of the Kennedy Administration was the formation of the United States Peace Corps volunteer movement. That movement has spread to Japan in the form of the Japanese Overseas Volunteers Corps (JOVC). Like its Peace Corps model, the JOVC has traditional strengths in agricultural, medical, and educational assistance to third-world countries. Such programs are relatively inexpensive compared to foreign aid. It costs roughly $1 million in overhead to open up a new program in a country and about $29,000 annually to support each volunteer. The greatest impact of overseas volunteers lies in the personal assistance and cross-cultural interaction.

Like its American counterpart the JOVC has grown rapidly in recent years (Goodman 1990, p. 227), and there are many more volunteers than volunteer slots available. What is particularly important about the JOVC from the standpoint of internationalization is that it appears to tap recruits from sources outside ordinary channels to internationalization. There are no statistically significant relationships between JOVC volunteering and sister-city ties (r = 0.12) or passport holding (-0.20). The JOVC appears to tap quite different types of persons interested in foreign culture or overseas experiences than general passport holders or sister-city enthusiasts.

The range is from 28.6 volunteers per million population in Kagoshima to 9.3 in Shiga. Inspection of this distribution does not lead to easy clues concerning the social dynamics that underlie these differences. The major urban populations cluster in the middle ranks. Rural prefectures close to major urban populations appear less likely to produce volunteers than distant rural prefectures. The visual impression is that Japanese in rural prefectures within easy commutes of the major cities have little reason to volunteer. Residents of Shiga are within easy commute of Kyōto; persons in Tochigi are close to Tōkyō, and Mie residents border on Nagoya. All of these prefectures contribute few JOVC recruits. By contrast, the highest rates of volunteering are in prefectures that are relatively isolated from major cities; for example, Kagoshima, Iwate, Aomori, Tottori, and Saga.

Among the various broad census categories for coding occupations (professional, technical, service, etc.) only crafts workers (0.48; $p < 0.05$) and farmers ($r = 0.38$; $p < 0.05$) have significant correlations with JOVC volunteering. However, the correlation between farming and volunteering turns out to be spurious while crafts work remains robust in a variety of regression analyses. Crafts workers explain about 25% of volunteer status in the JOVC after controlling for education, marital status, age, farm status, population density, and urbanization.

Unlike Peace Corps volunteers, age is not significant to JOVC-status. One in eight Peace Corps volunteers is over age 55, bringing years of practical experience to their tasks, but no such relationship exists in the JOVC data. Marital status is also not a predictor; widows, widowers, single persons, and married persons appear to be equally as likely to volunteer in the JOVC.

PASSPORT HOLDERS AND FOREIGN TRIPS

Another way to measure internationalization is to consider who shows interest in foreign travel and who actual goes abroad (Mowlana 1986). Students, scholars, immigrants, and diplomats are examples of important sources of face-to-face contact and human flow across national boundaries. Passport holding shows intent to travel abroad, as passports are a necessary condition for legal foreign travel for any reason. Figure 7—4 suggests that 4.4% of Japanese held passports in 1988. The amount of variation in passport holding is notable. Over eight times as many people in Tōkyō held passports as in Aomori and Akita which ranked at the bottom. Tōkyō is an outlier. Its residents hold nearly four times as many passports as persons in the average prefecture. Neighboring Kanagawa is also an outlier with over two and one-half times the normal rate of passport holding.

The cities of Tōkyō, Ōsaka, Kyōto, and Nagoya all must play an enormous role in the need for passports. There are no real differences across prefectures in reasons applicants give for obtaining passports. The correlations between reasons for passport holding — official diplomatic purposes, business, educational study, technical study, tourism, and permanent residency abroad — are all above 0.90, save technical study. The lowest correlation between technical-study and other reasons is 0.67.

This illustrates the extent to which some areas of Japan recognize the value of internationalism while others do not. That is, The Tōkyō to Ōsaka corridor contains the largest portion of passport holders. As one goes north of Tōkyō and west or south of Ōsaka, passport holding declines significantly. At least two reasons account for this difference: First, the majority of government, business, and academic institutions lie in those two major metropolitan areas. Second, the Tōkyō-to-Ōsaka corridor is the main repository of high disposable income. Although the original historical pressures to close off Japan germinated in the Kantō, the government quickly tried to catch up with the West as rapidly as possible starting in the Meiji Era. This meant encouraging exchange on a wide variety of levels. Passport holding should be a sign of such interest. The correlation of 0.97 between the percentages of persons holding passports and taking trips abroad indicates the strong overlap between the variables. It follows that the least internationally minded area is the Tōhoku region, succeeded by the islands of Shikoku and Kyūshū. Passport ownership and use are most necessary and useful for certain classes of persons. Government officials, mercantile traders, international businessmen, scientists, engineers, and certain educators often have reason to travel abroad. Wives and children of men with such occupations may wish to accompany their husbands on overseas trips. Finally, individuals with disposable income and a yen for foreign-travel experiences such as single women in the secretarial work world appear to be good candidates for passports. In actuality, about 80% of Japanese passport users were tourists in 1990, of whom 40% were affluent single women. Overseas tourism went through a phenomenal rise during the bubble-economy period of the late 1980s. From 1985 until 1990 there was a doubling of overseas tourists from approximately 5 million to just over 10 million.

Table 7—2 summarizes selected measures of status and passport possession. Unfortunately, comparable American data by states does not exist in such detail. However, some occupational data does exist. The correlation for American white-collar workers is 0.71, and is 0.62 for lawyers. These are close to the median correlations for the Japanese equivalents, suggesting similar cross-national reasons for passport holding. Occupational-status data provide an extremely interesting picture of the continuum of interest in foreign travel. At the high end are persons with such white-collar occupations as clerical workers, managers, and realtors, all of whom have close to a 75% chance of possessing a passport.[4] Laborers and housewives provide, perhaps, the largest surprise as they rank above such occupations as lawyers, sales persons, and professionals. Close to two out of three laborers and housewives owned a valid passport.

Among the remaining occupations with significant positive correlations, it is noteworthy that scientists and engineers appear to have much less interest in passport ownership than most other white-collar workers, and also than American scientists and engineers. The correlation for the 1980 American data (Stark 1992) is about 50% larger (r = 0.54), no doubt reflecting the more international orientation of American science and engineering (Mowlana 1986, p. 144).

---

[4]The square of a Pearson's correlation coefficient provides a useful measure of variation explained.

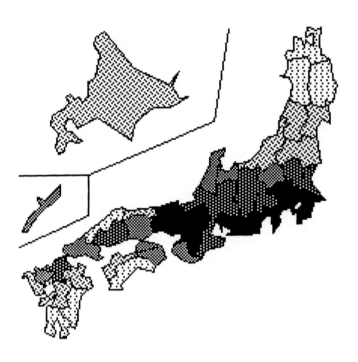

Tōkyō	16.1	Ibaraki	4.9	Niigata	3.2
Kanagawa	11.0	Hiroshima	4.8	Nagasaki	3.1
Chiba	9.2	Mie	4.8	Tokushima	3.1
Ōsaka	8.4	Tochigi	4.8	Tottori	3.1
Kyōto	8.2	Gunma	4.7	Yamagata	3.0
Nara	8.1	Ishikawa	4.6	Hokkaidō	2.9
Hyōgo	7.7	Toyama	4.4	Fukushima	2.9
Saitama	7.4	Okinawa	4.2	Ehime	2.9
Aichi	7.0	Okayama	4.0	Kōchi	2.5
Shiga	5.9	Kagawa	4.0	Shimane	2.4
Shizuoka	5.9	Wakayama	4.0	Kagoshima	2.3
Fukuoka	5.7	Saga	3.9	Miyazaki	2.3
Yamanashi	5.5	Yamaguchi	3.8	Iwate	1.9
Nagano	5.5	Kumamoto	3.8	Akita	1.9
Gifu	5.5	Miyagi	3.5	Aomori	1.8
Fukui	5.0	Ōita	3.2		

Figure 7—4   Percent of Population Holding a Passport by Prefecture

The structure of the negative associations is also enlightening. Farmers are the least likely to hold passports among all occupations shown in Table 7—2, followed by the self-employed, miners, educators, transportation workers, and those employed in the crafts. Once again, the American data is consistent. Farmers and self-employed Americans both have low correlations (r = -0.40 in both cases); and the correlation for American miners is -0.26. The American correlations are considerably weaker than their Japanese counterparts, but in the same direction. This suggests that Japanese farmers, self-employed persons, and miners are less internationally oriented than there American counterparts.

Interestingly, the moderately strong negative correlation for educators in the Japanese data replicates in the United States. American elementary and secondary school educators are unlikely to hold passports (r = - 0.26). With the outliers of Alaska and Hawaii removed, the correlation rises to -0.37 (p < 0.01) and is close to its Japanese counterpart. Part of the image problem both countries have may be the lack of interest in internationalization among those who teach.

Age statuses provide another handle on understanding interest in foreign travel. The American data show no correlations with age, but the Japanese data indicate more foreign travel at young ages. Indeed, some high schools became highly active in promoting overseas field trips during the 1980s. For example, during the 1986 school year, there was a 75% increase in the number of high school students taking school trips abroad. Although this represented a broadening institutional base, only 204 of the 5511 senior high schools participated in overseas school trips in 1986. The Foreign Ministry does not release information that would identify the types of high schools that participate. However, the correlational data presented in this chapter suggest schools in the Tōkyō and Kansai areas must have been most likely to be among this group. Furthermore, the correlational data in Table 7—2 suggests a clear relationship to cultural capital. Areas with higher-status occupations, elite universities, and higher library readership are the same areas in which those schools are most likely to be located.

In Japan, individuals over age 64 appear least interested in foreign travel, while those under age 15 are most interested. The negative correlations for widows and widowers reflects their age and possibly their low educational levels and lack of disposable income. The group most likely to be illiterate (less than a junior high education) consists of persons mostly born prior to World War II.

Japanese over age 64 are unlikely to have obtained enough foreign language skills to feel comfortable in foreign travel. Students in junior high, senior high, or college must take English as a second language. However, the age effect remains robust after controlling for various educational indicators (the percentage of youth going on to college, the percentage attending the top 40 universities).

Table 7—2

Results of Zero-Order Correlations between the Percentage
of Japanese with Passports and Selected Indicators of Status

Occupations	Correlations	Marital	Correlations
%Clerks	**0.88	Single female	** 0.69
%Managers	**0.86	Single male	** 0.64
%Realtors	**0.85	Divorced	-0.04
%Laborers	**0.79	# in household	* -0.31
%Housewives	**0.79	Widow	** -0.46
%Lawyers	**0.68	Widower	** -0.63
%Sales	**0.63		
%Professional/Technical	**0.59	Education	
%Service	**0.45		
%Scientists/Engineers	*0.38	Book rate	** 0.73
%Protective	0.01	Top 45 Univ	** 0.70
%Crafts	-0.22	% attend university	0.07
%Transportation	**-0.44	Under 6 yrs	* -0.33
%Educators	**-0.47		
%Miners	**-0.48	Owner/Renter	
%Self-Employed	**-0.67		
%Farmers	**-0.82	Rneter	** 0.51
		Owner	** -0.71
Age			
		Miscellaneous	
%age 0-15	** 0.78		
%age 15-64	** 0.57	Density	** 0.84
%age 64+	** -0.61	Industrial	** 0.79
		GPP per cap	** 0.71
		Foreigners	** 0.63
		Newcomers	** 0.61

* Significant at 0.05 level
** Significant at 0.01 level

Many Japanese confuse internationalization with instruction in English, most probably because it is viewed as the language of international business. Thus, while virtually all junior and senior high schools teach English, less than 2% teach French. Although Monbushō claims to promote languages other than English, as of 1990 only 5% of high schools offered lessons in other languages. Here again we see the pattern of privilege noted throughout education in Japan. Of the 89 high schools offering French in 1990, 55 were private and 36 were in Tōkyō. The same pattern existed for the 71 high schools teaching Chinese; the disproportionate number were private schools in the Tōkyō metropolitan area. Although the roots of modern Japanese medicine depend on a knowledge of German, only 54 high schools taught this language in 1988. The historical importance of nearby Russian and Korean borders, and Korean-Japanese populations would also lead to the expectation that these languages would play a significant role in Japanese education. Yet only 14 high schools taught Korean and 4 instructed in Russian in 1988. Thus, it is no wonder that few Japanese travel independently for long periods to non-English speaking countries.

RETURNEES FROM LONG-TERM OVERSEAS ASSIGNMENTS

By 1992, the Foreign Ministry reported that over half-million Japanese lived overseas with the right of permanent residence overseas (kaigai zairyū hōjin). Figure 7—6 visualizes the rapid increase in Japanese on overseas assignments for longer than 3 months from 1969 through 1986. Increasing Japanese investments plausibly explains the 500% increase in long-term overseas stays, as there is a 0.95 correlation between the two variables. Almost two-thirds of all long-term residents engage in trading, banking, and manufacturing businesses. Although Goodman (1990, p. 20) suggests that Japanese go to developed countries for education and developing countries for business, the prefectural-level correlations between reasons for passport issuance do not support him. The correlation between going abroad for technical training and business reasons is the lowest, but is still an impressive 0.67 in the 1988 data. Passports issued for all other reasons correlate at over 0.9 with business purposes.

Just as the number of adults going abroad for long stays increased rapidly during the post-war period, so did the number of accompanying children of school age. From 1966 to 1972, it increased over four-fold. It doubled again in the 12-year period from 1972 until 1984. Partly due to revision of the School Education law in 1987, which approved up to 30 credits for overseas study, the number of students studying abroad for more than 3 months continued to expand greatly. However, over three-fourths of such students studied in the United States with most of the remainder studying in other English-speaking countries like Australia, Canada, Great Britain, and New Zealand. By the end of the 1980s, over 100,000 Japanese youth had returned from extended stays overseas.

Nearly half of the returnees had attended nihon gakkō, with the other half going to host-country schools. Most of these returnees report readjusting to Japanese life after a year. Still, many report that they had trouble readjusting to life in Japan because students or teachers rejected them, confusion over cultural allegiance, or anxiety over being different from other Japanese. A survey of returnees to Kanazawa and Ishikawa Prefectures (The

Japan Times, March 9, 1990, p. 2) found that only 10% remembered anything positive about their return. More than half gave critical responses such as "There are too many rules and students," "privacy is not respected" or "My classmates act in a uniform way and do not disclose their real feelings." Rather than help integrate children into the advantages of internationalization, schools appear to focus children's visions on their local society (Iwamura 1987, p. 22).

No wonder then that workers assigned overseas appear reluctant to take their children out of fear that their education will suffer. The popular press refers to such men as part of the <u>tanshin fu'ninzoku</u> (bachelor-husband tribe). In particular, families show reluctance at taking their sons out of the competitive education race (Onoda and Tanaka 1988, pp.26-27).

This gender-bias shows up in the correlations in Table 7—2 where young single women are more likely than young single men to hold passports. Still, the fact that young people under age 15 are the most likely age group to hold passports suggests that the popular press has overblown the reluctance of Japanese to take or send their children overseas. More likely, the press has focused on the minority of horror stories at the expense of a more balanced picture.

Academics have generally not done much better at providing adequate comparisons. Research by White (1988) clearly delineates the problems of Japanese returnees from overseas without showing how they differ from children in other nations with similar overseas experiences, or even Japanese who move from one part of Japan to another. She lists challenges of children re-entering the educational system; problems women must overcome, as mothers, to protect their children and themselves from criticisms for their "foreign" ways; and the dilemmas that confront middle-class, white-collar male workers and professionals as they seek to reestablish themselves in their workplaces and to reshape career paths that may have been irrevocably altered by foreign assignments. None of these are problems that are unique to Japanese returnees.

White's classifications of returnees also suggest the self-imposed nature of many problems. Some returnees become "reassimilators" who "launder" themselves to try to erase all traces of their foreign sojourns. Next are the "Adjusters" who conform, but are less hypersensitive about revealing their foreign experiences. Then there are two groups of "internationals," who capitalize on their foreign expertise: elite internationals who can maintain their foreign contacts and habits because their other attributes of mainstream social status are so strong they need not worry about being stigmatized; and nonconformist internationals who are willing to sacrifice the possibility of mainstream status for the relative freedom and personal autonomy they can pursue as internationals.

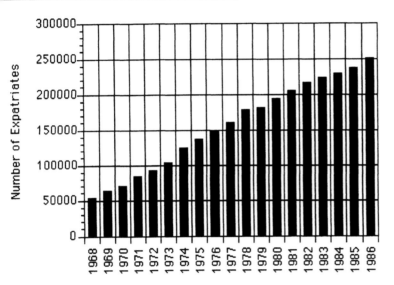

Figure 7—5   The Increase in "Long-Term" Overseas Expatriates 1969 through 1986

Sources: Kaigai Shijo Kyōiku Shinkō Zaidan, 1980: Monbushō, 1988:4.

In spite of the rich detail inherent in White's and other studies, Goodman (1990) points out that the returnee literature rarely uses control groups. For example, students who move from one Japanese school to another (tenkōsei) provide a natural comparison group because these students are the normal targets of bullying as we saw in Chapters 1 and 3. Yokoshima (1977) is one of the few academics who has compared tenkōsei with kikokushijo. As he points out "according to children, nothing is more unpleasant than changing schools." (p. 142)

Yokoshima's studies suggest more similarities than differences between students who return from overseas and those who move to new schools within Japan. Similarly, students from other nations often have negative experiences as foreign exchange students, regardless of the country where they study. But such natural comparisons escape most writers on the kikokushijo experience. Hence, the mass media focuses on negative experiences as if they are uniquely Japanese and rarely mentions positive outcomes.

Kidder (1992) provides another example of reviews of the problems of returnee status without comparison groups. She divides returnee problems into five areas: physical markers (unanticipated hair color changes), behavioral signs (more active communication), interpersonal styles (more direct, argumentative speech), and manners of speaking (loss of polite speech). None of these problem areas are inherent to returnees. Teachers are notorious in forcing any student with light-colored hair to dye it black. Students who move from one area of Japan to another often find their accents and dialects subject to ridicule. Thus, we are left wondering how much of the alleged deleterious effects of overseas stays is actually due to the well-known effects of self-fulfilling prophesy.

During the 1970s, returnees actually found themselves placed in classes for the mentally handicapped. The present Monbushō budget for returnees remains part of the funds designated for handicapped children. By the 1980s returnee discrimination became a more subtle "minority status" based upon the belief that exposure to a foreign culture creates social problems for reintegration. Some teachers and classmates referred to returnees as gakoku kabure (tainted by foreign contact). The stereotypic returnee was a threat to the Japanese ideal: aggressive, insubordinate, strange, intractable, and disrespectful of authority. Yet advertisements by companies looking for just such special skills increased during the 1980s with the recognition that individuals with stronger character might have their advantages in the international marketplace. Returnees appear to agree. Two-thirds of a sample of 163 returnees to the Tōkyō area stated that their overseas experience had aided them find employment, and half agreed that part of the attraction was the foreign language skills gained while living abroad (Goodman 1990, p. 186).

Some teachers make vague claims of returnees suffering disadvantages from their overseas experiences. Ironically, a Monbushō survey of teachers indicates that returnees are anything but handicapped. Teachers rated 51% of returnee children as above average (sugurete iru), 42% as average (futsū), and 7% as below average (ototte iru) in their class work (Goodman 1990, pp. 166—167). Indeed, the main thesis of Goodman (1990) concerning children who have returned from overseas stays is that they are a very privileged group; a "new international elite" rather than stigmatized by their experience as White (1988) argues.

If overseas travel were a stigma we would expect a strong negative correlation between the percent of children under age 15 and passport holding. The strong positive correlation of 0.78 between passport holding and percent of children under age 15 supports Goodman's over White's arguments. Also, roughly half of student returnees (kikokushijo) attend special reception schools (ukeireko).

Goodman argues that the returnee families in his convenience samples have families from the elite class in part because 90% of his sample have college-educated fathers. A survey of nearly 1000 parents with children in overseas Japanese schools corroborates the privileges bestowed on those with overseas experiences (Kawabata and Suzuki 1981; Kawabata and Suzuki 1982). This series of studies indicates that families on long-term overseas stays do much better than average in education; 90% of the men had college degrees, 35% of the mothers had a university degree and another 25% had two-year junior college diplomas. Furthermore, virtually all of the returnees come from the two most dynamic areas of industrialization. During the late

1980s over two-thirds of them came from the Tōkyō metropolitan area. When combined with the Kansai area, close to four out of five returnees can be accounted for.

The results of Table 7—2 are even more equivocal. The data on education suggests that passport holders are unusually well-educated and have graduated from the cream of the universities (r = 0.70) rather than any particular university (r=0.07). This supports an interpretation of the elite universities as internationally-oriented with other universities more parochially-oriented. Chapter 3 suggests that Japanese with education majors are more parochial than other majors because they tend to be trained in the prefecture in which they find employment. This implies that most teachers do not graduate from one of the elite universities, possibly explaining the low chance that educators hold passports. By contrast, American universities do not appear to have a similar elitist split. Attendance at universities in the United States correlates strongly (r = 0.61) with passport holding. This is consistent with data showing that the United States has become the major center of foreign students (Mowlana 1986. p. 145).

Other data in Table 7—2 also strongly support Goodman's elitist thesis. Disproportionately high numbers of Japanese passport holders have elitist occupations (managers, realtors, lawyers, professionals, scientists). Prefectures with large proportions of their youth attending the top 40 universities, more industrialization, and higher GNP are more privileged and have more passport holders. Indeed, Goodman (1990, p. 43) points out that many prestigious universities have special quotas called tokubetsu waku that grant preferential admittance to returnee children who have spent several years abroad. Approximately 25% of Japan's universities offer special admissions to returnees; more than half of the national universities, and the top two public (Tōkyō, Kyōto) and private (Waseda, Keio) universities do (Kyōiku joseikyoku zaimuka kaigai shijo kyōikushitsu 1988). A telling neologism is the label "Japanese-plus" implying that returnee students have something extra to offer due to their international experiences.

If they have more to offer than average citizens it is partly due to Monbushō's priorities. The Ministry spends considerably more on students with than without overseas experience. For instance, in 1984 Monbushō spent 44% more per capita on elementary students attending nihonjin gakkō (special overseas schools), 22% more on junior high students, and 15% more on high school students. Partly as a result of this favorable status, three-year assignments to the approximately 1000 overseas postings available at nihonjin gakkō are in great demand.

The demand for admittance to national and international schools in Japan also illustrates the advantages of being a kikokushijo. The 22 national and international schools are in great demand due to their small class sizes allowing for more individual attention, educational programs in English, and other perquisites. The advantage of overseas versus non-overseas experience on admittance to these schools is significant: it is five times higher for elementary students, over ten times higher for junior high students, and 35 times greater for high school students (Goodman 1990, p. 183) Here, again, Monbushō shows it ambivalence through institutional discrimination by categorizing students at such schools ineligible for educational loans. The result is that all but 5% of the students attending international schools matriculate at western institutions of higher learning (Willis 1983). Thus, the charge that returnees attending western universities are "dropouts" is chauvinistic (Shukan Shincho May 17, 1990).

The special status of returnee children shows up in schools especially built for them and subsidized by Monbushō. International Christian University (ICU) Senior High School, Gyōsei International Senior High School, and Dōshisha International Senior High School. Part of the prestige of schools set up for returnee children is due to the low student-teacher ratios (Furuhashi 1984). Hoshino (1983) studied returnees at ICU's Senior High School. Three factors predicted individual adjustment: (1) admitting to a long-term purpose in life; (2) having strong family ties; and (3) identifying as Japanese. Returnees who had spent over 6 years overseas had the most difficulty in maintaining the socially expected Japanese identity.

INTERNATIONALIZATION AND FOREIGNERS LIVING IN JAPAN

Without disputing the importance of individual-level factors to life after returning home, one might wonder if ecological differences might also play an important role in acceptance of foreign things. It seems reasonable to suppose that a returnee to Tōkyō or Ōsaka would feel less reverse culture-shock than in Iwate or Yamagata. Foreign influence is greatest in the two largest metropolitan areas. The correlation of 0.63 between trips abroad and percentage of foreign residents suggests a symbiotic relationship. More internationally minded Japanese appear to attract more ethnically diverse populations, and vice versa.

Although it may seem surprising at first glance that the Kansai is far ahead of the Kanto in foreign residents (over 2% of Ōsaka residents do not hold Japanese citizenship), in actuality this is because of the huge Korean-Japanese and Chinese-Japanese populations in the Kansai who are denied citizenship. Yamagata, which is at the bottom, has only one-twenty-fifth as many foreign residents as Ōsaka. The upshot is that the average citizen in the Kansai and Kantō regions has much more chance of daily contact with non-Japanese people and cultures.

Research conducted by Fukurai and Alston (1990) shows some hope of ameliorating neo-nationalistic, anti-internationalist behavior in Japan. They used path analytic techniques that suggest that prefectures with more ethnically diverse compositions showed significantly less conformity to the neo-Shintoist image of "racial purity." Also, they found that prefectures with greater in- and out-migration showed much less religious conformity. Their data indicate that greater ethnic and population heterogeneity of the Kantō and Kansai areas, in particular, have much more accepting climates for the growth of internationalism and reduced tolerance for conformism and neo-nationalism.

SUMMARY

Micro-level Japanese attitudes and behaviors toward, and the macro-level social structure underlying, internationalization allow one final glimpse of the mechanisms of learning and socialization. This chapter has demonstrated that government officials and the mass media present an oversimplified picture of a unified status quo. Official positions stress internationalization as a conundrum of rewards and costs understood and shared by all Japanese. However, statistics on flows of goods, services, people, technology, and information indicate consistent asymmetry across prefectures. As with other advanced nations, the most urbanized areas show the greatest signs of internationalization by almost any measure.

The irony is that although official propaganda stress uchi as Japanese and soto as non-Japanese, the real uchi and soto is urbanized versus rural Japan. Rigid, ascribed statuses of Japaneseness no longer constrict the elites in the major governmental and commercial centers as they did in the past. However, such achieved statuses as education, overseas experience, and occupation are in constant tension with traditional ascribed statuses. Furthermore, such ethnic groups at the bottom of the status ladder as the Korean-Japanese, Chinese-Japanese, foreign aliens, Burakumin, and Ainu suffer from the most severe constraints of ascriptive norms.

Korean-Japanese make up the largest and most visible group treated as outsiders. Splits between those who identity with North Korean, South Korea, and Japan exacerbate their fights to integration into the larger society. Chinese-Japanese are the second largest minority group. They have little in common with the Korean-Japanese other than their low status. They live in different areas and have engaged in less direct competition with their host country, making their status more invisible than the Korean-Japanese.

The hot economy of the 1980s attracted large numbers of Asian immigrants who could make more in Japan in one month than in their home country in a year. As in other industrialized countries their uncertain, and often illegal, statuses have led to systematic discrimination by brokers and employers who profit from their exploitation. Thus, although their sub-human treatment is inexcusable, it is little different from guest workers in Europe or "wetbacks" in the United States.

On the brighter side are signs of growing international cooperation, friendship, and exchange through sister ties among governments of different levels. Sister City ties appear partially to rectify the rural-urban inequities in internationalization. More urbanized, export-oriented prefectures have been less aggressive in seeking the benefits of sister ties than less developed prefectures. On the American side, these ties appear related to importing Japanese factories as a source of new employment opportunities and are sought mostly be persons with a college education. On the Japanese side, interest in learning, as measured by library-lending rates, and increased overseas tourism are good predictors of the seeking of sister ties. The Peace

Corps model of giving agricultural, medical, and educational assistance to third-world countries also shows the increasingly broadened base of internationalization in Japan. Persons with skills in various crafts and who live in rural areas are most likely to represent Japan in the Japanese Overseas Volunteer Corps.

The most notable increase in internationalization has taken place with the increasing disposable income of certain segments of the population. More elite occupations like managers, realtors, lawyers are over-represented among passport holders and users. Lower-status occupations like farmers, the self-employed and miners, by contrast, show the least interest in, or ability to use, passports. Younger, single persons who attended a top university and read library books also appear over-represented among passport holders.

The more dense, industrial prefectures with higher per capital gross prefectural profits (higher disposable income), larger numbers of foreign residents and more population movements also appear to display the most international behavior as measured by passport holding. One particularly important type of passport holder are returnees from long-term overseas assignments and their families. The analysis in this section corroborates Goodman's thesis that they make up a new elite group rather than being stigmatized by their experiences as some writers have charged.

Often lost in the concern over the individual sufferings of outsiders are the institutionalized disadvantages of the status quo to the whole society, and the structural advantages that accrue to those who adapt to changing conditions. It is clear that the Kantō and Kansai areas benefit the most from internationalization of most types discussed. Other regions presently get the crumbs, and not the bread.

It is also well to remember that the issues I have discussed are issues experienced in all industrialized countries. For many Japanese the returnees "way of thinking" is different and not compatible to a society accustomed to traditional conditioning. Much of the problem has been constructed by the news media, without benefit of comparison to other countries. The most industrialized, export-orient prefectures are overrepresented on most measures of internationalization. Most Japanese, like other nationals, readjust well within a year of return to their homeland. Internationalization and returnees are not really the problem--they are mirrors held up to society's own face.

JAPANESE GLOSSARY

The pronunciation of Japanese vowels is similar to Italian vowels. Give vowels double length when modified by a macron (e.g., ō,ū, Ō). Pronounce consonants similarly to English with the exception of r. R-sounds are halfway between the English r and l. Treat each element of a double consonant (e.g., pp, kk) separately with a slight pause after the first consonant and the release of a small explosion of breath with the final consonant. Pronounce words in an even fashion with little variance in pitch. G is hard. With the exception of the consonant 'n', all Japanese phonemes end in vowels. As an aid to understanding where to separate these phonemes I use the apostrophe (') as a separator mark. For example, 'fu'nin' is read 'fu-ni-n' rather than 'fun-in' or 'fun-i-n'.

Ainu: the aboriginal inhabitants of the Japanese archipelago, gradually pushed back to the northernmost island of Hokkaidō. Current estimates of near-pure-Ainu are about 25,000.

bungakubu: university liberal arts division.

Burakumin: an euphemism that replaces the more stigmatizing word 'eta'. It refers to the 2-3 million members of Japan's outcast group who the pre-Meiji government officially distinguished by their low-status occupations such as tanning and butchery.

Chōsoren : Acronym for the Federation of [North] Korean Residents.

dekasegi: farm workers primarily from the Tōhoku region who migrate principally to Tōkyō during the winter months to find seasonal employment.

Edo period: Also known as the Tokugawa period from 1603 until 1868 when the center of state power was based in Edo (present-day Tōkyō) under the Tokugawa military government.

eta: The original name for the untouchable class known now by the euphemism of Burakumin.

gambaru: verbal infinitive for exerting effort or persisting in the face of travesty, implying that effort is more important than individual ability.

gōgaku: extant word meaning 'village schools' that were set up during the Edo period and later became part of the state education system in the Meiji period. Divided into two types: hankō and terakoya.

hensachi: a quantitative measure similar to American S.A.T. percentile scores that is used to inform juku students of their relative standing on college entrance test-taking.

hoikuen: day nurseries funded by the Kōseishō.

honne: one's true intentions. Similar to the sociological concept of 'backstage behavior' (see tatemae)

ie: literally, house or household, but often used to refer to the prototypic social unit. A legal institution for the transmission of property rights.

juku: often translated into English as 'cram school'; these schools offer after-school instruction in how to pass the national university entrance exams for primary and secondary school students.

kaiimoji: describes the vast majority of Chinese characters as ideographs of social construction rather than pictographs.

kana: consists of the syllabic script for the 46 Japanese morphemes. The hiragana is used for everyday cursive phonetic writing and their katakana equivalents that are used mostly to write foreign loan words,

kanji: ideographic characters borrowed from the Chinese to write Japanese.

Kantō: the Greater Tōkyō Metropolitan Area, from the Chinese characters for 'East of the Barrier.'

kikokushijo: children who have spent time overseas with parents who are on a visa allowing them to stay at least 3 months in a foreign country.

Kōseishō: the Ministry of Health and Welfare.

koseki: the official village, town, or city registry of family members. Although tracing back to the 10th century, it was not established as law until the Meiji Era.

Kyōdai: acronym for Kyōto University.

kyōiku mama: refers to the implicit primary responsibility of mothers for their children's education.

kyōikubu: university school of education.

miai: traditionally, pre-marital form of introduction of prospective spouses through a nakōdo, but has come to include introductions through anyone who is one's senior such as a boss, former teacher, etc.

Meiji period: era of formal rule under the Emperor Meiji from 1868 until 1912.

Mindan: Acronym for the Association of [South] Korean Residents.

mitsunyūkokusha: persons smuggled into Japan; mostly refers to illegal Koreans returnees to Japan.

Monbushō: The Ministry of Education, Science, and Culture.

naishoku: the term may refer to more general sideline work outside of one's ordinary job, but it may also be used to refer to part-time, or piece work that married women do for pay in their homes.

nakōdo: traditional matchmaker or go-between. Originally, a fictive parent for the groom but now has degenerated into a superficial and temporary role.

nenkō jōretsu: "lifetime" job security system characteristic of white-collar employment in the largest Japanese companies.

Nichibenren: Japanese Bar Association.

nihonjin gakkō: special overseas schools supported by Monbushō to make re-entry back into Japanese schools easier upon the students' return.

nihonjinron: a genre of literature that examines what appears to be unique about the Japanese as a people.

Nihon Keisai Shinbun: Japanese Economic Journal, the daily national newspaper equivalent of the Wall Street Journal and the New York Times combined.

Nikkei: acronym for Nihon Keisai Shinbun.

Nikkyōso: the Japanese Federation of Teachers); the main teacher's union in Japan.

ren'ai: traditionally, marriage based on a love-match, although it has come to mean marriage through introductions by one's peers.

Ryūkyū: Okinawa is the primary island in this island chain which has prefectural status.

rōnin: from the Chinese characters for "masterless samurai", now used as a pejorative for high-school graduates who failed the college entrance examination and are preparing to retake it.

sakoku: closed country. A key phrase during the approximately 250 years of the Tokugawa Era (1615-1868) policy of closing Japan to the outside world.

sensei: although used to refer to one's teachers and professors this is also a general term of respect for one's seniors.

shūshin koyō: lifetime employment.

shijuku: private academies.

shōkeimoji: describes those few Chinese characters which have literal pictographic origins.

SSM: acronym for 'Social Stratification and Mobility', a decennial national probability survey drawn independently of official government samples in years ending with a "5" to test a variety of sociological questions contributed by cooperative sociologists.

tanshin fu'nin: practice of husbands who are assigned to outlying districts for company work and thus who live in separate quarters from their family for the greater part of the year. Also used to describe husbands who work overseas for extended periods while their families live in Japan.

tatemae: the official party line. Similar to the sociological concept of 'frontstage behavior'. (see honne)

teichaku ijūsha: an official "permanent-resident" status given to Korean and Chinese forced into servitude in Japan during the pre-World War II period and their offspring, and non-Japanese married to Japanese.

<u>tekireiki</u>: the most suitable age for marriage; traditionally, 23 for women and 28 for men.

<u>terakoya</u>: private Buddhist parish elementary schools. See <u>gōgaku</u>.

<u>Tōdai</u>: acronym for Tōkyō University.

<u>ukeirekō</u>: special schools for students who have returned from abroad to help readjust them to the demands of Japanese education.

<u>yobikō</u>: special private university entrance examination for high school graduates called <u>rōnin</u> who have previously failed them.

<u>yōchien</u>: kindergartens under control of <u>Monbushō</u>.

BIBLIOGRAPHY

Abu-Lughod, J. (1989) *Before European hegemony: The world system, 1250-1350 a.d.* Glendale: Oxford.

Amano, I. (1989). The examination hell and school violence. In J. J. Shields Jr. (Eds.), *Japanese schooling: Patterns of socialization, equality, and political control.* (pp. 111—123). University Park: Pennsylvania State University Press.

Amano, I. (1990). *Education and examination in modern Japan* (Cummings, William K. and Fumiko Cummings, Trans.). Tōkyō: University of Tōkyō Press.

Anderson, S. A., Bagarozzi, D. A., & Giddings, C. W. (1986). Images: Preliminary scale construction. *American Journal of Family Therapy, 14,* 357—363.

Barnes, G. L. (1990) "Ceramics of the yayoi agriculturalists." In *The rise of a great tradition: Japanese archaeological ceramics from the jomon through heian periods (10,500 b.c. - 1185 a.d.),* ed. Japan Society and Agency for Cultural Affairs. pp. 28—39. Tōkyō: Government of Japan.

Bartholomew, J. R. (1989). *The formation of science in Japan.* New Haven: Yale University Press.

Bauer, J. & A. Mason. (1992). The distribution of income and wealth in Japan. *Review of Income and Wealth.* 38: 403-428.

Bayley, D.H. (1991). *Forces of order: Policing modern Japan.* Berkeley: University of California Press.

Beauchamp, E. R. (1978). Shiken jigoku: The problem of entrance examinations in Japan. *Asian Profile, 6,* 523—560.

Beauchamp, E. R., & Rubinger, R. (1989). *Education in Japan: A sourcebook.* New York: Garland Publishing.

Becker, G. (1973). A theory of marriage: Part I. *Journal of Political Economy, 81,* 813—846.

Benjamin, G. R., & James, E. (1989). Public and private schools and educational opportunity in Japan. In J. J. Shields Jr. (Eds.), *Japanese schooling: Patterns of socialization, equality, and political control.* (Pp. 154—162). University Park: Pennsylvania State University Press.

Bennett, J. W. , H. Passin, & R. K. McKnight. (1958) "The innovative potential of american-educated Japanese." *Human Organization* 20: 246-251.

Billig, M. S. (1991). The marriage squeeze on high-caste rajasthani women. *The Journal of Asian Studies, 50,* 341-360.

Blake, J. (1989). *Family size and achievement*. Berkeley: University of California Press.

Bloosfeld, H. P., & Huinink, J. (1991). Human capital investments or norms of role transition? How women's schooling and career affect the process of family formation. *American Journal of Sociology, 97*, 143—168.

Blumberg, R. L. (1991). Introduction: The "triple overlap" of gender stratification, economy, and the family. In R. L. Blumberg (Ed.) *Gender, family, and economy: The triple overlap*. Newbury Park, CA: Sage Publications. Pp. 7—34.

Brinton, M. (1988). The social-institutional bases of gender stratification: Japan as an illustrative case. *American Journal of Sociology, 94*, 300—334.

Buswell, R. E. (1990) *Chinese Buddhist Apocrypha*. Honolulu: University of Hawaii Press.

Cahn, D. D. (1989). Relative importance of perceived understanding in developing male-female mate relationships. *Psychological Reports, 64*, 1339—1342.

Calder, K. (1988). *Crisis and compensation: Public policy and stability in Japan, 1949-1946*. Princeton: Princeton University Press.

Calhoun, J. A., Grotberg, E. A., & Rickley, W. R. (1980). *The status of children, youth and families, 1979*. No. 80-30274. U.S. Department of Health and Human Services.

Chambers, G. S., & Cummings, W. K. (1990). *Profiting from education: Japan-United States educational ventures in the 1980s*. No. 20). Institute of International Education, New York.

Cheatham, R. E. (1986). *Women in higher education: Traditions, transitions, and revolutions*. St. Louis: Saint Louis University Metropolitan College and SAASS.

Cheng, M. T. (1991). The Japanese employment system: Empirical findings. *Work and Occupations, 18*, 148—171.

Chinen, I. (1990). *Fukusō suru nansei shotō no bunka —kyūshū kigen dake de ha hodokenai bunka yōsō. Saishin nihon bunka kigenron. [Perspective on the nansei islands: Aspects of culture that are not clearly unraveled concerning the origins of Kyūshū. New theories on culture in Japan]*. Tōkyō: Gakken

Cho, C. K. (1987). Ethnic identity and political movement: A history of the Korean minority in Japan. Berkeley CA: Unpublished in manuscript.

Cogan, J. J. (1984). Should the u.s. mimic Japanese education? Let's look before we leap. *Phi Delta Kappan, 65*, 463—468.

Coleman, J. S. (1993) The rational construction of society. *American Sociological Review, 58*, 1—15.

Coleman, S. (1983). *Family planning in Japanese society: Traditional birth control in a modern urban society*. Princeton: Princeton University Press.

Cooperative Survey Staff of the Sande- Mainichi (1988, April 2, 1989). '88 zenkoku chomei 400 kōkō shuyō daigaku gōkakusū. (Leading university examination results for aspirants from the 400 best-known high schools in 1988.). *Sande- Mainichi (Sunday Mainichi)*.

Corley, C. J., & Woods, A. Y. (1991). Socioeconomic, sociodemographic and attitudinal correlates of the tempo of divorce. *Journal of Divorce and Remarriage, 16,* 47—68.

Coser, L. (1974). *Greedy institutions.* New York: Free Press.

DeCoker, G. (1989). Japanese preschools: Academic or nonacademic? In J. J. Shields Jr. (Eds.), *Japanese schooling: Patterns of socialization, equality, and political control.* (pp. 45—58). University Park: Pennsylvania State University Press.

De Mente, B. (1990). *Japan's secret weapon: The kata factor—The cultural programming that made the Japanese a superior people,* New York: Phoenix Books.

Deliberative Council for Buraku Assimilation. (1965) *Dōwa taisaku no genkyō. [The present condition of assimilation policy.].* Sōrifu [Prime Minister's Office]

DeVos, G. & H. Wagatsuma. (1966). *Japan's invisible race: Caste in culture and personality.* Berkeley: University of California Press.

Di Meglio, R.R., ed. (1970) *Arab trade with indonesia and the malay peninsula from the 8th to the 16th century.* Islam and the trade of asia: A colloquium. Philadephia: University of Pennsylvania Press.

Dodo, Y. & H. Ishida. (1990). "Population history of Japan as viewed from cranial nonmetric variation." *Journal of Anthropology and Sociology of Nippon* 98: 269—287.

Doi, T. (1973). *The Anatomy of dependence.* Tōkyō: Kodansha International Press.

Dore, R. P. (1986). *Flexible rigidities: Industrial policy and structural adjustment in the Japanese economy 1970 - 80.* Stanford CA: Stanford University Press.

Dore, R., & Sako, M. (1989). *How the Japanese learn to work.* London: Routledge.

Duke, B. (1986). *The Japanese school: Lessons for industrial america.* New York: Praeger.

Duke, B. (Ed.) (1989). *Ten great educators of modern Japan—A Japanese perspective.* Tōkyō: Tōkyō University Press.

Earns, F. (1993) "Language adaptation: European language influence on Japanese syntax." Ph. D. dissertation, University of Hawaii.

Edwards, W. (1989). *Modern Japan through its weddings.* Stanford, CA: Stanford University Press.

Ehara, T. (1984). *Gendai kōtō kyōiku no kōzō (The contemporary structure of higher education).* Tōkyō: Tōkyō Daigaku Shuppankai (University of Tōkyō Press).

Finifter, B. M. (1977) . "The robustness of cross-cultural findings." *Annals of the New York Academy of Sciences, 285:* 151—184.

Fujimura-Fanselow, K. (1989) "Educational opportunity for special groups." In *Japanese schooling: Patterns of socialization, equality, and political control.,* ed. James J. Shields Jr. Pp. 163—175. University Park: Pennsylvania State University Press.

Fujioka, K. (1908 [1985]) *Nihongo no ichi. Nihong no Keitō— Arutaikei to minamiajiakei to no ketsugō ni kanshite,* The Situation of Japanese. A short history and unification of the Japanese system with southeast Asia. Ōsaka: Izumishoin.

Fujita, H. (1989). A crises of legitimacy in Japanese education. Meritocracy and cohesiveness. In J. J. Shields Jr. (Eds.), *Japanese schooling: Patterns of socialization, equality, and political control* (Pp. 124—138). University Park: Pennsylvania State University Press.

Fukurai, H., & Alston, J. (1990). Divorce in contemporary Japan. *Journal of Biosocial Science, 22,* 453—464.

Fukutake, T. (1976). *Nihon nōson no shakai mondai [Social problems in Japanese agricultural communities].* Tōkyō: Tōkyō University Press.

Furuhashi, S. (1984). "Foreign in their own land: Returnee children's patterns of adjustments into Japanese schools." M. Ed., University of Hawaii.

Garfield, E. & Welljams-Dorof, A. 1992. Of nobel class: A citation perspective on high impact research authors. *Theoretical Medicine, 13,* 117—124.

Garon, S. (1987). *The state and labor in modern Japan.* Berkeley: University of California Press.

Glass, J., & Camarigg, V. (1992). Gender, parenthood, and job-family compatibility. *American Journal of Sociology, 98,* 131—151.

Glenn, N., & Shelton, B. (1985). Regional differences in divorce in the United States. *Journal of Marriage and the Family, 47,* 641—652.

Gluck, C. (1990) "Idea of Showa." *Daedalus, 119:* 1—26.

Goldberg, M. P. (1989). Recent trends in special education. In Tōkyō. In J. J. Shields Jr. (Eds.), *Japanese schooling: Patterns of socialization, equality, and political control.* (pp. Pp. 176—184). University Park: Pennsylvania State University Press.

Goode, W. J. (1963). *World revolution and family patterns.* Glencoe, IL: Free Press.

Goode, W. J. (1987, January 26). A citation classic. *Current Contents: Social and Behavioral Sciences,* p. 14.

Goodman, R. (1990) *Japan's "international youth": The emergence of a new class of schoolchildren.* New York: Oxford University Press.

Gordon, A. (1985). *Industrial relations in Japan: Heavy industry, 1853—1955.* Cambridge, MS: Council on East Asian Studies and Harvard University Press.

Guttentag, M., & Secord, P. (1983). *Too many women? The sex ratio question.* Beverly Hills, CA: Sage Publishers.

Hamaguchi, E. (1985). A contextual model of the Japanese: Toward a methodological innovation in Japan studies. *Journal of Japanese Studies, 11,* 289—320 (Trans: K. Shumpei & Mildred R. Creighton).

Hamashita, T. (1986) "Chōkō bōeki shisutemu to kindai ajia (The tribute system and modern Asia.) *Kokusai Seiji (International Relations), 82:* 42—55.

Hanami, T. (1989). Industrial democracy. In T. Ishida & E. S. Krauss (Eds.), *Democracy in Japan* Pittsburg: University of Pittsburg Press.

Hanihara, T. (1991) "Dentition of Nansei islanders and peopling of the Japanese archipelago: The basic populations of east asia, IX." *Journal of the Anthropology and Sociology of Nippon* 99: 399—409.

Hart, J. A. (1992) The effects of state-societal arrangements on international competitiveness: Steel, motor vehicles and semiconductors in the United States, Japan, and western Europe. *British Journal of Political Science, 22,* 255—300.

Hawkins, J. N. (1989). "Educational demands and institutional response: *Dowa* education in Japan." In *Japanese schooling: Patterns of socialization, equality, and political control.*, ed. James J. Shields Jr. Pp. 194—211. University Park: Pennsylvania State University Press..

Hayashi, K. (1989). "Family planning and population problems." *Sei no Igaku (Medical Science of Sex), 37,* 404—489.

Hechinger, F. M. (1986, March 11). School violence: The Japanese version. *The New York Times,* p. 25.

Heise, D. R., & Lewis, E. (1988). *Introduction to INTERACT [IBM-PC computer program].* Raleigh, N.C.: National Collegiate Software Clearinghouse.

Hendry, J. (1986). *Becoming Japanese: The world of the pre-school child.* Honolulu: University of Hawaii Press.

Hirschi, T. (1969) *Causes of delinquency.* Berkeley: University of California Press.

Hodge, R. W., & N. Ogawa (1991). *Fertility change in contemporary Japan.* Chicago: University of Chicago Press.

Hokkaidō Shuppan Kikaku Center. (1980). *Ainu-shi Shiryo-shu. [Ainu Historical Material.].* Sapporo: Hokkaidō Shuppan Kikaku Center.

Horan, P. M., & Hargis, P. G. (1991). Children's work and schooling in the late nineteenth-century family economy. *American Sociological Review, 56,* 583—596.

Hoshino, A., & Ryōko, N. (1983). "Atarashii kata no nihonjin no tanjō: Ibunka no naka de sodatsu kodomotachi (The birth of a new-style Japanese: Children raised in a different culture)." In *Ibunka ni sodatsu kodomotachi (Children brought up in a different culture.),* ed. Tetsuya Kobayashi. Tōkyō: Yūhikaku sensho, 1983.

Hsieh, W. (1992). *The historical nanyang trading world: Comparison with and critique of f. braudel's mediterranean world.* Midwest Conference on Asian Affairs.

Huber, J. (1990). "Macro-micro links in gender stratification." *American Sociological Review, 55:* 1—10.

Ichikawa, N. (1991). "Trends in the contemporary overseas Chinese studies of mainland China during the 1980s." *Kokusai Shogakubu Bulletin of Kyūshū International University* 2: 131—139.

Imai, K., & Itami, H. (1988). Allocation of labor and capital in Japan and the United States. In D. I. Okimoto & T. P. Rohlen (Eds.), *Inside the Japanese system: Readings on contemporary society and political economy* (pp. 112—188). Stanford: Stanford University Press.

Inoue, M., & Kobayashi, T. (1985). Nihon ni okeru SD hō ni yoru kenkyū bunya to sono keiyōshi taiyakudo kōsei no kaikan (The research domain and scale construction of adjective-pairs in a semantic differential method in Japan). *Kyōiku Shinrigaku Kenkyū (Japanese Journal of Educational Psychology), 33,* 253—260.

Ireland, T. (1982). *Whole life control.* Boston: Little, Brown.

Israel, J. I. (1989). *Dutch primacy in world trade, 1585 - 1740.* Oxford: Clarendon Press.

Ito, T. K., Murray, V., & Loveless, R. U. (1991). Computerized matchmaking. *Mangajin,* p. 16—20.

Iwakabe, Y. (1989). "On the Jurisdiction over Chinese Subjects and Citizens of other Non-Treaty Powers in the Later Tokugawa Regime." *Bulletin of the Kanagawa Prefectural Museum - Cultural Sciences* 15: 43—77.

Iwakabe, Y. (1990). "On the registration of Chinese subjects in the Meiji Period." *Bulletin of the Kanagawa Prefectural Museum - Cultural Sciences* 15: 1—77.

Iwama, H. F. (1989). Japan's group orientation in secondary schools. In J. J. Shields Jr. (Eds.), *Japanese schooling: Patterns of socialization, equality, and political control* (Pp. 6—15). University Park: Pennsylvania State University Press.

Iwamura, A. (1987). *Urban Japanese housewives: At home and in the community.* Honolulu: University of Hawaii Press.

Iwao, S. (Ed.). (1976). *Onna no manzokukan — onna no ikigai [Women's satisfaction — women's meaning in life].* Tōkyō: Taiseido.

Jacobson, W. J., & Takemura, S. (1986). *Analysis and comparisons of science curriula in Japan and the United States.* New York: Second International Science Study, Teacher's College, Columbia University.

Jansen, M. 1992. *China in the tokugawa world.* Cambridge: Harvard University Press.

Japanese Post and Communications (1982). "Japan investigates TDF." *Transnational Data Report* 5 (8 (December): 421—423.

Johnson, C. A. (1982). *MITI and the Japanese miracle: The growth of industrial policy: 1925-1975.* Stanford: Stanford University Press.

Johnson, R. J. & Kaplan, H. B. (1991). Developmental processes leading to marijuana use: Comparing civilians and military. *Youth and Society* 23, 3—30.

Jones, F. C. (1949). *Manchuria since 1931.* London: Oxford University Press.

Kaneko, M. (1978) "Buraku: Housing conditions in a discriminated buraku community in Japan." *Archictectural Association Quarterly* 10 : 20.

Kashioka, T. (1982). "Meiji Japan's study abroad program: Modernizing elites and reference societies." Ph.D. dissertation, Duke University.

Katsillis, J., & Rubinson, R. (1990). Cultural capital, student achievement, and educational reproduction: The case of Greece. *American Sociological Review, 55,* 270—279.

Kawabata, M. & M. Suzuki. (1981). "Kaigai nihonjin no jidō, seito no tame no kyōiku ni kansuru kisoteki kenkyū (Toward a general theory of education for children overseas) Part I." *Kōbe Daigaku Kyōiku Gakubu Kenkyū Shūroku* 68 : 29-39.

Kawabata, M. and M. Suzuki. (1982) "Kaigai nihonjin no jidō, seito no tame no kyōiku ni kansuru kisoteki kenkyū (Toward a general theory of education for children overseas) Part II." *Kōbe Daigaku Kyōiku Gakubu Kenkyū Shūroku* 69: 21-31.

Keene, D. (1982) *The Japanese discovery of europe: Honda Toshiaki and other discoverers, 1720-1798*. London: Routledge & Kegan Paul, 1952.

Keisatsu C. (1990). *Keisatsu hakusho (White paper on crime)*. Tokyo: Okuroshō Insatsukyoku.

Kenkyūkai, D. (1986). *Tokushū rōnin-yobikōsei no shinrosentaku ni kansuru ishikichō sa daiichiji hōkoku* [A preliminary report on consciousness regarding career choices among rōnin]. *Daigakushingaku Kenkyūkai*, 7(March) , 6.

Kerr, G. H. (1958). *Okinawa: The history of an island people*. Tōkyō: Charles E. Tuttle.

Kesavan. K. V. (1989). "Contemporary Japanese politics and foreign policy." *Asian Affairs, 21*, 114—120.

Kidder, L. H. (1992) "Requirements for being "Japanese:" Stories of returnees." *International Journal of Intercultural Relations* 16: 383—393.

Kikuoka, T. (Ed.) (1970). *Japanese newspaper compounds: The 1,000 most important in order of frequency*. Tōkyō: Charles E. Tuttle, Co.

Kimura, Y. (1981). *Reading and writing in English and Japanese children: A cross-cultural study*. D. Phil, Oxford University.

Kinsley, W.D. (1990). *Industrial harmony in modern Japan: The invention of a tradition*. London: Routledge.

Knowles, J. H. (1980). "Health, population, and development." *Social Science and Medicine* 2 (1980): 67—70.

Kohn, M., Naoi, A., Schoenback, C., Schooler, C., & Slomczynski, K. M. (1990). Position in the class structure and psychological functioning in the United States, Japan, and Poland. *American Journal of Sociology, 95*, 964—1008.

Kojima, H. (1991). *Determinants of first marital formation in Japan: Does the sibling configuration matter?* American Sociological Association annual meeting presentation, Cincinnati, Ohio.

Kōseishō [Ministry of Health and Welfare] (1989). *Showa 62 Nen Dai 9 jishussanryoku Chōsa (Kekkon to Shussan ni kansuru Zenkoku Chōsa) (The Ninth Japanese National Fertility Survey in 1987)* Volume II). Tōkyō: Kōseishō Jinkō Mondai Kenkūjo (Ministry of Health and Welfare, Institute of Population Problems).

Kozintsev, A. G. (1992). "Prehistoric and recent populations of Japan: Multivariate analysis of cranioscopic data." *Artic Anthropology* 29: 104—111.

Kumagai , F. (1984). *The life cycle of the Japanese family. Journal of Marriage and the Family, 46*, 191—204.

Kurashima, A. (1990). "Los angles no sara arai tachi." In *Dōjidai hihyō bukkuretto 3: Tōkyō nanmin sensō. [Booklet #3 of contemporary criticism: The Tōkyō immigration strife.*, ed. Noboru Okaniwa. Tōkyō: Seihōsha, 1990.

Kurosu, S. (1991). "Suicide in rural areas: The case of Japan 1960-1980." *Rural Sociology, 56*, 603-618.

Kyōiku joseikyoku zaimuka kaigai shijo kyōikushitsu (1988). *Kaigai kinmusha shijo kyōiku no genjō (The current situation of education for overseas children).* Tōkyō: Monbushō.

Langreth, R. (1991). Surprise! U.S. sometimes beats Japan in understanding science. *Science, 251,* 1024.

Lebra, T. S. (1984). *Japanese women: Constraint and fulfillment.* Honolulu: University of Hawaii Press.

Lebra, T. S. (1992). "Introduction." In *Japanese Social Organization,* ed. Takie Sugiyama Lebra. Pp. 1—21. Honolulu: University of Hawaii Press.

Lee, S., T. Graham, & H. W. Stevenson. (in press) "Teachers and teaching: Elementary schools in Japan and the United States." In T. Rohlen (Ed.) *Teaching in Japan.* Berkeley: University of California Press.

Lewis, C. C. (1989). Cooperation and control in Japanese nursery schools. In J. J. Shields Jr. (Eds.), *Japanese schooling: Patterns of socialization, equality, and political control.* (Pp. 28—44). University Park: Pennsylvania State University Press.

Lie, J. & E. Fujieda. (1992). The *"problem" of foreign workers in Japan, c. 1990.* Paper presented at the 87th Annual Meeting of the American Sociological Association, Pittsburgh.

Liedka, R. V. (1991). Who do you know in the group? Location of organizations in interpersonal networks. *Social Forces, 70,* 455—474.

Lynn, R. (1988). *Educational achievement in Japan: Lessons for the west.* Armonk, N.Y.: M. E. Sharpe, Inc.

Maeyama, T. (1984). " Ishitsu no mono e no katarikake no shiza—Zainichinikkei nihonjin no ron (A viewpoint for talking to heterogeneous elements: A theory of overseas Japanese in Japan)." In *Kokusaijin no jōken (The condition of internationalists),* ed. Hideo Uchiyama. Tōkyō: Mitsumine Shobō.

Mainichi Shinbun Tōkyō Honsha Shakaibu (ed.). (1990) *Jipangu: Nihon wo mezasu Gaikokujin Rōdōsha [Foreign Workers in Japan.].* Tōkyō: Mainichi Shinbunsha.

Martin, S. E. (1975). *A reference grammar of Japanese.* New Haven: Yale University Press.

Martin, S. E. (1966). "Lexical evidence relating Japanese to Korean." *Language* 42: 185—251.

Masnick, G., & Bane, M. J. (1980). *The Nation's Families: 1960-1990.* Cambridge, Mass.: Joint Center for Urban Studies of MIT and Harvard University.

McKinstry, J., & McKinstry, A. (1991). *Jinsei annai, "life's guide": Glimpses of Japan through a popular advice column.* Armonk, N.Y.: M. E. Sharpe.

Mellott, R. L. (1990). "Ceramics of the asuka, nara, and heian periods (AD 552—1185)." In *The rise of a great tradition: Japanese archaeological ceramics from the jomon through heian periods (10,500 b.c. - 1185 a.d.),* ed. Japan Society and Agency for Cultural Affairs. Pp. 56—66. Tōkyō: Government of Japan.

Merton, R. K. (1938). Social structure and anomie. *American Sociological Review* 3: 672—682.

Miller, R. A. (1981). The lost poetic sequence of the priest manzei. *Monumenta Nipponica.* 36: 133—172.

Min, Y. G. (1993). Comparison of the Korean minorities in China and Japan. *International Migration Review, 26*, 4—21.

Miyahara, K. (1988). Inter-college stratification: The case of male college graduates in Japan. *Sociological Forum, 3*, 25—43.

Miyazaki, K. (1977). Juvenile delinquency in Japan today. In *Proceedings of the* Taipei: *First Asian-Pacific Conference on Juvenile Delinquency,* 1 (Pp. 105—110).

Miyazaki, K. (1982). Problems of juvenile delinquency in school and family. In Seoul: *Proceedings of the Second Asian-Pacific Conference on Juvenile Delinquency,* 2 (pp. 193—199).

Mizuno, T. (1987). "Ainu: The invisible minority." *Japan Quarterly* 34: 143-148.

Monbushō (Ministry of Education, Science, and Culture) (1989). *Kyōiku hakusho (Annual white paper on education).* Tōkyō: Monbushō.

Moriyama, A. T. (1985). *Imingaisha: Japanese emigration companies and hawaii, 1894—1908.* Honolulu: University of Hawaii Press.

Morse, R. A., & Samuels, R. J. (1986). *Getting America ready for Japanese science and technology.* Princeton: Woodward Wilson International Center.

Mosk, C., & Johansson, S. R. (1986). Income and mortality in Japan. *Population and Development Review, 12*, 415—440.

Motoki, K. (1989). *Jinken to kyōiku: Shakai keihatsu no kisō riron. (Human rights and education: A fundamental argument for social enlightenment.).* Ōsaka: Kaihō Shuppansha.

Mouer, R., & Sugimoto, T. (1985). *Images of Japanese society: A study in the structure of social reality.* London: Routledge, Chapman, & Hall.

Murakami, Y. (1984). *Ie:* Society as a pattern of civilization. *Journal of Japanese Studies, 10*, 281—363.

Murakami, Y. (1989). Bullies in the classroom. In J. J. Shields Jr. (Eds.), *Japanese schooling: Patterns of socialization, equality, and political control.* (Pp. 145—151). University Park: Pennsylvania State University Press.

Muramatsu, M. (1978). Estimation of induced abortions: Japan, 1975. *Bulletin of the Institute of Public Health, 27*, 93—97.

Nakane, C. (1970). *Japanese society.* Berkeley: University of California Press.

Nakatani, I. (1990). Effectiveness in technological innovation: *Keiretsu* versus conglomerates. Günter Heiduk & Kozo Yamamura (Eds.) *Technological competition and interdependence: The search for policy in the United States, west Germany, and Japan.* Seattle: University of Washington Press. (pp. 151-162).

Naoi, M., & Schooler, C. (1990). Psychological consequences of occupational conditions among Japanese wives. *Social Psychology Quarterly, 53*, 100-116.

Neary, I. (1989). *Political protest and social control in pre-war Japan: The origins of buraku liberation.* Atlantic Highlands, NJ: Humanities Press International.

Nihon Rōdō Kenkyūsho [Japanese Labor Studies Bureau] (1981). *Japanese industrial relations series: Problems of working women* Tōkyō: Rōdōshō.

Nihon Zaigai Kigyō Kyōkai [Japanese Overseas Industrial Society] (1981). *Kaigai hakenmono no shijo kyōiku mondai ni kansuru teigen (A proposal concerning the educational problems of children sent overseas.)* Tōkyō.

Nyūkankyoku [Immigration Bureau], Hōmusho [Ministry of Justice]. (1988). *Shutsunyūkoku kanri. [Immigration Administration.]*. Tōkyō: Okurosho Insatsukyoku.

Ogawa, C. (1991). "Archives in Japan: The state of the art." *American Archivist*, 54, 546—554.

Onoda, E. & K. Tanaka. (1988) "Ibunkataiken no chōkiteki ishiki (A long-term perspective on the experience of other cultures)." In *Kikokushijo no tekio ni kansuru tsuiseki kenkyū (Follow-up research on the adaptation of returnee children*, ed. Tetsuya Kobayashi. Kyōto: Kyōto Daigaku Kyōiku Gakubu.

Osgood, C. E., Suci, G. J., & Tannenbaum, P. H. (1957). *The measurement of meaning*. Urbana: University of Illinois Press.

Ota, H. (Ed.). (1989). *Political teacher unionism in Japan*. University Park: Pennsylvania State University Press.

Okubo, S. (1983) *Hoshū jugyō kō (Supplementary lesson schools)*. Tōkyō: Fukazawa Kyōkai Insatsubu.

Onuki-Tierney, E. (1987) "Pollution in the folk belief system." *Current Anthropology* 28: 565—572.

Otsubo, S. (1992) *The central-local relationship in the early tokugawa ruling system: The case of tsushima han*. Annual Midwest Conference on Asian Affairs.

Paradis, M., Hagiwara, H., & Hildebrandt, N. (1985). *Neurolinguist aspects of the Japanese writing system*. New York: Academic Press, Inc.

Passin, H. (1970). *Japanese education: A bibliography of materials in the english language*. New York: Teachers College Press.

Peak, L. (1991). *Learning to go to school in Japan: The transition from home to preschool life*. Berkeley: University of California Press.

Peak, L. (1992). Formal pre-elementary education in Japan. In R. Leestma & H. J. Walberg (Eds.) *Japanese educational productivity*. (Pp. 35—68) Ann Arbor: Center for Japanese Studies, The University of Michigan.

Pearson, R. (1990). "Jōmon ceramics: The creative expression of affluent foragers." In *The rise of a great tradition: Japanese archaeological ceramics from the jomon through heian periods (10,500 b.c. - 1185 a.d.)*, ed. Japan Society and Agency for Cultural Affairs. Pp. 15—27. Tōkyō: Government of Japan.

Plummer, K. *The Shōgun's reluctant ambassadors: Sea drifters*. Tōkyō: Lotus Press, 1984.

Powers, R. G., Kato, H., & Stronach, B. (Ed.). (1989). *Handbook of Japanese popular culture*. Westport, Conn.: Greenwood Press.

Pursell, S., Banikiotes, P. G., & Sebastian, R. J. (1981). Androgyny and the perception of marital roles. *Sex Roles, 7*, 201_215.

Reischauer, E. O. (1988). *The Japanese today: Continuity and change.* Cambridge, Mass: Harvard University Press.

Rohlen, T. F. (1974). *For harmony and strength: Japanese white-collar organizations in anthropological perspective.* Berkeley: University of California Press.

Rohlen, T. F. (1983). *Japan's high schools.* Berkeley: University of California Press.

Rohlen, T. F. (1985/86). Japanese education: If they can do it, should we? *The American Scholar*(Winter), 29—43.

Rotberg, I. C. (1990). I never promised you first place. *Phi Delta Kappan, 72,* 296—301.

Rōdōshō Staff (1991). *Kōyō Dōko Chosa (Survey of Employment Trends)* Rōdōshō (Ministry of Labor).

Rubinger, R. (1989). Continuity and change in mid-nineteenth-century Japanese education. In J. J. Shields Jr. (Eds.), *Japanese schooling: Patterns of socialization, equality, and political control.* (pp. 224—233). University Park: Pennsylvania State University Press.

Sakamoto, A., & Chen, M. D. The effect of schooling on income in Japan. *Population Research and Policy Review., 11,* 217—232.

Sakade, F., Mori, K., Friedrich, R., & Ohashi, S. (1959). *A guide to reading and writing Japanese: The 1,850 basic characters and the kana sylabaries* (Second edition (revised), 1961 ed.). Tōkyō: Charles E. Tuttle.

Sansom, G. B. *Japan in world history.* Tōkyō: Tuttle, 1951.

Sansom, G. B. *The western world and Japan.* New York: Knopf, 1962.

Saso, M. (1990). *Women in the Japanese workplace.* London: Hilary Shipman.

Schaub, M., & Baker, D. P. (1991). Solving the mathematics problem: Experimental mathematics achievement in Japanese and American middle grades. *American Journal of Education, 99,* 623—642.

Science Watch (1992). The world's most prolific scientists., *255,* 283.

Shibutani, M. (1990) *The languages of Japan.* Cambridge: Cambridge University Press.

Shields, J. J., Jr. (1989). Introduction. In J. J. Shields Jr. (Eds.), *Japanese schooling: Patterns of socialization, equality, and political control.* (pp. Pp. 3—7). University Park: Pennsylvania State University Press.

Shimahara, N. (1971). *Burakumin: A Japanese minority and education.* The Hague: Martinus Nijhoff.

Shōji, K. (1990) "Japan and East Asia." In *The Cambridge History of Japan,* ed. K. Yamamura. pp. 396—446. Vol. 3. New York: Cambridge University Press.

Singleton, J. (1989). *Gambaru:* a Japanese cultural theory of learning. In J. J. Shields Jr. (Ed.), *Japanese schooling: Patterns of socialization, equality, and political control.* (Pp. 8—15). University Park: Pennsylvania State University Press.

Smith, R. J. (1972) "Small families, small households, and residential instability: Town and city in 'premodern' Japan." In *Household and Family in Past Time.,* Peter Laslett ed. London: Cambridge University Press.

Sodei, T. (1982, July 13). Josei no shurō wa katei wo hakai suru ka? [Will women's work destroy the family?]. *Ekonomisuto, 28*—33.

Sōrifu [Prime Minister's Office] (Ed.). (1983). *Fujin no genjo to shisaku (Kokunai kodō keikaku daisankai hōkokushō) [Governmental policies and the curent state of women: The third report on the National Action Program]*. Tōkyō: Gyōsei.
Spencer, S. A. (1993) Illegal migrant laborers in Japan. *International Migration Review., 26*, 754—786.
Stark, R. (1992). "MicroCase 2.0." 3.0 ed., Bellevue, WA: MicroCase Inc..
Steelman, L. C., & Powell, B. (1991). Sponsoring the next generation: Parental willingness to pay for higher education. *American Journal of Sociology, 96*, 1505—29.
Stevenson, D. L., and D. P. Baker (1992). "Shadow education and allocation in formal schooling: Transition to university in Japan." *American Journal of Sociology, 96*, 1639—1657.
Stevenson, H. W. (1989). The asian advantage: The case of mathematics. In J. J. Shields Jr. (Eds.), *Japanese schooling: Patterns of socialization, equality, and political control.* (pp. 85—95). University Park: Pennsylvania State University Press.
Stevenson, H.W. (1993). Mathematics achievement of Chinese, Japanese, and American children: Ten years later. *Science, 259*, 53—58.
Sueo, M., & Miwa, Y. (1986). *Konnichi no buraku sabetsu [Buraku discrimination today]*. Ōsaka: Buraku Kaihō Kenkyujo.
Suzuki, A. & Y. Takahama. (1992). "Tooth crown affinities among five populations from Akita, Tsushima, Tanegashima, (sic) Okinawa in Japan,(sic) and middle Taiwan." *Journal of the Anthropological Society of Nippon* 100: 171—182.
Suzuki, T. (1989). Shokonnan no Chiiki Kōzō (Regional patterns of the marriage squeeze in Japan). *Jinko Mondai Kenkyuu (The Journal of Population Problems), 45*, 14—28.
Taeuber, I. B. (1962). Japan's population: Miracle, model or case study? *Foreign Affairs*(July), 595—603.
Taira, K. , & Levine, S. B. (1992). Education and labor skills in postwar Japan. In R. Leestma & H. J. Walberg (Eds.), *Japanese Educational Productivity*. Ann Arbor: Michigan Papers in Japanese Studies.
Tani, N. (1985). "Trade with the Continent." In *Seventy-seven keys to the civilization of Japan.*, ed. T. Umesao. Ōsaka: Sōgensha, 1985.
Taylor, S. & K. Yamamura. (1990). "Japan's technological capabilities and its future: Overview and assessments." In *Technological competition and interdependence: The search for policy in the United States, west Germany, and Japan.*, ed. Günter Heiduk & Kozo Yamamura. 25—63. Seattle: University of Washington Press.
Thibaut, J., & Kelly, H. (1959). *The social psychology of groups*. New York: Wiley.
Thornton, A., & Freedman, D. (1979). Changes in the sex role attitudes of women. *American Sociological Review, 44*, 832—842.
Tobin, J., Wu, D. Y. H., & Davidson, D. H. (1989). *Preschool in three cultures: Japan, China, and the United States*. New Haven, CT.: Yale University Press.

Tonkin, H., & Edwards, J. (1987). The role of the university in America and Europe: Similarities and differences. *CRE Information, 77*, 119—135.

Tsukada, M. (1991). *Yobiko life: A study of the legitimation process of social stratification in Japan.* Berkeley: Institute of East Asian Studies, University of California.

Tsuneyoshi, R. (1992). Ningenkeisei no nichibei hikaku: Kakureta karikyuramu. (Socialization in Japan and the United States: The hidden curriculum) Tō kyō:Chuōkoronsha .

Tsuya, N. O. (1986). Japan's fertility: Effects of contraception and induced abortion after world war II. *Asian and Pacific Population Forum, 1*, 7—13.

Turner, C. G. II. (1987). "Late pleistocene and holocene population history of East Asia based on dental variation." *American Journal of Physical Anthropology* 73: 305—321.

Twine, N. (1991). *Language and the modern state: The reform of written Japanese.* London: Routledge.

U.S. Bureau of the Census (1990). *Current population reports, populations characteristics, Series P-20, No. 448.* Washington, D.C.: U.S. Government Printing Office.

Umakoshi, T. (1991). "The role of education in preserving the ethnic identity of Korean residents in Japan." In *Windows on Japanese Education.*, ed. Edward R. Beauchamp. Pp. 281—290. New York: Greenwood Press.

Umemoto, S. (1975) *Manshu.* Tōkyō: Manshūkai.

Umino, M., Matsuno, N., & Smith, H. W. (1991). A Japanese semantic differential dictionary. In D. Heise (Eds.), *INTERACT: Expert simulation program for the IBM PC* Durham, N.C.: Duke University Press.

Underhill, A. P. (1990). "A guide to understanding ceramic change." In *The rise of a great tradition: Japanese archaeological ceramics from the jomon through heian periods (10,500 b.c. - 1185 a.d.),* ed. Japan Society & Agency for Cultural Affairs. pp. 10—14. Tōkyō: Government of Japan.

Upham, F. K. (1987). *Law and social change in postwar Japan.* Cambridge, Mass: Harvard University Press.

U.S. Government Printing Office (1965). *Historical abstracts.* Washington, D.C.: U.S. Government Printing Office.

U.S. Government Printing Office (1980). *Statistical abstract of the United States, 1980.* Washington, D.C.: Government Printing Office.

van Wolferen, K. (1989) *The enigma of Japanese power: People and politics in a stateless nation.* London: Macmillan.

Vogel, E. F. (1979). *Japan as number one: Lessons for America.* Cambridge: Harvard University Press.

Vogel, S. (1986). "Toward understanding the adjustment problems of foreign families in the college community: The case of Japanese wives at the harvard university health services." *Journal of American College Health, 34*, 274—279.

Wallerstein, M. B. (1984). *Scientific and technological cooperation among industrialized countries: The role of the United States.* Washington, D.C.: National Academy Press.

Watanabe, M. (1991). *The Japanese and western science.* (Otto Theodor Benfey, Trans.). Philadephia: University of Pennsylvania Press.

Weeks, J. R. & R. G. Rumbaut. (1991) "Infant mortality among ethnic groups." *Social Science and Medicine* 33: 327—334.

White, M. (1987). *The Japanese educational challenge: A commitment to children.* New York: The Free Press.

White, M. (1988). *The Japanese Overseas: Can They Go Home Again?* New York: Free Press.

Whiting, R. (1989). *You gotta have wa.* New York: Macmillan.

Whyte, W. F. (1956). *The organization man.* Garden City, NJ: Doubleday Anchor Co.

Wiener, M. (1989) *The origins of the Korean community in Japan, 1910-1923.* Atlantic Highlands, NJ: Humanities Press International.

Willis, D. (1983). " International schools in Japan." *International Schools Journal* 5: 21-25.

Wilson, W. J. (1987). *The truly disadvantaged: The inner city, the underclass, and public policy.* Chicago, IL: University of Chicago Press.

Yagi, K. (1980). *Sabetsu no ishiki kōsō. [The structure of discriminatory consciousness.].* Ōsaka: Kaihō Shuppansha.

Yamada, J. (1992) Asymmetries of reading and writing kanji by Japanese children. *Journal of Psycholinguistic Research,* 21: 563—580.

Yamamoto, F. (1984). "Nihon shakai kōseiin to shite no gaikokujin. [Foreigners as future generations of Japanese society.]." In *Zainichi gaikokujin to nihon shakai. [Foreign residents and Japanese society.],* ed. Masuo Yoshioka, Fuyuhiko Yamamoto, and Yong Dai Kim. 13—56. Tōkyō: Shakai Hyō ronsha.

Yamashita, K. (1990). "A cultural geographical study on regional characteristics of the Chinese society in Japan: A comparison with the Chinese society in Southeast Asia." *Memoirs of the College of Education, Akita University* 41: 149—159.

Yasumoto, Y. (1989). *Origins of the Japanese language: A factor analysis.* Kyōto University.

Yokakaihatsu Center (1987). *Kigyō no okeru rōdōjikan to yokakyoju kankyo ni kansuru chōsa (An industrial survey of labor hours and leave provisions)* Tōkyō: Yokakaihatsu Center.

Yokoshima, A. (1977). "Tenkōsei no tekio ni tsuite no kangaekata (Considerations concerning the adjustment of transfer children)." *Utsunomiya Daigaku Kyōiku Gakubu Kiyo* 27: 139—153.

Zimmerman, S. L. (1991). The welfare state and family breakup — the mythical connection. *Family Relations,* 40, 139—147.

SUBJECT INDEX

abortion, 113, 162, 165
  practices, 178
  rates, 166, 167
absenteeism, 64
academic calendar year, 96
academic instruction, 42
academics, 95
achieved statuses, 213
ACT, 19, 78
adult education, 107
  interference, 43
  population, 23, 26
  supervision, 169
  workers, 6
adultery, 175
affirmative-action programs, 15
affluence, 169
age homophily, 120
age of marriage, 137
age statuses, 231
age-homogamy, 122
age-specific sex ratios, 115, 131
Aichi, 74, 75, 117, 119, 121, 124,
  126, 132, 152, 163, 164, 200, 216,
  220, 223, 224, 230
Ainu, 3, 14, 184, 191, 241
Ainu people, 206
Akikawa High School, 77
Akita, 18, 24, 74, 75, 117, 119, 121,
  124, 126, 132, 152, 163, 164, 173,
  200, 216, 220, 224, 228, 230

alcohol abuse, 170
alien registration cards
  (gaikokujin tōroku shōmeisho),
  213
alimony, 176
alumni gifts, 82
amae, 40
amaeru, 41
American culture, 30
ancestor worship, 203
Aomori, 23, 24, 74, 75, 117, 119, 121,
  124, 126, 132, 152, 153, 163, 164,
  173, 200, 216, 220, 224, 228, 230
appearance of equality, 77
Archivists, 105
arranged marriage (miai) system,
  113, 141
ascribed statuses, 213
ascriptive, 15
Assimilationist policy, 206
assistant professor, 35
assistants" (joshu, 104
Atayal, 184
atotori, 129
attitudes, 34
  toward women, 149
aunt, 156
authority, 36
average enrollment expenses, 84
average rental expense, 84
awards, 99

baby-sitting, 145, 146
bad behavior, 40
Belgian, 31
birth rate, 177
birth-control pill, 162
blame, 66
blind, 35
blue-chip corporations, 100
body beautification, 42
books, 25, 210
boss, 157
brain drain, 23, 25, 205
bread-winning role, 146
bride, 158
Britain, 5
broken homes, 168
Buddhism, 185, 186, 197
Buddhist, 45
bully, 33, 34
bully's victim, 33, 34
bullying, 62, 63, 235
bungakubu, 14, 241
Buraku, 194
Buraku discrimination, 204
Buraku Liberation League, 199
Burakumin, 3, 12, 21, 196, 197, 198,
    199, 201, 202, 203, 204, 241
Burakumin Liberation League, 198
bureaucrats, 6

cabinet officials, 89
Cambodian, 184
career patterns, 57, 144
career patterns for Japanese
    academics, 99
career women, 146
careers, 40
censuses, 8
change, 177
change and stability in the modern
    Japanese family, 141
chaos level, 44
chastity, 175
Chiba, 61, 74, 75, 100, 117, 119, 121,
    124, 126, 132, 151, 152, 163, 164,
    200, 216, 220, 223, 224, 230

Chicago, 9
child dependency ratio, 47
childhood identities, 40
child-oriented roles, 177
child-rearing, 39, 146
chimei sōkan, 203
China, 11, 42, 185
Chinese characters, 2, 186
Chinese language, 22
Chinese women, 115
Chinese-Japanese, 3, 181, 213, 218,
    219
choral recitation, 52
Chōsoren, 215, 241
christianity, 189
citation-count analyses, 30
civil servant, 157
class, 1
class size, 52, 54, 55, 69
classmate, 34
classroom time, 57
clerk, 157
club memberships, 83
clubs, 96
cluster analysis, 90
cohort analysis, 142
college
    attendance, 12
    entrance examinations, 20
    graduates, 100
    matriculates, 120
    presidents, 99
    prestige as a screening
        device, 80
college-educated worker, 102
college-recruitment process, 100
college-student culture, 226
colonialist government policies, 193
commercial, 72
community, 151
community services, 202
commuter patterns, 75
company loyalty, 138
comparison-level alternative
    (CLalt), 33
computerized matchmaking, 133,
    135

concept of "community", 97
condoms, 162
conflict, 1, 7
conflict between marriage and
    work, 143
conform, 1
Confucianism, 185
consensus, 1
conservative social values, 175
consistent methods, 2
consulting fees, 82
consumer's prices, 18
consumer's, citizen's, or rights-of-
    worker's literacy movement, 28
contraception, 162, 178
cost differential, 83
cost of land, 97
costs of preschool education, 57
costs of schooling., 85
courts, 14
cram schools, 68
creativity, 30
credentialing, 80
crime, 167, 178
crime statistics, 168
crime and delinquency, 202
criminal arrests, 167
criminal cases, 14
cross-cultural research, 85
cross-district registration, 15
cross-national differences, 38
crude birth rate, 141
crude divorce rate, 141
crude marriage rates, 138
crude sex ratio, 114
cultural capital, 15, 39, 84

danchi, 151
Date Masamune, 188
daughter, 156
day nurseries, 41, 47, 51, 54
day nursery groups, 44
day-nursery attendance, 41
de facto discrimination, 15

de-population, 4
deaf, 35
deans, 99
decentralization, 7
decentralized community-based
    system, 11
decision to marry, 113
deconstruct, 2
definition of internationalization,
    210
dekasegi, 174, 241
delegating authority, 52
delinquency, 59, 169, 178
delinquency rates, 8, 171
delinquent from school, 34
democratization, 134
demographic projections, 84
Dentsu, 93
depopulation, 205
deviant educational roles, 33, 34
deviant roles, 33
diet, 89
discipline, 45, 65
discrimination, 198, 201, 217
discriminatory, 13
dislocation of men, 173
divorce, 3, 171
divorce rates, 172, 174, 175, 176, 178
divorce-statuses, 172
divorced, 115
divorcee, 158
doctoral work, 102
domestic chores, 147
domestic violence, 66
Dōshisha, 24, 72
dōwa chiku, 199
dress for women, 175
dress restrictions, 65
dropout rates, 167
dropouts, 11
drug offenses, 170
dual structure of enterprises, 148
Dutch, 189
duty, 3
dyadic power, 175

early childhood education, 69
early childhood socialization, 40, 41
ecological level poverty, 204
economic capital, 39
economic stability, 133
economy, 2
Edo period, 191, 242
education, 202
education majors, 101
educational, 120
    attainment, 153
    background of women, 122
    costs, 46
    credentialism, 28
    discrimination, 14, 215
    expenditures, 58
    life cycle, 3, 31
    opportunity, 6, 11, 15, 20
    opportunity in Japan, 73
    pressures, 63
    staffer, 35
    statuses, 31
    stratification, 7, 50
educator, 35
educator roles, 35
Ehime, 74, 75, 117, 119, 121, 123, 124, 126, 132, 152, 163, 164, 200, 216, 220, 224, 230
elderly, 21
elderly dependency ratio, 47
elementary school, 6, 57
    funding, 58
    spending, 58
elite universities, 76
emigration, 191
emotional gratification and support, 120
emotional maturity, 120
employment discrimination, 149
employment pattern for educators, 101
empty-nesting, 143
endowments, 82
engineering, 11
engineers, 27
English, 29

English expressions, 29
English language, 30
entrance examinations, 34
entrance-exam scores, 71
eta, 12, 197, 242
ethnic variation, 182
ethnographic, 21
Eugenic Protection Law, 165
Everest-ites, 2
examination hell, 165
excuses, 40
exposure to a foreign culture, 236
extra-school studying and tutoring, 59, 69

factor analysis, 93
factor scores, 95
faculty meetings, 99
faculty system, 98
failing, 20
familial conflict, 176
familial roles, 177
family, 138
    and kinship identities, 155, 156
    care, 44
    conflict, 176
    courts, 14
    formation and process, 159
    income, 8
    life cycle, 142
    planning, 160, 166, 177
    roles, 144
    size, 56, 160
    values, 172
farm occupations, 49
farmers, 47, 54, 231
farmers, fishers, and lumber workers, 153
farming, 49, 85
father, 17, 156
father's occupation, 7
features peculiar to Japanese universities, 95
fellowships, 103
felonies, 167

female labor-force participation,
51, 151, 174
female work-force participation,
130
females, 12, 21, 48
females in the labor force,
47, 49, 53
feminist movement, 87
feudalist, 6
filiocentric, 13
final exams, 97
fishing, 85
five-day-school week, 59
flunk out, 34
forced laborers, 196
foreign
  bridal market, 116
  brides, 221
  influence in Japan, 187
  labor, 210
  laborers, 123, 222
  language instruction in
    Japan, 29
  language skills, 231
  students, 210, 211
  travel, 231
  trips, 228
  workers (gaijin rōdōsha),
    181, 219
foreign-resident status, 14
foreigners, 42
front-stage" behavioral, 4
Fukken Dōmei, 197
Fukui, 74, 117, 119, 121, 124, 126,
  132, 151, 152, 163, 164, 200, 216,
  220, 224, 230
Fukuoka, 24, 74, 75, 83, 117, 119,
  121, 124, 126, 132, 152, 163, 164,
  199, 200, 216, 220, 223, 224, 230
Fukushima, 24, 64, 74, 75, 117, 119,
  121, 124, 125, 126, 132, 152, 163,
  164, 192, 200, 216, 220, 223, 224,
  230
functional literacy and
  numeracy, 20

gaijin rōdōsha, 181
gakoku kabure, 236
Gambaru, 17, 34, 58, 60, 242
genbun'itchi, 191
gender
  bias, 234
  differences, 37
  differentiation, 145
  segregation, 142
  -stratified power, 154
geographic, 182
geographical mobility, 173
German, 31
German science, 190
Germanic "chair" system, 104
Germany, 5
Gifu, 74, 117, 119, 121, 124, 126, 132,
  152, 163, 164, 200, 216, 220, 224,
  230
glue sniffing, 170
goodness, 31, 35, 37, 60, 99
government statistics, 13
government-run survey, 33
gōgaku, 6, 242
graduate assistant, 35
graduate programs, 83
graduate-level education, 12
graduates from top high schools, 47
graduation rates, 11, 59
grandfather, 156
grandmother, 156, 158
grants, 99
Greater Tōkyō, 25
greedy institutions, 142
grievances, 202
Gross Prefectural Profits (GPP),
  47, 54
group cohesion, 43
group identity, 197
group-centeredness, 54
groups, 44
Gunma, 12, 74, 117, 119, 121, 124,
  126, 132, 152, 163, 164, 200, 216,
  220, 224, 230

Hachinohe, 191
Hachiōji Koryo High School, 77
hair rules, 64
hair style rules, 65
hakushi, 40
handicapped, 35, 236
handicapped student, 72
harmony, 4, 64, 66
having lower expectations, 52
Hawaii, 192
health, 202
health-care system, 201
Heian period, 185
hensachi, 78, 93, 242
hensachi system, 78
hierarchical-society thesis, 148
hierarchy, 104
higaisha ishiki, 62
high school, 7, 11, 21, 39, 50, 109
    diploma, 72
    dropout rates, 78
    graduation, 10
    graduation rates, 10
    history textbook, 195
    teacher, 35
high-school-entrance, 11
higher education of women, 87
hinin, 197
hiring-practice, 88
Hiroshima, 12, 24, 74, 81, 117, 119,
    121, 124, 126, 132, 152, 163, 164,
    173, 192, 200, 216, 218, 220, 223,
    224, 230
hobo, 44
hoikuen, 43, 44, 46, 69, 242
hoikuen education, 49
Hokkaidō, 57, 74, 92, 117, 118, 119,
    121, 124, 126, 132, 150, 152, 153,
    163, 164, 182, 189, 191, 200, 206,
    216, 220, 224, 230
Hokkaidō Prefectural
    government, 14
Hokkaidō University, 89
home economics, 14
home ownership, 151
homemaker, 147
homemaking, 146

homework, 9
homogamy, 120
homogeneity, 11, 64, 66
homogeneous society, 4
Hōmushō, 213
Hong Kong, 26
honne, 242
Honshū, 182, 191, 199
Honshū area, 168
Honshū immigrants, 206
household composition, 202
household income, 154
housekeeping, 146
housewife, 87, 158
housing, 202
human capital, 5
human rights of children, 65
human-capital advantage, 145
Hungary, 26
husband, 156
Hyōgo, 74, 75, 100, 117, 119, 121,
    124, 126, 132, 152, 163, 164, 199,
    200, 216, 220, 224, 230
hypergamy, 111

Ibaraki, 74, 117, 119, 121, 124, 126,
    132, 152, 163, 164, 200, 216, 220,
    223, 224, 230
ideal mate scale, 120
identity, 156, 158
ideographic systems, 23
ideographs (kaiimoji), 22
ie, 154, 242
ie household system, 203
ijimerarekko, 62
illegal drugs, 169
illegitimacy, 175
illiteracy, 20, 21, 23
immigration, 217
imperial universities, 8
in-class education, 28
income distribution, 86
individual, 3
    choice, 54
    traits, 112
industrial competition, 88

industrialization, 10, 63, 176
industry-university cooperation on
    research and development
    projects, 102
infant mortality, 201
infants, 41
inferiority-superiority, 147
information transfers, 210
innumeracy, 21
insider statuses, 213
insider-outsider discrimination, 181
insiders, 3
Institute for Scientific
    Information, 31
institutional scale, 95
institutional status, 8
institutionalized racism, 217
institutionalized sex
    discrimination, 87
instructional time, 9
instructor, 35
intellectual
        and emotional
            relationship, 138
        companion, 120
        flexibility, 85
intelligence, 17, 120
International Association for the
    Evaluation of Educational
    Achievement, 26
International Core Test
    of Science, 58
international marketplace
    of ideas, 105
international trade, 187
internationalism, 210
internationalization, 3, 181, 190,
    207, 209, 222, 228, 232, 238, 239
internationalization of
    academia, 106
intervening, 52
invasion, 193
IQ, 17
Ishikawa, 47, 74, 117, 118, 119, 121,
    124, 126, 132, 152, 163, 164, 200,
    216, 220, 223, 224, 230

Iwate, 24, 74, 117, 119, 121, 124,
    126, 132, 152, 163, 164, 173, 200,
    216, 220, 233, 224, 228, 230
Iwate Prefecture, 115
Izanagi, 182
Izanami, 182

janitor, 157
Japan Amateur Sports
    Association, 14
Japan Newspaper Publishers and
    Editors Association, 24
Japan Prize, 30
Japan Sea, 46
Japan Teacher's Union, 10
Japanese language, 22, 184
Japanese missions, 185
Japanese Overseas Volunteers
    Corps (JOVC), 227
Japanese written language, 190
Japanese-Manchurian
    immigrants, 193
Jesuits, 189
jimujikan, 102
jinmyaku, 99
Jinmyaku ("old boy" networks), 99
job, 108
    market, 102
    stability, 151, 153
Jōmonese, 183
journalists, 92
juku, 7, 9, 17, 30, 33, 61, 86, 242
jūmin, 214
jumping grades, 20
junior colleges, 13, 44
junior high schools, 60, 64, 66, 68
justifications, 40
juvenile delinquency, 168

kabushigaisha, 22
kachō, 102
Kagawa, 74, 117, 119, 121, 124, 126,
    131, 132, 152, 163, 164, 200, 216,
    220, 224, 230

Kagoshima, 64, 74, 75, 117, 119, 121, 124, 126, 132, 152, 163, 164, 200, 216, 220, 224, 227, 228, 230
kaiimoji, 242
kaikoku, 181
Kamakura, 187
Kamakura bakufu, 187
kan no mushi, 40
kana, 242
kana syllabary, 45
Kanagawa, 24, 73, 74, 75, 100, 117, 119, 121, 124, 126, 132, 151, 152, 163, 164, 175, 200, 216, 220, 223, 224, 228, 230
Kanazawa, 233
kanji, 22, 23, 242
Kansai, 33, 46, 50, 68, 73, 88, 93, 130, 165, 231, 238
Kantō, 7, 46, 50, 73, 75, 90, 165, 173, 229, 238, 242
Kantō-Kansai area, 59, 93
kata, 2
kata ni hameru, 42
Keio, 72
keiretsu, 5
kikokushijo, 181, 235, 237, 242
kindergarten, 18, 41, 45, 46, 47, 48, 50, 51, 55
kindergarten attendance, 41
kinship identities, 157
kitaeru, 42
Kōbe, 61, 64, 219
Kōbe Bar Association, 64
Kōchi, 13, 47, 74, 75, 117, 118, 119, 121, 124, 126, 132, 152, 153, 163, 164, 200, 216, 220, 224, 230
kojiki, 182
kokumin, 214
kokuritsu, 81
kokusaika, 181, 209
Korea, 11, 185, 194
Korean Atomic Bomb Victims Association, 217
Korean kingdoms, 186
Korean peninsula, 182, 188
Korean Yi dynasty, 189
Korean-Japanese, 3, 181, 213, 214

Koreans, 12, 21, 195, 196
Kōseishō, 44, 49, 242
Kōseishō-controlled preschools., 51
kōseki, 197, 212, 243
kōseki system, 197
kōshi, 22
Kumamoto, 74, 117, 119, 121, 124, 126, 132, 152, 163, 164, 165, 200, 216, 220, 224, 230
Kutami migrants, 194
Kwansai Gakuin, 72
Kyōchōkai, 5
Kyōdai, 81, 243
kyōiku, 51
kyōiku mama, 66, 69, 243
kyōikubu, 14, 243
Kyokuchō, 102
Kyōto, 24, 73, 74, 75, 81, 100, 117, 119, 121, 124, 126, 132, 150, 151, 152, 163, 164, 199, 200, 215, 216, 220, 223, 224, 228, 230
Kyōto Universities, 80
Kyōto University, 73, 88, 89
Kyūshū, 46, 67, 81, 100, 197, 229
Kyūshū University, 88, 89

labor force, 48
labor movements, 5
labor shortages, 159
labor-force participation, 144, 145
labor-force participation of Japanese women, 143
laborers, 47
land prices, 86
languages, 184
large classes, 54
large-group daily activities, 52
LaSalle, 73
latch-key children, 168
latch-key environments, 169
law school, 13, 80
law, engineering, medicine, 81
lawsuits, 149
lawyer, 157
learning, 190
learning process, 57

lecturer, 35
legal informality, 28
legal resident aliens, 221
legalized abortion, 165
liberal arts, 14
Liberal Democratic Party, 10
Li-Ito Convention, 193
Liaotung peninsula, 193
libraries, 83
    and books read per capita, 24
    per capita, 25
library books, 225
library budgets, 104
life spans, 143
lifetime employment (shūshin
    koyō), 148, 150, 177
lifetime job system, 8
"lifetime" job security system
    (nenkō jōretsu), 123
linguists, 184
literacy, 26, 27
literature, 14
liveliness, 31, 35
living conditions, 222
living space, 160
living standards, 151
loan words, 29, 189
location, 95
love-based (renai) marriage, 13, 186
low-weight babies, 201
lower social status, 79
loyalty, 150

M/F college matriculation, 122
mainstream education, 14
male
    dominance, 13
    labor-force participation, 153
    raters, 37
male-to-female ratio, 118
male-to-female ratio for college
    matriculation, 122
managerial jobs, 127
managers, 47
manga, 24, 26
Mantetsu, 193

Man'yōshu, 186
marital and work-related roles, 158
marital choice, 174
marital life-cycle, 3
marital marketplace, 114
marital status, 142
marriage, 3, 112, 130
    bureaus, 135
    markets, 111, 113
    patterns, 162
    rates, 137
    squeeze, 111, 118, 122, 137
Marriage Squeeze Index, 122
mass education, 19, 191
mass media, 23
mass testing, 19
mass transportation system, 131
masshiro, 40
master's level graduates, 102
mastery of English, 28
matchmaking fees, 135
mathematics, 9
mathematics majors, 11
Matsumae fiefdom, 189
mean spousal difference in age at
    first marriage, 131
Meiji Era, 190, 191
Meiji period, 243
Meiji Reformation, 6
Meiji Restoration, 197
memorization, 19
meritocracy, 7, 17, 85
methodology, 2
miai, 136, 243
Mie, 24, 74, 117, 119, 121, 124, 126,
    132, 152, 163, 164, 200, 216, 220,
    224, 228, 230
migrant worker, 173
migration, 178
Minatogawa, 183
Mindan, 215, 243
miners, 231
Ministry of Education, 69
Ministry of Finance, 13
Ministry of Health and Welfare,
    13, 69
Minneapolis, 57

minority groups, 15
Mintoren, 217
mitsu'nyūkokusha
    (hidden immigrants), 217
mitsunyūkokusha, 243
Miyagi, 52, 53, 74, 117, 119, 121,
    124, 126, 132, 150, 152, 163, 164,
    200, 216, 220, 223, 224, 230
Miyazaki
Miyazaki, 24, 25, 74, 75, 117, 119,
    121, 124, 126, 132, 152, 153, 163,
    164, 200, 216, 220, 224, 230
modernization, 134
Mombushō, 7, 10, 45, 64, 81,
    82, 98, 243
Mombushō-controlled preschools, 51
Monbushō officials, 33
morality, 43
mother, 17, 40, 156, 158
mother's complexes, 112
mother-in-law, 158
motherhood, 159
Motorola Corporation, 21
Muromachi bakufu, 187
musical cues, 52
mutual cooperation, 147
mythistory, 1

Nada, 61
Nagano, 47, 53, 74, 117, 119, 121,
    124, 126, 127, 132, 152, 163, 164,
    200, 216, 220, 224, 230
Nagasaki, 25, 74, 75, 117, 119, 121,
    124, 126, 132, 152, 163, 164, 189,
    200, 216, 218, 219, 220, 224, 230
Nagoya, 81, 92, 150, 173, 223, 228
Nagoya University, 89
Naha, 100, 205
naishinsho, 64
naishoku, 144, 243
nakōdo, 136, 243
Nanyang world-system, 187
Nara, 24, 74, 75, 100, 117, 119, 121,
    124, 126, 132, 151, 152, 163, 164,
    199, 200, 216, 220, 224, 230

national
    curriculum, 17
    education policy, 103
    educational standards, 10
    science and engineering
        academy honors, 98
    test in Japan, 78
    tests, 8, 81
    universities, 88, 109
    university exams, 78
Nationalism, 209
nationwide school system, 6
Nebuta, 191
nenkō jōretsu, 243
Nepalese, 184
Neputa, 191
newspaper, 23
    circulation, 25
    readership, 24, 25, 225
Nichibenren, 65, 243
nihon gakko, 233
Nihon Keisai Shinbun, 243
Nihon-machi, 188
Nihongi, 182
nihonjingakkō, 192, 237, 243
nihonjinron, 1, 112, 243
Niigata, 24, 74, 117, 119, 121, 124,
    126, 132, 152, 163, 164, 200, 216,
    220, 224, 230
Nikkei, 27, 244
Nikkyōso, 7, 244
ninjo, 1
Nobel Prize, 30
noise, 44
noise and liveliness levels, 42
noise level, 52
non-college educated men, 123
non-disposable income, 151
non-humans, 197
normal childhood roles, 33
normlessness, 145
norms, 2
North Korean government, 215
Northern Japan, 125
nuclear families, 47
numeracy, 27

nursery aide, 158
nursery and kindergarten
   attendance, 48
nursery school, 47, 51
   attendance, 48, 49

obedience, 64
occupational status, 151
occupations, 27, 85
Ochanomizu Women's
   University, 45
office worker, 125
official abortion, 165
official juvenile delinquency
   rates, 169
Ōita, 74, 75, 117, 119, 121, 124, 126,
   132, 152, 163, 164, 200, 216, 220,
   224, 230
Okayama, 74, 117, 119, 121, 124,
   126, 131, 132, 152, 163, 164, 200,
   216, 220, 224, 230
Okinawa, 57, 67, 74, 75, 78, 88, 100,
   117, 119, 121, 123, 124, 126, 132,
   152, 153, 161, 163, 164, 188, 191,
   192, 199, 200, 203, 206, 216, 220,
   224, 230
Okinawans, 205
old maid (o-rudomisu), 158
omote, 212
on-the-job training, 6, 102, 108
onna no michi, 13
opening of Japan, 190, 197
opportunities, 68
organization-man syndrome, 137
origami, 45
originality, 19
Ōsaka, 15, 24, 73, 74, 75, 81, 92, 93,
   116, 117, 119, 121, 124, 126, 127,
   131, 132, 150, 151, 152, 153, 163,
   164, 173, 199, 200, 206, 214, 215,
   216, 220, 221, 223, 224, 228, 230,
   238
Ōsaka Municipal government, 14
Ōsaka University, 13, 21, 89
Ōsaka-Kōbe area, 7
Ōsaka-Kōbe-Kyōto areas, 25

Ōsaka-Kyōto, 215
otoko no michi, 12
outcast status, 204
outlier or deviant case, 25, 75
outsiders., 3
overachievers, 58
overseas, 96
   business offices, 173
   tourism, 229
   travel, 236
oversupply of young men, 139
owners (of businesses), 47
oyabun-kobun (parent-child, 107
oyakata, 154
oyako, 154

Pacific Ocean prefectures, 58
Paleolithic, 183
parents, 134
parents' background, 8
part-time workers, 143
passport holders, 227, 228, 229
patri-locality of residence, 160
Pax Neerlandica, 189
pay for teaching, 8
pecking order, 104
pedagogical practices, 9
peer-group approval, 52
peopling of Japan, 183
per capita educational spending, 47
per-capital high school
   expenditures, 75
per-pupil expenditures, 18
perceived family socioeconomic
   status, 16
perceptions of fairness
   and justness, 16
permanent residence overseas
   (kaigai zairyū hōjin), 233
permanent residents
   (teichaku ijūsha), 181, 213
persistence, 17, 60
personal freedom, 133
personal responsibility, 40
philanthropy, 103
physical illness, 67

pictographs (shōkeimoji), 22
placement, 19
policy of non-interventionism, 63
political science, 133
politics, 2
pool of eligible men, 136
population composition, 4
population density, 47, 48, 54, 129, 169
population size, 226
Portuguese, 189
post-baccalaureate education, 101
poverty, 167, 204
power, 1, 31, 177
    advantage, 157
    relations, 3
powerfulness, 35
premarital sex, 165
preschool, 39, 42, 43, 47, 53
    attendance, 48, 51
    education, 42
prestige, 11, 83
primary industries, 79
primary-sector industries, 151
Prime Minister Nakasone's, 20
principal, 35
private
    and public education, 18
    grants, 82
    kindergartens, 47, 51
    spending, 59
    universities, 83
probability-sampling methods, 33
professional and technical workers, 47, 50, 127
professional roles, 36
professions, 27
professors, 35, 36, 99
property crimes, 168
proto-forms, 184
PTAs, 17
public, 72
    expenditures, 58
    opinion polls, 113
    servant, 125
    universities, 83, 92

public versus private
    universities, 81, 90
public-private, 54
purchasing power parities (p.p.p.)
    of ¥205=$1.00, 18

quality, 83

race, 1
racial, 182
racism, 209
raising children, 87
Rakusei, 68
Ranking of high schools, 16
Ratings of Goodness, 36
Ratings of Goodness, Powerfulness,
    and Liveliness, 32
receptionist, 157, 158
recruiting season for new
    employees, 99
refugees, 210, 211
regional patterns of recruitment, 99
regional-market segmentation, 100
regression analysis, 128
regression of population density, 48
relationships, 48
relationships between statuses, 3
religion, 81
remarried, 158
remedial classes, 15
ren'ai, 136, 244
repetition, 20
research
    collaboration, 96
    facilities, 104
    laboratories, 83
researcher, 35, 36
resident aliens, 219
returnee problems, 235
returnees, 211, 233, 234, 240
Revisionists, 1
rhythm, 162
rice, 116
rites of passage, 3, 39

role of women, 106
Roppongi, 221
rotations, 108
rote memorization, 72
royalty, 6
rōnin, 34, 61, 78, 84, 86, 244
rōnin status, 79
rural, 4
    areas, 53
    regions, 131
    school system, 10
ryūgakusei, 185
Ryūkyū, 12, 24, 244
Ryūkyū archipelago, 191
Ryūkyū Islands, 205
Ryūkyū kingdom, 187
Ryūkyūs, 206

Saga, 67, 74, 117, 119, 121, 124, 126,
    132, 152, 163, 164, 200, 216, 220,
    224, 228, 230
Sahkalin Island, 182, 196
Saitama, 12, 18, 58, 74, 75, 100, 117,
    119, 121, 124, 126, 132, 152, 163,
    164, 200, 216, 220, 223, 224, 230
sakoku, 181, 244
sakoku jidai, 190
sakoku period, 186
Salariman, 137
samurai, 6
Sapporo, 100, 191
SAT, 19, 78
Sawauchi Township, 115
scholar, 35, 36
school, 192
    absenteeism, 62, 64, 167
    achievement, 56
    delinquent, 33
    dropout, 34, 66
    friends, 63
    groups, 56
    history, 196
    laggard, 33, 34
    vandalism, 62, 64
    violence, 32

schooling, marriage, child bearing,
    and job-hunting statuses, 145
science, 11
science and engineering, 97
"science city" areas, 103
scientists of international repute, 95
SD
    data, 37
    ratings, 32, 33
    scores, 34
secretary, 106, 157, 158
Seikō Gakuin, 68
Select Forty-Five Universities, 88
self
    -control, 45
    -defense force, police, fire
        fighters, 205
    -directedness, 85
    -discrimination, 146
    -employed, 47
    -employment status, 49
    -fulfilling prophesy, 8
    -image, 78
    -improvement movements, 198
    -regulation, 45
semantic differential (SD), 31, 60
semester exam periods, 97
Sendai (Miyagi Prefecture), 9, 33,
    57
seniority, 101, 102
sensei, 35, 244
sex
    discrimination, 13, 63
    discrimination in
        education, 12
    role identities, 37
    stratification, 15
sex-age ratios, 111
sex-ratio
sex-ratio, 13, 77, 113, 114,
    127, 129, 133, 174, 175
    limits, 77
    prospects, 131
    theory, 3
sex-specific roles, 159
sexual life, 41

shadow-education systems, 86
shame, 4
Shanghai, 192
Shiga, 74, 117, 119, 121, 124, 126,
    132, 152, 163, 164, 200, 216, 220,
    223, 224, 227, 228, 230
shijuku, 6, 244
Shikoku, 46, 67, 199, 229
Shimane, 74, 117, 119, 121, 124, 126,
    132, 152, 163, 164, 200, 216, 220,
    224, 230
Shinto, 45
shitsuke, 42
Shizuoka, 74, 117, 119, 121, 124,
    126, 132, 152, 163, 164, 200, 216,
    220, 224, 230
shōkeimoji, 244
Shudan Seikatsu, 52, 53
shūshin koyo, 148, 244
Siam, 188
Siberia, 182
single, 158
sister city ties, 222, 239
sister ties, 223, 226, 227
social calendars, 95
social stratification and mobility
    (SSM), 84, 109, 244
social stratification and mobility
    (SSM) studies, 8
social studies texts, 196
social-capital theory, 3
social-ecological maps, 4
socialization, 39
sociologist, 36
sociology, 14
son, 156
sorting machine, 19
sorting mechanisms, 39
soto, 212, 239
soto-uchi thesis, 212
Soviet, 31
spousal satisfaction, 120
spouse selection, 111
spurious, 48
stability, 177

standardization, 17
status, 3, 31, 177
    attainment, 8
    relationships, 3
stereotypes, 1
stock market, 86
stratified, 60
streaming, 9
structural barriers, 14
structural power, 175
student
    ability and effort, 15
    honors, 34
    identities, 35
    overall ratings, 34
    populations, 93
student-to-teacher ratios, 52, 55
sub-cultural support for deviant and
    criminal roles, 170
subordinate, 157
subsidizes, 82
subsistence income, 154
substandard housing, 222
Suiheisha, 198
Suiheisha (Equality Society), 198
Supreme Court justices, 89
surplus (disposable) income, 154
surrounding community use of
    campus facilities, 98
surveys, 8
suspended student, 34
Suzuki marriage-squeeze index, 129
Suzuki's Marriage Squeeze index,
    122

tabula rasa, 40
Taihō Code, 185
taiso, 52
Taiwanese, 9, 184
tanshin fu'nin, 16, 244
tanshin fu'ninzoku, 234
tatemae, 244
tax breaks for donations to non-
    profit organizations, 103

teachers, 28, 44
elementary school, 35
head, 35
intervention, 42
junior high, 35
kindergarten, 35
nursery school, 35
quality, 8
ratios of women to men, 56
recruits, 56
teacher's pet, 34
teaching assistantships, 103
technical high schools, 72
technical schools, 71, 93
teichaku ijūsha, 181, 244
teineigo, 29
tekireiki, 136, 137, 245
television, 24
television watching, 24
tenkōsei, 235
tension, 7
tenure, 104
terakoya, 6, 245
textbooks, 10
three-generational household,
141, 168
Tibet, 185
time, 9
Tochigi, 74, 117, 119, 121, 124, 125,
126, 132, 152, 163, 164, 200, 216,
220, 223, 224, 228, 230
Tōdai, 78, 92, 245
TOEFL, 29, 30
Tōhoku, 24, 81, 92, 115, 173, 199, 229
Tōhoku University, 35, 89
Tokugawa, 154
Tokugawa family, 188
Tokugawa Period, 189, 197, 207
Tokugawa shogunate, 189, 190
Tokunoshimans, 183
Tokushima, 12, 74, 117, 119, 121,
124, 126, 132, 152, 163, 164, 200,
216, 220, 224, 230
Tōkyō, 23, 24, 50, 53, 61, 64, 73, 74,
75, 81, 100, 116, 117, 119, 121,
124, 125, 126, 127, 130, 131, 132,
134, 150, 151, 152, 153, 161, 163,

164, 173, 175, 191, 199, 200, 206,
215, 216, 220, 223, 224, 228, 230,
231, 238
arts, 93
engineering, 93
metropolitan school
system, 76
public elementary school
expenses, 58
residents, 25
science, 93
Stock Exchange, 89
University, 3, 7, 13, 73, 89
Women's Normal School, 45
Tomakomai, 191
Tomama, 74, 117, 119, 121, 124, 126,
132, 152, 163, 164, 200, 216, 220,
224, 230
Tottori, 13, 74, 117, 118, 119, 121,
124, 126, 132, 151, 152, 163, 164,
200, 216, 220, 223, 224, 228, 230
tourism, 205
Towa University, 83
town-gown" relationships, 98
Toyama, 10, 11, 12, 88, 151, 161
(tōyō)1850 kanji, 22
Toyotomi family, 188
trainee, 157
transportation, 71
treaty of Shimonoseki, 193
tribute-trade system, 187
truancy, 62, 65, 67
truancy rates, 68
truants, 66
Turkish, Mongol, and Tungus, 184
tutorial schooling, 16
tutoring, 59
types of occupations, 128

uchi, 212, 239
ukeireko, 245
uncle, 156
underachievers, 58
undergraduate student culture, 96
undergraduate university
structure, 80

undesirability of farm life, 116
unemployment, 202, 215
unemployment rates, 201
uniform military-like schooling, 10
United States, 5, 42
universal theory, 2
university, 83
    club activities, 96
    education, 82
    entrance tests, 16
    president, 35
    professor, 16, 36
    reject (rōnin), 34
    stratification system, 88
unrepresentativeness of Tōkyō, 25
unskilled foreign workers, 211
upper blue-collar workers, 85
ura, 212
Ural-Altaic languages, 184
Ural/Altai (Mongolian, Tungusic,
    Japanese, Korean, etc.)
    languages, 184
urban, 4
urbanization, 10, 86, 169

values, 2
vandalism, 64
vertical relationships, 148
victimization, 63
violent offenses, 168
virginity, 175
voting rights, 214

wa, 4, 28
wage differentials, 143
Wakayama, 74, 117, 119, 121, 124,
    126, 132, 152, 163, 164, 200, 216,
    220, 224, 230
Waseda, 92
wealth, 11
white flight, 15
white-collar workers, 16, 85
widow, 156, 158
wife, 156, 158
wives, 146

women, 13, 14, 134
women
    aspirations, 123
    in academia, 107
    in higher education, 13
    teachers, 56
    rising expectations, 131
    work patterns, 177
work, 3
    commitment, 176
    force shortage, 211
    identities, 158
    roles, 144, 177
    superior, 157
working women, 55
world trade, 186
World War II, 115

xenophobia, 4
xenophobic, 190
xenophonia, 113

Yakuza, 202, 204
yakuza membership, 204
Yamagata, 74, 75, 117, 118, 119,
    121, 124, 125, 126, 132, 134, 152,
    153, 163, 164, 173, 199, 200, 216,
    220, 221, 223, 224, 230, 238
Yamaguchi, 74, 117, 119, 121, 124,
    126, 132, 152, 153, 163, 164, 192,
    200, 216, 220, 224, 230
Yamanashi, 74, 100, 117, 119, 120,
    121, 124, 126, 132, 152, 163, 164,
    165, 200, 216, 220, 224, 230
Yamato, 186
yamato damashi, 27
yamatogokoro, 1
Yayoi, 183
yobikō, 17, 79, 86, 245
yōchien, 43, 44, 45, 46, 69, 245
yōchien attendance, 47
Yokohama, 170, 219
Yōrō Code, 185
yosomono, 209